ALL TO PLAY FOR

ALL TO PLAY FOR

THE ADVANCE OF
RISHI SUNAK

MICHAEL ASHCROFT

Biteback Publishing

This revised edition published in Great Britain in 2023 by
Biteback Publishing Ltd, London
Copyright © Michael Ashcroft 2020, 2023

ISBN 978-1-78590-796-8

10 9 8 7 6 5 4 3 2 1

A CIP catalogue record for this book is available from the British Library.

Set in Minion Pro and Futura

Printed and bound in Great Britain by
CPI Group (UK) Ltd, Croydon CR0 4YY

FSC
www.fsc.org
MIX
Paper | Supporting
responsible forestry
FSC® C171272

CONTENTS

AUTHOR'S ROYALTIES

Lord Ashcroft is donating all author's royalties
from *All to Play For* to charity.

INTRODUCTION

Since this book was first published as *Going for Broke* in the autumn of 2020, the governing Conservative Party, and by extension the country, has endured sustained turbulence thanks to having three Prime Ministers in quick succession. After Boris Johnson's chaotic premiership collapsed in July 2022, Britain was subjected to the strange interlude of Liz Truss's six-week administration, before Rishi Sunak's hastily arranged coronation that October. Even though Sunak's abilities had been widely recognised since his earliest days in the House of Commons, nobody could have predicted just how quickly he would find himself in 10 Downing Street. Aged forty-two, he was the youngest occupant of that august address since Lord Liverpool came to power in 1812. Equally remarkably, he was the fifth person to hold the highest office in the land since June 2016.

Going for Broke looked back at Sunak's life before he entered politics with the help of the recollections of those who have known and worked with him. It also examined the trajectory of his political career from the time he was first elected an MP in 2015, through his appointment as a junior minister in the local government department in January 2018, until he became the Chancellor of the Exchequer in February 2020.

Reaching one of the four great offices of state so early was unusual enough, yet the fact that he was plunged into defending the British economy from the devastating effects of the coronavirus crisis within weeks of arriving at the Treasury made an exceptional situation more extraordinary still. Such a task would have daunted far more seasoned political operators. By spending billions of pounds a week trying to protect jobs, businesses and public services, he exploded the budget deficit and, for a spell, became the most popular politician in Britain.

The speed of his ascent and the magnitude of the public health emergency meant that Sunak went from being relatively unknown to a household name almost literally overnight. How he managed to apply himself to this gargantuan task intrigued me. I chronicled his early months as Chancellor and his part in the government's response to the biggest catastrophe to have confronted Britain in peacetime and gathered some thoughts on what he might possibly do next.

This fully revised and updated edition of his biography builds on this, taking in his increasingly strained relationship with Boris Johnson and other Cabinet members, his sceptical view of how the Covid crisis was dealt with, his eventual resignation as Chancellor in July 2022 and his first – failed – bid for the Tory leadership that summer, as well as the first nine months of his premiership.

When Sunak became leader in October 2022, the various crises that had engulfed the Conservative Party since it won an eighty-seat majority in December 2019 prompted some to consider it not so much a governing party as a circus. Bereft of heavyweight figures, riven by internal disputes, prone to self-indulgence (or worse) and seemingly exhausted after a dozen years in government, it was, unsurprisingly, written off as a spent force.

Yet Sunak did not only have to try to reinvigorate a fatigued party. Far more importantly, he also had a country to run. On Johnson's watch, a once-in-a-generation opportunity to realign British politics had been largely squandered. Under Truss, Britain was portrayed around the world as so lacking in stability that it came to be regarded as something of a joke. The disarray of their respective tenures in Downing Street, coupled with the £400 billion Covid bill and the war in Ukraine, helped to saddle the nation with myriad problems, not least in its public services, a situation worsened by persistent strikes and soaring inflation. What sort of person would want to take on such pressures? And would he be able to fix a broken economy and make the Conservative Party popular again?

This book sets out to answer these questions, offering readers the chance to understand more about Rishi Sunak via the convoluted route he took to 10 Downing Street. Having had the privilege of being able to speak to some of those who know him best, I hope that this volume will offer worthwhile insights into his approach to the top job as Britain gears up for a general election whose outcome will be pivotal.

Michael Ashcroft
September 2023

ACKNOWLEDGEMENTS

Dozens of people agreed to be interviewed for the purposes of this book. Some were willing to be named, while others, for understandable reasons, were not. I am grateful to every one of them for sharing their stories and impressions of Rishi Sunak, including his friends, colleagues and other observers, both inside and outside the political world. For ease of reference it should be assumed that, unless otherwise attributed, all quotes are taken from interviews conducted exclusively for this book. Thanks must also go to the formidable Angela Entwistle and her team, as well as to those at Biteback Publishing who were involved in the production of this book, and to my chief researcher, Miles Goslett.

CHAPTER 1

FRENCH CRICKET

Nobody can say definitively which ingredients are necessary to create a happy childhood, but most people would surely agree that they would have to include loving parents, a stable home environment and the absence of want or fear. Add to these advantages some siblings to play with, being raised in a pleasant neighbourhood, the best schooling money can buy and plenty of time spent with one's family, and it would be unusual if anybody who was exposed to such a start in life did not emerge as a well-rounded individual.

Rishi Sunak, who was blessed with all of this and more during his formative years, is a shining example of how such contentment can be converted into success. His parents left their home countries to come to Britain and worked all hours to give their three children a comfortable life.

'They were not political,' Sunak has said. 'We never talked about politics. They were a classic Indian family. They came here, and their general view was that they were going to work really hard and they want to provide a better life for their kids.'

The image of parents working, striving and making sacrifices in order to give opportunities to their children seems familiar, but the Sunaks' history is quite remarkable. The story of a family that values determination, endeavour and the pursuit of education and opportunity goes back generations and covers three continents. It is the story of a family ready to take big risks in search of a better life.

Sunak's father, Yashvir, is from an upper-middle-class Punjabi family who, before partition, came from Gujranwala, now in Pakistan. His parents, Ram Dass and Suhag Rani Sunak, were themselves both from educated families with strong ties to the British Raj – Yashvir's maternal grandfather, Mr Luthera, was the postmaster of the Abbottabad Post Office, a prestigious role awarded to those considered especially loyal.

By 1935, tensions were rising between Hindus and Muslims and the future looked bleak on the subcontinent. With Britain needing skilled workers in east Africa, Ram Dass found himself a job as a clerical officer in Nairobi, Kenya. Taking a young bride to a new and unknown country was not considered safe, so he bought a one-way ticket aboard a ship and promised to send for his wife in time. After taking courses to qualify as an accountant, he became a civil servant in Harambee House, now the office of the President of Kenya, and subsequently at the Treasury in Nairobi.

Upon Ram Dass's departure to Africa, his young wife, Suhag Rani, migrated to New Delhi with her parents-in-law to ensure they had a footing in Hindu India. It meant an emotional goodbye not just to their ancestral home but to the happy, successful life they had enjoyed there, surrounded by centuries-old traditions. In 1937, Suhag Rani joined her husband in Nairobi and the couple began to put down roots in a country vastly different from the one in which they had grown up.

Once settled in Kenya, Sunak's paternal grandparents had six children, including Sunak's father, Yashvir. For their higher education, the girls eventually returned to India, the country the family still considered its homeland. The boys, meanwhile, looked west. Harish Sunak, Yashvir's elder brother, was offered a place at Liverpool University to study electrical engineering in 1966 – an opportunity that he was able to take up with the help of grants, scholarships and the savings the family had managed to cobble together. The same year, Yashvir joined his brother in Liverpool to complete his A-levels. The pair lived together in student accommodation with sparse furniture and an even smaller income. A few years later, Ram Dass, Suhag Rani and the rest of the family joined the two boys in the UK.

Sunak's mother, Usha, also grew up in a family of Hindu Punjabis. However, while her father, Raghubir Berry, grew up on the Indian side of the Punjab, her mother, Sraksha, was born in rural Tanganyika (now Tanzania) in a remote hut surrounded by lions. Although Sraksha grew up learning Swahili and considered Tanganyika her home, her family – like her future son-in-law's – retained close ties with India.

At the age of sixteen, Sraksha entered an arranged marriage with Raghubir. Hers is a tale of extraordinary bravery: a few years later, with next to nothing in her pocket, she would head to the UK alone, acting as an advance guard for the rest of her family.

Before that, however, this clever and confident young woman persuaded her groom to move to Africa and build a new life with her there – a reversal of the usual 'bidaai' whereby the bride leaves her childhood home to join her husband. Raghubir soon found a job as a tax official in his new country, and the couple had three children – Usha and her two younger brothers.

By the late 1960s, the family was keen to move to Britain – especially Sraksha, who was attracted to the land of Oxford and Shakespeare. While immigration rules made the move possible, finances were more of a problem. The future Prime Minister's grandmother sold her wedding jewellery to buy her one-way ticket, leaving her husband and children behind in the hope – by no means certain – that they would be able to join her later.

Arriving in the UK in 1966 with no family or friends to greet her, Sraksha made her way to Leicester and rented a room in the home of an acquaintance. Having already learned to type, she made the most of a head for numbers and found a job as a bookkeeper with a local estate agent. She saved every penny she earned and in 1967 – her daughter Usha now aged fifteen – was able to send for her family. The anglicised name Berry was probably adopted at this point to help with integration; the original surname is likely to have been the traditional Punjabi Beri. Raghubir joined the Inland Revenue, eventually receiving an MBE after many years of service.

After passing his A-levels, Yashvir went on to read medicine at Liverpool University, graduating in 1974. Usha, meanwhile, had graduated in pharmacology from Aston University in 1972. Introduced by family friends, the couple were married in Leicester in July 1977.

Their first child, Rishi, was born on 12 May 1980 at Southampton General Hospital. The happy parents took him home to 54 Richmond Gardens, their sizeable 1930s redbrick house in the city's Portswood district, a couple of miles from the surgery on Raymond Road in Shirley where Yashvir now worked as a family doctor. Usha had been working as a manager at a local chemist before she became pregnant for the first time, but she knew that with a young baby the role would be too much, and she left shortly before her son was born, hoping that in due course she could become a locum – a well-paying and flexible job enabling her to keep up her skills. As the family grew, with another son, Sanjay, arriving in 1982, followed by a daughter, Raakhi, in 1985, the couple decided to move to a pleasanter area of Southampton.

On the face of it, there was nothing very special about 21 Spindlewood Close, where the future PM spent much of his childhood. Built in the early 1980s, it was the sort of thoroughly ordinary-looking modern brick property that can be found in the suburbs of every city in England. With six bedrooms, two bathrooms and a double garage, it was ideal for a growing family. To the back of the detached house in a quiet tree-lined cul-de-sac lay Bassett Woods, where the children could play hide and seek and build dens. To the fore, the quiet road was the perfect place for local youngsters to join in a spot of French cricket. It was the remarkable community spirit and friendships formed between families in the street that made it such an attractive place to live and meant many of those who moved in stayed for decades.

People in Spindlewood Close still remember the small boy with jet-black hair, a ready smile and lovely manners who used to wheel around on a bike with the other kids or kick a ball about with his little brother Sanjay. Janet and David Parnell moved into the house next door to the Sunaks in September 1984, when Rishi was four. Their children Luke, born in 1978, and Alice, born in 1981, grew up alongside the future PM and his siblings. 'They were lovely neighbours,' recalls Janet.

The kids all used to play together ... There were at least a dozen children on the close ... It was such a safe place to play, a really lovely spot. The whole Sunak family, including the children, were very friendly, very personable. Rishi was chattier than his brother Sanjay; always very polite and friendly.

Everyone in the street seems to have liked Yashvir and Usha, who regularly invited neighbours round for dinner. 'They often had dos with other people in the street. They cooked Indian food, and sometimes we did barbecues. Usha did one of the best curries we have ever had,' Janet recalls. Politics was not discussed on these occasions. Instead, conversation revolved around the usual middle-class preoccupations: work, holidays, school fees and the children's progress.

Neighbours were left in no doubt that the Sunaks were fiercely ambitious for their brood. 'The parents were very supportive of all their children and their education – not pushing them; just wanting the best for them,' Janet says, adding that all the siblings were good at talking to adults.

The first school Yashvir and Usha chose for their elder son was Oakmount, an old-fashioned prep school which acted as a feeder for minor public schools. The couple had always believed that their children should have the best possible education, and the state primary school in the area at the time was, as one neighbour put it, 'dire'. Its catchment area encompassed various downtrodden housing estates and blocks of social housing and was not viewed as an option by many local middle-class parents. Most either sent their children to church schools (which, given they were Hindus, was not a route open to the Sunaks) or went private.

Located just two miles from Spindlewood Close on the other side of Southampton Common, Oakmount made for an easy school run and had an excellent reputation. It had just 150 pupils and had been operated by the Savage family for generations. The Sunaks liked the look and feel of the place. Rishi's education would begin there at the age of four.

Andy and Liz Claughton, who lived two doors down from the Sunaks in Spindlewood Close, sent their son John, two years Rishi's senior, to the same school and describe the place as a 'little anachronism' populated by the children of middle-class professionals, for whom the fees were within reach. 'It was a traditional small prep school, of which there were many around here, back in the day,' recalls Mr Claughton, a retired naval architect. 'These schools were much of a muchness; they weren't like the prep schools that feed Eton, but they did a good job.' Mrs Claughton, a retired nurse, has a clear recollection of the head of kindergarten, a Mrs Everest, predicting that the young Rishi would go into medicine. 'She always used to say that he'll be a brain surgeon, or a heart surgeon. She knew how bright he was.'

Indeed, Sunak was so academically able that he appears to have been moved up a year at Oakmount. The Claughtons say that despite being almost two years younger than their son, Sunak was in the same year group.

Then, in 1989, came a shock: the little school was closing. One minute, pupils were enjoying their Easter break; the next, they were being told that summer term would be their last at Oakmount. The letter from the headmaster, bluntly informing them that the schoolhouse and playing fields were being sold for development, sparked a stampede for places at other local independents.

The Sunaks chose Stroud, a prep school for boys and girls aged three to thirteen and the main feeder for King Edward VI, an independent secondary school in the area. They were relieved to get places for Rishi and Sanjay: the Claughtons recall it all being 'a bit of a scramble', as 'everyone rushed to Stroud'.

Despite the upheaval, Sunak quickly settled in his new school, the transition eased by the fact that so many of his Oakmount friends had made the same move.

There were plenty of other boys and girls of a similar heritage, generally children of Asian medics.

Olly Case, who was in the same year at the school as Sanjay Sunak – two years below Rishi – and who went on to become a teacher there, describes life at Stroud as 'idyllic', saying, 'There were lovely grounds, not massive, but lovely, with playing fields, woods and a pond. It had a real family atmosphere, and everybody knew each other. It wasn't a big school, and most children came from professional working parents. The staff were lovely and caring.'

Case remembers that the future PM was quickly identified as a high achiever.

He was someone that was talked about; the teachers would say, 'He's going to be a Prime Minister.' I know that because since I started working at the school and have spoken to some of the teachers who taught me, they remember the former deputy head and former head discussed it and thought he'd be the first Asian-background Prime Minister and things like that. He was very well regarded, and that was literally something they said about him.

At Stroud, Sunak played hockey, football and cricket. He also took part in athletics, but it was cricket at which he excelled. He became captain of the team and is remembered as a confident batsman and an excellent bowler.

Every year, the school put on a musical: during Sunak's time, there was *Fiddler on the Roof* and a production based on various tales by Hans Christian Andersen. Though he did not have starring roles, Sunak seems to have enjoyed treading the boards and is remembered for playing Benjamin in a production of *Joseph and the Amazing Technicolor Dreamcoat*. Case recalls, 'He would have been in a number of these musicals. He wasn't one of the big, out at the front, leading types in drama, I guess, but he still enjoyed it.'

He remembers Sunak as a 'really nice guy' who was 'very caring' and was involved in the community. These qualities made Sunak an obvious pick as head boy in his final year, a role which provided some early practice in public speaking, as his duties included giving a small speech at end-of-term assemblies.

In addition to being what Case describes as an 'all-round good egg', young Rishi was working hard. His parents were clear: education was everything, and he should apply himself rigorously. 'My parents' view was, we should work as hard as we can ... That's an ingrained value in our family. That's how you provide a better life. That was fundamentally what they believed in,' Sunak has said.

Tim Wardle, whose wife was in Rishi's class, says she and Sunak were 'the class swots', adding, 'She's never met anyone so competitive. Today, every time we turn on the news, she says, "I can't believe little Rishi became Chancellor and married a hot billionaire, while I... [voice trails off]."'

While most Stroud pupils went on to King Edward's, Yashvir and Usha were aiming higher. They knew their elder son was exceptionally bright and were keen to get him into the sort of school that would help him achieve his full potential. They set their sights on Winchester College, not only one of the most famous public schools in the country but also fairly conveniently located for Southampton.

The couple now had three children at private day schools, already a huge drain on the family finances, and Winchester, whether Sunak attended as a boarder or as a day boy, would represent a significant additional burden. Without the benefit of inherited wealth, it was a stretch, so they encouraged Sunak to try for a scholarship. At Winchester, these highly competitive awards were not automatically accompanied by a reduction in fees and were more sought after for the academic prestige they conferred. Nonetheless, a scholarship would make a bursary easier to obtain, and so they thought it was worth a try. In a manner that would become a feature of the way he approached challenges in later life, Sunak did everything possible to prepare for what he knew would be an incredibly rigorous set of exams. The scholarship tests – known at Winchester as 'Election' – took place over several days. Meanwhile, Yashvir secured a part-time job as an occupational health adviser for John Lewis. This role produced some very welcome extra income, and he would keep it up for two decades.

With so much of the family budget going on the children's education, holidays were not extravagant. Sunak has recalled happy summers on the Isle of Wight, an easy ferry ride from Southampton, and remains fond of the island. Some days were beach days; others were for exploring places like Carisbrooke Castle, the spectacular Needles chalk stacks, which rise thirty metres out of the sea off the island's westernmost extremity, or Blackgang Chine, the UK's oldest theme park.

From time to time, the family also went abroad, accepting invitations to stay at David and Janet Parnell's holiday apartment in Alcossebre, Spain. The apartment complex, about fifteen minutes by bike from the village, had a tennis court, a big draw for Yashvir and Usha, who were both keen players. 'It's a very rural, quiet place, and they just went to the beach and played tennis and cycled,' David recalls.

Despite the protests of the Parnells, the family always insisted on paying something to cover bills.

Money was not too tight for other modest treats, including trips to watch Southampton Football Club. Yashvir had a season ticket and passed on a love of the club to his elder son, who remains a passionate supporter today. Sunak's childhood hero was the team's star player Matt Le Tissier, and he could often be seen sporting a replica of Le Tissier's No. 7 shirt.

On special occasions, the family would go out to dinner at Yashvir and Usha's favourite Indian restaurant in Southampton, which was owned by a popular local businessman who had become a close friend. Kuti Miah had moved to Southampton around the same time as Yashvir and Usha were beginning their married life in the city and has known Rishi since he was a baby. A fellow first-generation immigrant – he had moved to the UK from Bangladesh in 1975 and worked as a waiter for years before opening his own restaurant – he met the Sunaks through his then boss, who was one of Yashvir's patients. He was still working as a waiter when they were first introduced, and a lifelong friendship began.

In 1983, he was diagnosed with tuberculosis and spent three months in hospital. He has never forgotten how Yashvir supported him during what was a difficult and frightening time. 'He was like a brother to me. Fantastic man,' he says.

For three decades, the Sunaks would go to Miah's restaurant every Christmas Eve. Recalling Rishi as a child, the father-of-three says he was 'intelligent, playful and hyper. He would laugh and joke,' adding that he always knew the young man would go far. 'I always say I saw lights on Rishi from day one. I'm not saying it because he is famous now – it's just he's so charismatic, like his dad. And like his dad, he is a very kind guy.'

Miah's restaurant business thrived, and he was proud to be able to send his own son to King Edward VI – a decent first division school which was the next step for most of Rishi's year group at Stroud. However, the boy who would become Prime Minister was going up a league.

In the event, he had not quite made the grade to enter Winchester as a scholar. His parents had always been realistic about his chances: getting a scholarship to Winchester – one of the most selective schools in the country – was a tall order for any boy. Tim Johnson, an Old Wykehamist who is a year older than the PM, also sat the scholarship exams and says, 'They were the hardest exams I've ever taken, up to and including my finals. I remember the French oral being done in Senegalese, so not only was it in French, it was also in West African French.' Nonetheless, Sunak had done well enough in the tests to be offered a regular place and it was agreed that he would attend as a day boy. It seems his parents may have been offered some financial help by the school: he has since said somewhat vaguely that he was 'helped along the way with support and scholarships here and there'.

At the time, his achievement in getting into such an elite establishment was something of a talking point among teachers and fellow pupils at Stroud. 'It is quite a rarity,' recalls Olly Case. 'To get in, you have to be well above normal ability across the board, really. And Rishi wasn't your stereotypical, nerdy, good-at-books type – he was more rounded than that; a lot more personable.'

The year was 1993 and Sunak had just turned thirteen. For the Conservative government of the time, these were dark days indeed. Re-elected in 1992 with a majority of just twenty-one, John Major's administration had lurched from crisis to crisis, from the storm over the Maastricht Treaty through Black Wednesday, when the UK was forced to withdraw from the Exchange Rate Mechanism following a run on the pound. The Prime Minister was in office, but, as his former Chancellor Norman Lamont would cuttingly declare, there was little sense that he was in power. In summer 1993, Major staggered through an unofficial vote of confidence in his leadership, and the Maastricht Treaty was finally ratified, but his troubles were far from over. The beleaguered premier was about to cause himself a lot of bother with his notorious 'back to basics' initiative. Before long, the phrase would be uttered only with derision, as it emerged – in toe-curling detail – that the values he was attempting to promote were not being upheld by a string of senior figures in his own Cabinet.

It seems unlikely that Sunak was preocupied by these political dramas, however. His parents were not politically active and there is no evidence that they were even very interested in current affairs. In any case, Sunak had more typically teenage concerns, not least because he was about to embark on a new life, as a pupil at one of Britain's finest public schools.

CHAPTER 2

TEENAGE KICKS

According to his sister Rachel, at the age of four Boris Johnson expressed the hope that he would grow up to be 'world king'. Eton College, where the future premier went to school, prided itself on turning out supremely confident young men and would not have discouraged such lofty aspirations. It had, after all, produced no fewer than eighteen Prime Ministers by the time Johnson took up his place, a record of which it was fiercely proud.

By contrast, Winchester College, the school Yashvir and Usha Sunak chose for their son, has always been more interested in intellectual ability. Until 2022, it was the alma mater of only one Prime Minister, Henry Addington, who entered Downing Street more than two centuries ago. Nevertheless, it has always taken great satisfaction in beating Eton in academic league tables. Unlike some public schools, it is simply not accessible to the 'rich but thick' and every boy who makes it through the rigorous entrance exams joins a ferociously bright community. The world Sunak entered as a nervous thirteen-year-old was – in the words of one former pupil – 'intellectually arrogant', and from the moment he arrived it would have been clear to him that he was going to have to work hard to compete.

Tim Johnson, who was in the year above him at Winchester, says:

If Eton's problem is generally social arrogance, then Winchester's is intellectual arrogance. What you get told an awful lot – if not spelled out then implicitly – is that by being there, you're among the very brightest of your cohort. But you also know very quickly that you're not the brightest in the room, because there is always someone cleverer than you. Whether that gives you arrogance and humility at the same time, I don't know ... Someone like Boris Johnson would have found it much harder to bluff through Winchester than he found it to bluff through Eton, I think. The premium is on intelligence not social skills.

It is not hard to imagine how daunting it must have been for the young teenager as his parents dropped him off to begin the next stage of his education. The grandeur of the medieval buildings and the sheer size of the place – there are some 650 boys – must have added to the sense that he was stepping into a very different world from his relaxed little prep school. In Sunak's case, he also stuck out because unlike the vast majority of other boys there, he was a day pupil. What made the transition considerably easier was the traditional house system, designed to create an extended family, in which new boys have plenty of support from teachers and older pupils and form lifelong friendships.

Sunak was placed in a house called Trant's, though its official name was Bramston's. Home to about sixty boys aged thirteen to eighteen, Trant's had its own dining hall, squash court, music room and large recreation room with snooker and pool tables. Thrown together in this way, new arrivals were unlikely to feel lonely for long and quickly learned to mix with pupils from a variety of backgrounds.

Many fiercely academic schools begin preparing pupils for

GCSEs from the moment they arrive, but the attitude to public exams at Winchester College is different. Proud as it has always been of its exam results, the school refuses to be constrained by the curriculum. Far from encouraging pupils to sit as many exams as possible, it does not even bother entering pupils for some subjects. According to Tim Johnson, in Sunak's day the school 'didn't rate GCSEs very highly' and there was no pressure on the most able pupils to sit subjects to rack up extra A grades. 'We hardly took any GCSEs,' he explains. 'We didn't do history, we didn't do English literature.' When it came to A-levels, the school was so confident in pupils' ability to do well that instead of spending two years teaching the curriculum, they covered it in just one, devoting the first year of sixth form to educational material that would not form part of the exams but was nonetheless indirectly relevant.

Johnson describes the overall set-up as 'very academic', with pupils 'rigidly' divided into sets according to ability. As at Eton College, exam marks were publicly displayed, an approach that fuelled intense competition. 'Everyone knows where everyone else sits in the academic hierarchy.'

Sunak has described his time at Winchester College as 'absolutely marvellous'. As a teenager, he is remembered as a 'joiner' who threw himself into everything the school had to offer and made friends easily. 'He was a nice, unpretentious, un-difficult person; a good chap, always pleasant and polite,' recalls another Old Wykehamist.

Sports-wise, he was up against keener competition than he had been at Stroud, and though he was still a decent cricketer, he only made the Thirds. Sport was compulsory until sixth form and he was required to participate in various inter-house competitions, where, being fit and athletic, he did not let the side down. Perhaps to his relief, since he was very slight and shorter than most of his peers, there was no rugby. Instead, pupils played a complicated game unique to the school called Winchester College football, which Sunak enjoyed and was sufficiently good at to represent his house.

For A-level, Sunak chose English literature, economics and maths. He also took AS-levels in biology and French. His parents were not entirely convinced by this selection. 'They're kind of classic Indian immigrant parents. They said do a degree that leads to a very specific job, and then have security of income – that was their driving mindset,' Sunak has said. 'When I said I was going to study economics at A-level, that was something my mother was very worried about, because it was not obvious what job that would lead to, in her mind.' Nonetheless, economics quickly became his favourite class. He has described it as 'absolutely my major academic love'.

For English literature he recalls having 'two amazing teachers' to guide him through set texts which included Milton's *Paradise Lost* and Chaucer's *Canterbury Tales*. 'As well as teaching us English, they combined it with teaching us a little bit about the history of the era as well. Which was really great, it just really brings it to life … But economics was my major nerdy passion,' he would later recall, in an interview with pupils at a school in his constituency.

*   *   *

Winchester College liked to treat pupils as if they were young men, not children, an aspect of the culture Sunak particularly appreciated. As we have seen, his parents had encouraged him to work hard from a very young age, a discipline that was gently, but firmly, reinforced. Now he was at a boarding school, albeit as a day boy, he had to manage his own time, which he believes was one of the most valuable skills he acquired. Reflecting on his years at Winchester, he has said:

> It was really teaching you to be able to just figure out your own life a bit … Homework was not 'here it is today, hand it in tomorrow'. It was much more 'here's all the stuff you need to do for next week' – you kind of organise your own time and figure out when you're going to do it … You can't get your parents to help you with everything, so it teaches you that independence and that self-motivation. That's probably the biggest kind of life lesson.

Liberation from parental supervision at boarding schools can create an atmosphere of mischief-making, particularly in relation to alcohol and cigarettes, even for day students. The most senior pupils were allowed to buy a limited amount of beer at a sixth-form club and seem to have been able to get away with drinking quite a lot. This relatively laid-back approach must have presented significant temptations. However, Sunak seems to have stayed firmly on the straight and narrow. While the Hindu faith does not prohibit the consumption of alcohol, and Sunak's father enjoys an occasional glass of red wine, the young Rishi simply did not like the taste or effect of alcohol – and never would. A friend says, 'Rish tried lots of different types of alcohol growing up, but it just never really appealed. His friends kept encouraging him to, but it's just not his thing.'

Such abstinence cannot have made the periodic discos with girls from neighbouring schools any easier. Even for the most confident boys these were awkward events, involving busloads of teenage girls suddenly descending on what was then a single-sex school for what Johnson describes as a 'strictly policed dance'. The artifice of these social occasions did not diminish the excitement they generated, particularly among those who benefited from Dutch courage.

While more daring boys were sneaking spirits into the school and occasionally experimenting with illicit drugs, it seems the naughtiest thing Sunak ever did at Winchester College was to smuggle a hand-held television into the school so that he did not miss any key games of Euro '96. The contest took place in England that June, around the time he was finishing his GCSEs, and, along with the rest of the nation, the teenage Sunak was swept up in the excitement. 'It was a big deal, because we hadn't had a big football tournament in England for a very long time,' he has recalled.

[A friend and I] had managed to smuggle into school this chunky thing with a big aerial that you could receive a TV signal from, but which obviously didn't work brilliantly … During the time when we were meant to be doing our homework in the evening, he and I nipped up to the top of the school, this attic, to go and watch TV … There was some England game, someone had scored, and we were jumping up and down, singing. It was like a scene from a movie: we were totally absorbed in the moment – and then obviously turned round and standing at the doorway was our teacher, who was nonplussed … He'd already busted us once a few days before, and told us to take this thing home, which we obviously didn't listen to. We were in full embrace, screaming and shouting 'Three Lions'.

It was around this time that Sunak first experienced racism. It had never been an issue in the relatively affluent neighbourhood in which he grew up, nor reared its ugly head in any of the schools he attended, where there were many ethnic minority pupils. He has said that broadly speaking, it was not something he had to endure. However, he has never forgotten one incident, which took place when he was out with Sanjay and Raakhi.

'I was probably a mid-teenager,' he has said.

We were out at a fast food restaurant, and I was just looking after them. There were people sitting nearby who – it was the first time I'd experienced it – were just saying some very unpleasant things. The 'P' word ... And it stung. I still remember it; it's seared in my memory. You can be insulted in many different ways ... but that stings in a way that's hard to explain really. Particularly because my little sister was quite young, as was my brother. I just took them away, and just removed ourselves from the situation.

Now the children were growing up, Usha had more time on her hands. In the mid-1990s, after years of working as a locum, she decided to establish her own pharmacy. She bought a somewhat dilapidated premises a couple of miles from Spindlewood Close, on Burgess Road, and set to work smartening it up. During school holidays, Sunak would support his mother's fledgling business. He helped with the accounts and book-keeping, a role that fostered a growing political awareness. Seeing how fiscal policy affected company profits, he began taking an interest in fluctuations in National Insurance and VAT rates and paying attention to what the main political parties were saying about tax and spending. He was also becoming increasingly conscious of the importance of the role his parents played in the local community in their capacities as a doctor and a pharmacist. He admired what they were doing and began thinking about how he might live up to the example they had set.

This was an exciting time to become interested in politics as the Conservative administration entered its death throes. After eighteen long years, the party was exhausted and divided, while Labour was surging into the ascendancy under its charismatic new leader, Tony Blair. As the seminal 1997 general election approached, Sunak devoured the news and comment pages in national newspapers.

It was not, however, a fashionable time for young people to be Tories, even in public schools. Tim Johnson describes it as 'the less comfortable intellectual position to take' at that time, even at Winchester College. Nonetheless, the Conservatives were the party with which Sunak identified most. For all its troubles, he felt it still represented the aspirational values he espoused: hard work not hand-outs; the crucial importance of education; and the primacy of the individual over the state. He has said that he felt the Conservative Party were 'kind of on the side' of people like his parents, who had poured everything into creating a better life for themselves and their children.

Sunak was just shy of seventeen when Major went to the country in May 1997, the PM having put off the day of reckoning until the last possible moment. Nationally, Labour was some twenty points ahead in the polls, but in Winchester, the Liberal Democrats were the main threat to the Tory incumbent, Gerry Malone. Sunak briefly got involved, helping out with some leafleting. On the night of an election that would topple 178 Tory MPs, including, in one of the most memorable moments, Defence Secretary Michael Portillo, Sunak settled down to watch the BBC's Election Night special. Keeping one eye on Peter Snow's swingometer as it showed the country turning from blue to red, he was also writing a piece for the school magazine.

The results were only beginning to come in, but jubilant crowds had already gathered outside Blair's home, waving Union Jacks. Sunak considered this display of national pride 'ironic', on the grounds that a Labour landslide was certain to be bad for Britain. In his magazine article, he acknowledged that the Tories deserved to lose, writing that 'nobody elects a divided party' or rewards 'weak leadership, sleaze, a poorly run campaign'. However, he did not accept that Labour deserved to win. In a long essay, he warned of looming tax rises and criticised the Labour Party's refusal to commit to keep spending below 40 per cent of GDP. Quoting a piece in the *Daily Mail*, he attacked what he described as Blair's 'discredited belief' that 'state training schemes, not entrepreneurialism' created jobs and expressed concern that trade union 'brothers' Blair had strategically cold-shouldered would soon begin to flex their muscles.

Sunak's article is remarkably sophisticated for a sixteen-year-old. Musing on how a New Labour administration would evolve, he was prescient about the likelihood of the hard left returning to the fore, predicting that 'slowly but surely the Labourites of Old will emerge and make their voice more strongly felt. Tony Benn, Margaret Beckett, Robin Cook, Jack Straw and most importantly of all John Prescott might well become fed up of Tony Blair's centre-right concessions after a while,' he wrote. With the exception of Jack Straw, who never seemed uneasy about the party's shift to the centre, and perhaps Margaret Beckett, who never gave the new leader any trouble, all of those he named would in due course struggle with the new direction of the party, just as he had anticipated.

In two further accurate predictions, he suggested Peter Mandelson was likely to lose control of 'the [New Labour] project' (the spin doctor resigned eighteen months later); and that the media would quickly become interested in Labour sleaze (the first scandal came just six months later). Though these observations were not particularly original – the article drew from secondary sources including *The Times* and *The Spectator* – Sunak's arguments were well crafted and revealed certain political positions, particularly on the EU, that he never changed. Aged sixteen, he was already clearly Eurosceptic and fearful of the creation of a European 'Super State', voicing concern that New Labour rhetoric sounded 'worryingly pro-Europe' and noting that 'avid pro-Europeans' were already being sent to Brussels.

At the same time, he had no truck with the 'knee-jerk, overdone Euroscepticism' of figures like John Redwood, arguing that the latter was as much to blame for the Tory Party's downfall as Europhile Ken Clarke. This measured Euroscepticism was exactly what he would display almost two decades later, as a referendum on the UK's membership of the EU approached.

More controversially, at sixteen, Sunak bitterly opposed Labour's proposed minimum wage and the introduction of the Working Time Directive, lambasting these measures as 'proven job-destroyers'. Today, it is hard to find any Conservatives who remain hostile to the minimum wage, but the position was quite common among Tories at the time. Sunak also believed public sector pensions would eventually 'bankrupt Britain'.

Writing about what lay ahead for the Conservatives, he listed the strengths and weaknesses of various potential leadership contenders, seeming impressed by William Hague. The party needed to be 'revitalised and modernised under someone young', he said.

On the morning of 2 May 1997, Blair entered Downing Street with a majority of 179 seats. The Tories had been reduced to a rump, in their worst general election performance since 1906.

In Winchester, a seat the Conservatives had held since 1950, the election result had been too close to call and there had been no fewer than three nail-biting counts. In the end, Malone lost his seat by just two votes. Adamant that he had been robbed, he launched High Court proceedings, claiming that fifty-five ballot papers had been wrongly excluded from the total because they had not been correctly security stamped. A court accepted his argument and the result was subsequently declared void. In a by-election later that year, Malone expected to regain the seat. However, in a sign of the depth of the crisis engulfing the Conservative Party, the Lib Dem candidate Mark Oaten was returned to Westminster with a majority of more than 21,500 – leaving Malone with more than a little egg on his face.

Having leafleted for Malone, Sunak followed the drama with interest, but his A-levels were looming. Fascinating as the political landscape was, academically he could not afford to take his foot off the gas. His time at Winchester was drawing to a close, and he needed brilliant results. With excellent predictions, he had decided to apply to Lincoln College, Oxford, to read philosophy, politics and economics (PPE). This was one of the most prestigious courses at one of the university's most highly regarded colleges. After beating some intense competition, he was offered a conditional place.

Though he had not been a scholar at Winchester, his intelligence, self-confidence and easy charm, along with his enthusiasm for all the school had to offer, had consistently been on display. It was no surprise to his peers when he was appointed 'Sen. Co. Prae', meaning head boy.

Explaining Winchester's unusual head boy system, a friend says:

> The way it works at Winchester is that there are two head boys. One is known as Aul. Prae – Head of House from the scholars' House (called 'College'). That person is Aul. Prae all year. But the main Head of School is Sen. Co. Prae and they change each term – meaning that there are three in total in any given year. Rish was Sen. Co. Prae for the first term – chosen by the Heads of Houses at all the other ten-plus houses at Winchester.

As we have seen, he had also been head boy at his prep school, suggesting a consistency in leadership qualities and good character – a record arguably all the more remarkable given that at Winchester he was one of the few day boys and will have had to work harder to make his mark.

On his eighteenth birthday, Sunak received a card signed by the entire Southampton football team – a gift that became one of his most prized possessions. Southampton would always be home, and the Saints would always be his team. He was about to venture out into the world, however – beginning in the city of dreaming spires.

CHAPTER 3

THE AIRPORT TEST

If Rishi Sunak's political career hits the buffers, he could well be snapped up for primetime television. It is hard to imagine the Prime Minister in the *I'm a Celebrity* jungle, but a spot on *Strictly Come Dancing* seems entirely conceivable – especially as he already has some of the skills required. In a talent he has kept well hidden, it turns out that Sunak is something of a natural at ballroom dancing. Though no expert, he once took part in a competition, so impressing judges with his slinky moves that he is said to have made it to the semi-final.

This secret skill is a throwback to his time at Oxford University, where the academic pressure was even more intense than it had been at Winchester. He was one of just nine undergraduates accepted to study philosophy, politics and economics at Lincoln College and there was no hiding place. In addition to attending lectures and tutorials, during his first year of study he was expected to read widely around all three subjects of his degree and produce two essays a week, the contents of which would be dissected by dons, often in front of other students.

All this was less of a shock to someone of his academic background and ingrained work ethic than it would have been to many others, but he still needed to let off steam, and in his spare time explored other aspects of student life, including volunteering to take part in the ballroom dancing contest. The event was organised by Oxford University's DanceSport Club, where students can learn a range of dance genres including Argentine tango, salsa and rock 'n' roll.

Sunak was roped in by a fellow Lincoln undergraduate named David Weston, who was looking for a novice to take part in an inter-college competition. Mirroring the *Strictly* format, the 'Cuppers' contest required that at least one member of each dance partnership should be new to the sport. This meant that success depended as much on the natural aptitude of the novices as it did on the moves of the more experienced performers.

Weston, an engineering and computer science student, was a brilliant Latin American dancer who would go on to achieve considerable success at national level. Casting his expert eye over the potential talent at Lincoln, he felt the future PM had what it took on the dance floor. Weston recalls, 'I was looking for some volunteers, and Rishi agreed to learn to waltz for the competition. I think he did quite well and made the semi-final, though that's a ridiculously hazy memory. But I taught him to waltz... or it may have been quickstep.' He remembers Sunak as a 'lovely guy, very kind, very amenable, very charming'. There is no evidence that he kept up the dancing, but his readiness to accept the challenge was entirely characteristic of his self-confidence and spirit.

Founded more than 600 years ago, Lincoln is among Oxford's most revered colleges. It has some of the university's most beautiful buildings, including a stunning medieval hall and three quadrangles. All first-year students are accommodated within the college, and many choose to live in for the entire three years of their studies, a privilege unavailable at many other Oxford colleges. Having been immersed in the academically rigorous atmosphere of Winchester College for five years, the transition to university life was no great leap for Sunak, and he quickly settled into the new routine.

While PPE is a classic choice for future politicians, Sunak was not actively involved in student politics, either through the Oxford University Conservative Association or with the Oxford Union, the debating society which has been a training ground for generations of statesmen and women. He knew he wanted to enter public life at some point, but first he wanted a career in the City.

To this end, he joined the Oxford University Investment Society, a club that fosters links between students and the financial world. Sponsored by investment banks such as Credit Suisse and Merrill Lynch, the society hosted speakers from organisations like the Bank of England, the IMF, the World Bank and the London Stock Exchange. It also staged role-play exercises designed to give students a flavour of life as an investment banker. Sunak loved it. Eager to help shape the programme of events – and spotting a valuable networking opportunity – in his second year he became president of the club, a role that expanded to fill the time available.

In 2000, a *Sunday Times* reporter observed the society in full swing, describing how members threw themselves into the mock financial scenarios.

From the sidelines a sharp-suited banker screams: 'There's been a change of government, what do you do?' Thirty-five students immediately shout new share prices. There is a bedlam of hurried negotiations, scribbled note making and pained anticipation of a slump in the market. A drama society rehearsal, perhaps? No, this is a meeting of the Oxford

University Investment Society, the 'must join' group for undergraduates aiming to be the next generation of big-money City bankers.

Asked what the society offered, Sunak told the reporter it was an opportunity to 'meet the people who really matter'. It wouldn't guarantee them a job, he acknowledged, but meeting future employers in this relaxed setting would help undergraduates get through what Sunak called 'the airport test': 'showing employers that they could spend an eight-hour stop-over in your company'.

Being very competitive, he particularly enjoyed trying to make more money than others in various trading room scenarios. 'It's exciting, with the buzz of the real situation – especially when the bankers compute which team has made the most money,' he told the paper.

Sunak still had another year or so of his studies, but it seems he personally had already passed 'the airport test'. He has said that at university he was 'really focused' on getting a good job and he spent a great deal of time firing off applications for internships and graduate training schemes. His efforts paid off: the same article reported that the enthusiastic young president of the society had already secured offers of internships from a number of top investment banks.

In the meantime, like most students, he needed cold hard cash, which meant finding a job during university vacations. This proved easy: his parents' old friend Kuti Miah, who had always been very fond of him, was delighted to offer him work at the Indian restaurant where the family were regulars. The restaurateur prefers not to use the word 'waiter' in relation to the role Sunak performed, considering it demeaning. Instead, he says the future PM was more like an 'entertainer' whose job was to ensure diners had a great experience, a challenge he apparently more than met.

'He was very warm, explaining, laughing, always had a smile on his face,' Miah recalls. 'He would talk to every table, in the way that I do ... He was charming with every single person – it was not just customers but every other member of staff that liked him.' He says Sunak was conscientious and never cut corners. 'Whatever he does, he does it from his heart – he's not going to sleep unless he's done his job. Everything he does, he does it passionately. He tried his best, his level best.'

As a close family friend, Miah is of course biased, but university contemporaries also remember Sunak as something of a 'golden boy'. He was never a big name at Oxford like those involved in student politics or the Union, and did not seek the limelight, but nonetheless seems to have had what another Lincoln contemporary describes as 'star quality': 'My overall impression of him was always very positive. I just remember him being a really nice guy. When I saw he had become Chancellor, I just thought, "Yeah, Rishi, he's awesome."' His tutors also thought highly of him. One of his former Oxford tutors recalls a 'smart, hard-working student who I liked and admired'. PPE students would normally have been supported by an economics fellow at Lincoln, but for some reason this post was vacant during Sunak's time at the college. A don who taught his cohort remembers them being 'collectively quite annoyed' that they were one tutor down but observes that the situation 'had the positive effect of encouraging them to support each other'. 'They were very rewarding to teach when I arrived,' recalls the tutor, who has vivid memories of what was an exceptionally talented year group.

Professor Michael Rosen, who taught Sunak philosophy, has gone further, describing him as a 'remarkable' student and saying no PPE cohort at Oxford has been equalled before or since. Seven out of nine of the group – including Sunak himself – went on to be awarded first-class degrees, giving the college its best ever results. 'That was an absolutely astonishing figure. No college, let alone Lincoln, has ever managed that before or since, to my knowledge,' Professor Rosen, who now teaches at Harvard, has said. He remembers Sunak as well organised and an 'implicit' Conservative and recalls that he clearly wanted to go into politics in due course.

It was no surprise to any of his tutors when Sunak graduated with first-class honours. He had sailed through his finals, enjoying a traditional showering with champagne and glitter when he finished his last exam. Next move: the Big Smoke.

* * *

Of the various offers that came his way, the graduate position Sunak accepted was with Goldman Sachs, one of the world's largest – and, for its critics, most rapacious – investment banks. Asked in the 1970s what made the company stand apart from the competition on Wall Street, its managing partner boasted, 'At Goldman Sachs we're greedy, but we're long-term greedy.' Gus Levy was proud of this approach, emphasising that Goldman bankers weren't out to make a quick buck but sought fat returns on investments that might take years or even decades to come good. For a long time, this strategy proved extraordinarily successful – at least for those who ran the bank, who became very rich indeed. However, it was not necessarily so great for all their clients. In due course, the obsession with maximising profits from clients would poison Goldman's corporate culture. Following the global financial crisis of 2008, insiders labelled the company 'morally bankrupt' and a slew of reports emerged of the deep disdain some senior company figures displayed towards clients they secretly labelled 'muppets'.

Writing in the *New York Times* in 2012 on his last day in his job, Greg Smith, executive director and head of the firm's US equity derivatives business in Europe, the Middle East and Africa, declared that the firm's values no longer bore any resemblance to those it had espoused when he joined, fresh out of college, just a year before Sunak arrived. 'I can honestly say that the environment now is as toxic and destructive as I have ever seen it,' he wrote, adding, 'It makes me ill how callously people talk about ripping their clients off.'

All this was yet to come when Sunak made it through endless rounds of face-to-face interviews to secure a coveted place on the firm's 2001 graduate training scheme. Only about 4 per cent of those who applied for these positions were successful. Being a straight-A student was never enough. Indeed, according to a former recruiter for the firm, Goldman was quite sniffy about 'excellent students with a first in economics and ten internships', saying these were not the ideal. 'We were actually fairly anti hiring these people, whom we referred to as "plug and play". Yes, they've got the track record, but they're not exciting.' What the bank really sought were individuals with 'unusual profiles'. It was all about 'trying to attract a diverse group of applicants, who've studied history or English literature instead of just finance'.

Unusually for the industry, Goldman did not make potential recruits sit numerical tests or attend assessment centres. It was more interested in character. Particular attention was paid to the covering letter applicants had to submit with their CV. 'There were some students who were excellent until we got this letter: people who sent the same application letter to ten different banks and who weren't writing specifically about why they wanted to work for Goldman,' the recruiter recalls. 'We looked for creativity and effort.'

What Goldman prized above all else, however, was drive. 'The bottom line is that Goldman really wants to hire people who are ambitious. You need to be personable, and you need to be seriously ambitious.'

Sunak's school career left little doubt that he fit the bill and, being of Indian heritage – and from a family who had grafted for everything they had got – he stood out from the barrage of applicants from privileged backgrounds who had never had to try very hard. Goldman was keen to promote diversity, and while he was more than qualified for the position in any case, his ethnicity would not have been a disadvantage.

Sunak's new position was in Goldman's Private Investment Area (PIA), the bank's internal private equity unit, and it would begin that summer with a two-month induction programme in New York, or 'Goldman Sachs bootcamp', as one former GS man puts it. 'This is where they try to make the firm seem human, and they do a pretty good job of it,' the source says.

The attempt to make new recruits feel good about their new employers was smart, because the three-year training programme that followed the induction course would be brutal. For any new hire, the long hours and lack of control over one's schedule were a huge culture shock, but for the 2001 graduate intake, plunging into this strange new world was an even greater adjustment. They were barely through the door when terrorists struck New York's World Trade Center and the Pentagon in the 9/11 attacks, plunging global markets into turmoil.

The deadliest terror attack in US history claimed thousands of lives and brought the world's leading financial centre to a halt. The New York Stock Exchange, the American Stock Exchange and the Nasdaq remained closed for the rest of the week – the longest NYSE shutdown since 1933, one of the darkest years of the Great Depression. Trading in bond markets also stopped for two days and the Federal Reserve was forced to step in to prevent a financial crisis, lowering interest rates and buying massive quantities of government bonds.

No Goldman employees died in the attacks, but many lost relatives and some of the company's properties were affected. In a voicemail to all employees that week, the company's then CEO Hank Paulson highlighted how staff pulled together to support the company's New York operation. A history of Goldman Sachs recalls: 'Offices around the world shouldered the workloads normally handled in New York. Team members slept on floors, relocated offices to nearby Princeton, New Jersey, and eventually went to great lengths to return to the firm's Manhattan offices once it was deemed safe to do so.'

It is hard to imagine a stranger introduction to life in the City than this. One of Sunak's former colleagues in the London office recalls:

When it hit the City, it completely stopped any activity for a week. People just sat there in the office going, WTF just happened? I'll never forget it. I walked into Goldman, and they had a big billboard up, by the escalator, saying, these guys not only attacked New York City; they attacked us. And we stand with America and freedom, or something like that.

In the Private Investment division, Sunak was required to learn hard and fast. His boss was Richard Sharp, a formidable figure who would go on to become chair of the bank's Principal Investment business in Europe and, later, BBC chairman. The Goldman veteran was not the sort to be easily impressed, but he saw something special in Sunak. 'He came there very bright, very willing, very eager, and he had this mentality of flawless execution,' Sharp recalls.

The culture at the bank was one in which those who did well moved rapidly up the ladder while those who failed to inspire were issued with a P45. This unsparing approach to human resources was informally known as 'up and out' within the company at the time. To avoid being in the 'out' category, Sunak not only had to survive the punishing hours – a bad day might begin before 8 a.m. and finish in the middle of the night – but also dazzle (or at the very least not alienate) both his bosses and his peer group. In an approach that encouraged every employee to develop first-rate interpersonal skills, the firm operated a '360-degree review process', in which staff were actively encouraged to report back on each other. To climb the ladder, new recruits could never afford to forget that everyone with whom they worked had a line into the HR department – and could stab them in the back.

'The result is that you have to constantly manage your brand, i.e. how people in the company see you,' explains one familiar with the system. 'It's an exhausting game and as a new recruit, it governs your life.'

The years Sunak spent walking this tightrope may go some way to explaining how well he would come to be regarded at Westminster fifteen years later. At Goldman, he could never stop being mindful of the impression he was creating, and of the necessity of keeping colleagues onside. This is an extraordinarily useful transferable skill, particularly in politics, where diplomacy is less prized and less immediately rewarded than ambition and cunning but nonetheless pays big long-term dividends. While many MPs have been in managerial positions in previous careers, few have been subjected to the kind of brutal continual assessment Sunak faced at this impressionable age at Goldman, such that a highly respectful attitude to all colleagues became second nature.

Sharp agrees that the emphasis on teamwork at Goldman probably shaped the way Sunak would work for the rest of his career. 'Often in our first job, we establish certain values,' he says.

A critical value I sought to establish was one of prioritising teamwork as a performance issue. We believed in hiring outstanding people – that was necessary, but it wasn't sufficient. What was necessary was a willingness to work truly as part of a team; to use your competitive forces externally not internally … He slotted very well into that culture.

In truth, interacting with colleagues was probably a welcome relief from the majority of his work, which would have been quite solitary. 'Most of his intimate relationships would have been with spreadsheets. He would have spent a lot of time making love to Excel,' observes a former banker wryly.

For the first two years, he would have been cannon fodder. In that position, you basically don't see daylight for two years. A late night would be 3 a.m. or 4 a.m. If you're a grunt on the desk, your job is grunting and being on the desk. It's not sleeping, eating or having any fun.

Sunak's line managers were struck by his stamina. Sharp freely admits that the work was 'highly intensive; 24/7, for weeks on end' and that 'not everyone can hack the pace'.

'He hacked it in spades,' Sharp says, adding that Sunak was 'very engaging as an individual'.

The one concern was whether one of his most attractive character traits at that age – a kind of happy innocence – might backfire on him in the ruthless private investment world. His bosses wondered whether he had the nous to detect deceit in a world in which unscrupulous operators routinely artificially inflate or even falsify figures. 'The thing that people underestimate is how persuasive liars can be. We need intelligent cross-checking and due diligence – you can't just accept someone's forecast; you need to check it against other evidence,' Sharp says.

It was during this period that Sunak began to learn the art of financial modelling, a skill that would prove a huge asset when he entered the Treasury. Put simply, this was about making financial projections, using historical performance to figure out how an entity might fare in future. Very few Treasury ministers have this background and officials were delighted by his level of expertise.

In addition, Sunak would also have had to study for a Chartered Financial Analyst qualification, a certificate issued at the end of three years of applied study in finance, broadly equivalent to a graduate degree. 'Investment banks give all their kids the CFA syllabus,' a former Goldman source says. 'Notionally, it gives them some on-the-job training and – in a further win for the banks – it divides the serious candidates from the less serious candidates. The serious ones study their butts off.'

Between his day job and studying for the CFA exams, Sunak

had precious little time to do anything else, though Goldman did at least boast one of the finest gyms in the City. Sneaking away for a quick workout was about as good as it got, in an environment in which everyone lived in fear of being pushed out. In the wake of 9/11, pressure on new recruits was particularly intense as the firm sought to reduce its headcount. 'A lot of people who had just started work were let go, because transactions just collapsed,' a former Goldman employee recalls.

> The investment banking side went from being relatively busy – 2001 was a very good year for the first nine months – to a sudden stop. Getting a gig at PIA isn't easy. Holding onto a gig at PIA isn't easy. For Sunak to stay on for three years after that suggests that he found his way into … a group of [more senior] people who protected him when HR came looking. The industry is presented as being inhumane, and it really is. If the firm thinks you're good, it wants to hold onto you; if not, it wants to use your space for someone better. It's brutal, but both sides are aware of the deal.

By the time Sunak reached his third year at Goldman Sachs, many of his peers had fallen by the wayside. He had impressed his bosses, but he was getting twitchy. When he joined the company, he may have imagined he was entering a glamorous world of high finance. For a graduate, the remuneration was generous: a starting salary of around £60,000 per annum with a performance-related bonus ranging from 50 per cent to 300 per cent of base. ('If you got 50 per cent, you seriously screwed up,' is how one former employee puts it.)

However, as he soon discovered, the work was exhausting

and often mundane, and it would continue to be so for many years before he reached a level of seniority in which the ability to make a vast amount of money more than offset the drudgery.

'By the time he got to three years in, he knows what the job's about, he's eaten a lot of free sushi, and it's probably all becoming a bit political. It's quite normal for people at that stage to start thinking about their next move,' says a Goldman veteran.

Sunak's employers had always known that he was fiercely ambitious, one of the qualities that had attracted them to him in the first place. Ironically, it was the reason he wouldn't stay. Having completed his three years' training, he was impatient to move up the ladder faster than Goldman's corporate structure allowed. As he contemplated his next step, he talked at length to a senior Goldman colleague named Snehal Amin. The older banker encouraged the future PM to broaden his horizons, suggesting he consider studying for an MBA at one of the world's most prestigious business schools. It meant another two years of intensive study in another country – but it would change his life for ever.

CHAPTER 4

SILICON ROMANCE

In a five-bedroom bungalow on a street named La Jennifer Way, a company that would change the world was just beginning to take shape. The year was 2004 and the unremarkable property was in Silicon Valley, a part of California that was rapidly becoming synonymous with revolutionary business start-ups. Among the occupants was one Mark Zuckerberg, who along with his housemates was busy building a company called Facebook. Before long, he would be one of the richest men on earth.

It was during this exciting period in Silicon Valley history that Sunak was embarking on a two-year MBA course just a hop, skip and jump away from 'Facebook House' at Stanford University. The course is expensive, with tuition fees and living costs easily running into six figures. As a result, the 375 or so graduates who beat off competition from thousands of applicants to secure a place are not only exceptionally bright but often exceptionally wealthy. For very high-calibre candidates from a less moneyed background, however, there is a way to make it affordable. The Fulbright Program offers scholarships to talented overseas students to study at the most prestigious academic institutions in America. It was to this scheme that Sunak applied in the hope of securing financial help – and he was successful.

Fulbright alumni include sixty-two Nobel Prize recipients, eighty-nine Pulitzer Prize winners and forty-one current or former heads of state or government. Evidently, sharp-eyed selectors felt Sunak had the potential to join these illustrious figures. The two years the future PM spent at the Stanford Graduate School of Business and in Silicon Valley had a profound impact on his view of the world, filling him with excitement about entrepreneurialism and giving him a thoroughly global outlook. 'It is an incredible place to work,' he has said, describing the concentration of creativity and innovation as 'intoxicating'.

Taking a ten-minute drive through the Bay area of San Francisco, it is possible to pass the headquarters of technology giants such as Apple and Google and hundreds of other businesses which have changed the way we live our lives today ... I found working among all this young talent truly inspirational.

After Oxford and Goldman, Sunak was no stranger to hard work, and the pressure of the MBA course, which involved continuous assessment, did not faze him. Only around a dozen or so of his fellow students were British, but many had banking backgrounds, including Deepak Sarpangal, another Goldman Sachs man who had been in the New York and London offices at the same time as Sunak. The two became firm friends.

The course involved a great deal of teamwork, to which Sunak was well suited. Maria Anguiano, a fellow student from the class of 2006 who remembers the future PM well, says:

It was a very intense programme ... My calendar was booked from 8 a.m. to 10 p.m. every night, with studying, work teams and projects. I don't think I've ever been that busy. Rishi coped very well. He was always very positive … I've never been with a group of such intelligent people. Everyone was very hard-charging – that was just the environment out there.

Graduate students live off campus and sky-high property prices in the area mean many have to look beyond Palo Alto for accommodation. Geography notwithstanding, the MBA course is a hugely sociable experience, and few students let the demands of the course prevent them from having a good time.

'Basically, the scene is a house party scene,' according to an American familiar with the Stanford graduate MBA social circuit.

Frankly, the average American doesn't know how to cook, so they don't do dinner parties. What happens is that someone will buy wine, someone will buy some cheese, and a lot of alcohol is consumed. Rishi may not drink, but believe me, his classmates would have. Part of the appeal of going to Berkeley or Stanford is that you are basically studying in wine country.

Another student who joined the graduate MBA course in 2004 at the same time as Sunak recalls that while he did not drink at these soirées, he occasionally played cards for money. Rashad Bartholomew, who is now director of commercial sales at software company Vercel in San Francisco, says, 'We'd have a poker night every now and again … It would be $20 hands, something small – then whoever wins would treat everyone to meals or drinks.'

Bartholomew describes the atmosphere among those on the course as highly competitive, though 'not in some dark and stormy way'.

> You're competing in such a way that others [on the course] are helping you become the best version of yourself. It was a lot of hard work, but it didn't really feel like work to me personally – I really enjoyed it. I think most of us enjoyed it and the competition that went with it, to be the best we could be.

As at Winchester and Oxford, Sunak was well liked by his peers. 'Was he popular? It's funny, because Stanford Business School is by nature a gathering of all the popular kids,' Bartholomew muses, meaning that the course was packed with 'Alpha' personalities. 'He was definitely well liked and had his own crew. He was very positive, very decent.'

It is sometimes claimed, not entirely in jest, that Stanford MBA graduate students are not only shopping for a business qualification but also for a spouse. Many do meet lifelong partners on the course, and so it was for Sunak.

Until this juncture, his love life is something of a mystery. At university, he became very close to a fellow student named Anoushka, but it does not seem that they were romantically involved. Any ex-girlfriends from his time at Goldman Sachs remain well below the radar. At Stanford, however, he would meet the person with whom he wished to spend the rest of his life: a young woman from an extraordinary Indian family whose parents were self-made billionaires.

* * *

Akshata Murthy did not have a moneyed start in life. In a touching open letter to his daughter, Narayana Murthy, now the third richest tech billionaire in India, has told how he learned of her birth through a friend, because he and his wife Sudha could not afford a telephone at home. 'My then colleague Arvind Kher came all the way from our office in Nariman Point [on the southern tip of the Mumbai Peninsula] to our house in Bandra [a northern suburb of Mumbai] to tell me that your mother had delivered you, back in Hubli, her hometown,' he recalled. For the first time in his life, Narayana said, he felt 'a compelling need to become a better person'.

It was 1980, and Narayana and his wife were both struggling to establish careers. In Sudha Kulkarni, Narayana had married a force of nature: a fiery, feminist surgeon's daughter who was highly educated and had taught her grandmother to read. In a most unusual choice for a high-caste Indian woman of her generation, Sudha had studied electronics engineering and technology at university, becoming the first female engineer at India's auto manufacturing giant Tata. She landed the job after firing off a postcard to the chairman complaining of the 'men-only' gender bias at the firm, a move which secured her an interview, after which she was hired immediately as a development engineer. It was during this period that she met Narayana, an equally ambitious engineer who was building a career in computer systems. They married in the late 1970s.

In the early years of their lives together, the couple struggled with work–life balance, and Akshata, their first child, who arrived in April 1980, was initially brought up by her grandparents. In his letter to his daughter, published in a collection of missives from eminent parents to their daughters, Narayana explained:

Two months after your birth in Hubli [some 300 miles south of Mumbai] we brought you to Mumbai, but discovered quickly enough that it was a difficult task to nurture a child and manage careers side by side. So, we decided that you would spend the initial years of your life with your grandparents in Hubli. Naturally, it was a hard decision to make, one which took me quite a bit to come to terms with.

Every weekend, Narayana would take a plane to Belgaum, around sixty miles from Hubli, and then hire a car for the final leg of the journey to see his daughter. This routine was extremely expensive, but he missed her too much not to return regularly. During these visits, he was always reassured by how happy his little girl seemed, surrounded by her grandparents and a set of adoring aunts and uncles.

When Akshata was one and Narayana in his mid-thirties, he founded Infosys, along with six other software professionals. This was the company that would make his fortune. The initial capital injection of 10,000 rupees – around £540 at the time – was provided by Sudha, who served as CEO from 1981 to 2001. It was not an overnight success, not least because India was such a difficult place to do business at that time. Slow processes and endless red tape meant just setting up the basics was a battle: Narayana recalls waiting a year to get a telephone connection and three years for a licence to import a computer. 'We used to have a joke: half the people in the country are waiting for a telephone, the other half are waiting for a dial tone,' he has said.

Other features of India in the 1980s were on his side, however. There was a growing demand for customised software, creating an opportunity for India-based suppliers. Since independence in 1947, successive governments had also made a concerted effort to encourage the development of technology, resulting in a glut of engineers searching for work. This enabled Narayana's start-up to recruit very smart, innovative people. In the 1990s, economic reforms also made overseas travel and importing goods much easier, and Infosys, launched with just one customer, eventually took off. Now a multinational corporation with more than 343,000 employees, the company provides business consulting, information technology and outsourcing services.

According to *Forbes* magazine, in 2023 Narayana Murthy's net worth was $4.5 billion. However, the family studiously avoids ostentatious displays of wealth. Though both Narayana and Sudha came from fairly privileged backgrounds, money was tight when their two children were small. On one occasion, when Akshata was at her all-girls school in Bangalore, she was selected to take part in a school drama, for which she was required to wear a special dress. It was the mid-1980s, Infosys was in its infancy and her parents did not have any money to spend on non-basic goods. Sudha told her daughter that it would not be possible to buy the dress and that she would have to drop out of the performance, a huge disappointment to the little girl. Recalling the episode in the letter to his daughter, Narayana said, 'Much later, you told me that you had not been able to understand or appreciate that incident. We realise it must have been a bit drastic for a child to forgo an important event in school, but we know you learnt something important from that – the importance of austerity.'

As the couple became richer, they went to great lengths to keep their children grounded. Narayana has said that his lifestyle 'continues to be simple' and that when he returns home from work every night, he still cleans his own lavatory.

'We have a caste system in India where the so-called lowest class ... is a set of people who clean the toilets,' he has explained. 'My father believed that the caste system is a wrong one and therefore he made all of us clean our toilets ... That habit has continued, and I want my children to do that. And the best way to make them do it is if you did it yourself.'

In his letter to Akshata, published in 2016, he recalls how Sudha insisted that her children travel to school by rickshaw, even though the family could afford a chauffeur.

> I remember discussing with your mother the issue of sending you kids to school by car once we were a little comfortable with money, but your mother insisted that Rohan and you go to school with your classmates in the regular autorickshaw. You made great friends with the 'rickshaw uncle' and had fun with the other kids in the auto. The simplest things in life are often the happiest and they are for free.

In the late 1980s, Narayana and Sudha bought a nice house in an affluent part of Bangalore, where the children went to school. However, the property was not grandiose, and the couple remained determinedly unmaterialistic. 'The only emphasis we had in our house was on education,' Akshata's younger brother Rohan Murthy has said, adding that after Infosys floated and his father became a household name in India, his parents taught him and his sister not to pay any attention to gossip about the family wealth. '"All this is transient," they said. "The only things that remain with you are how you interact with people and what bonds you forge with them, and what knowledge you acquire. That is something nobody can take away from you,"' he has recalled.

In her quest to raise serious-minded children, Sudha decided that they should not have a television in the house, to create more time for studying, reading, talking together and meeting friends. When Akshata and Rohan were teenagers, the hours between 8 p.m. and 10 p.m. were dedicated to pursuits that brought the family together in what Narayana has called 'a productive environment'. Rohan started computer coding at the age of eight. By the age of twelve, his dinner conversations with his father were about operating systems. 'My parents never pushed me into anything, only to gain weight. But they were very supportive. If I wrote ten pages of code, my father, even if he had just come back from a long journey, would sit with me and go through it and explain things,' he has said. He went on to study for a PhD and became a junior fellow at Harvard before joining the family firm.

For her part, Akshata was more interested in fashion than computers. 'Ever since I was a little girl, I have always loved clothes,' she has said, adding that her 'no-nonsense engineer' mother was 'always baffled why I would spend so much time creating different outfits from my wardrobe'.

After school in India, she studied economics and French at Claremont McKenna College, California. She might easily have finished her education there – in which case she would never have met Sunak. Inspired by her parents, however, she was serious about making a success in the world of business. With money no object, the eye-watering fees for a Stanford MBA were no problem – and so it was that she found herself embarking on the same course as Sunak, in 2004.

It is easy to see why the pair were so drawn to each other: the parallels in their upbringings are remarkable. Both had grown up in households in which education and achievement were obsessions and hard work and decency were prized above all else. Both family units were rock-solid, and Hinduism played a big part in their lives.

At Stanford, in keeping with the way she had been brought up, Akshata never flaunted her wealth, and many of her peers were unaware that she was an heiress. Maria Anguiano says:

> I wasn't super-close friends with her, but I will say the entire time in our first year I didn't even know that her family was wealthy. I literally didn't know until the second year of our business programme and that was because we had a study abroad-type programme and a group of students went to India and she helped organise it and that's when I realised how important she was, but before that I never ever would have guessed because there was nothing about her that indicated that.

The fortnight-long study trip took in Delhi, Mumbai and Bangalore, where students met key business figures and politicians to develop their understanding of what made the country tick. Anguiano describes it as a fantastic experience, partly thanks to Akshata's contribution:

> I was born and raised in California as a first-generation college student myself, so I'd never really travelled too much. It was a really amazing, eye-opening trip to see another country and get such an inside view of it. [The organisers] did a fabulous job, really giving us access to understanding the economy … We had a dinner with some of the political leaders and they spoke about the current issues facing India at the time, so it was very well done.

With outgoing personalities and preppy good looks, Sunak and his new girlfriend quickly became something of a power couple at Stanford. They were 'both very committed to each other and both very, I think, focused on making an impact', Anguiano says. 'I'm not sure if I remember them having political ambitions, but I know that they were very impact-orientated people.'

Rashad Bartholomew seconds this, recalling: 'They definitely complemented one another, they're definitely a beautiful, powerful power couple, a good-looking couple, a smart couple ... Their hearts are in the right place.'

There does not seem to have been much talk of party politics, but Akshata in particular is remembered as an idealist. 'Folks in business school at Stanford tend to think they can actually make an impact and change the world, so that was definitely a part of just the general vibe of the campus and our programme, but they actually went out and did it,' says Anguiano. Bartholomew had the same impression. 'She was always interested in pushing positive social agendas,' he recalls, adding that she was especially keen to explore how not-for-profit programmes could improve society.

After two incredibly formative years, in summer 2006 Sunak's time in Palo Alto was coming to an end. He had successfully completed his MBA and now had to decide how to use it. He and Akshata also had a difficult personal decision to make. Sunak was heading back to London while Akshata, who had been in the States for many years, felt rooted and had decided to stay. She enrolled on a postgraduate course in apparel manufacturing at the nearby Fashion Institute of Design and Merchandising, with the goal of launching her own fashion label. Meanwhile, Sunak was returning to the City, having secured a plum job at The Children's Investment (TCI) Fund, a hedge fund run by the billionaire financier Chris Hohn. He had been recommended for the role by his old mentor Snehal Amin, who had left Goldman Sachs to work with Hohn, and was thrilled at the opportunity to work with him again.

Though Sunak had not abandoned his long-term plan to enter politics, he had never wanted to be a career politician and felt he would have more to contribute to public life if he continued to build on his experience of the financial world. 'I think Parliament benefits from Members who have had experience outside of politics. If you can bring that experience from another career into the Houses of Parliament, that will help you be a better politician and make good policy. So for me, I guess it was a late transition,' he has said.

Despite the geographic challenges, he and Akshata were committed to each other and would stay together. For now, theirs would have to be a long-distance relationship. For the next few years, the couple would live between London, California and New York, the latter being a much more practical place for them to meet, if Sunak was flying from the UK.

In 2009, Sunak would take up a job that allowed him to relocate to California, where they were able to live together, but for the time being it was a question of criss-crossing the Atlantic to see each other as often as work allowed.

CHAPTER 5

NO TAMASHA

When Rishi Sunak's painstaking financial projections were blown up by coronavirus, the sickening feeling he experienced was not an entirely novel sensation. Back in 2008, he had learned the hard way what it is like to sign up to a job in good times only for everything to be blown off course by *force majeure*.

Armed with his MBA from Stanford, in 2006 Sunak had joined what was probably the UK's best-performing hedge fund. For a while he and his new colleagues were riding the crest of a wave. Then the financial crisis struck, and they watched as balance sheets plummeted into the red and all their grand plans for future growth were plunged into doubt. For Sunak, seeing hundreds of millions of pounds wiped off the value of investments was a bitter foretaste of the terrifying uncertainty he would face as Chancellor more than a decade later when the UK economy plunged into recession. As with coronavirus, the spectacular reversal in fortunes at the hedge fund happened almost overnight.

Sunak's new boss, Chris Hohn, was one of the most successful and feared hedge fund managers in the world. Within the industry, it was a coveted position. In 2006, Hohn – a man who openly described himself as an 'incredible money maker' – was riding high. In the four years since he had founded his

London-based investment firm, this Jamaican car mechanic's son had established a reputation as one of the most fearsome shareholder activists in the industry. His talent for spotting undervalued stocks and forcing companies in which he had a substantial stake to do things his way had made billions. When Sunak joined The Children's Investment Fund, his boss was at his most confident and aggressive. He was making his investors an average return of 40 per cent – a multiple of what rival hedge funds were generally able to achieve. At one point, he was delivering returns in excess of 50 per cent. Other hedge fund managers could only look on in awe. In the twelve months to August 2008, his outfit would make a profit of more than £555 million.

Then the global financial crisis struck, walloping TCI's flagship funds. Sunak watched in horror as everything blew up. 'It was extraordinary,' he later recalled. 'Once in a lifetime. This hadn't happened since the 1930s, this scale of dislocation in the financial markets. So the speed of what was happening, the scale of what was happening, was unprecedented, even for people who had been doing it for a while.'

One of the things Sunak loved about investment banking was the responsibility. 'You are highly accountable. That's what I like about it – it's very directly accountable. You are responsible for your investments; either they are good or bad; things work out or they don't, and there's not many other people to blame; there's nowhere to hide,' he has said.

That was all very well when things were going in the right direction, but it was another story altogether when clients were losing money. Sunak suffered many sleepless nights: 'Living it was stressful. When you've that scale of loss, financially, that you have responsibility for… when you are looking after people's savings, and that is all evaporating before your eyes, that is quite a thing to live through.'

Hohn was not just brilliant at making money; he was also good at giving it away. As the name of the fund implied, one of its core missions was to generate cash for children's charities. For Sunak, the philanthropic dimension of the business had been one of the key reasons he accepted a job there. Every year, Hohn would donate the majority of the fund's profits to a charitable foundation run by his then wife, Jamie Cooper. Unusually, this charitable giving was built into the firm's fee structure. In 2008 alone, before the financial crash struck, The Children's Investment Fund Foundation received £486 million from TCI Fund Management. Hohn's largesse enabled the charity to build up a £1.5 billion endowment to fund projects supporting children in the developing world.

Working for a hedge fund is always high-octane, but Hohn's aggressive shareholder activism gave it an extra edge. In a spectacular win in the early days of TCI, he managed to thwart an attempt by Deutsche Börse to buy the London Stock Exchange, resulting in the ousting of both the company's chief executive and its chairman. Hohn was triumphant: a 2006 New Year card he and his wife sent friends and family described an 'exceptionally exciting year overthrowing German CEOs'.

It seems unlikely that Sunak took such pleasure in ousting senior figures from their jobs: he was of an altogether gentler disposition. Nonetheless, when the future PM joined the small, highly select team at TCI, he was quickly drawn into similar battles, including an extraordinary wrangle with an American railroad company called CSX Corp that ended in court. It centred on an audacious attempt by TCI to overthrow the board of directors at the Fortune 500 company and install a new team, spearheaded by Hohn himself. Sunak was asked to help. Later that year, CSX filed a lawsuit against TCI, alleging violations of federal securities laws. A judge would later criticise the way Hohn's outfit had behaved, particularly their use of indirect shareholding instruments to increase their stake without declaring it to the company – though as a bit-part player, Sunak himself was not seen to have done anything wrong.

In the same period, Hohn was also embroiled in a high-profile and ultimately unsuccessful attempt to challenge corporate culture in Japan by acquiring a controlling stake in one of its biggest energy wholesalers. By the time of the global financial crisis, however, he was tiring of these missions, and the atmosphere at TCI was very different from the buoyant mood that had prevailed when Sunak had first joined.

Hohn's anxiety and self-doubt were exposed in private emails to TCI colleagues, disclosed as part of the discovery process relating to the CSX lawsuit. According to a lengthy feature in *Institutional Investor* magazine, the messages revealed his fears about the credit crisis, his portfolio's volatility and what he saw as his team's failures to foresee price movements in their key positions.

By mid-2008, he had lost not just money but confidence. Perhaps most painfully of all, the financial crash was hitting his charitable foundation. (The following year, TCI's donation to the foundation fell to just £19 million, a fraction of what he had been giving before.) At an investor day in New York for 300 of his clients, Hohn shocked the industry by declaring that he would now take a less activist stance.

'We are going to be more cautious about it when we look at making new investments, because quite frankly activism is hard,' he admitted in an interview. 'It has been very profitable for us, but it is unpredictable and expensive,' he added, pointing to the US$10 million bill TCI had racked up on the proxy fight with CSX.

Of course, Sunak could not know it then, but being at TCI at such a turbulent time would stand him in good stead when he became Chancellor. Through all the market turmoil, Hohn held his nerve. Before long, TCI's performance bounced back and Hohn recovered his mojo. By 2011, he was once again at the top of his game. An audacious acquisition of almost US$1 billion of shares in Rupert Murdoch's News Corp at the height of the phone-hacking scandal earned the fund a 57 per cent return when the stock rallied two years later. By the time Sunak became Chancellor in 2020, Hohn had also returned to his activist ways and was piling pressure on portfolio companies to reduce greenhouse gas emissions and disclose their carbon footprint.

TCI had been buffeted by events beyond its control, and Hohn had picked fights with big beasts that created huge additional challenges, but the business eventually emerged stronger. Sunak had learned how to weather a storm.

*   *   *

In January 2009, Sunak proposed to Akshata. They had been together for several years, sometimes living thousands of miles apart, but despite the geography and work schedules that often left little time for romance, they both knew they wanted to be together for ever.

For Narayana Murthy, news of the engagement was bittersweet. 'It is quite a well-known fact that when a daughter gets married, a father has mixed feelings,' he would tell Akshata later, admitting to a twinge of jealousy at having to share her with a 'smart, confident, younger man'.

However, the moment he and Sudha met their future son-in-law, any misgivings evaporated. Rishi Sunak was everything Akshata had said he was. In his open letter to his daughter many years later, Narayana was gushing about her choice. 'I found him to be all that you had described him to be – brilliant, handsome, and most importantly, honest. I understood why you let your heart be stolen. It was then that I reconciled to sharing your affections with him,' he wrote. The couple set the date for their wedding at the end of August 2009.

Weddings are an obsession in India and prominent families lavish huge sums on ostentatious celebrations, with multiple ceremonies and receptions held over several days. So when society magazines learned that the daughter of one of India's foremost industrialists was to be married, there was much excitement. To the disappointment of gossip columnists, however, Narayana and Sudha Murthy were not about to abandon the quiet modesty with which they had chosen to live their lives, even for their daughter's wedding. This would not be a crazily extravagant affair. 'We'd have loved to know more about the wedding and share the same with *WeddingSutra* readers,' one magazine reported disconsolately, admitting information about the event was thin on the ground. 'Much as we're dying to learn this, we can't tell you where Akshata picked the pretty pink saree that she wore for the [blessing ceremony] or ... who designed the beautiful orange lehenga choli [three-piece traditional Indian dress].'

In accordance with Hindu tradition, the first stage of the formalities was a pre-wedding *puja* – a ceremony to invoke the elephant god Ganesh, with the two families praying that the wedding go smoothly and that he bring prosperity to the couple's life.

To say that the venue for this part of the nuptials was not flash is an understatement. A marketing video for Chamaraja Kalyana Mantapa in Bangalore shows a cavernous, utilitarian hall that looks much like a school gymnasium. The venue did not allow alcohol or non-vegetarian food. The main attraction appeared to be the sheer size of the place: it could seat 800 guests, with standing room for a further 700.

The wedding reception itself was held somewhere significantly more glamorous: the spectacular five-star Leela Palace hotel in Bangalore. A modern palace built in 1997 with stunning tropical gardens, a spa and twenty-nine suites which come with a butler service, it promises to make guests 'feel like a Maharaja' and 'take back memories of a regal experience'.

For once, the characteristically self-assured Sunak was nervous, so much so that it appears he may have temporarily broken his lifelong habit of eschewing alcohol. A friend says, 'Apparently he promised friends that he would have some shots in advance of his wedding, and he did.'

WeddingSutra magazine did at least manage to uncover details of the menu, reporting breathlessly that the caterers specialised in the traditional regional fare of the state of Karnataka in south-west India, where the Murthy family were based. 'The satvik (no onion and garlic) meal was a traditional Mysore Brahmin fare (Narayana Murthy is from Mysore) with the Dharwad touch (Sudha Murthy's home town).' The highlight of the menu was mandige – a sweet dish from Hubli, where Akshata was initially raised – and the food was served in plain, biodegradable plantain leaves.

The article described the whole affair as 'no tamasha' – an expression meaning that there was no grand show – reporting that while many guests were surprised by the low-key festivities, others were 'amazed' that one of India's richest families could host such a no-fuss traditional affair. Neither the bride nor her mother wore many diamonds; nor did they indulge in the heavily embroidered outfits and gaudy accessories often favoured by wealthy bridal parties. 'Both the bride and her mother wore subtle make-up, a natural look hairstyle and what by Indian wedding standards could be considered minimal and basic jewellery,' the magazine declared.

There were some celebrity guests, however, including Indian business tycoon Azim Premji, known as the tsar of the Indian IT industry and a man even richer than his hosts; Indian billionaire entrepreneur Kiran Mazumdar-Shaw, chair of a biotechnology company based in Bangalore; Indian cricketers Anil Kumble and Syed Kirmani; former champion badminton player Prakash Padukone; and the Indian actor Girish Karnad.

What of the bridegroom in all this? The Indian press showed only a passing interest in Sunak, simply describing him as 'a British citizen of Indian origin' and noting that he was a Fulbright scholar who had studied at Oxford and Stanford. As his best man, Sunak had selected his best friend, James Forsyth. The pair had known each other for more than fifteen years, having been at Winchester together. While Sunak was in the City, Forsyth had gone into political journalism and was a rising star at the Conservative-supporting *Spectator* magazine, where he would soon be promoted to political editor.

For now, the relationship between these two supremely bright young men was primarily personal not professional, but as Sunak became more engaged in UK politics, this would change. In time, they would become even more important to each other as they navigated their respective careers. When Sunak decided to make the leap from the City to politics, he was able to tap into Forsyth's network of Tory contacts and insider knowledge about the Conservative Party. Later, when Sunak became Chancellor, Forsyth and his journalist wife Allegra Stratton found themselves with a direct line into one of the most powerful political figures in the country. During the coronavirus crisis, Sunak selected Stratton as his director of strategic communications, one of the most senior media jobs in government. In December 2022, Forsyth too entered the political fray when he was appointed political secretary to the Prime Minister.

*   *   *

A few years after the financial crash, Sunak's old boss Chris Hohn received a knighthood for services to philanthropy and international development. Despite the most expensive divorce in British history – his split with Jamie Cooper cost him a reported US$500 million – he had continued giving huge sums to charity. The pressure had taken its toll, however, creating a rift at the very top of TCI. In January 2009, Patrick Degorce, a co-founder and partner at the firm, walked.

For a while, the former French naval officer lay low, having cited 'personal reasons' for his departure. But by the summer of 2009 he was back on the scene, launching a rival hedge fund, Theleme. In a move that must have infuriated Hohn, he then set about poaching a string of TCI's senior staff – including Sunak.

Based in Mayfair with offices in the US, Theleme was typically secretive, with a minimalist website that offered only the basic information required by financial regulators. Sunak would be with old friends, however. By February 2012, no fewer than seven ex-TCI managers and analysts had jumped ship to Theleme, including Snehal Amin. As we have seen, he and Sunak had always enjoyed working together, and they had often talked about setting up an investment firm together. Friends say Amin was instrumental in Sunak's decision to leave TCI. One of the primary attractions of Theleme was the opportunity to relocate to America, where he could be with Akshata. Putting her fashion ambitions on hold, she had taken up a job in San Francisco with a Dutch company called Tendris that invested in businesses offering clean technologies. The couple decided to begin married life in California.

By spring 2011, they were expecting their first child. As well as planning for the new arrival, Akshata had been thinking about her own career. While she wanted to make beautiful clothes, she had never forgotten something her mother had said when she was young: 'If you cared as much about your studies as you do about fashion, you could change the world.' Encouraged by Sunak, she began working on plans for a range of designer clothes that would benefit Indian workers. Her ambition was that the western-style garments she designed would not only be beautiful in their own right but also promote Indian culture. The plan was to use luxury traditional fabrics: silk from Mysore; chanderi, a cotton yarn woven with silk to create a shimmering effect; and ikat, a colourful material made with a certain dyeing technique. Explaining her vision to *Vogue India* magazine in 2011, she said: 'I'm about the story behind a particular garment, its authenticity, craftsmanship and protecting a rich heritage. I care about doing something in India, for India because it's part of our family's DNA.' Her new label was to be called Akshata, which means 'immortal' in Sanskrit.

For an unknown designer, a feature in *Vogue* was dream publicity, and for a while there was quite a buzz in fashion circles about the launch of the new label. Akshata was the first to acknowledge that her start-up would not have attracted anything like this level of attention had it not been for her father's public profile. In interviews, she made clear she did not want to ride on his coat tails and expressed a determination to be a success in her own right. 'I understand that there may be some curiosity around what I'm doing given my parents' achievements, but I hope that one day this business is able to stand on its own feet and I'm able to speak on its merit rather than anything else,' she told one online publication.

Akshata had clearly had big ambitions for her new company, investing a huge amount of time and effort getting it off the ground, much of it while heavily pregnant. Despite her huge private wealth – her personal share in Infosys is worth hundreds of millions of pounds – she made it very clear that she was not just dabbling in this new venture. Launch publicity suggested that her designs would be 'sold in stores all over America' and at a boutique in New Delhi called Moon River.

In reality, her clothing line just fizzled out. The company Akshata Designs Inc. was incorporated on 11 February 2010 and dissolved little more than two years later, on 1 November 2012.

After all that hard work, and the kind of publicity other new designers could only dream of, what went wrong? Timing, for a start. The joyous arrival of the couple's first baby, Krishna, later that year made it difficult to focus on the fledgling business. Quite simply, Akshata's priority was now her daughter.

(A few years later, a second daughter would follow. The couple called her Anoushka, nicknamed 'Nou'.) Additionally, friends say she discovered she didn't much like the fashion world. 'All that air kissing just wasn't her,' says a friend. Such superficiality was, after all, completely alien to her upbringing. Quietly, she decided to let her fashion label wither on the vine.

Fatherhood had changed Narayana Murthy, and he proved a devoted grandparent too. In his open letter to Akshata, he told of his joy at seeing his new granddaughter for the first time. 'I wondered, whether from now on, I would have to behave like a wise, grand old man! But then I realised the bonus to growing older and becoming a grandparent. I would have the joy of pampering a child silly!'

Wrapping up the letter, he gave his daughter a final piece of advice, now she was a mother.

As you pursue your goals and live a contented life, remember that there is only one planet for us to live in and that planet is now becoming endangered. Remember that it is your responsibility to pass on this planet to Krishna in a better condition than you got it from us.

Sunak would spend another three years in finance, but he too was beginning to think about what he could do to make the world a better place. The time was coming to make the transition into politics.

CHAPTER 6

THE LEAP

In spring 2014, an influential think tank published a report that startled Middle England. It revealed how the face of the UK was changing and featured a striking statistic: by 2050, ethnic minorities would make up a third of the population. A series of eye-catching tables and charts showed huge increases in certain communities, including a doubling of the black African population and an 85 per cent rise in mixed-race groups since 2001. Most of these communities lived in deprived inner-city areas, predominantly in London, Manchester and Birmingham, the report said, but in due course they would move into suburbs and surrounding towns. The socio-economic implications were huge.

The report was a worry for many organisations, not least for the Conservatives. Produced by Policy Exchange, an organisation with close links to the party, the research was not ostensibly political, but the message was clear: the party would need to change its attitude to black and minority ethnic communities – or lose power. The default position for immigrants and their families had always been to vote Labour. For a long time, Tories had been able to win elections without the support of these groups. Now they had a problem.

While most Tory strategists were grateful for the wake-up call, behind the scenes some senior figures were annoyed. In particular, Lynton Crosby, who had masterminded Boris John-son's triumphant mayoral campaigns in a city with millions of ethnic minority voters, did not feel he needed any lessons on this subject. Who were these think tank types to imagine they knew more about it than he did? The tough-talking Austral-ian wanted to know who was behind the study. The answer? A young man named Rishi Sunak, head of Policy Exchange's newly established Black and Minority Ethnic Research Unit.

The previous year, Sunak had started getting serious about moving into politics. He and Akshata also felt it was time to move back to the UK. Sunak missed his parents and wanted them to be able to see more of their granddaughters. The couple also wanted their girls to go to school in England. By now California felt very much like home, however, particu-larly for Akshata, so they decided to maintain a base in the States where they could have regular holidays and catch up with friends. To that end, they bought a fabulous penthouse in a smart complex in Santa Monica called the Waverly.

From the outside, the apartment block did not look par-ticularly impressive. This was deceptive: the property, bought in Akshata's name, was in a prime location, with views of the Santa Monica mountains and the Pacific Ocean. All apart-ments in the complex boast 'beautifully detailed kitchens' with 'sea pearl quartzite counters, custom oak cabinetry and polished home hardware'. Bathrooms are kitted out in what the developers call 'Imperial White marble' with walnut vanity units and polished chrome hardware. Residents can 'unwind in the Zuma soaking tub' or wash away their trou-bles in the 'shower accented with a tortoise shell, glass mosaic wet wall and floor'. Naturally, such luxury came at a price: US property website Redfin estimates the apartment Akshata bought is worth $7.2 million. In years to come, however, she and the family would make good use of it.

Maintaining this foothold in the States, they were now ready to return to England. While he began exploring how to become an MP, Sunak would work at his father-in-law's investment company, Catamaran Ventures, with which Akshata was also involved.

The next opportunity to enter Parliament would be the 2015 general election. As nobody in the Tory Party knew who he was, he did have not much time to figure out how to make it happen.

Sunak approached this mission in the same way as he had always approached the big challenges in his life: with meticulous research and preparation. He knew he would be up against hundreds of other impressive hopefuls. He did have one very significant advantage, however, in the shape of his best friend, James Forsyth. As political editor of *The Spectator*, Forsyth was brilliantly connected and liked and trusted at the highest levels in the Tory Party. The journalist helped him get a foot through the door. He began quietly introducing his old friend to some key players, starting with a veteran Tory aide named Dougie Smith.

Smith was a colourful figure who had been around the party in various capacities since the John Major years. In the 1990s, he had been an adviser and speechwriter to several senior right-wing figures, including Referendum Party founder Sir Jimmy Goldsmith and Michael Howard. It would later emerge that he had a much racier side hustle, organising sex parties for the super-wealthy. Nobody at Westminster ever quite forgot this unusual feature of his CV, but the scandal over his Fever Parties orgies, which broke in the early 2000s, did not hold him back for long. By 2005, he had been rehabilitated and was working as a speechwriter for David Cameron. Later, he would marry Munira Mirza, then a Deputy Mayor of London and one of Boris Johnson's key advisers. In short, he knew everyone there was to know.

Forsyth's recommendation was enough to encourage Smith to take a keen interest in Sunak. He made it his business to set him on the path to becoming an MP, not only helping make useful contacts in the party but also guiding him through the process of joining the party's long list of approved prospective parliamentary candidates.

Recalling how he made his way into politics, Sunak has told friends, 'I came back from America and only knew James. No one else in politics. He introduced me to Dougie and between them, that was that.'

Among other influential figures Sunak met through Forsyth and Smith were Downing Street aides Oliver Dowden and Ameet Gill, who were also generous with time and advice.

Knowing people in high places would not be enough, however. Sunak knew he would have to do something special to stand out from everyone else seeking a place on the Tory Party's list of approved prospective parliamentary candidates. After all, he had not proved his commitment to the cause as a councillor or a grassroots activist. Nor had he been a special adviser or parliamentary researcher. He had not even written a column for the *Daily Telegraph*. What to do?

What came out of his conversations with Tory insiders was the importance of identifying himself as a 'thinker'. He should join a Conservative-leaning think tank, he was told, and write some interesting policy papers. That way, he would be taken seriously.

To that end, Sunak met the directors of Policy Exchange and volunteered to undertake some research on a subject close to his heart: Britain's minority communities. For too long, he felt, the media had treated BAME groups as if they were a single entity, when more than 100 different languages were spoken in London playgrounds alone. As Sunak knew first-hand, people like his parents who came to Britain from India or east Africa in the 1960s and 1970s were very different from people from the Caribbean, who had arrived in the UK much earlier, and different again to more recent arrivals from countries like Somalia. Politicians needed to understand these groups better in order to cater to their needs, Sunak believed. The directors of Policy Exchange liked his pitch, and he was given the go-ahead. Co-authored with former Tory special adviser Saratha Rajeswaran, his report on Britain's BAME communities was published on 5 May 2014 – almost a year to the day before the general election.

Neither Sunak nor anyone else at Policy Exchange had expected it to make such a bang, especially since the key statistics had all been previously published elsewhere. What the study did was pull together existing information about ethnic minority populations from a variety of sources and present it in a clear and concise way, as 'A Portrait of Modern Britain'. Key data about education, employment and income for different sections of society was now all in one place. Packaged in this way, it made compelling reading. Having imagined that it might attract passing interest among highbrow commentators, Sunak found the content splashed all over newspaper front pages. Suddenly, he was in high demand for media interviews.

'Lynton wasn't happy about it,' recalls a senior Tory Party strategist. 'He was like, who is this guy, talking about BME voters, when I know more about it?'

Crosby might not have liked it, but he could not have complained about the way Sunak handled the attention. In an exhausting round of TV, radio and newspaper interviews, the investment banker did not put a foot wrong.

Mark MacGregor, deputy director of Policy Exchange from 2013 to 2015, thought he had done brilliantly.

> Here was a guy who had never done a TV interview, never done a radio interview, never done a newspaper interview. And I'd told him, 'We might get *some* coverage, but…' and lots of people would sort of breeze in, thinking, 'I'll be fine, then.' But he took it incredibly seriously. He got some proper media training, as you should do. He prepared properly as if it were going to be a series of interviews. And in the end it was a hugely long day with the media. I think he started at 6.30 a.m. and he was still going late at night. I think there was even a piece on *Newsnight* about it.

If the aim had been to get noticed as well as contribute to an important debate, Sunak had pulled it off in spectacular style. In an indication of just how well his report was received, he was invited to the Home Office to brief Home Secretary Theresa May – a real coup.

Looking back on the fuss over 'A Portrait of Modern Britain', MacGregor is struck by Sunak's courtesy to colleagues at Policy Exchange.

> He said thank you. I tell you what, how often in politics do people say thank you? I've worked for MPs in elections where I've given up like three weeks of my holiday and brought tens of people with me to help them in their seats,

and barely received a thank-you. So often people don't thank you, and he is so polite, and I think that is an incredible strength for him.

As a first step towards a political career, it was a great start. He had made a tangible contribution by setting out in stark terms the scale of the demographic challenge the Tory Party faced. Party strategists could now start thinking about solutions. Sunak had enjoyed the experience and was eager to do more.

Luckily, his family supported his proposed career change. His father-in-law was particularly encouraging. Sunak had mentioned his ambition to go into public life to his parents-in-law when they first met, and Narayana had made it clear he approved. The billionaire was increasingly engaged in Indian politics and enjoyed meeting representatives from the main parties, though he considered himself too old to seriously enter the fray. It was a job for younger people with more energy, he felt. Sunak would later describe Narayana as his 'number one supporter' as he made the transition from the world of business and finance into politics. 'There have been many conversations, from a very early time. He's known it's always been an ambition of mine, and he's been incredibly supportive,' he told an Indian broadcaster.

Akshata too was positive, though she knew it would mean huge changes to their lives. Until he was selected for a particular seat, they would not be able to make any long-term plans, since they did not know where he would be based. Her attitude was to get on with her own work at Catamaran Ventures, where she was also a director, and continue bringing up their two little girls.

William Hague, who came to know her well, believes she has always been entirely comfortable with Sunak's career.

She is a brilliant woman in her own right. Sometimes with people's partners, in politics, you find they say, 'I'm not doing this; I'm not doing that,' but she was very, very supportive of his choice of career. I've never detected the slightest doubt or reservation in Akshata with what he's doing, even though it's meant quite an upheaval.

Sunak had laid the foundations for a formal entry into politics. Now the challenge was to find a seat.

CHAPTER 7

BLUE WELLIES

Shortly after the Conservative Party conference of autumn 2014, Sunak found himself on a train trundling north on what he felt was likely to be a wasted journey.

This was a febrile time for the Tory Party. Following four years of relative stability in coalition, they were heading towards a general election in which they risked a routing over Europe. Day-to-day government was becoming increasingly difficult as the Liberal Democrats sought to differentiate themselves from their coalition partners over tax and spending policy, leading to particularly fraught negotiations over the Treasury's Spending Review and Autumn Statement. Somehow David Cameron would have to hold the joint administration together for another eight months while Nick Clegg's party fought to set its own course ahead of what was expected to be a brutal day of reckoning at the polls for the Liberal Democrats. Meanwhile, the UKIP juggernaut was gathering momentum. In a devastating blow to the Prime Minister's authority, on the eve of the Conservatives' annual gathering in Birmingham, Tory MP for Rochester and Strood Mark Reckless announced that he was joining Nigel Farage's forces, declaring that voters had been 'ripped off and lied to' by the Tory leadership about Europe and immigration.

Douglas Carswell, formerly Tory MP for Clacton, had also

recently defected, and rumours swirled that others might follow suit. The 23.1 per cent of votes secured by the Tories in the European Parliament elections earlier that year was the lowest recorded vote share for the party in a national election. Within the leadership, there was mounting alarm that if they did not respond to public impatience over Europe, they faced an electoral wipe-out.

As Sunak stepped off the East Coast Main Line train at the market town of Northallerton, he was no doubt reflecting on all this, and how he might respond to questions about how the party should position itself in the months ahead. He would also have been casting surreptitious glances at other passengers alighting at the station, trying to work out which of them might be heading in the same direction. His destination was a dreary business park on the outskirts of town – but the opportunity it represented was anything but dull. Along with nine other hopefuls, he was on his way to the headquarters of Richmond Conservative Association for the chance to represent one of the Conservative Party's most prestigious parliamentary seats.

That summer, William Hague had announced that he was stepping down as Foreign Secretary and would not seek re-election to the Commons in May 2015. He had clocked up twenty-six years as MP for the rural constituency of Richmond in Yorkshire, during which time he had become Leader of the Opposition in the early years of Tony Blair's premiership and de facto Deputy Prime Minister under Cameron. Now he was expected to head to the House of Lords.

His decision to retire as an MP opened up one of the safest Tory seats in the country, and the race for selection as the local parliamentary candidate was now on. Sunak's task that day was to put in a sufficiently solid performance to make it to the next round of interviews, and from there, to make the cut to a final shortlist.

Privately, he felt it was something of a long shot. After all, he had no connection to the area and could not even claim to have been brought up in the countryside. He had also just been roundly defeated in the selection contest for Hertsmere in Hertfordshire, where Cameron's deputy chief of staff, Oliver Dowden, had stormed to victory after winning more than 50 per cent of the vote in the first round. Sunak had come a respectable second, but it was a blunt reminder of the calibre of the competition he faced. His original plan had been to find a seat somewhere near where he grew up in Southampton, but that had not proven straightforward.

Stephen Parkinson, now Lord Parkinson of Whitley Bay, who was also on the longlist for Richmond, recalls:

> He had been applying for other seats that had come up that summer, but he was particularly keen on a Hampshire seat, having grown up in Southampton. North East Hampshire – held by James Arbuthnot – and North West Hampshire – held by George Young – were both known to be coming up, and I think his sights had been on those, as a Hampshire boy and a Southampton fan and all the rest of it. But that's never how these things work out with parliamentary seats. So I think he was surprised but delighted to have been called for an interview in such a rural northern seat, having no rural northern credentials.

Always well prepared, Sunak knew who and what he was up against in Richmond. Hot favourite was Wendy Morton, who had not only been leader of Richmondshire Council but was also chair of the association. Her local knowledge and connections were unrivalled and there was clearly no doubting her commitment to the party and to local causes. On paper, she looked hard to beat. She was not Sunak's only problem, however. Also on the longlist were two senior Tory aides who had clocked up long years of service for the party. Nick Timothy and Stephen Parkinson both worked for Theresa May in the Home Office and were highly respected in senior Tory circles. They too seemed to have better credentials than Sunak for the job. It was hard to imagine how an almost unknown outsider could trump this formidable trio, but Sunak consoled himself that even if he bombed, it would be worth the experience. For the winner, a glittering prize awaited. The constituency was not only in one of the loveliest parts of rural England; it was also true blue, having been represented by Tory MPs for more than a century. Hague would be bequeathing his successor a 23,000-strong majority.

Applications for the seat had opened in August 2014, prompting a flurry of excitement. There was some speculation that Boris Johnson, approaching the end of his second term as Mayor of London and keen to return to Parliament, might have his eye on the patch; certainly, many associations were eager to snap him up. To the relief of other prospective candidates, that threat did not materialise, but some ninety others threw their hats into the ring, setting the scene for one of the fiercest selection contests in the country.

Eventually, the CVs were whittled down to the ten candidates who headed to Northallerton that October day. The first round of interviews took place at Omega Business Park and involved a roleplay activity. 'We were split into two groups and I was in the same group as Rishi,' Parkinson recalls.

I can't remember what the roleplay was about, but it was designed to see how you interact with your fellow applicants and what kind of person you were, and that was the first time I ever met Rishi. It was very clear how suave and smart and presentable he was. He didn't push himself forward too much, but that's a very wise thing in the environment. If you get too loud and too pushy, that can definitely count against you.

Heading to Northallerton Station after the event, Parkinson and Sunak soon realised they would be on the same train back to London. Parkinson admits his heart sank.

I thought, 'This is going to be the longest train journey ever: two and a half hours back to London with one of the people I'm competing against.' But he was just really friendly and charming, and we had a really pleasant and interesting chat. He was a very likeable person. By the time we got back to King's Cross I'd have voted for him myself.

During their conversation on the train, Sunak downplayed his chances of succeeding in Richmond, saying he was just happy to learn more about the selection process. This air of natural modesty would have gone down well with selectors.

While Morton was the obvious choice for the seat, this was never going to be a coronation. For decades, Richmond Conservatives had been represented by MPs who had distinguished themselves at Westminster. Hague's predecessor had been Leon Brittan, who had several ministerial roles in Margaret Thatcher's government, including Home Secretary. Prior to Brittan's tenure, the seat was held by Sir Timothy Kitson, who had been an aide to Ted Heath when he was premier. Both took a keen interest in the question of Hague's successor. With such an illustrious history, the association, which had an unusually strong branch network with many active members, was set on finding another high-flyer.

'There was huge excitement from the association,' Parkinson says. 'They were picking their parliamentary candidate for the first time in a generation. They were intensely proud of William Hague and everything he'd achieved, and there was a real buzz about who was going to step into his very large shoes.'

The second round of longlist interviews was held in the Golden Lion Hotel in Northallerton a week or so after the first, in front of the association executive, branch chairmen and representatives. In the front row sat Brittan, then president of the association. Behind him were ranks of farmers, former military types and businesspeople, most of whose families had lived in the constituency for generations.

One by one, candidates were called forward to present themselves. To win over the fifty-strong audience, they first had to provide a compelling account of why they wanted the job. Whenever anyone asked why he wanted to go into politics, Sunak's answer was always the same: it was about following the example his parents had set.

Speaking about what motivated him to enter politics some years later, he said:

It was actually my parents that motivated me... but not in a political way. My dad was a GP, my mum a pharmacist, and I grew up working in their surgery; in the pharmacy; delivering medicines to people who couldn't pick them up.

People would always stop and talk to me about my mum and dad, saying, 'Oh, you're Mrs Sunak's son, Dr Sunak's son.' And then they'd have some story about how my parents had helped them, or their parents, or children, and I thought that was amazing. They had done the same job in the same place, a mile from each other, for thirty years, and it was pretty clear that they as individuals were able to have an amazing impact on the community around us, and that I found pretty inspiring. And that was really my motivation for becoming an MP – it was to be able to make that same difference in a community as well, and I hope I am able to do that in North Yorkshire.

Heartfelt though it may have been, such an explanation hardly marked him out: most candidates probably referenced a role model, and all would have talked about wanting to serve the community. Sunak's real opportunity to shine would come during the twenty-minute grilling that followed, where he would have to show his ability to deal with whatever might be thrown at him.

The association was particularly anxious to ensure they did not select anyone who might embarrass them on social media: just a week or so earlier, on the eve of the Tory Party conference, Brooks Newmark, Conservative MP for Braintree and the Minister for Civil Society, had been forced to resign in a mortifying sex scandal, involving the sending of explicit photographs to an undercover reporter.

'Everyone was asked, "Have you ever done anything embarrassing on social media?" because the eve of party conference was when Brooks Newmark had his unfortunate incident in the tabloids, so I think that was very much on people's minds,'

Parkinson recalls. He describes the audience as 'blunt York-shire folk' who would 'tell it like it is'.

Voting took place immediately after the interviews, while candidates were still present. Parkinson, Timothy and four others were knocked out of the contest at this stage, leaving four finalists: Morton, Sunak, a former soldier named Chris Brannigan who had also been a Tory aide, and Robert Light, the former leader of Kirklees Council.

The final selection took place at Tennants of Leyburn, a famous local auction house. Angus Thompson, a farmer who now chairs Richmond Conservative Association, says that about 800 people turned up to watch as a panel put the candidates through their paces. What impressed the selection board was Sunak's positivity. Questioning was led by Julian Smith, now MP for Skipton and Ripon, and nothing he directed at Sunak seemed to faze him. 'He could just bounce back – no matter what the [selection panel] chairman asked,' Thompson recalls.

The same questions were put to all the candidates; they had about twenty-five minutes each. It didn't matter what – he always had a positive answer. He couldn't answer questions about agriculture up the Dales, but he could talk his way through it. While the other candidates would say, 'Oh, I'll have to look into it; I'm not sure,' he was just so positive – saying what his intentions would be, to sort out this and that issue, if he were elected.

By the end of the session, the selection panel was in no doubt who they wanted. One of those who witnessed Sunak's performance said he simply 'blew them away'. 'He was outstanding.

Wendy [Morton] is very nice indeed and is impressive too, but Sunak was just in another league to everyone.'

The result was a huge disappointment for Morton, who simply could not match Sunak's star quality that day. A few weeks later, she was selected for another seat, Aldridge-Brownhills, in the West Midlands, and has since been Minister for Transport and, briefly, Chief Whip.

Becoming an MP for any party is generally a long hard slog. A lucky few are 'parachuted in' to safe seats when there is a snap general election, but for most, the process is time-consuming, expensive and often dispiriting. Tory high command generally expects candidates to prove their worth by contesting an unwinnable seat, where they must increase the party's share of the vote before they can expect promotion to a constituency they might stand a chance of winning. Talented individuals like Morton can spend years cultivating a particular seat, doing everything in their power to demonstrate their commitment while waiting for the incumbent to step down – only to be supplanted at the eleventh hour by someone else or fall victim to a national swing against the party on polling day.

Sunak's experience was entirely different. He was only rejected once and did not have to spend years fighting hopeless campaigns in Labour or Liberal Democrat strongholds. There had been no leg-up from Central Office. He had overcome formidable hurdles to become parliamentary candidate for Richmond purely on merit – aiming high, doing his research, then dazzling everyone. Quite simply, he outclassed the competition.

For the next eight months, he could have done very little in Richmond and he would still have found himself heading to Westminster with a thumping majority. That was not in his nature, however. It was time to get to know his new patch, and he was eager to get started.

* * *

The shadow of William Hague seemed to follow Sunak everywhere in those early days following his selection, and he was acutely conscious of its presence. Once, he arranged a visit to one of the remotest parts of the constituency, a tiny village that was so difficult to access he thought Hague might never have been there. Just this once, he thought, he might outdo his predecessor. On arrival, he discovered to his chagrin that Hague had not only held a surgery there quite recently but had arrived in a Harrier jet, having flown in from meeting the President of the United States.

As he began familiarising himself with the constituency, dutifully making his way round primary and secondary schools, meeting key employers, networking with farmers and small-businesses owners and visiting pubs, health clinics and old folks' homes, Sunak constantly talked about the 'big boots' he had to fill, sometimes going so far as to say that following in Hague's footsteps felt 'impossible'. It was obvious to him that Hague had been very popular, and Sunak was aware that locals would be looking at him with a critical eye and secretly wondering if he would ever match up to his distinguished predecessor.

Sunak handled this burden by playing the apprentice, constantly deferring to the outgoing MP and making frequent public references to the magnitude of the act he had to follow. Somehow, he managed to pull this off without sounding either obsequious or insincere, attracting those he met with an obvious eagerness to learn and an easy charm.

On a more practical note, the huge life change he was making, from City hedge fund manager to Yorkshire politician, was going to require a new wardrobe – and fast. Within days of being selected, he would literally be walking up hill and down dale, day after day, often in battering wind and rain. He was going to need the right kit. Here he had less success fitting in. In an early presentational error, he purchased a pair of blue wellington boots, the choice of colour immediately marking him out as a 'townie' in the farming community, where the standard colour is green. It did not go unnoticed, but nobody judged too harshly, and his Barbour jacket, though it had clearly not yet been anywhere near a field or farmyard, was more in keeping with his new working environment. For less formal engagements he generally wore a waxed jacket, expensive-looking dark blue jeans and a crisp white shirt under a green or navy cashmere Ralph Lauren jumper. Top to toe, there would have been little change from four figures for these casual outfits, and the preppy country look oozed City money, but at least he was not pretending to be anyone other than himself. In more formal meetings he always wore tailored suits.

There were still eight months before the election, expected on 7 May 2015. However, Sunak was not impervious to the mounting panic in the party over UKIP's advance. A significant swing in the vote towards Nigel Farage's outfit would cost many Tory MPs their seats, and however comfortable Sunak's position seemed in Richmond, complacency would have been very bad form.

He therefore made arrangements to devote most of his time to the constituency, working with Richmond Conservative Association to set up a packed programme of engagements. The aim was to meet as many people as possible, familiarise himself with the geography and develop a feel for the big local issues.

Sunak's commitment and energy during this period did not go unnoticed. During his first working week, he visited Northallerton Police Station to learn about crime rates; met executives from NYnet, an organisation set up to improve connectivity and broadband services across the north of England; toured the local NHS hospital; went to Northallerton Auction Mart to talk to farmers; did his first question-and-answer session at Northallerton College; attended a Bonfire Night fireworks display; visited the local Fire and Rescue team for a briefing on emergency services; met a local employer to talk about apprenticeships; toured a department store and other businesses in Northallerton; attended a local teaching conference; and visited a horticultural charity for adults with learning disabilities.

This was a remarkably energetic start, which set the tone for the rest of his campaign. That weekend, he could justifiably have put his feet up, but instead, on the morning of Saturday 8 November, he set up his first street stall in front of Northallerton Town Hall, to continue his progress. Alongside dozens of market traders, at a stand complete with balloons and a gazebo, he talked to shoppers about local and national issues.

That Sunday he took part in Richmond's Remembrance Day ceremony, walking in the parade and attending a church service at St Mary's. He was honoured to lay a wreath on Hague's behalf at the War Memorial in Friary Gardens. Despite being a practising Hindu, he felt no discomfort in attending the religious service, listening attentively to the 'excellent' sermon by Reverend John Chambers. 'Two elements ... stayed with me,' he reported in his early campaign diary. 'He asked us to consider what we had done and what we were doing today with the sacrifice of our forefathers. And he also reminded us that "the best way to honour the dead is to care for the living".'

As the weeks slipped by towards Christmas, this was how Sunak spent his time, tirelessly touring Yorkshire hamlets and villages, going to schools and colleges, visiting local charities, attending meetings in church halls, talking to shopkeepers and local business owners, visiting food banks, and never looking or sounding anything less than boyishly keen. After Christmas, there would be little change to this routine, save that it would pick up pace.

After the sophistication of Silicon Valley, the buzz of India and the intensity of the City, rural North Yorkshire must have been quite a culture shock. If the insularity of the community and mundanity of many of his engagements ever tested his enthusiasm, he never showed it publicly. He could console himself that after the general election, this would only be part of the job. Meanwhile, he knew he must keep his eye on the prize.

CHAPTER 8

JEDI KNIGHTS

Now he was in the constituency full time, Sunak needed a base. Most parliamentary candidates in such circumstances rent a modest flat or cottage, but it came to Sunak's attention that there was a fabulous manor house on the market in the village of Kirby Sigston, Hambleton, about four miles east of Northallerton. The Grade II listed building was set in many acres of parkland and had a beautiful lake. It offered both the space and the privacy he felt his family would need in the months ahead. He and Akshata were used to multi-million-pound price tags for swanky apartments in London and Los Angeles. Reflecting the very different property market in Yorkshire, this stately home was a snip at just £1.5 million.

Tempting as it was to buy it on the spot, Sunak knew this would look presumptuous: he could not afford to be seen to be measuring up the curtains before he had even been elected. So he struck a deal with the owner to rent the place for a few months with a view to buying it as and when he became the local MP. This was quite a presentational risk: no PR adviser would recommend a prospective parliamentary candidate base themselves somewhere as ostentatious, for fear of accusations from political opponents that they were out of touch with the locals. Strangely, however, he got away with it. Either the candidates representing other parties were insufficiently on the ball or (somewhat to their credit) they simply didn't have the appetite for negative personal campaigning. The overwhelming strength of support for the Conservative Party in the constituency made it unlikely that such attacks would have found a particularly receptive audience in any case. These pitfalls successfully avoided, Sunak and his family now had somewhere comfortable to stay when they came up from London and the many spare rooms would prove useful for friends and relatives who came to lend their support.

As Sunak's campaign gathered momentum that spring, his father Yashvir became increasingly involved, having recently retired as a full-time doctor. Angus Thompson, chair of Richmond Conservative Association, says the GP gave his son 'a lot of help' during this period, and that Sunak threw his heart into the campaign every single day.

> It was six days a week, full on, every door was knocked on. His father was out a lot too. There was always a team of young enthusiastic people. Rishi had a lot of helpers; five or six, probably students. He was absolutely 100 per cent committed and full on. If he said he'd be there to meet you at 9.30 a.m., he was there. He's just one of these dynamic people, who just goes, goes, goes.

The geography of this huge rural seat could present logistical challenges: soon Sunak was clocking up hundreds of miles a week in what he called the 'family van'. The demographic was a more delicate problem. When Sunak originally applied for the seat, he was well aware that it was one of the whitest constituencies in the country. It certainly didn't put him off – the colour of his skin had never affected his career trajectory

– but in a seat like this, he knew it could present an additional challenge.

According to the 2011 Census, 85.2 per cent of people in Richmond were born in England, and many of the remainder (6.3 per cent) in Scotland, Wales or Northern Ireland. Almost 70 per cent of the local population describe themselves as Christians, with only 1 per cent saying they are Hindus and 0.3 per cent describing themselves as Muslim. (In answer to the question on religion, some 123 people in Richmond described themselves as 'Jedi knights', presumably being even more devoted than their Tory candidate to *Star Wars*.) In an area with so little ethnic diversity, Sunak was always going to stand out, and he fully expected to come up against some form of racism.

Thompson says that while he was never subjected to any overt abuse, he did have to overcome latent prejudice among some older voters, and that he handled this with ease.

> At times, I felt as though there were people who played the racist card. It was local people – older people in their seventies or so, who had just thought of ethnic minorities as people who lived in Bradford. They didn't see him as fitting in, in rural Yorkshire. He dealt with that brilliantly. If people said, 'We remember William Hague, we like William,' he would say, 'I'm the next William Hague; I've just got a better tan!' He dealt with it very well.

By April, Sunak had done most of the groundwork he felt was required in Richmond. Nationally, the campaign was an unusually flat affair, with none of the blunders and dramas that politicians are desperate to avoid but which at least enliven proceedings for voters. No punches were thrown; nobody prominent was caught saying anything embarrassing after accidentally leaving their microphone on; and there was a general absence of politicians shooting themselves in the foot. The Conservatives had taken the wind out of Farage's sails by making an in/out referendum on the UK's membership of the EU a key plank of their manifesto and their coalition partners no longer posed much of a threat in marginal seats. Having used the Liberal Democrats to keep them in government for five years, they could largely stand back and let Nick Clegg's party pay the price of an alliance the grassroots had never liked. Meanwhile, Labour under Ed Miliband was struggling. A towering stone tablet, swiftly dubbed the 'EdStone', onto which the party's six key election pledges had been carved was widely lampooned and voters found it hard to imagine Miliband in Downing Street. In the final stretches of the campaign, polls pointed to a hung parliament. There was little expectation that voters would reward the Tories for five years of austerity, but Labour continued to struggle to cut through.

In Richmond, the big themes were much the same as they were everywhere else at the time: Europe, immigration and the economy, with the usual local worries about bus services, the state of the local NHS and the future of small businesses thrown in.

Sunak's campaign fell into a regular pattern: during the day, he and his team would knock on doors talking to people about what mattered to them; in the evening, he would hold question-and-answer sessions in village halls. During his first week, he was joined by work experience students from all over the constituency. 'They helped design some literature specifically targeted at young people and got their first taste of a political campaign. Although I think we learned as much from them as they did from us,' he noted in his campaign diary.

That Easter, which fell at the end of the first week of the campaign, Sunak took a day off for his younger sister's wedding. Career-wise, the siblings had followed very different paths. While Sunak had spent his spare time at Oxford learning about investment banking and cultivating contacts in the City, Raakhi, who also went to Oxford, had thrown herself into good causes. As an undergraduate in 2006, she founded the university's UNICEF Society, enrolling some 400 members and raising several thousand pounds. In recognition of her contribution, she was invited to join the charity's delegation to the House of Commons. In her early twenties, she was a restorative justice intern at the UN Development programme in Jamaica. After graduating, she worked as an adviser to Y Care International, the YMCA's aid and development charity, before joining the Department for International Development, where she rapidly rose through the ranks. At the time of her marriage to international aid specialist Peter Williams, she was policy and programme adviser for DfID in Dar es Salaam, Tanzania.

All these jobs suggest her political views differ sharply from those of her brother: it is of course a generalisation, but those helping refugees and asylum seekers, working for human rights organisations and supporting international aid programmes tend to be left-leaning. While Raakhi's voting record is unknown, those who know her admit that when she and her older brother discuss politics, the debate can be lively. 'They certainly have quite differing views,' says a source who knows them both.

For Sunak, the wedding was a welcome change of scene. Having spent all week out on the stump, he was relieved that he hadn't been asked to give any kind of speech at the reception and that his official role was limited to a reading. It was refreshing to forget the campaign for a few hours and talk about something other than broadband connections and sheep-tagging.

Cameron launched the Tory manifesto during the second week of the so-called short campaign, pledging to ensure a 'good life' for British workers and their families. The Prime Minister declared that he wanted to 'finish the job' of rebuilding Britain for working people, promising to pass a law to keep those on the minimum wage out of tax. He claimed Britain was 'on the brink of something special' and warned that voting Labour would take the country 'back to square one'.

North of the border, however, back at square one was exactly where frustrated nationalist voters wanted to be. Having lost the 2014 referendum on independence by a very clear margin, the SNP had set its sights on a replay. The party leadership appealed to Scottish voters to send an army of SNP MPs to Westminster to be a thorn in the side of the UK government and demonstrate that Scottish independence was not going away. The rallying cry was working, with polls suggesting Nicola Sturgeon's party was on course to win almost every Scottish seat.

In Yorkshire, the idea that the SNP might hold the balance of power in another hung parliament was a source of mounting concern, and Sunak spent a surprising amount of time during the campaign explaining his position on Scottish independence. 'Everywhere I go, people are worried about the prospect of the SNP being part of a Westminster government.

What will that mean for England?' he noted in his campaign diary. 'For me, we must have some measure of English votes for English Laws – simply put, only English MPs should be able to have a say on matters that affect only England. That's what happens on Scottish matters and it should be no different for us here in England.'

Given the history of the seat, it is virtually impossible to imagine circumstances in which Sunak would not have won this campaign with thousands of votes to spare. Yet he took nothing for granted. House to house, farm to farm, village to village, he made the most of every day that remained to influence the Richmond electorate. It took almost two hours by car to get from one end of the patch to the other, but the hard work was on foot, as he tried to reach as many of the 80,000 electors and 42,000-odd homes as he could. 'By the end of the campaign I am sure I will have walked a few marathons at least,' he noted – which was no exaggeration. By the final week of the campaign, according to an app on his smartphone, he was walking eighteen miles a day.

Among those who came to help was Narayana Murthy, who was delighted by his son-in-law's move into politics. Sunak armed him with a stack of campaign leaflets to deliver, appealing to his gregarious father-in-law not to get drawn into too much debate on doorsteps, or they would never get the job done. It was a novelty for the billionaire to be told what to do, but he pulled his weight.

In marginal seats, election day is an ordeal for candidates, whose fate sometimes rests on just a handful of votes. The agony can be protracted as snippets of information and misinformation about turnout in particular wards point to a positive or negative result. For candidates defending huge majorities, upsets are rare, making for a much more relaxed experience. As the big day dawned on 7 May, Sunak and his team were never in any doubt about the result. Indeed, they were so relaxed that they did not show up to the count until the very last minute, prompting word to go round that he had actually missed the big moment when the results were announced. Sunak claims his late appearance was in fact an act of courtesy to the tellers, which seems more plausible, since he is neither disorganised nor arrogant. 'I wanted to come when I wasn't able to disturb people,' he breezily told reporters that night. 'Because we're not allowed to talk to the counting agents when they're getting on with their work, I wanted to make sure that I was able to go round and say thank you to everyone personally, which I was able to do.'

In any case, after months of hard slog, he was home and dry, having secured more than 51 per cent of the vote. The total number of people who voted for him was 27,744, almost 6,000 fewer than had backed Hague five years earlier, reducing the Tory majority in Richmond to 19,550. The fly in the ointment had been Farage's party, which fielded a candidate in the constituency for the first time. UKIP's Matthew Cooke had come second with 8,194 votes, accounting for most of the old Tory support that had fallen away.

None of that mattered on what was a night of euphoria for the Conservatives nationally. For the first time since 1992, they had secured a majority – albeit only twelve seats strong – in a result that had not been predicted by pollsters, the media or the markets and which arrived on the back of a near-total rout for Labour in Scotland at the hands of the SNP.

As for Sunak, after months in rural Yorkshire, he was heading back to the bright lights of the capital – and the corridors of power.

* * *

Only a handful of MPs were in the Commons debating chamber to witness one of their brightest new colleagues make his maiden speech. Nonetheless, Sunak was surrounded by allies who could be relied upon to make approving noises at the right moments and laugh at his jokes. As he rose to his feet, looking and sounding not in the slightest bit nervous, he was flanked by Tom Tugendhat, newly elected MP for Tonbridge and Malling, who had already been marked out by Westminster observers as a rising star. Like Sunak, Tugendhat had written a number of well-received papers for the think tank Policy Exchange, in his case on the pursuit of veterans over allegations of historical abuse. There was widespread expectation at Westminster that he would not remain on the back benches long.

Sunak was of course a confident orator – his public-school education and time at Stanford had ensured that – but nothing quite prepares a new MP for the feeling when they address the Commons the first few times. Even the most accomplished performers can feel overwhelmed by the historic surroundings and a sense that they are following in the footsteps of great statesmen. Thankfully maiden speeches are fairly formulaic, requiring little creativity, and take only a few minutes. After paying tribute to their predecessor, MPs wax lyrical about their new constituency; talk about how honoured they are to represent such a special place; and emphasise their commitment to public service. Following general elections in which lots of seats change hands, there are hundreds of these performances, mostly very dull – which is why there were not many people in the Commons when, more than a month after he was elected, Sunak's turn finally came. His speech was an impressive example of the genre, featuring plenty of self-deprecating quips, and the laughs it elicited from his audience were genuine. 'Some have wondered about William Hague's future,' he observed jauntily, following the requisite tribute to his predecessor. 'Perhaps he will heed the advice of the Prime Minister, who suggested he ought to become the new James Bond. In the Prime Minister's own words: "He's fit, he's healthy, he does yoga, he can probably crack a man's skull between his kneecaps. Hard to beat!"'

The rest of the five-minute speech was standard stuff: promises to protect local hospitals and schools, a pledge to stand up for farmers, and talk of fighting for better broadband. Courteous as always, Sunak did not forget to make a special mention of Hague's predecessors the late Lord Brittan and Sir Timothy Kitson and he ensured he paid tribute to the armed forces, so important in his constituency. What was striking about his performance was just how assured it was. There was nothing about his demeanour to suggest he was anything other than relishing this moment and, having been an MP for only a few weeks, he addressed the chamber with no less ease than he would display five years later when he delivered his first Budget.

Sunak had quickly found his feet in his strange new work-place. The unique environment is a culture shock for anyone unfamiliar with the bewildering geography of the sprawling parliamentary estate, the curiously garbed officials and the archaic customs and traditions. Following general elections, MPs usually have to hot-desk for several days or even weeks while party whips allocate offices according to seniority. Returning MPs generally go back to their old rooms, but there is always a competition for prestigious spots vacated by senior figures who have either lost their seats or gone to the Lords. The most popular offices are generally in Portcullis House, the modern wing of the Houses of Parliament which opened in 2001 to accommodate 213 MPs. These rooms are bright, airy and comfortably furnished, with anterooms for staff. Many have spectacular views over the River Thames. By contrast, offices in the older buildings tend to be dark and poky, with tiny latticework windows, dubious electrics and no air conditioning – an ordeal in summer. Mice are far from an unusual sight. The upside for MPs based in these dingy quarters is the thrill of working in such a historic and atmospheric place.

Least coveted of all are the rooms in 1 Parliament Street, accessed from Whitehall, and in Norman Shaw Buildings, which lie just north of Portcullis House. MPs based in these buildings can feel a bit far from the action – not to mention the only decent coffee, which is to be found in the atrium of Portcullis House.

After the usual kerfuffle, Sunak was allocated a room. Walking into his new office, he was somewhat taken aback to find that someone had left a high-visibility jacket and hard hat – a symbol of the sorry state of repair of much of the parliamentary estate.

His focus did not move entirely to Westminster, however. Back in Richmond, he hired Malcolm Warne, the former editor of the *Darlington & Stockton Times*, to manage communications locally. He was determined to keep up his local profile and develop a reputation for being committed to the constituency – not something that all MPs with safe seats manage to maintain.

Nationally, the election result had left socialists reeling. Appalled by the prospect of five years of undiluted Conservatism, in the weeks after the election left-wing activists staged a number of rowdy demonstrations outside the House of Commons, decrying austerity and chanting abuse about Tory MPs. Battling his way through one of these protests in Parliament Square not long after he had been elected, Sunak was shocked at the vitriol being aimed at politicians.

> I was walking across Parliament Square with a colleague, who's also a new MP at the time, and we were strolling along, and… people were hurling abuse at us, saying, 'bloody politicians, you are all useless', etc etc. It was a few weeks in, and kind of like, wow, quite hard to take.

His colleague Jeremy Quin MP, the newly elected MP who was walking across the green with him, was more phlegmatic. 'I glanced at him, and he was grinning!' Sunak recalled. 'And I said to him, "Jeremy, do you hear what they are saying about us politicians? It's not particularly flattering." And he said, "Rishi, my dear boy, you have to understand – I used to be an investment banker!"'

Uncomfortable as they were for young MPs yet to develop a thick skin, the protests came to nothing. Indeed, David Cameron would look back on this period as one of the happiest of his premiership. Liberated from the constraints of coalition government, he was at the peak of his power as a party leader, finally free to shape the Cabinet as he saw fit and pursue a policy agenda that did not constantly need to be modified to suit the Liberal Democrats. The reshuffle immediately after the election cemented George Osborne's status as the second most powerful figure in government. The reappointed Chancellor was now de facto Deputy Prime Minister, and a clutch of his acolytes were given top jobs, reinforcing his power and influence. At Westminster, he was widely seen as Cameron's likely successor, but a vacancy in No. 10 seemed a distant prospect: the incumbent was riding high.

Writing about this period in his memoirs, Cameron would later remark that he had 'never felt more content' in his own skin 'or more excited about where I was taking the country'.

'I felt I had everything on my side: experience and energy, plus my party and my country.' The worst of the austerity years were over, and his vision was for what he called a 'Great British take-off' that would leave nobody behind.

Within a year, Cameron would be out of office – these dreams shattered by the tidal wave of the EU referendum. But for Sunak, the journey was just beginning.

CHAPTER 9

'IN GOD WE TRUST'

Less than a year after entering Parliament, Sunak took a risk that would shape his political career. It was his first winter as an MP and the novelty of his ringside seat on some of the momentous decisions taken in the House of Commons – and Westminster's archaic traditions – had yet to wear off. Still marvelling at the strange ceremonies and costumes surrounding set-piece occasions, he had watched wide-eyed as the parliamentarian he had replaced in the Commons took up his seat in the House of Lords, in a ritual dating back to 1621.

Accompanied by two supporters in flowing ceremonial robes, Lord Hague of Richmond, as he would thenceforth be known, was led into the chamber by Black Rod, the parliamentary official who represents the monarch in the upper house, to swear an oath of allegiance.

When Sunak relinquished the City for politics, some banker friends sniffed that global investors like his old boss Chris Hohn and corporations such as Amazon and Google had more power and influence than almost anyone in Parliament. But as he immersed himself in day-to-day business at Westminster during the autumn of 2015, Sunak was overcome by the magnitude of some of the matters at stake, feeling vindicated in his conviction that this was no backwater. In the space of a few short weeks, the government not only published a long-awaited Strategic Defence Review, setting out how the armed forces and intelligence services should meet the greatest threats to national security, but also unveiled plans for the public finances for the rest of the parliament in an Autumn Statement associated with some £4 trillion of future public spending. Even the most arrogant City types could not scoff at these figures.

Prime Minister David Cameron had also delivered a sombre statement on Syria in response to a report by a cross-party committee of ordinary MPs. Sunak felt this underlined how much influence even the lowliest backbencher could exert – an impression that was reinforced when Cameron spent more than two hours fielding some 100 questions from MPs. Meanwhile, parliamentarians were being asked to vote on whether to extend air strikes to Syria, a debate scheduled to last ten hours to allow for contributions from more than 150 Members. Few would dispute the gravity of such a decision.

'For those who question the relevance of Parliament in the modern age and the role it plays in holding Government to account, these events have demonstrated its importance,' Sunak observed in the weekly column he wrote in his local paper. 'The decisions taken in the House of Commons over these 12 days affect us all and have set the course for our nation for the remainder of the parliament.'

A former minister recalls that Sunak positioned himself well as a new MP. 'He wasn't too pushy,' he says. 'When you come into the House, you want people to notice you, but you don't want to look like you're really pushing. So people just thought he's bright, he's good, he's one of the people in this intake who we'd expect to get somewhere.' At the same time, he managed to be loyal without looking like a toady. 'I would say he wasn't unhelpful, but he wasn't a sort of creep either. You get some people who basically spend their lives in the chamber trying to do the Whips' Office's bidding ... But I wouldn't have put him into that group of people who the whips always identify as their sort of absolute bankers.'

Significant as the issues before the new parliament were, there was an even bigger strategic question facing all MPs: how to vote in the looming EU referendum. Though a date for the plebiscite had yet to be set, it had been a key plank of the Conservative Party's general election manifesto and, sooner or later, it would have to take place.

Though Cameron talked up the prospect of 'renegotiating' the UK's relationship with Brussels, it was increasingly clear that whatever the outcome of those discussions, the Tory Party leadership was in favour of remaining in the EU. Young MPs who backed Brexit would thus be setting themselves at odds with those they needed to impress to be in with a chance of promotion – the very opposite of the ultra-loyal approach Sunak had hitherto adopted.

The problem was that he was increasingly drawn to Brexit. With an internationalist outlook stemming from his links to India and his time in the United States, he instinctively felt the UK would be better off outside the EU. Sunak never made big decisions based on instinct, however. In an interview with an Indian TV channel shortly after he was elected, he explained that when it came to difficult issues, he always followed his father-in-law's advice, which was to focus on the facts. 'One of my favourite quotes of his is: "In God we trust, but everyone else needs to bring data to the table." It's something I try to live by ... I'm always interested in getting the data; getting the facts.'

Adopting an analytical approach to whether the UK should leave the EU, he examined the potential for economic innovation, the scope for better trading relationships and the UK's ability to control immigration. To him, all of this pointed to Britain being better off out. Nonetheless, he was not keen to find himself on the losing side of the argument – few in political circles at the time believed the UK would vote to leave. Moreover, it preyed on his mind that William Hague, for whom he had the greatest respect, was leaning towards Remain. The former Foreign Secretary loathed the dreary, overbearing institutions of the EU and was deeply uncomfortable about the lack of democratic accountability in Brussels. However, he feared what might happen if the bloc unravelled. A week before Christmas 2015, he penned an article for the *Daily Telegraph* which left little doubt over the way he would vote. He remained as scathing as ever about much of the EU, but he had come to the view that it was 'manifestly not in our interests' for it to fall apart. He worried, too, about giving Scottish nationalists any excuse to demand a second referendum on independence. Hague did not quite say it would be 'foolish' to leave, but that was the word that appeared in the *Telegraph* headline – a characterisation that must have been unsettling for his nervous young successor in Richmond.

By the New Year, pressure was mounting on Cameron over his effort to secure what he called a 'new settlement' for Britain in Europe. Attempts to have a substantive discussion at the European Council just before Christmas had failed, with the agenda dominated by terrorism and migration. The new target date to reach an agreement was the summit due to take place on 18 February. Among the concessions the Prime Minister sought were limits to the right of EU migrants to claim welfare benefits; safeguards to ensure the UK would not have to participate in eurozone bailouts; opt-outs from some EU employment directives; and an end to Britain's backing for the collective commitment to 'ever-closer union' enshrined in the EU treaties.

Shortly before the House returned from the Christmas break, Cameron had announced that he would lift the principle of collective responsibility underpinning Cabinet decision-making to allow ministers to vote as they saw fit in the referendum – a move driven more by necessity than choice. Several Cabinet ministers were vocal Brexit supporters and would have been forced to resign from government without this freedom.

Nonetheless, Sunak was anxious. Though he was not yet even a parliamentary private secretary (PPS), an unpaid role that is normally the first stage towards securing a junior ministerial job, he was mindful of the fate of other young independent-minded MPs who had previously voted with their consciences. Cameron and Osborne had shown how unforgiving they could be, consigning Rory Stewart, the talented MP for Penrith and the Border, to the back benches for years after he rebelled over House of Lords reform. Another rebel, Jesse Norman, the MP for Hereford and South Herefordshire, had also been blackballed. The circumstances were quite different – Stewart and Norman had defied a three-line whip – but the hard line taken by the party leadership was hardly encouraging.

According to a friend and lobbyist who knows him well:

When Rishi became an MP, he was advised to keep a low profile for a while. One of the things he did very sensibly was buddy up with Oliver Dowden, who was deputy chief of staff to Cameron. Oliver and Rishi became firm pals in that 2015 intake. Oliver guided him to keep his head down. He told Rishi, 'Don't paint a target on your back; don't do any big press interviews.' And Rishi took that advice. Going in another direction from the leadership on Brexit was not following that strategy and I know he was nervous about how it might play out.

Sunak would be gambling that if the nation voted to remain in the EU, Cameron and Osborne would not bear grudges against those who had argued the opposite.

In one of his first television appearances, a regional segment of the BBC's *Sunday Politics* show on 17 January, he was asked bluntly which side he would be on when it came to the vote. He avoided giving a direct answer but declared that the UK's relationship with the EU needed 'major reform', citing immigration as 'central' and a 'real concern'. It had been 'too high for too long', he said, and it was too easy for immigrants to 'come here and very easily tap into the welfare system'.

At this stage, he was still tentatively clinging to the hope that Cameron's renegotiation might deliver the necessary change. Early indications were not promising. All the signs were that the EU would reject the Prime Minister's key demands on migration on the basis that such changes would threaten the founding principle of free movement of workers. If that were the case, Sunak would have to vote Out.

The crunch summit was not the triumph No. 10 needed. Cameron did not exactly return empty-handed, but the few symbolic concessions he secured on migrant rights to benefits, the UK's exposure to eurozone financial bailouts and an

opt-out on the commitment to ever-closer union were nowhere near enough to satisfy most Eurosceptics. The verdict
in the Eurosceptic press was damning: the Prime Minister's
diplomatic offensive had failed.

Announcing that the referendum would be held on 23 June,
Cameron insisted that he still believed it was in Britain's best
interests to remain, but Sunak's mind was made up. 'On June
23 I will vote to leave the European Union,' he declared in a
column for his local newspaper.

> It pains me that I have reached a different conclusion to
> people I greatly respect; notably the Prime Minister and my
> illustrious predecessor, Lord Hague. For me, this is a once
> in a generation opportunity for our country to take back
> control of its destiny. Of course, leaving will bring some
> uncertainty, but on balance I believe that our nation will be
> freer, fairer and more prosperous outside the EU.

A senior figure in the Vote Leave campaign says they considered it 'really quite a coup' for Sunak to come down on their
side of the argument.

> The Eurosceptics are easy to caricature as the men in grey
> suits who have been banging on about this for thirty years.
> Here is a young, liberal, modern MP with no particular
> history of Euroscepticism saying that in this referendum,
> for a variety of internationalist and democratic reasons, I'm
> going to vote to leave.

He also acknowledges the potential risk Sunak took with his
political future.

Backing Leave, which at that point was definitely not expected to win, was an unusually brave thing to do. He marked
himself out again as an interesting, independent-minded
MP ... There were definitely people who would quite happily
have backed Leave but felt that the loyal thing to do to David
Cameron, or the careerist and sensible thing to do, would
be to chew their lip and say they were a reluctant Remainer.

Sunak had made his choice; the die was cast.

*   *   *

While Sunak's decision to back Brexit was partly about immigration – a theme he knew resonated with more voters than
the nitty-gritty of tariffs and quotas – what really exercised
him was the EU's record on trade negotiations. One glance at
their 'dismal' trade policy was enough to undermine the case
for Remain, he argued, singling out a painstakingly reached
trade deal for particular criticism. The free trade agreement
with South Korea, the EU's first with a major developed
economy, did not happen until fifty-four years after the bloc's
founding members relinquished the power to negotiate their
own trade deals, he lamented. In a hard-hitting article for the
Daily Telegraph, he pointed out that South Korea's economy
is only half the size of Britain's; that it took the EU five years
longer to sign the deal than it took Switzerland; and that –
after half a century – the EU still did not have a free trade deal
in place with a single top-ten economy.

His global connections through his wife and the time he
had spent in the United States, as well as his business career
investing in companies from Silicon Valley to Brazil and

Bangalore, had left him in no doubt that what he called the 'scales of the global economy' were tipping eastwards – and that the UK was in danger of being left behind, dragged down by membership of an organisation that had failed to recognise the shift. Europe's major economies were still fixated with European markets, he argued, when they needed to adopt a more global approach. As the only major EU economy that exported more outside the EU than within it, the UK, he felt, was instinctively more outward-looking – yet fettered by its ties to an organisation with a profoundly different agenda. 'The result is that our country's trade policy is now run by an organisation with fundamentally different trade priorities to our own. For Britain that means too few trade deals, too slowly, with mismatched partners,' he wrote.

Explaining his decision to back Brexit to his constituents in his weekly column, he skimmed over immigration and sovereignty – the two issues most frequently cited by Leave-supporting voters – emphasising instead what he saw as Europe's failure to keep up in an increasingly competitive global market.

Since we joined the Common Market, Europe's share of the world economy has halved and is still falling. Whilst China's GDP has doubled since the recession, Europe is the only continent in the world (alongside Antarctica, that is) that has failed to grow at all. Canada, South Korea and South Africa all trade freely with Europe without surrendering their independence. As one of Europe's largest customers, I see no sensible reason why we could not achieve a similar agreement.

Sunak recognised that harping on about global trade deals was unlikely to cut much ice with one of the most important communities in his constituency, however: farmers. Many were nervous about the potential loss of EU subsidies. From the moment he was selected as the Tory Party's parliamentary candidate for Richmond, Sunak had been at pains to cultivate this influential group. Following his initial faux pas with the blue wellies, he had replaced them with a green pair, standard footwear at the various agricultural shows and markets where he went to press the flesh. He applied himself to learning as much as he could. One of his first engagements was a morning at the livestock market at Northallerton, where he began to familiarise himself with industry terminology. 'A great morning at the Auction Mart,' he enthused. 'I got to test out my knowledge of liveweight and deadweight, fat stock, store stock and cull cows, and was even given a quick test on identifying different breeds!'

His discussions with dozens of farmers at the market, which has been a twice-weekly fixture in Northallerton for more than a century, was just a taste of the kind of issues that really matter to the many people in Richmond whose livelihoods depend on the land. Over the months that followed, Sunak made it his business to grasp the way supermarkets drive down milk and livestock prices and to develop an understanding of the many EU regulations affecting the way farmers move and manage land and animals.

The contrast with his old life in Silicon Valley could hardly have been more extreme, but if he was bored by the intricacies of the 'six-day standstill rule', a measure introduced during the 2001 foot-and-mouth disease outbreak preventing the movement of any livestock for six days after the arrival of a new animal on the premises, he never showed it. Soon he would be an expert in problems with electronic sheep-tagging, frustrations over new environmental obligations linked to EU subsidies, and the failure of the European Commission to enforce pig welfare rules, which put compliant pig farmers in Richmond at a competitive disadvantage. By the time he joined the House of Commons Environment, Food and Rural Affairs Select Committee shortly after entering Parliament, he could speak with authority on such matters.

In the run-up to the referendum, Sunak was at pains to reassure farmers that if the UK quit the EU, they would not be left swinging in the wind. The government could create a bespoke British Agricultural Policy of subsidies to replace the flawed Common Agricultural Policy (CAP), he argued.

> I care a great deal about supporting our local farmers ... If we leave the EU, we will immediately save £20bn. UK farmers currently receive £2.5bn from CAP so the UK will certainly have the resources to put in place a British Agricultural Policy. Not only could we financially support our farmers but we could also free them from the most costly European regulations.

Towards the end of May 2016, he embarked on a roadshow designed to explain his decision to back Brexit to as many voters on his patch as possible. While Richmondshire would subsequently back Leave by some margin, Sunak was conscious that it was not an overwhelmingly Leave-supporting constituency and that he needed to make the case. To that end, between 30 May and 2 June he arranged four consecutive town hall meetings in Northallerton, Stokesley, Richmond and Leyburn, chaired and moderated by a local journalist and various councillors, in a question-and-answer format. These meetings 'will not be about me campaigning for Brexit', he emphasised, but about airing the issues. 'In the end, this is not about my vote or that of any other politician. Our future European relationship will be decided by all of you, the British people.'

During this frenetic week, he spoke to more than 500 people, writing somewhat schmaltzily in his weekly column that he had been 'humbled by the vibrancy and intelligence' with which people on both sides of the debate had taken part. These Q&A sessions underlined the extent to which Sunak's decision to back Brexit was not, as it was for millions of voters, a question of the heart – an instinctive sense that Brussels had become overbearing and that the UK would be better shaping its own destiny. It was entirely cool-headed. 'The best way I can think of explaining how I came to my own decision was by breaking the question down into five categories: the economy, immigration, UK contributions to the EU budget, security and sovereignty', he explained. Having examined each of these areas, he acknowledged that whichever way the UK voted, there were 'risks, benefits and uncertainties' on all five fronts.

Chris Lloyd, chief feature writer at the *Northern Echo* and Sunak's local paper, the *Darlington & Stockton Times*, who chaired the Q&A event in Northallerton Town Hall, was impressed by the manner in which he engaged with constituents.

At these town hall meetings, you could see he was trying to be honest. He admitted that the Brexit decision was a very close-run thing for him; that there would be downsides to it; but that he felt there would be opportunities. I remember him talking about a global view of a world. His audience were not internationalist at all – they were mostly local farmers – so it could have been quite a difficult message to get across.

As the referendum campaign reached fever pitch, with a furious row over a Brexit slogan on the side of a bus, and farcical scenes surrounding rival Remain and Leave flotillas clashing on the Thames, a terrible event put everything firmly into perspective. In a crime that appalled the nation, Labour MP Jo Cox was shot and stabbed multiple times on the steps of her constituency surgery. The 41-year-old died at the scene. In the hours after her murder, police confirmed they were investigating reports that the suspect, Thomas Mair, shouted 'Britain first' as he carried out the frenzied attack. Campaigning on both sides was immediately suspended as a mark of respect, as politicians reeled from the loss of one of their own. Behind the scenes in the Brexit campaign that weekend, there was mounting alarm over the political repercussions. Cox had been a prominent Remain supporter. Coupled with the suggestion that she had been killed by a British nationalist, it looked like a disaster for Leave.

As referendum campaigning juddered to a halt, Sunak threw himself into constituency events. This at least took his mind off things. In the space of forty-eight hours, he attended two village fêtes, started a 10km race and fun run, judged the parade floats at a festival and picked the best young handler in a dog show. Somehow, he managed to end up in the stocks in both Great Ayton and Bedale – not quite the role he had envisaged for himself when he entered politics. Still, it was difficult to fret about Brexit when his head was being pelted with wet sponges by giggling Boy Scouts.

Whether this would be a metaphor for the fate of all of those on his side of the argument in the EU referendum campaign was now out of his hands. With just four days to go until the vote, there was little he could do but hold his breath and wait.

* * *

Torrential rain and flash floods brought chaos to parts of the UK on polling day, but for once the downpours were not in Yorkshire. As almost a month's worth of rain drenched the capital in the space of a few hours and urgent flood warnings were issued for south-east London and Essex, Sunak was home and dry (both literally and politically, as it would turn out).

He spent that historic day, 23 June, quietly in his constituency, carrying out a strictly non-Brexit-related official engagement: the launch of a new monthly friendship club designed to combat loneliness in rural areas. More than thirty people pitched up to the Black Bull at Moulton, a famous Yorkshire pub, for a subsidised meal, including Sunak, looking slightly out of place in his formal attire.

As polling day drew to a close, he sat drinking tea in the late evening sunshine – having cast his own vote – with his friend and neighbouring MP Kevin Hollinrake, who had supported Remain. The bitterness of the campaign meant that many old friendships between politicians on opposing sides of the debate did not survive – most dramatically, the relationship between David and Samantha Cameron on the one hand and Brexit supporters Michael Gove and Sarah Vine on the other. The Prime Minister's close personal friendship with his former policy chief Steve Hilton and his wife Rachel Whetstone was another casualty. Sunak and Hollinrake had never fallen out over Brexit, however, and were determined that whatever the outcome, they would remain friends. That evening, the pair talked about the dramas of the campaign, and the parts they had both played on different sides of the argument and agreed that whichever side won, they would continue to work together for the benefit of their North Yorkshire constituents. Naturally, they also chewed over the dreadful events of the preceding week and how Cox's murder might affect the way MPs worked. The initial shock had given way to a practical debate at Westminster over the safety of politicians, with calls for panic alarms and other extra protection for MPs.

For his part, Sunak felt strongly that the tragedy should not undermine the longstanding principle that MPs should be accessible to their constituents. He recalled a story Hague had told him from his days as Foreign Secretary. The former Tory leader had been attending an important overseas summit with his American counterpart Hillary Clinton, then Secretary of State in the US, but had had to leave before it closed, in order to attend his regular surgery with constituents in Richmond. According to Sunak, Clinton was 'amazed – and very impressed' that a government minister in such an elevated position continued to carry out such routine duties.

He was determined not to change the way he went about his business. 'Whatever weighty matters we might be dealing with in Westminster, we always have to remember the needs of the people back home who elected us,' he wrote in a column published ten days after Cox's death. 'That means we have to have regular and meaningful contact. The regular surgeries I and other MPs hold are just one way of maintaining that relationship and assisting those who need our help.'

Just hours after Sunak and Hollinrake's pleasant tête-à-tête, the political landscape would change for ever. By 5 a.m. on 24 June, the verdict was clear: the UK had voted Out, by a margin of 52 to 48 per cent. Remain campaign strategists, who had been quietly confident they had the edge, were reeling. David Cameron's director of communications, Craig Oliver, would later reveal he was physically sick on hearing the extraordinary outcome. Later that morning, the Prime Minister would resign, privately telling aides that his heart just wasn't in staying in No. 10. The prospect of clinging on to his job while under constant fire from the winning side was 'miserable', he told Oliver, saying it would be an invitation to critics to 'come and punch me as hard as you like'.

In backing Brexit, Sunak had both voted with his conscience and landed on the winning side of the argument. In theory, he was now very well positioned politically for a post-Cameron regime. After all, the Prime Minister's successor seemed almost certain to be a Brexiteer. Having notched up a year in Parliament without upsetting anybody and stood out from the crowd as one of a minority of young MPs in the 2015 intake to support Brexit, promotion from the back benches seemed within grasp.

Nobody would have bet on what happened next.

CHAPTER 10

GREASY POLE

Shortly after the referendum, Sunak was forced to embark on something of a damage-limitation exercise. It was July 2016 and Westminster was stunned. The vote to leave the EU had been a profound shock to MPs on all sides. Many were struggling to adjust to their new duty to implement a decision with which they overwhelmingly disagreed. Meanwhile, the Tory leadership contest triggered by David Cameron's sudden resignation had turned into an extraordinary drama that shattered old loyalties and presented MPs with a completely new political landscape.

Within a week of the referendum, former frontrunner Boris Johnson's campaign lay in tatters after he was stabbed in the back by his running mate, Michael Gove. Three hours before nominations closed, Gove had suddenly declared he had 're-luctantly' come to the conclusion that the former Mayor of London could not 'provide the leadership or build the team for the task ahead' and (having repeatedly denied he had any interest in the top job) announced that he was running himself. A humiliated Johnson felt he had little choice but to withdraw.

Gove, whose behaviour revealed a side to his character many erstwhile admirers found more than a little distasteful, was swiftly eliminated from the contest, setting the scene for a final play-off between Home Secretary Theresa May and Energy Minister Andrea Leadsom. Before the party membership had the opportunity to choose between the pair, however, Leadsom's campaign was derailed by an interview in which she appeared to suggest that being a mother gave her a better political perspective than her childless rival. In the ensuring furore, Leadsom lost her nerve and withdrew from the contest, leaving May unopposed. Combined with Brexit, the leadership soap opera was head-spinning. MPs were left struggling to work out where to fix their allegiances.

At the beginning of the leadership contest, Sunak had quietly backed Johnson, assuming, like many others at Westminster, that he would win. According to colleagues, however, privately he was always keener on Gove. There is no suggestion that the young MP for Richmond was actively involved in what came to be known at Westminster as the 'cuckoo's nest plot' to kibosh Johnson, but unlike many of Johnson's backbench supporters, who were loath to reward Gove's treachery by backing his leadership campaign, Sunak overcame any reservations he might have had and stuck with him. When Gove, too, crashed out of the contest, Sunak found himself in the uncomfortable position of having backed the wrong horse not once but twice.

For ambitious young MPs, party leadership contests are perilous indeed. The clear advantages of allying oneself with the eventual winner at the earliest possible opportunity – a gamble that is often rewarded with swift promotion – must be balanced against the grave dangers of backing a loser. As many talented individuals can attest, the wrong call can result in years of backbench obscurity. Having made two such errors, Sunak refrained from publicly backing either of the final two contenders.

It was in this awkward context that, shortly after a victorious Theresa May stood on the steps of No. 10 and declared her intention to address the 'burning injustices' facing the nation, Sunak felt the need to pen an article about what a brilliant Prime Minister she would make, perhaps hoping that his fulsome tribute would not go unnoticed in Downing Street. Whatever he may privately have thought of the new party leader before she entered No. 10, he now asserted publicly that she would 'do a great job' and was 'the experienced and skilled politician the UK needs'. Her twenty years at the top table in politics and government would be 'invaluable in the days and months ahead', he declared, while her 'record-breaking six years as Home Secretary' would be 'ideal preparation for the top job and evidence of her strong, proven leadership qualities'. In the gushing column, published in his local newspaper, Sunak also paid tribute to May's 'well-established reputation' for 'mastering the detail of issues', her 'vision for the country', and her commitment to 'serious social and economic reform'. Like many other Brexiteers, he had been reassured by the former Home Secretary's apparent determination to set aside her personal reservations over Brexit and deliver on the verdict of the 17.4 million people who backed Leave. 'Her attitude is positive, seeing it as an opportunity, not a problem, and I am sure she can get the best deal for Britain,' he wrote optimistically, adding that he was looking forward to working with her.

By the time this somewhat cringeworthy tribute was published, May had been Prime Minister for a little over forty-eight hours. Though she had already made key Cabinet and senior ministerial appointments, she was still putting the finishing touches to the new administration. If Sunak hoped the piece might catch the eye of the new Chief Whip,

Gavin Williamson, as No. 10 considered which promising young backbenchers to recommend for elevation, however, he was to be disappointed. A long list of junior ministerial appointments and government aides was announced, and his name was not among them. He would have to slog it out on the back benches for another year before finally getting his foot on the bottom rung of the ladder.

In the meantime, he tried to make the best of the opportunities to affect policy via his role on the Environment Committee and on various Bill Committees, in which cross-party groups of MPs scrutinise proposed legislation. A seat on the Digital Economy Bill Committee that autumn would have tested the patience of most MPs, but for Sunak, whose rural constituency is beleaguered by poor broadband, it was a chance to push for new statutory obligations on providers to give all customers a decent connection. With his keen eye for detail, the meticulous analytical work of these committees quite suited him.

He also used his position on the cross-party Commons Environment Select Committee to lobby for farmers, advocating a British Agricultural Policy to replace the Common Agricultural Policy when the UK left the EU, telling newly appointed Environment Secretary Andrea Leadsom that the new system of farm payments would have to be much simpler and more efficient. He also pressed for lighter-touch regulation of the industry and a level playing field for pig farmers struggling to compete with European producers still using cruel intensive farming systems – knowing all this would go down very well in Richmond.

If this part of his job was worthy but dull, there was often more excitement to be found in the debating chamber. In a welcome break from Brexit, towards the end of July, MPs were asked to vote on another highly emotive and divisive issue: the future of Trident, the UK's nuclear deterrent. Sunak had been compelled to develop a rapid interest in defence because of the heavy military presence in his constituency. Just three miles south of Richmond is Catterick Garrison, the biggest British Army base in the world, and RAF Leeming, which has played a crucial role in the war on terror, is also in his constituency. With thousands of constituents in the armed forces, there was never any prospect that Sunak would vote against plans to spend £31 billion renewing the continuous at-sea deterrent.

Nonetheless, he was keenly aware that the policy was opposed by others on his patch, some of whom felt strongly enough about the UK's nuclear weapons arsenal to travel from North Yorkshire to London to stage a protest in Parliament Square on the day of the vote. Sunak took the trouble to study a long and complicated government-commissioned review of potential alternatives to Trident (secured by the Liberal Democrats during coalition negotiations and published in 2013) and came away feeling that sticking with the existing system was the only viable option. Writing in his weekly column, Sunak acknowledged that spending such a huge sum on nuclear missiles that were never expected to be used was not an easy option. In the context of overall government spending, however, he believed it was good value for money, pointing out that it amounted to twenty pence in every £100 the government spends. 'To me, that's a very cheap premium to renew an insurance policy that has kept Britain safe for almost 50 years and will do so for almost another half century,' he argued.

In the end, despite the clamour in Parliament Square and the intervention of various celebrities, MPs voted overwhelmingly in favour of renewal, with almost the entire Conservative Party and more than half of Labour MPs backing the move. Sunak had enjoyed playing his part in such a historic decision, but, unlike his anxieties over Brexit, it had not been difficult for him to choose a side.

*　　*　　*

The call Sunak had been waiting for finally came more than two years after he entered Parliament, when he was invited to become a parliamentary private secretary in the Department for Business, Energy and Industrial Strategy (BEIS).

To MPs who have had distinguished careers outside politics, the lowliness of this rank can feel demeaning. Very often, talented young MPs find themselves having to defer to older ministers who are fairly obviously less able than themselves – a naturally frustrating position. Yet the unpaid role as a glorified bag carrier to one or more ministers is a chance to observe how they go about the job and how the civil service operates. Crucially, it is also an opportunity to impress party whips. Effectively, it is the first rung on the ministerial ladder, and in due course those who do well can expect promotion to the next tier: Parliamentary Under-Secretary. As Sunak's own career would show, from this jumping-off point, the rate of ascent can be dizzying.

Just how rewarding the role of a PPS proves to be depends greatly on the nature of the relationship with the minister or ministers to whom they are attached. Some Cabinet ministers, like former Chancellors Ken Clarke and Philip Hammond, acquire a reputation at Westminster for generosity towards colleagues who are just starting out, inviting them to contribute to a wide range of meetings and allowing them to sit in on the most interesting – and often sensitive – private briefings. Other old hands may be threatened by the presence of ambitious young Turks and guard their positions in a way that makes the PPS role less fulfilling. Greg Clark, Business Secretary at the time, did not obviously fall into either camp, but in any case, Sunak would not have a great deal to do with him. The promotion, in June 2017, was even more modest than it sounded, because Sunak was the second PPS in the department, a tier below his colleague Kelly Tolhurst, who was appointed as Clark's personal PPS. This left Sunak to support other ministers in the department: Margot James, Claire Perry, Richard Harrington and Jo Johnson. Nonetheless, it was a step in the right direction. In a symbol of his new status, during business debates in the Commons, Sunak could now be found sitting on the second row behind the front bench.

With a first-class degree from Oxford, an MBA from Stanford and several stellar years in the City under his belt, Sunak clearly outclassed many of those who surrounded him in the BEIS department. Yet he was not too proud to be excited by his new role. 'Being a PPS is a tremendous opportunity for me to be involved in the day-to-day business of government and contribute in a small way to the formulation of policy for the developing industrial strategy and enterprise,' he enthused in his weekly column.

He approached the job with characteristic charm and professionalism. Margot James, with whom he worked closely, says that she found him 'exemplary'. 'As a PPS, if you're any good, you're dramatically overqualified for the work involved – it's like an apprenticeship. He was incredibly proactive and always a step ahead.'

What Sunak did *not* do was attempt to cultivate the Secretary of State, a natural strategy for a PPS impatient to make the next move up. According to departmental colleagues, out of a respect for hierarchies and courtesy to Tolhurst, Sunak concentrated on making himself indispensable to the junior ministerial team and did not seek out opportunities to ingratiate himself with Clark. This says something about his character: a more ruthless political operator would have vied for position with a fellow PPS. Perhaps conscious of his political inexperience, Sunak seems to have been content to make the best of the hand he had been dealt. Either way, his new job allowed him to attend weekly meetings with ministers and departmental officials, liaise between the ministerial team and backbench MPs and, in his own words, 'make sure that Ministers are aware of what members are thinking on BEIS issues'. This meant acting as eyes and ears to his bosses in the Commons tea rooms, passing on useful gossip and alerting them to any trouble brewing. It would not be long before he would find out himself just how valuable such sources of intelligence can be.

* * *

Indirectly, Sunak owed his next promotion to pornography. In June 2017, May blew her Commons majority in a snap general election that was designed to secure a stronger mandate for her Brexit proposals but which achieved exactly the opposite. Sunak's own majority in Richmond increased by more than 3,500, but for the Tories nationally the picture was grim. The Labour Party, under Jeremy Corbyn, made a net gain of thirty seats. Only a confidence and supply agreement with the Democratic

Unionist Party kept the Conservatives in government. Fatally weakened, May was in no position to execute anything more than a minor reshuffle following the election, until a spate of Cabinet resignations in the run-up to Christmas forced her to do so. The departure of her deputy and old friend Damian Green for lying to colleagues over X-rated material found on his computer – hot on the heels of the resignation of International Development Secretary Priti Patel over secret meetings with Israelis, and the resignation of Defence Secretary Michael Fallon over the #MeToo scandal – meant the beleaguered Prime Minister had to make a number of changes at junior ministerial levels, and Sunak was a beneficiary.

The call from No. 10 came in the early afternoon of 9 January 2018. Would Sunak be available to meet the Prime Minister in half an hour? He later claimed he had 'no inkling of what might happen at that point', but as he set off from his Westminster office across Whitehall to Downing Street, accompanied by his backbench colleague Lucy Frazer, he knew there was only one reason for the summons: he was about to be offered a job. The question was what.

Approaching the forbidding iron gates to Downing Street and seeing the throng of journalists and cameramen monitoring the comings-and-goings through the famous black door to No. 10, Sunak felt a thrill of excitement and nerves. He was glad he was not running the gauntlet of the media by himself and that he and Frazer, who had received a similar summons, were facing the cameras together.

Inside No. 10, after a brief wait, he was called into the Cabinet Room, where he sat across the Cabinet table from the Prime Minister. Would he like to become a junior minister in the Ministry of Housing, Communities and Local

Government (MHCLG)? Delighted, Sunak accepted immediately, telling the Prime Minister he was 'honoured'. The rest of their brief discussion concerned May's vision for the department. She was expanding the ministerial team at MHCLG, she said, because it was so important to increase the supply of new housing. Following another short meeting with Downing Street aides and the Chief Whip, Sunak headed straight to his new offices on Marsham Street, a few minutes' walk away, to start his new job as a member of Her Majesty's government.

What followed was a whirlwind of meetings and briefings, as he was introduced to the civil servants with whom he would be working, the ministerial team led by Secretary of State Sajid Javid and Minister of State Dominic Raab, and got to grips with his new responsibilities.

His new job title was Minister for Local Government and his brief was wide, including local authority funding policy, council workers' pensions, adult social care, parks and green spaces and 'troubled families'. Dull as some of this might sound, Sunak comforted himself that his remit covered issues that really impacted everyday lives. In an enthusiastic post to his Yorkshire constituents, he stressed that 'it underpins the services provided by our local council whether it is emptying our bins, maintaining most of our roads [or] caring for the elderly'. One of his first tasks would be pushing through plans to allow councils to keep 75 per cent of business rates paid in their area to spend at their discretion, shifting billions of pounds of public money from central to local government control.

Meanwhile, he was anxious to avoid the impression that he would now be too busy for the people of Richmond. 'Being a Government Minister in no way lessens the importance of my constituency,' he emphasised. 'On Thursday evening as normal I was back home in North Yorkshire and on Friday holding an advice surgery in Hawes and visiting the Wensleydale Creamery to hear of their exciting development plans.' Showing he remained committed to the constituency, on the same Friday, he opened a new 'forest school' for young children at High Bank Nursery at Stapleton in the far north of the constituency and visited a large dairy farm, managing to find time for a quick visit to the barber's in Northallerton. With a sharp new haircut to match his elevated status, he finally headed home to spend a cosy Friday night – and the rest of the weekend – with the 'voluminous contents' of his new ministerial red box.

CHAPTER 11

KEEN BEAN

There are junior ministerial jobs that come with fabulous perks that more than make up for the anti-social hours, rubbish pay and limited power. At the Foreign Office, it's the opportunity to travel all over the world meeting diplomats and dignitaries. At the Ministry of Defence, there is the thrill of warzones and boys' toys. At Culture, Media and Sport there are free tickets to the hottest shows, the best seats at rugby and football internationals, and endless invitations to cocktail parties and sell-out concerts where the politicians rub shoulders with showbiz stars.

In the Ministry of Housing, Communities and Local Government, however, the glamour does not extend much beyond dreary annual dinners for local councillors, for which ministers generally struggle to muster much enthusiasm.

Not so Rishi Sunak, who eagerly sought opportunities to press the flesh with some of the decidedly stolid stakeholders in his department and made a very good show of enjoying the experience. Some months into the job, the new minister impressed in local government circles by actively requesting to attend an annual bash for Tory councillors laid on by the Local Government Association. That night, he made it his business to talk to as many people as he could.

Former chair of the LGA Gary Porter, now a member of the House of Lords, recalls:

> Each of the political groups have a dinner. Conservatives have about 240 people. He asked if he could come and went round every single table. Every person he spoke to, it was like he was really talking to them. It was like a direct conversation rather than pleasantries. I had to drag him out – he was twenty minutes late getting into the car. I have never seen a politician do this.

Local government types were delighted to have such an energetic new representative. Porter says that they are wearily accustomed to junior ministers they do not rate highly, and that Sunak was very obviously different. 'Fantastic, such a switched-on cookie,' is how Porter puts it.

> With all respect, normally in that position, they're not the sharpest tools you ever come across in politics and he was in a completely different league. You only had to tell him or show him something once, and he got it. If you didn't show him something for five minutes, he started to get twitchy about learning something else; always keen to figure out how to do the job ... He really impressed me, and it just got better and better.

Sunak's appointment came at a critical point in the calendar for local government, when negotiations over the annual budget allocation from central government were nearing completion. A decision on the final settlement was imminent, and lobbying was reaching fever pitch. A ministerial colleague who worked with him at MHCLG remembers him throwing himself into debate, spending long hours liaising with the queue of MPs appealing for additional funding for their area. 'He absolutely nailed it,' according to the source.

> Any MP who had any issues with any council, Rishi talked it through with them, absolutely knowing all the numbers. He did a huge amount of homework – he would have lost weekends over it, because that is the time you can get hold of councillors. He would have spoken to over 100 leaders and then probably thirty MPs.

One of many backbenchers attempting to wrest more money from the government for their constituency was the MP for the Isle of Wight, who managed to secure parliamentary time to make his case. The energetic Bob Seely led a Westminster Hall debate on the proposed settlement for the island, which required a minister to attend and respond. It was Sunak's first Westminster Hall debate in his new role. As always, he was meticulously well prepared, drawing on happy childhood memories of visits to the island to underline his familiarity with and affection for the constituency before rattling off a barrage of facts and figures relating to the increase in resources islanders could expect. It was a characteristically professional performance which seemed to have satisfied Seely.

The final national settlement required legislative approval from MPs, and no vote could be taken for granted. In the event, Sunak's careful outreach work paid off, and the relevant bill passed through the Commons without a hitch. It helped that the deal would see a real-terms increase in resources to town halls in the two years that followed, and that many councils were being given the opportunity to hold on to all cash raised in local business rates. 'There were no rebellions, no votes against, no amendments put down,' the former colleague recalls. 'Sunak did a superb job.'

Financial settlement out of the way, Sunak homed in on other aspects of the brief that he found interesting, particularly opportunities associated with digital technology and so-called channel shift, the move from traditional forms of communication with voters to the use of smartphones and other devices.

Porter met Sunak once or twice a week during this period and got to know the minister very well. Though Sunak was still little known beyond his own intake of Tory MPs, Porter knew he was dealing with a politician who would go very far. He stresses, however, that while it was clear at this stage that Sunak was very ambitious, he did not display it 'in that grasping way'. 'Normally the sharper political people have more pointy elbows. He isn't a pointy-elbow person. He just seems keen to do well. Whatever you give him, he wants to do it good, and there's an inbuilt pride in that.'

Porter observes that Sunak is both instinctive and methodical, an unusual combination, and acknowledges that he never witnessed the minister having to backtrack, a tricky but essential political skill to master. It would not be long before he had plenty of opportunity to learn the art of that manoeuvre.

*   *   *

While Sunak was grafting away at MHCLG, Theresa May was struggling to make headway on Brexit. Following the triggering of Article 50 – the mechanism via which an EU member state gives Brussels notice of intention to leave – the clock was ticking towards the date of the UK's departure, on 29 March 2019. Multiple hurdles remained, both in negotiating the nature of the future relationship with the EU and in passing the necessary associated legislation through the Commons and the Lords. Both Houses were dominated by Remainers.

Emboldened by the loss of the Conservative majority, a phalanx of anti-Brexit Tory MPs was doing everything possible to frustrate almost every aspect of the process. In cahoots with the opposition, they now had the parliamentary numbers to thwart the Prime Minister at every turn. Throughout 2018, negotiations with Brussels were tortuous – especially when so many of the senior civil servants on whom May relied struggled to hide their antipathy to the Brexit agenda – but managing the Tory parliamentary party was much worse than dealing with EU negotiators. As time went by, she became completely enmeshed: by Brussels, by her own officials and, worst of all, by Cabinet ministers who fundamentally disagreed with the direction she was taking.

The first major showdown came in July 2018, following the now infamous Chequers summit. After a marathon meeting at the Prime Minister's country retreat in Buckinghamshire on 6 July 2018, the Cabinet appeared to have backed a blueprint for post-Brexit relations with the EU. This was a big breakthrough for May. The agreement paved the way for a softer Brexit, but while some ministers were uncomfortable, they seemed to accept it was the only realistic way forward. As the last of a long line of ministerial limousines swept off down the drive for the journey back to London, the Prime Minister felt sufficiently confident to announce details of the 'collective agreement' the Cabinet had reached that day. A landmark statement from Her Majesty's government published that evening set out what it described as a 'substantial evolution' in proposals for the UK's future relationship with the EU, involving a 'free trade area for goods' with the EU, allowing frictionless trade and thus avoiding the need for a hard border with Northern Ireland.

Downing Street claimed the deal would 'end free movement', giving the UK control of Britain's borders, and 'restore the supremacy of UK courts'. The UK would also be leaving the Common Agricultural Policy and Common Fisheries Policy. The problem was that the proposed new trade area involved a 'combined customs territory' – meaning the UK would be forced to collect tariffs on goods on behalf of Brussels and mirror many European rules and regulations.

The verdict from Brexit campaigners was swift and brutal: the deal was a sell-out. Yet there were no immediate ministerial resignations. That weekend, furious Leavers rounded on the government for betraying the 17.4 million people who had voted for Brexit. Pressure mounted on Eurosceptic ministers to make their feelings known. In a shattering blow to May's authority, on the morning of Monday 9 July, David Davis quit as Brexit Secretary, with another Eurosceptic minister, Steve Baker, immediately following suit. That same day, Boris Johnson resigned as Foreign Secretary, declaring that the UK was headed 'for the status of colony' if May's soft Brexit plans were adopted. Dominic Raab, Davis's successor at the Department for Exiting the EU, would last only a matter of months in the job.

Throughout this turbulent period, Sunak kept a low profile. He resisted the temptation to express any disquiet either about May's handling of the negotiations or about the nature of the future relationship with the EU she envisaged. His quiet loyalty meant that on the issue that dominated the news agenda and overshadowed and stymied almost everything else the government was trying to achieve he was by and large invisible.

A key figure in Downing Street at the time recalls:

He was just a very good, competent minister. He was a safe pair of hands, clearly very smart, got on with his Secretary of State. If you hear about junior ministers at No. 10 it's usually because they're doing something wrong – they're being a nuisance, they're not doing their box, they're doing unscheduled appearances, they've fallen out with their Secretary of State, but there was none of that.

Sunak was simply being pragmatic. Though he backed Brexit, he did not feel sufficiently strongly about the detail of Britain's departure from the EU for it ever to represent a resignation issue. For an ambitious junior minister, there was simply no upside in rebelling when it would not change the course of events and there was no knowing how long May would remain in power. In any case, others with significantly less to lose were more than willing to take a stand.

As the No. 10 source puts it:

There were a lot of people who got the satisfaction of writing a resignation letter, but that didn't really alter very much in the great scheme of things. Rishi correctly realised that resigning as a Parliamentary Under-Secretary of State at MHCLG would probably not change the course of history. Whereas other Parliamentary Under-Secretaries of State concluded differently.

A friend who talked to him about these matters at the time says

Sunak was deeply underwhelmed by the Chequers agreement, which was incompatible with his vision of Brexit. However, he did not feel in a position to make much difference.

> I think he found having to deliver the 'line to take' during that period quite uncomfortable. His idea of Brexit was all about big free trade, not getting tied down in a customs union and so on. Chequers made a fool of his particular version of Brexit. But when you're a junior minister, you can't guide what the government is saying one way or another. I think he felt constrained. He was too straight to be a resigner; too mainstream and too shrewd. While he definitely saw himself as a Brexiteer, it wasn't the be-all and end-all of what he thought. It's just the logic of his vision about an entrepreneurial global Britain. His view was that the deal was unwise but would unwind itself.

Sunak was right. That autumn, the government lurched from crisis to crisis as May's grip on her administration ebbed away. A withdrawal agreement with the EU was taking shape but would need to be endorsed by a majority of MPs in a meaningful vote in the House of Commons. May's problem was that nothing she could negotiate with the EU satisfied enough Tory Brexiteers to overcome the devilish parliamentary arithmetic. The Democratic Unionist Party (DUP), on whose MPs she relied to prop up her foundering administration, remained bitterly opposed to the Irish backstop, a fallback customs arrangement designed to avoid the need for a hard border. While it remained in place, they would not throw their weight behind her proposals. A handful of Labour MPs who represented Leave constituencies were ready to back the government, but there were nowhere near enough of them to offset the Tory rebels.

Westminster was now a seething mass of plotters: Remainers plotting to thwart Brexit, Brexiteers plotting to oust May, and the Downing Street machine juddering from one day to the next like an old car on a long journey stuttering towards a destination that seems ever further away, with an engine that is overheating and all the passengers know is about to blow up.

Like every other government minister, Sunak was privately despairing about the political deadlock over Brexit, but he resisted the temptation to get involved. Amid all the sound and fury, he told himself that the day-to-day work of government must continue, so he focused on his ministerial brief and the policy changes he could help make that might not feature on newspaper front pages but would nonetheless benefit many people. An example was an announcement about improved housing for armed forces veterans, an important issue for the thousands of military personnel in his constituency.

In his capacity as Local Government Minister, Sunak was pushing the Treasury for more money for councils to spend on social care. He was constantly being lobbied on this issue, and though the additional funding he eventually helped to secure was a drop in the ocean relative to the scale of the problem, he felt his persuasive powers had achieved something when Chancellor Philip Hammond announced a £650 million boost to adult social care funding in the Autumn Budget.

On 4 December 2018, MPs began the first of five days of Brexit debates leading up to the meaningful vote scheduled for 11 December. To no avail, May pleaded with MPs to recognise that there could be no deal with the EU without the controversial Northern Irish backstop, but it was painfully clear she faced heavy defeat. In the first of a series of humiliations, on the eve of the crunch votes she pulled the legislation, acknowledging that the proposals had no hope of getting through the Commons. Within twenty-four hours, she faced a vote of no confidence in her leadership of the Conservative Party.

This was a botched coup, orchestrated by arch-Brexiteers who seriously miscalculated the number of critics ready to topple the premier at a critical juncture in negotiations with Brussels. In theory, little more than three months remained before the UK was leaving the EU. Privately, the vast majority of Tory MPs accepted that May was a busted flush. However, her removal was likely to trigger a long and potentially bitter party leadership contest, further derailing the Brexit process. Meanwhile, even the most ambitious potential contenders could see that steering the UK out of the EU was a near-impossible job. Few were keen to enter No. 10 in such circumstances.

Whether Sunak supported or opposed May in the secret ballot is not a matter of public record. However, his silence as more than 188 MPs publicly pledged their backing for the PM may be telling. In any case, May survived, securing 63 per cent of the total vote: enough to stagger on and, crucially, enough to protect her position for at least another twelve months, during which no further challenge could be mounted, under Tory Party rules.

In Downing Street, there were no celebrations: May had lost the confidence of one third of her MPs, and her ability to drive her Brexit Bill through the Commons hung in the balance.

When MPs returned to the Commons in 2019, no amount of cajoling from Downing Street operatives would be enough to salvage the Prime Minister's Brexit agenda. May was running out of road. On 15 January, she lost the meaningful vote she had deferred in December. Surviving a vote of no confidence in the government tabled by the opposition was of only minor consolation, as the clock ticked inexorably towards the deadline and her administration seemed unable to achieve anything. On 13 March, MPs voted to rule out a no-deal Brexit. Since the Commons had refused to back the withdrawal agreement she had negotiated with the EU, there would be no choice but to write to EU leaders requesting an extension.

For two years, May had repeatedly promised that the UK would leave the EU on 29 March 2019. She had simply been unable to deliver. Events were now moving very fast. By midsummer, she would be out of Downing Street – and Sunak would be heading to the Treasury.

CHAPTER 12

TEAM BOJO

Who could save the Tory Party from annihilation by delivering Brexit?

That was the question that had been exercising Tory MPs for months and could now no longer be avoided.

When the EU departure date of 29 March came and went, and Downing Street was forced to ask Brussels if the UK could stay in the bloc for a bit longer – and then request a second extension when that deadline also passed – even Theresa May's closest allies ceased to believe that she was the answer.

Furious Leave campaigners were on the march – quite literally, in the case of a band of Brexiteers who trekked from Sunderland to Parliament Square in Westminster to make their point at a noisy rally.

The marchers were the least of May's problems, however. Days after she failed to meet her March deadline, a brand-new political party burst onto the scene, threatening to strip away the Tory vote. Though it was led by Nigel Farage, the newly formed Brexit Party bore little resemblance to the shabby operation he had presided over at UKIP. This was a highly professional political machine with supporters from all walks of life, and it had no shortage of cash; the frustrated former Tory donors lavishing money on Farage's new outfit were a source of mounting panic in the Tory ranks.

A day of reckoning loomed, in the shape of European elections on 23 May 2019 – a trial the party's leadership had desperately hoped to avoid. To Downing Street's chagrin, voters were not celebrating Britain's departure from the EU but being asked who they wanted to represent them in Brussels for the next four years. There was no need to invite pollsters to predict the result.

Sure enough, when polling day came, disillusioned Leavers exacted their revenge on the government, voting in droves for the Brexit Party. Farage's party triumphed in nine out of the UK's twelve regions, securing twenty-nine out of seventy-three seats in the European Parliament. The pro-EU Lib Dems came second, pushing the Tories into a humiliating fifth place behind Labour and the Green Party.

The bitter divisions within the Conservative Party, and the determination of Tory Remainer MPs to join forces with the overwhelmingly pro-European opposition parties to defeat the government at every turn, now made an early general election inevitable. Tory MPs were terrified: if the Prime Minister was forced to go to the country before the UK left the EU, many of those representing Leave-supporting constituencies seemed likely to lose their seats. Fighting for their political lives, they knew their only hope was to get May out of Downing Street.

Under Conservative Party rules, a formal challenge could not be mounted until at least December, but the pressure on May to quit was now unbearable. On 24 May, she finally announced that she would step aside, setting 7 June as the date for her resignation. Sunak now had to decide whom to support in the forthcoming leadership contest. In the previous leadership contest, he had backed the wrong horse, but as a backbencher it hadn't mattered too much. Now that he was a minister itching for promotion, he needed to get it right.

In a sign of the near-total collapse of party discipline following the routing at the European elections, the contest got under way weeks before May officially conceded she would leave, with Rory Stewart announcing his candidacy as early as 2 May, just a day after he had been promoted to the Cabinet as International Development Secretary. Others were scarcely more delicate: less than a week after Stewart's declaration, Andrea Leadsom revealed she was 'seriously considering' a tilt at the top job, while Esther McVey made clear her intention to stand the following day. On 16 May, Boris Johnson was asked if he too would be a candidate, and did not beat about the bush, replying, 'Of course I'm going to go for it.' The moment May's leaving date was announced, Jeremy Hunt, Matt Hancock and Dominic Raab also entered the contest, with Michael Gove, Sajid Javid and Kit Malthouse soon following suit. James Cleverly and Mark Harper would later join the race, making an opening field of twelve candidates.

Instinctively, most Tory MPs felt that May's successor would have to be a Brexiteer – a view Sunak shared. The fact that the outgoing Prime Minister did not originally support Brexit and had voted Remain in the referendum had dogged her premiership. For all her protestations that she was a convert to the cause, Brexiteers continued to question whether her heart was truly in it.

If the next leader had to be a 'true Brexiteer', Sunak's options narrowed considerably, to candidates who had played an active role in the original Leave campaign. That ruled out Stewart, Hunt, Javid, Hancock, Malthouse and Harper, leaving Johnson, Gove, Leadsom, Raab, Cleverly and McVey.

While Sunak had once felt that he was a 'Gove man', he now believed that Johnson was the only answer to the crisis engulfing the Tory Party – and the country.

Before committing himself, he discussed the options at length with his old ally Oliver 'Olive' Dowden. Cambridge-educated Dowden had years of political experience, having worked in the Conservative Research Department before becoming a special adviser and later David Cameron's deputy chief of staff, and the pair were now firm friends. Dowden agreed with Sunak that the party faced an existential threat and that only Johnson could see off both Nigel Farage and Jeremy Corbyn.

A Tory peer who discussed the leadership contest with Dowden at the time remembers him arguing that it would take someone exceptional to save the party.

I asked Olive what he was doing, and he said he was supporting Boris. I remember very clearly what he said when I asked him why. He said, 'The Conservative Party is in a small prison cell, with the walls closing in on it. On the one hand, the Lib Dems; on the other, the Brexit Party. We are going to get crushed. But there's a small window, right high up, near the ceiling of that cell. If only someone can climb out through that window and jump out, we can stop this. There is only one person who can shimmy up the wall with a ladder and just squeeze through the window, and that person is Boris.'

Looking back on that leadership contest, it might seem that Johnson was always a shoo-in. That is not the case. The former London Mayor had many fierce detractors within the parliamentary party, who questioned his principles, his self-discipline, his appetite for mastering policy detail, and his complicated private life. These concerns were shared by a sufficient number of Tory MPs to allow several rival candidates to gain momentum, with Hunt soon emerging as second favourite and Stewart, a Remainer who began the race as a rank outsider, picking up a surprising number of endorsements.

Sunak's view was that while Johnson was not perfect, voters liked him and trusted him on Brexit – a huge advantage given that a general election could be called any day. On 5 June, a week before the first ballot was due to take place, he joined forces with Dowden and Robert Jenrick to announce that he was backing Johnson. The three men penned a joint letter to *The Times*, admitting that the Tories were in 'deep peril' and arguing that only Johnson could get them out of the mess.

The crisis facing the Conservative Party was not just a difficulty or a bump in the road, they argued, but a question of survival. Only an exceptional leader could see off the dual threat posed by a resurgent Farage and the Brexit Party on the one side and Labour Marxists on the other. The trio reasoned that there was simply no time for a less well-known figure to earn public trust on Brexit, and that Johnson had already proven he had the necessary credentials to enter No. 10. He commanded the 'instant credibility' needed to achieve public support for a renegotiated deal, they argued, noting that he was willing to leave the EU on World Trade Organization terms if necessary – a crucial point of principle for many Leave voters. Beyond Brexit, they believed Johnson was 'one of life's optimists' who could inspire a weary electorate with his vision for the nation and set the Tory Party back on course. Finally, they emphasised his ability to win elections. Among those with reservations about Johnson's character at that time, there was nonetheless a widespread notion that he was a 'winner', as evidenced by his victory in successive mayoral elections in Labour-supporting

London and his role in the EU referendum. 'Twice in London and in the referendum, he defied all the odds and won when nobody else could have,' the trio argued, concluding that this was 'a moment in British politics like no other' and that Johnson would take the fight to Farage and Corbyn – and triumph.

Sunak's endorsement was influential among colleagues. He and his co-authors were barely known outside Westminster, but among Tory MPs, who would decide which two candidates reached the contest's final stage, they were seen as rising stars who represented the future of the party. Both Sunak and Jenrick were still in their thirties, underlining Johnson's appeal to a younger generation of MPs, while Dowden (in his early forties) had been a Remainer, suggesting he could draw support from that segment of the party. Johnson's campaign team was delighted. A Minister of State recalls, 'That article by Sunak, Dowden and Jenrick was quite influential. There was a feeling among some of us that those three sort of represented the future of the Tory Party, and for all of them to think Boris was the way ahead was significant.'

Now they had Sunak on board, Johnson's campaign team began considering how they could use him. From his assured performance in his maiden speech to his handling of questions at the despatch box in his capacity as a junior minister, Sunak had demonstrated that he was a good communicator, and in the days that followed they encouraged him to accept broadcast invitations to press their candidate's case. On a local radio station, he waxed lyrical about what he described as Johnson's unique ability to engage people. 'He … can broaden our appeal and our message to parts of the country we need to reach – he's the man to do that,' Sunak argued, before moving on to his Brexit credentials, and – rather less convincingly

– Johnson's domestic policy record. Challenged over incidents where Johnson had been 'caught out in public', a reference to various controversies over his private life in the past, Sunak replied that voters no longer wanted 'incredibly polished, line-perfect' politicians. What they were after, he contended, was 'a bit more raw honesty, a bit more authenticity, a bit more people being themselves'.

Ironically, Sunak himself had always been 'incredibly polished'. For now, he had done enough to ensure that when Johnson triumphed – beating Foreign Secretary Jeremy Hunt by two to one in the final run-off vote among party members after other contenders were eliminated – he would be suitably rewarded.

On 24 July 2019, Johnson entered No. 10 promising to defy 'the doubters, the doomsters, the gloomsters' by completing Brexit with a deal by 31 October that year.

As for Sunak, his time as just another Parliamentary Under-Secretary whom few outside Westminster had ever heard of was rapidly coming to an end. Extraordinarily, in little over six months, he would be moving into No. 11.

CHAPTER 13

STERLING EFFORT

An age-old parlour game at Westminster involves trying to identify which obscure young MPs might one day become Prime Minister. This guessing game provides endless entertainment for politicians and journalists, but it is also a serious business: figuring out who could make it to the top long before it happens is a huge political advantage, allowing ambitious colleagues to position themselves accordingly.

One of the first MPs to identify Rishi Sunak as an exceptional talent was Sajid Javid. A former banker, Javid had been an MP for five years by the time Sunak entered the Commons. He had spent eighteen months in the Treasury with George Osborne and was already onto his second Cabinet job. Nonetheless, the pair had much in common, both in background and in political outlook.

Like Sunak, Javid was the son of immigrant parents who had arrived in the UK in the 1960s in search of a better life. His father was a hard-working Pakistani Muslim nicknamed Mr Night and Day by friends because of the long hours he worked in a cotton mill and as a bus driver. Like Yashvir and Usha Sunak, Javid Sr instilled a fierce work ethic in his son. Without the benefit of a private education or any useful connections, the teenage Javid set his sights on a career in the City and determined to do whatever it took to secure the necessary qualifications. By the age of twenty-five he was a vice-president at Chase Manhattan in the US, later moving to Singapore to work for Deutsche Bank. As we have seen, Sunak had a much more privileged upbringing, but he too had worked very hard, from prep school through to university and his early days in the City. In their youth, both he and Javid had admired Margaret Thatcher, Javid's interest in the financial markets having been sparked by her government's privatisations.

Javid says that when he and Sunak first met, there was an instant connection:

I met him before he became an MP, when he was looking for a seat. Someone introduced us and I gave him some tips. We got on well immediately, because we had very similar backgrounds in banking to start with. Our political heroes were similar. And we are both ethnic minorities ... We stayed in touch and he got elected. After that, we would chat regularly, usually informally in the lobby.

Javid is a key figure in Sunak's story, having sensed early on that they would work well together. He felt Sunak would be an asset to any department and says that when he was Communities Secretary he specifically asked Downing Street whether the MP for Richmond could join his team.

I knew that Theresa May was thinking about making some ministerial changes. And I then fed in ... that Rishi is someone I would love to have in that department, especially in a finance role. She was thinking of making him a minister anyway and I got him in. And he was really, really good. He got things very quickly.

Four months after Sunak joined MHCLG, on 30 April 2018, Javid was promoted to the Home Office following the resignation of Home Secretary Amber Rudd over the Windrush scandal. Naturally, the pair now saw less of each other, but they kept in touch. In a sign of how highly Javid rated Sunak's political judgement and communication skills, that autumn he asked the younger man to help him prepare for his keynote speech at Tory Party conference.

When May resigned in 2019, Javid joined the leadership contest. As we have seen, Sunak did not support him, choosing instead to throw his weight behind Johnson, but Javid remained eager to work with him. 'Rishi told me right up front that he would support Boris,' Javid recalls. 'He thought it was time for a big shake-up and we needed someone completely new. He thought we needed a leading Brexiteer to deliver Brexit. He was very open and honest.'

When Javid was eliminated from the contest, he too declared for Johnson, sparking rumours that he was positioning himself as the frontrunner's future Chancellor.

This speculation was on the money: Javid did indeed have his eye on this job; and moreover, Johnson thought he would be a good fit for the post. Towards the end of the leadership contest, he and Javid privately discussed the possibility of Sunak also going to the Treasury. Javid recalls: 'Before I became Chancellor, I was chatting to Boris. I told him that if I became Chancellor, I wanted Rishi as Chief Secretary. Boris didn't commit; he said he would make a decision at the last minute.'

The proposed move was very much Javid's idea. However, he says that it was clear from this conversation that Johnson intended to promote Sunak to the Cabinet in some position or other. 'Boris definitely really liked him; he was definitely destined for the Cabinet,' he says.

Johnson's triumphant arrival in No. 10 on the morning of 24 July marked the beginning of a very long day for Sunak. He had every reason to believe he was in line for promotion, but as the hours ticked by, there was no word. Javid's appointment as Chancellor of the Exchequer had been one of the first announcements, but still Sunak's phone did not ring. The suspense was agonising. Ever the professional, he did his best to busy himself with routine matters at MHCLG while he waited to learn his fate.

In Downing Street, a radical overhaul of the government was under way. Though there had been no general election, Johnson was determined to present this as a very different administration. Out went seventeen of May's former senior ministers to make way for a string of Brexiteers and Johnson allies. Dominic Raab became Foreign Secretary, Priti Patel was installed in the Home Office, Jacob Rees-Mogg was made Leader of the House of Commons and Michael Gove was awarded the title Chancellor of the Duchy of Lancaster, a coveted and influential senior ministerial role without portfolio.

Sunak had almost abandoned hope of hearing anything that day when the call from the Downing Street switchboard finally came. It was almost 10 p.m. He was asked to make his way over to No. 10. Darkness had now fallen, but Downing Street was buzzing with reporters preparing for the all-important 10 p.m. news bulletins. As Sunak made his way through security at the gates, news anchors were in mid-flow. Resisting the temptation to respond to any shouted questions, Sunak slipped through the famous black door to No. 10 and was ushered into the Cabinet Room, where Johnson was waiting.

Without much small talk, the Prime Minister invited him to be Chief Secretary to the Treasury.

This was the job Sunak had wanted. After eighteen months dealing with local government finance, he had a good grasp of the way the Treasury worked; and he knew he and Javid would make a good team. Without hesitation, he replied that he was honoured to accept and to serve the country at such a defining moment in the nation's history.

Sunak would later observe that there are not many jobs for which candidates are 'interviewed' at ten o'clock at night and start work immediately afterwards. It was no exaggeration: despite the late hour, he headed straight from Downing Street to Her Majesty's Treasury just around the corner on Horse Guards Parade. As a mandarin escorted him into his new office, a few doors along from the Chancellor's rooms on the second floor, he noticed a wall bearing photographs of previous office holders, including former Tory PM Sir John Major and Lord Brittan of Spennithorne, who had also served as MP for Richmond. Once again, Sunak was struck by the footsteps in which he was following, and by the sense that he must try to match their contribution to public service.

By 11 p.m., Sunak had met his new team and received a preliminary briefing from officials. 'Already my ministerial folder was bulging with matters which had to be dealt with – there and then. Summer holidays were promptly cancelled,' he reported later in his weekly newspaper column. Introductions made, he headed home to snatch a few hours' sleep.

The extent to which he was already trusted by No. 10 is highlighted by his appearance on primetime television the following morning. Unusually for a new Cabinet appointee, he was encouraged to participate in the 'morning media round' of television and radio interviews and accepted a 7.15 a.m. slot on the BBC's flagship *Breakfast* TV show. Looking none the worse for sleep deprivation, by 7.20 a.m. he was confidently fielding questions on live TV about 'fiscal headroom' and contingency plans for a no-deal Brexit. Interviewed in the huge makeshift stand the Corporation had erected opposite the Houses of Parliament on College Green, Sunak was asked if he would be just another 'yes man' on Johnson's team. Would anyone in the new Cabinet have the courage to disagree with the premier, the presenter asked? Such a question might have disconcerted a less assured performer, but Sunak did not miss a beat, cheerfully batting it off with a response that would not cause trouble. 'One thing I've really enjoyed over the course of the campaign and having some conversations with him around policy and other things is that he very much enjoys the intellectual challenge of debating policy ideas,' he replied evenly, adding that Johnson was 'not at all afraid' to be challenged, and indeed enjoyed a robust debate.

Johnson's first Cabinet meeting took place just a few hours later and was captured on camera by a handful of pool photographers who were allowed to observe the start of proceedings. In broadcast footage, the new Chief Secretary to the Treasury can be seen sitting at the head of the table – the premier traditionally sits in the middle – drumming his hands enthusiastically as the PM declared that all of those assembled were now 'committed to leaving the European Union on 31 October, or even earlier – no ifs or buts'.

Among those who joined in the applause that accompanied these bullish words was Work and Pensions Secretary Amber Rudd. Within a few weeks, she would not only quit the Cabinet but also resign the Conservative whip as the new administration was plunged into disarray over Brexit.

The weeks that followed would see more extraordinary political drama as the revised deadline for the UK's departure from the EU approached once again. Fortunately, Sunak had no ideological difficulty with Johnson's determination to leave by the deadline. Nor could he afford to be drawn into the political soap opera. His new list of responsibilities covered almost every aspect of the government's spending, from strategic planning to Spending Reviews, and big tests of his abilities lay just around the corner.

*   *   *

If the Chief Secretary to the Treasury didn't have such an obscure job title, the position would probably enjoy a considerably higher public profile. The strange name disguises the amount of responsibility and influence associated with the role, which is effectively that of Deputy Chancellor. Just how much power the office holder enjoys is heavily contingent on the nature of the relationship with the Chancellor of the Exchequer. If the two ministers trust each other, the Chief Secretary can be privy to a great deal of sensitive information and involved in critical decision-making at the highest level. If, on the other hand, the occupant of No. 11 is paranoid or territorial, or there is a personality clash, a Chief Secretary to the Treasury can feel something of an adjunct and find themselves shut out of the most interesting and important meetings.

The relationship between the previous occupants of these two offices had been dysfunctional, to say the least. Philip

Hammond, a committed Remainer, had barely hidden his distaste for delivering on the result of the Brexit referendum, and his antipathy towards a no-deal scenario was clear. As time went by and May became ever more embattled, he became increasingly entrenched in his position and dogged by the knowledge that his political fate was inextricably linked to hers, however much he might disagree with her strategy. By contrast, his Chief Secretary, Liz Truss, was a Brexiteer and had at least one eye on a future tilt at the Tory Party leadership. Disgruntled Treasury aides and officials, struggling to maintain the appearance that the department remained rock-solid as it was battered by the daily Brexit tsunami, muttered about the amount of time and energy she devoted to her Instagram account.

Hammond's reaction to the fundamental ideological differences between himself and Truss was to freeze her out. Treasury officials were accustomed to the pair operating in silos and worked on the basis that the Chancellor would not want to share key information with the Chief Secretary, still less seek her views on how to manage the impossible business of planning for Brexit with no idea when or how the UK would actually leave. A former Treasury adviser recalls:

There were huge differences in personality as well as over Brexit. Liz was very focused on her own promotion and didn't follow the rules that other ministers follow, in terms of getting approval for media interviews or covering for other ministers if they can't carry out certain duties. Normal teamwork – standing in for others at the despatch box and so on – she just didn't do. She was definitely her own force. There was tension there, and Hammond's team were often thinking about how much to restrict what to tell her about things.

Within the Treasury, this difficult dynamic was not regarded as particularly unusual. Nonetheless, at times the relationship between Hammond and Truss had been sufficiently dysfunctional as to remind civil servants of the torrid 'TB–GB' years during Tony Blair's second and third administrations, when Nos 10 and 11 were at near-constant loggerheads. In his book *Coalition*, David Laws (a former coalition Chief Secretary) writes that the role of Chief Secretary had 'almost no influence' during that period: 'Tony Blair, when Prime Minister, used the Chief Secretary's post primarily to spy on Gordon Brown … Those who served during Gordon Brown's time as Chancellor were often regarded with ill-disguised suspicion by their Treasury boss, and were often also kept in the dark about key decisions.'

Sometimes Treasury officials were even used as tools in the long war of attrition between Brown and Blair. Laws writes that his successor, Danny Alexander, was shocked to discover that mandarins had on occasion been asked to give Chief Secretaries deliberately misleading figures. 'Gordon Brown was very clear that we should not give away the Budget contents to the Chief Secretary,' a civil servant is reported to have told Alexander. 'He was worried that it would get back to No. 10. So we had to talk the then Chief Secretary through a bogus scorecard. It was all most embarrassing.'

By contrast, Cameron and his Chancellor, George Osborne, were close personal friends and had enjoyed a remarkably smooth working relationship. Having been PPS to Osborne before being promoted to Economic Secretary and later Financial Secretary to the Treasury, Javid had seen how much better the Treasury functioned as a result.

A former aide says that when it became apparent to Javid that Johnson was serious about installing him in No. 11, he gave careful consideration to who would be the best fit as his de facto deputy:

> When we thought about Chief Secretaries, we thought Rishi would be ideal. The nature and importance of that relationship is really underappreciated. Under Hammond, the issues were not just with Liz but with No. 10. Hammond's people thought a lot about what to hold back from No. 10. We really wanted to be going in the same direction as Downing Street. There was going to be a conscious effort to align these things, in a way that had not happened with Hammond and May.

The post of Chief Secretary had been created in 1961 to reduce some of the burden on the Chancellor. The office holder is responsible for the control and management of public spending, which accounts for over 40 per cent of the economy. While the position is often considered among the most junior in Cabinet, there is an old protocol under which Cabinet colleagues who wish to see the Chief Secretary must always travel to the Treasury, rather than the reverse, which often enhances the office holder's sense of status.

Sunak swiftly settled into his new role during what was an unusually positive period in the Treasury. The department had been given a clear remit: to turn on the spending taps. Of course, it was never expressed quite like this, but privately Johnson had made it plain to Javid that he wanted his new administration to mark the end of austerity. The Chancellor was under orders to come up with eye-catching public spending initiatives to be unveiled at the Spending Round six weeks later.

The Spending Round, scheduled for 4 September, was designed to set out the government's spending plans for the year ahead. The Comprehensive Spending Review, meanwhile, was a much bigger exercise, setting departmental budgets for three to four years, not due to take place until 2020. Downing Street's instructions were that the short-term package should reflect what they called 'the people's priorities': high-quality healthcare, decent schools and resources for policing. Somewhat optimistically, No. 10 also hoped the exercise would give both Whitehall and the devolved administrations the financial certainty they needed to focus on delivering Brexit on 31 October. Johnson wanted to be able to tell the Commons, and the nation, that the package represented the fastest planned real growth in day-to-day departmental spending for fifteen years. With this in mind, Javid was instructed to be as generous as possible. 'Normally, a Chancellor will only allow a few absolute must-haves in terms of spending, but there was a real imperative to show that this was genuinely a new government, not just a new face in No. 10,' recalls a former adviser. 'There were some grumbles in the department, but it was an agreed strategy.'

This was not just about Johnson courting personal popularity but about laying the ground for a snap election that the Tory Party would have much preferred to avoid. Few Conservative MPs relished the prospect of being forced to go to the polls before the UK was out of the EU, but if there was no way out of it, party strategists wanted something positive to tell voters. An announcement just three days after Johnson entered Downing Street that the government would fund a faster rail route between Leeds and Manchester to 'turbo-charge' regional growth was designed to set the tone. 'There was an imperative and strategy to be popular in order to help push Brexit through. If you want an election to be a credible threat, then people need to think you've got a good chance of winning,' the same aide recalls.

From the outset, Sunak was fully engaged in this challenge. Together, he and Javid set about devising a package that represented some £13.8 billion in extra day-to-day spending – the equivalent of a 4.1 per cent real-terms increase. Claire Coutinho, a former investment banker who became a special adviser at the Treasury, recalls the hurtling pace at which they worked:

We came in at the end of July, and Spending Reviews normally take six months. The task was to get it done by early September. We would generally get into the office about 7 a.m. or 8 a.m. That Spending Review, we were leaving at close to midnight, and coming in at weekends as well. It was a really interesting period to see Rishi in motion. There were mountains of paperwork. He'd have these back-to-back meetings; and the Treasury stops serving food after 4.30 p.m., so it would get to about 3 p.m. and one of us would remember we'd need to go and do the dash to the canteen before everything shut.

For the first time since the Spending Review of 2002, no department would face a budget cut. Nonetheless, there were difficult negotiations with Cabinet ministers who wanted more resources. Coutinho was impressed by the way Sunak navigated this difficult terrain.

That two weeks we had of negotiating in August and September could have been quite awkward. Rishi was newly in that Cabinet position; he had to personally negotiate with Cabinet ministers. It could have been really challenging if tussles had played out in the press. But he's very polite and charming and on top of the detail. He had done a lot of preparation, which really showed.

Despite the frantic pace, officials were pleasantly surprised by how smooth the process proved, thanks in part to Sunak's energetic input and the extent to which he and Javid co-operated to meet the deadline. 'We had to work very quickly. There simply wasn't time to deliberate over big decisions in the normal way. One of the reasons we were able to turn it around so fast was that we had a good ministerial team, including Rishi,' says an adviser who was involved at the time.

One of the things Saj did very quickly was to bring Rishi into meetings. That was quite an institutional change for the Treasury. Officials were always asking Saj, 'Do you mind if we share this with the Chief Secretary?' They were used to seeing the Chief Secretary's office as a relationship they had to manage – a separate empire. We just demolished that wall and said there was no reason to withhold anything from Rishi.

When it came to key policy decisions, Saj would have Rishi next to him. Saj is quite a listener in style in meetings. After officials had all done their thing, Saj would turn to Rish and say, 'What do you think, Rish?' And Rish would give a thoughtful view, which more often than not Saj would agree with. So the whole thing would be done and dusted in that meeting. We had a lot to do in a short amount of time, and the relationship meant they could get through it.

While Javid was generous in involving Sunak at every level, Spending Reviews are always presented to the Commons by the Chancellor, with the Treasury ministerial team relegated to a quiet supporting role. When the big day came, Sunak would not have to do much more than sit next to his boss to offer a discreet prompt should the Chancellor require some unexpected detail, and nod encouragingly at the right moments.

This was the most significant Spending Review in years and Javid could have been forgiven for expecting some glory. After all, following years of austerity, he was splashing the cash. Unfortunately for all concerned, however, the event would be completely blown out of the water. A series of dramas in the Commons and within the Tory Party combined to create one of the most tumultuous weeks in modern political history. In all the excitement, the statement attracted far less than the standard level of attention.

For all Johnson's bombast when he entered office, his administration had been on a knife-edge from the outset. The parliamentary arithmetic had not changed. May's withdrawal deal – the only one on the table – remained unacceptable to MPs, the majority of whom were nonetheless unwilling to leave without a deal. Meanwhile, the Fixed Term Parliaments Act, designed by David Cameron and Nick Clegg to lock two very different political parties into a joint administration for five years, meant the new premier had no executive power to call a general election. For Johnson and most Brexiteers, the least-worst scenario was that the EU would refuse to grant the UK yet another extension, but Brussels had no appetite for a chaotic no-deal withdrawal. The new PM was therefore completely boxed in.

That August, Farage's Brexit Party roared around the

country staging rabble-rousing rallies that put the fear of God into both Tory and Labour MPs in marginal seats. Meanwhile, leading Conservative Remainers spent the summer plotting with opposition allies to derail Johnson's Brexit agenda. While Downing Street strategists war-gamed all the potential scenarios in the hope of wrong-footing the wreckers, rebels led by Sir Oliver Letwin, former Chancellor of the Duchy of Lancaster, and Dominic Grieve, former Attorney General, conspired to find legal ways to take over the order paper of business in the Commons. In cahoots with Remain-supporting Speaker John Bercow, they pored over ancient parliamentary precedents, seeking constitutional devices to prevent the government from leaving the EU without a deal. The minute MPs returned to the Commons in September, they were ready to pounce.

On the eve of the Spending Round, Johnson lost what little remained of his party's majority when Remain-supporting backbencher Phillip Lee crossed the floor to join the anti-Brexit Liberal Democrats. This was small beer relative to what was to follow. Before the week was out, several ministers – including Johnson's own brother Jo Johnson and the Work and Pensions Secretary, Amber Rudd – would resign, and twenty-one Conservative MPs, including two former Chancellors and Winston Churchill's grandson Sir Nicholas Soames, would be expelled from the party. Johnson's attempt to force an early general election was also defeated. The Prime Minister could only hope that Corbyn's reluctance to face the electorate amid dire Labour Party poll ratings would rapidly become unsustainable.

It is no surprise that amid all this turmoil, the Spending Review was a complete sideshow. The Chancellor delivered the statement as planned, but few at Westminster were really listening. The following day, Javid and Sunak's sterling effort would not even make newspaper front pages. Nonetheless, the Treasury team chalked it up as a success. None of their big announcements had instantly unravelled, as can happen with rushed spending decisions, and in so far as anybody was listening, the announcements had been broadly well received. That night, the exhausted Treasury team tumbled into the Two Chairmen pub, a favourite Treasury haunt near Westminster, where they were amused to bump into Gordon Brown's former director of communications Damian McBride – a veteran of many a Spending Round himself.

A week or two later, Sunak hosted a thank-you dinner for special advisers and civil servants who had been instrumental to making the Spending Round a success. The venue was Chutney Mary's, an upmarket Indian restaurant on St James's Street. Those who attended remember it as a very relaxed and enjoyable evening and say that Sunak, who picked up the entire tab, was extremely generous. 'It was quite lavish. It's a very nice restaurant, and he paid for everything. There must have been twenty or so of us there,' says a friend.

> For all his personal aversion to alcohol, by all accounts Sunak is surprisingly knowledgeable about wine, and he has a reputation as a generous and attentive host … He loves making cocktails and always has a well-stocked wine store. If you are a guest of his and you turn away from your glass for a second, you usually turn back to see him topping you up. His parents, wife and family all drink.

For the Treasury team, there was no more time to savour their success, however: the Autumn Budget was less than two months away, at a time when all hands were already on deck with no-deal preparations.

*   *   *

While Javid and Sunak were occupied with preparing the Spending Round, Johnson's inner circle had been plotting something extraordinary. In a move they knew would enrage Remainers, they planned to shut Parliament down for a full five weeks to limit the scope for MPs to block Brexit. This wasn't quite as extreme as it sounded – there is always a three-week parliamentary recess in September for party conference season – but under the circumstances, it was highly provocative. Downing Street knew it would cause uproar, but if Johnson was going to deliver on his promise to leave the EU on 31 October, 'do or die', they were running out of options. This was now 'government in name only', or 'GINO', as it soon became known by critics. Aided and abetted by a Commons Speaker whose family car sported a 'Bollocks to Brexit' sticker (which he insisted belonged to his wife) and who had all but abandoned the pretence of impartiality, Remainers had effectively seized control of the parliamentary agenda. The Prime Minister was getting desperate.

In late August, he asked the Queen to announce that business in both Houses would be suspended from 9 September until 14 October – the longest prorogation since 1945. The decision triggered the expected furore, with parliamentarians, constitutional experts and elder statesmen queuing up to condemn it as a travesty. Three former Prime Ministers weighed in, including Gordon Brown, who accused Johnson of 'shredding the constitution', and Sir John Major, who threw his weight behind an immediate legal challenge brought by anti-Brexit campaigner Gina Miller.

Since he could not publicly admit he was trying to run down the clock, Johnson justified the shutdown on the basis that the government needed a great deal of time to prepare for the Queen's Speech. This was clearly nonsense. Everyone at Westminster knows that these parliamentary set-pieces can be pulled together in a few days, and in any case, he would be in no better a position to implement a legislative agenda when MPs returned after the long unscheduled break. The real motive was obvious: to prevent Remainers boxing him in any further before 31 October. In reality, it was already too late. In early September, by 327 votes to 299, MPs had backed a bill forcing him to ask Brussels for an extension if a deal had not been agreed by mid-October.

Shuttered in the Treasury, Sunak refused to be deflected by all the noise, applying the remarkable self-discipline that had already carried him so far to preparing for the two next big events in his calendar: the Tory Party conference and the Budget. Those who have observed his Westminster career cite this ability to apply a laser-like focus to the task in hand – however new the subject is to him and however great the distractions – as pivotal to his rise. 'He's always quite method-ically sorted out his thoughts in his head and quite quickly comes to a strategy,' says William Hague.

Chief Secretaries are less involved in the Budget than they are in Spending Reviews, the latter falling directly within their remit. Once again, however, Sunak was fully engaged in the process. Groundwork for the event, scheduled for 6 November, provided a welcome opportunity to road-test policies that might feature in a Tory manifesto. The combination of

Downing Street's clear determination to spend more and the sense that Corbyn would not be able to resist calls for a general election for much longer meant the Treasury was being bombarded with ideas from ministers, lobbyists and think tanks. That autumn, dozens of proposals were subjected to rigorous testing to identify the fiscal implications. 'We knew an election was coming, and it was an opportunity to filter out a few bad ideas. It was very useful – when the election came, it meant we were able to cost things in a credible way,' an aide recalls.

The Labour Party was in the middle of its annual conference in Brighton when the Supreme Court declared Johnson's decision to prorogue Parliament unlawful. In a sensational ruling, Baroness Hale – whose enormous spider brooch became almost as famous as its owner – announced that there had been 'no justification' for a move which had had an 'extreme effect' on the 'fundamentals of democracy'.

For Downing Street, it was more of an embarrassment than a development that was likely to significantly change the course of events. Johnson was forced to make an uncomfortable call to Buckingham Palace to apologise for having drawn the monarch into what had now been confirmed as a gross constitutional breach. Meanwhile, Remainer MPs immediately began returning to the Commons, demanding the resumption of parliamentary business. The debacle overshadowed Corbyn's fifth conference as party leader, which had been a thinly attended affair.

From the Conservative Party's point of view, at least, Labour's annual gathering had not been a waste of time. A slew of policy announcements reminded voters of the party's radical redistributive agenda in a way that Tory strategists felt would soon play into Johnson's hands. Sunak was encouraged:

observing the event from afar, he felt it boded well for the showdown that was coming.

'Actually, it gives us something to go after, because the curtain has been pulled back,' he told a Conservative audience a few days later.

> If you own a house, if you've started a business, if you've got savings – according to Jeremy Corbyn, none of that is yours, essentially. All of that is the state's and they will take it if they want to. They will decide when you sell it, what price you sell it at, what wages you pay will be decided by the unions, they will take money from your pension if they want to – that is a fundamental change in how our economic discourse is working, and I think that will really resonate with people once we start having that conversation with them.

The Tory Party conference in Manchester in early October was a strange event, with the threat posed by the Brexit Party an increasing anxiety. If, when the general election finally came, the UK was not out of the EU, and Farage's party insisted on fielding candidates in Conservative seats, dozens of Tory MPs in marginal constituencies would be doomed. In hotel bars and on the conference fringe, the question of whether the party should break with tradition and strike some kind of deal with Farage was a continual talking point.

Sunak's own conference diary featured the usual exhausting round of appearances at fringe meetings; breakfasts, lunches and dinners with journalists; evening receptions with constituency and lobby groups; and various ad-hoc media appearances. He also had an important supporting role during Javid's keynote speech, which he watched from the conference floor with a group that included the Chancellor's mother.

'Twenty years ago, Mum thought it was a big deal when she watched the first Asians move into Coronation Street here in Manchester. Well, now she's watched the first Asians move into Downing Street,' Javid declared, to rapturous applause.

Little did the audience know that the next occupant of No. 11 would also be Asian.

CHAPTER 14

RISHI'S RED WALL

If a man is known by the company he keeps, then Sunak's political friendship group marked him out as a thinker who is drawn more to serious debate than to superficial banter in Westminster bars. Following Theresa May's ill-fated 2017 snap election, he became increasingly close to a number of Tories in their thirties and forties who had previously worked in government at the highest level and were alarmed by the parlous state of the party. The Conservatives seemed to face an existential crisis. Since 1997, the party had managed just two years of majority government, during which period they had presided over utter turmoil. They had failed to anticipate the growing appetite among younger voters for Corbyn's brand of hard-left politics; they had acquired an unfortunate reputation for slashing public services; and they had fallen apart (again) over Europe. Worst of all, they were completely unable to deliver on the result of a referendum they had repeatedly promised to honour. The question was how – or even whether – they could recover.

Every few months, Sunak would dine out with a discreet clique of ex-Downing Street and Treasury special advisers and pore over these matters. Sunak was invited along by virtue of his friendship with Oliver Dowden. The others were Ameet Gill, former Downing Street director of strategy; Nick Timothy, former joint chief of staff to Theresa May; and Rupert Harrison, former chief of staff to Chancellor George Osborne. Also in the informal dining club were former Tory special advisers Paul Stephenson and Henry de Zoete. This was elite company for a little-known junior minister. Unlike the others, Sunak had not earned his stripes as an aide at CCHQ or as a lowly Commons researcher. He had only been actively involved in politics for a few years. However, it was clear that he was smart and going places and he was accepted into the gang.

'We would get together ... and discuss the state of the Tory Party,' one member of the group recalls.

Rishi was very engaged in what needed to happen next, who the next leader should be, when the election should be, and how we could win ... Even at the worst of times – like what happened with the prorogation and the purges [of Tory rebels from the party] – he was very firm. He didn't get wobbly. He was clear this stuff had to be done.

Following the EU referendum, Stephenson and Gill had set up a public affairs company called Hanbury Strategy which picked up various contracts with the Conservative Party. In 2019, Hanbury analysts began modelling how the Tories could win the next election by breaking Labour's grip on the north. The strategy involved targeting a string of constituencies that Corbyn and his acolytes had assumed would always vote their way – areas that the Tory Party had long considered beyond its reach.

In September 2019, Gill and Stephenson shared some of their research during one of their regular dinners. Hanbury had identified sixty-three post-industrial, Leave-leaning seats which had not been represented by a Conservative MP for several decades. Their research suggested that the primary reason these constituencies remained solidly Labour-supporting was cultural: most voters in these areas simply did not think the Tory Party represented people like them. Viewed on a political map, these seats formed a 'Red Wall', which Johnson would have to smash if he were to win the next election.

The first and biggest stretch of the wall ran from north Wales through Merseyside and Lancashire to Yorkshire. The second was in the north-east of England and the third in the Midlands. The widespread suspicion of the Tory Party in these areas was never going to disappear overnight, or even over a period of years: it was too deep-seated for that. However, many longstanding Labour supporters in these seats were bewildered and exasperated by Corbyn's position on Brexit and could not see him as Prime Minister. According to the Hanbury crew, if the Tories rejected the received wisdom that such areas were unwinnable, they had a real chance of securing a majority and could win as many as 360 seats, including Labour strongholds like Scunthorpe, Bassetlaw, Bishop Auckland and Great Grimsby.

Sunak was excited. Though his own constituency was very different from these downtrodden parts of the UK, he had seen for himself how little Labour had delivered for voters in these areas. Indeed, privately he had been talking up the potential for the Conservatives to wrest such constituencies from Labour since at least the beginning of the year. Claire Coutinho says it was something he enthused about the first time they met.

I met Rishi at a drinks do in early 2019. He talked to me about optimism, saying it was one of the things we needed in politics at that time. We were in the Brexit quicksand, and he said, we need people talking up the country, as opposed to people having a negative view. I hadn't heard a lot of people talking in those terms and his positivity was exciting. He talked about Teesside: I remember him mentioning Redcar and Darlington. I remember him saying, we can do this, if we deliver Brexit. He was saying, we really can win these seats. His view was that people in the area were swinging towards the Conservatives.

Sunak was encouraged to hear that Hanbury's modelling was being taken seriously in Johnson's inner circle and resolved that when the election came, he would spend as much time as possible supporting colleagues campaigning in the new target seats.

There was of course one enormous problem: Nigel Farage. The more apparent it became that Johnson would be unable to deliver on his promise to leave the EU by 31 October, the more voters flocked to the Brexit Party. By summer 2019, it was polling at around 20 per cent and was ready to contest every constituency, threatening to split the vote in Leave-supporting seats. The Tories could only hope that, in due course, Farage could be persuaded to stand down his candidates.

Two days before the UK was due to leave the EU, MPs finally voted in favour of a pre-Christmas election. It had taken four attempts for Johnson to get the motion through the Commons. Now there was a mass exodus from Westminster, as MPs headed to their constituencies for the campaign.

Despite Sunak's 23,000 majority, the threat from the Brexit Party could not be entirely discounted. Most people in Richmond wanted to leave the EU, and in the past, strong UKIP candidates had taken a substantial slice out of the Tory vote. In any case, it was not in his nature to take anything for granted, and so within a few hours of the election being called he was hot-footing it back to Yorkshire.

By now he was well liked and trusted by Downing Street, having consistently demonstrated both 'people skills' and first-class intellect. He had also developed a reputation for calm, clear-headed competence. William Hague says that what particularly marks him out from others is that these qualities come without arrogance. 'That is very unusual in politicians,' the former Tory leader observes, noting that politicians as clever as Sunak have a tendency to be overbearing and self-important. It was becoming increasingly apparent to senior Tory strategists that Sunak had 'the complete package'. As a result, Downing Street saw him as a key asset to the national campaign, and the weeks that followed would see him criss-crossing the country for media engagements and trips to support colleagues in marginal seats. Of the many high-profile ministers the Tory campaign chiefs could have chosen to put up for the all-important BBC *Andrew Marr Show* the Sunday after the election was called, it is significant that they asked Sunak. Introduced by the presenter as a 'rising star in Boris Johnson's government', he handled the challenging encounter with aplomb, brushing aside accusations that the decision to call the election would turn out to be a 'terrible, terrible mistake' and never looking anything other than completely sure of himself and the facts. Watching from CCHQ, Tory Party strategists promptly moved him to the top of their list of ministers who could be wheeled out for the most important media appearances in weeks to come.

Back in Richmond, Sunak was facing a number of local difficulties, particularly in relation to the future of the local hospital. Known as the Friarage, the Northallerton district general had been in difficulty for years and was a growing source of concern to voters in the constituency. At the heart of the problem was the hospital's inability to recruit enough staff to maintain round-the-clock emergency care, a situation that threatened to lead to a reduction in some services.

Matters came to a head in February 2019 when South Tees Hospitals NHS Foundation Trust suddenly announced that some critically ill patients could no longer be treated locally and would have to be transferred to hospitals in Middlesbrough or Darlington. The issue was not money but the difficulty in persuading consultants to work full time in a district general hospital where they were simply not dealing with enough patient cases to develop their expertise. For some time, the trust had been muddling along by borrowing anaesthetists and critical care consultants from Middlesbrough's James Cook University Hospital, but it had not proven enough. Hospital bosses now deemed the situation unsafe. Without warning, the Friarage's Accident and Emergency Department was downgraded to an urgent treatment centre and a number of services were suspended.

By his own characteristically level-headed standards, Sunak hit the roof. He was never rude, but his carefully chosen words left little doubt of his fury. He publicly lambasted local NHS bosses, fired off a barrage of letters to key decision makers demanding meetings and made crystal clear that he believed the crisis could have been avoided.

Writing in his local newspaper, he described protecting the Friarage as his single highest priority as an MP and vowed to do everything in his power to save emergency services.

Like you, my family rely on the Friarage. From fixing broken bones to treating allergic reactions, the doctors and nurses at the hospital have been there for us, just like they have for thousands of you ... So last week's news was extremely disappointing to me personally.

It was also frustrating that this unwelcome change was sprung upon us suddenly by the South Tees NHS Trust. Because this change is not driven by money, but by recruitment and staffing issues which have been known about for a long time. Indeed, I've been pressing the Trust on this specific issue for over a year.

In the months that followed, Sunak staged a series of public events, arranging for doctors and health chiefs to attend Q&A sessions with constituents and personally subjecting them to a forensic grilling. That April, he took the extraordinary step of drafting in a leading healthcare management consultancy company to scrutinise plans for the future of the hospital, picking up the bill for their services himself. It would be hard to find any other MP with a sizeable majority who has dipped into their own pocket for such an exercise. Announcing the move on his website, Sunak said he had hired London-based Carnall Farrar to hold senior doctors and NHS managers to account, promising to 'leave no stone unturned' in the quest to protect services. 'It is important that we have independent advice to help us scrutinise the Trust's actions and what the doctors tell us about their vision for the future of the hospital,' he declared, adding that he did not take anything he was told at face value.

Planned hospital closures always represent an opportunity for political opponents and are especially difficult for MPs on the ministerial payroll to defend. They face a dilemma: either they condemn the proposed cuts, putting them at odds with their own government, or they defend the changes, a position which might well cost them their seat. No wise politician takes such a situation lightly. Nonetheless, the amount of time – and money – Sunak devoted to campaigning on this issue went well beyond what would normally be expected from an MP in one of the safest seats in the country.

The truth is that he was frustrated by what he saw as managerial incompetence – yet aware that he was not fully informed about a problem he recognised was probably more complex than it looked. The Stanford MBA graduate in him could see that the trust had not exhausted all potential ways to address staff shortages, and he was unwilling to stand by while it failed to explore alternative solutions. So he set about identifying a specialist doctor recruitment agency and suggesting the trust incentivise doctors at the James Cook to cover the Friarage rotas. He also wanted to understand the bigger picture. His decision to draft in management consultants was due diligence: if the issue was going to rumble on, he wanted to be sure he knew what he was talking about. It was back to his father-in-law's old saying: 'In God we trust, but everyone else needs to bring data to the table.'

Sunak also genuinely cared about the NHS. Both his parents were healthcare professionals and the NHS was a huge part of their lives. In a connection he has never felt the need to advertise, his younger brother is also a doctor: Sanjay Sunak is a consultant clinical psychologist. Having spent years working for the NHS, he now works for a private clinic and health insurers BUPA.

Sunak's careful political positioning on a potentially toxic issue is worth noting. He did not want to find himself on the back foot, so he immediately made clear his determination to hold the local NHS to account – while assiduously avoiding doing or saying anything that could be perceived as an attack on doctors or nurses.

In quieter times, all this might have attracted more media attention. Luckily for Sunak, there was far too much else going on for what was fundamentally a local drama to generate wider interest. The independent report he had commissioned into emergency services at the Friarage also helped, in fact going a long way towards vindicating the trust's decision to reconfigure services. It concluded that it was extremely rare for a hospital as small as the Friarage to be able to maintain full accident and emergency provision and highlighted that much larger hospitals had already had to go down a similar route. Following the controversial changes, the new urgent treatment centre was actually treating more children than had been seen before, and there was no evidence of any increase in mortality linked to longer ambulance journey times for the 10 per cent of adult patients who would previously have been treated at the Friarage and were now taken elsewhere. By the time the election was called, the heat had largely gone out of the issue. This was just as well, because Sunak was about to be propelled onto the centre of the national stage.

*　　*　　*

Had anyone at Westminster wondered whether Sunak was in line for promotion to one of the great offices of state, his appearance as a stand-in for the Prime Minister in two critical televised debates would surely have dispelled any doubt.

Of course, the Conservative Party still had to win on 12 December and victory was far from certain. Nonetheless, Johnson's decision to select the Chief Secretary to the Treasury to represent the party on primetime television was a huge vote of confidence in both Sunak's public appeal and his ability not to screw up.

Sunak's big opportunity arose because, having already participated in two televised debates, neither Johnson nor Corbyn deigned to appear in two further debates involving seven political parties: a BBC programme hosted by Nick Robinson in Cardiff and a show hosted by ITV's Julie Etchingham in Manchester. Designed to give fair representation to smaller parties, the seven-way format had proved awkward in the past, with the number of participants impeding a free-flowing debate. With so many voices to be heard, there was little scope for individuals to shine. There was still plenty of opportunity for error, however. Sunak – still a relatively inexperienced TV performer – knew that the slightest slip could go viral on social media. As always, his approach was to be meticulously prepared, and he spent hours poring over briefings from Tory campaign headquarters and rehearsing responses to possible lines of attack.

By now, the Conservatives had a commanding lead over Labour in the polls and the Brexit Party was slumping towards oblivion. This was an extraordinary turnaround. Towards the end of May's leadership, support for the Tories had plummeted to a twenty-year low, falling to 17 per cent in one shocking YouGov survey for the *Sunday Times* in June. This was nine points behind the Brexit Party, which had streaked ahead of all the other parties. Fortunately for the Conservatives, these figures proved to be the nadir. Within days of Johnson taking over, Tory ratings bounced into the 30s, while support for Farage's outfit began a sharp decline. By November, the Brexit Party was consistently polling single figures, and it would not be long before it would fall below five points.

To the enormous relief of Tories in marginal seats, on 11 November the Brexit Party announced that it would not contest 317 constituencies won by the Conservatives at the last election. By the time of the televised election debates, Tory ratings had soared into the 40s, with Labour languishing around ten points behind. Johnson's campaign slogan – 'Get Brexit Done' – coupled with the message that anything other than a Tory majority would simply drag out the misery over leaving the EU was working and had driven support for Farage's party off a cliff.

Against this backdrop, Sunak's mission in the TV debates was to hammer home the party's key messages and avoid making any blunders. Nobody at Tory campaign headquarters expected – or wanted – anything more imaginative.

Those involved in preparations for the debate say Sunak accepted the need to stick to a script, even though he knew it would not make for exciting television. When the cameras rolled, he did just that. 'Those performances were unbelievably disciplined,' recalls veteran Tory adviser Lord Finkelstein.

They were boring – but far from that being a downer, that's an exceptional skill. As a party, you have got a campaign message; what you want is people who are willing to put the campaign message above their own dignity sometimes. It can be a little undignified to go onto the TV and use the campaign slogan. Some politicians don't make the calculation that the sacrifice of dignity is a good thing, at the margin. Rishi was very disciplined about that – he did the best he could to try not to sound a bit clunky, but the most important thing was he got the message across.

Finkelstein says that Sunak did 'explicitly consider' whether simply delivering pre-agreed lines would sound inauthentic but concluded that it was 'a price he was willing to pay'. 'I was very impressed by that discipline,' the peer says.

Even *The Guardian* conceded that he gave a steady performance, concluding that it 'wasn't so much a bad night as a boring one for the chief secretary to the Treasury'. Describing him as a 'very safe pair of hands, who repeatedly pressed home his party's central message – that it is imperative to "get Brexit done"', the paper acknowledged that Conservative campaign bosses were probably content with the outcome. An assessment of his second performance was less kind ('cheesy and wooden ... all his lines sounded precooked') but conceded that he had made it through the two-hour ordeal 'without incident' and that party strategists would once again be pleased.

Minus the two main party leaders, these debates felt decidedly like B-list affairs and were quickly forgotten by most viewers, but they had propelled Sunak into a new league. He had proven that he could perform under intense pressure and scrutiny and could stick to a script without sounding so robotic that it grated.

Back in Richmond, Sunak's campaign was going well: the argument that voting Conservative was the only way to break the impasse was working on the doorstep. It was not just about Brexit, however. Fighting his third general election campaign in five years, Sunak knew that local issues were what usually mattered most to voters. In a significant coup, he had managed to persuade NHS chief executive Simon Stevens to visit the Friarage, a clever bit of PR which reinforced his commitment to the hospital.

Moreover, Sunak had a positive story to tell about the Conservatives' record in the area since 2010. In statistics he liked to trumpet, unemployment in Yorkshire and the Humber had fallen by 56 per cent, tens of thousands more young people had started apprenticeships, and the number of small businesses had grown by 96,200. 'More jobs, more skills and more enterprise' was how he put it, arguing that all these gains would be jeopardised by Labour. On the doorstep, he could tell voters that from 2021 to 2022, Tories would increase the amount spent on every secondary school student by £5,000, with an extra £4,000 for every primary school pupil. As the wider campaign to demolish the Red Wall gathered pace, he also underlined his party's determination to pour resources into the north. 'For too long, the north of England was overlooked by Westminster. So we will carry on supporting the Northern Powerhouse, delivering the critical infrastructure such as improved roads and railways which will spur Yorkshire's growth in the decades to come,' he declared.

How much difference all that talk about the Northern Powerhouse made in Richmond is a moot question. Before midnight struck on 12 December, it would become apparent that the combination of the pledges to 'get Brexit done' and to invest in the north had worked in many of the Tories' target seats. Just as the strategists at Hanbury had planned, the Red Wall had come tumbling down. By the following morning, Johnson would be back in Downing Street, having delivered the party's best election result since 1987.

Sunak's own result was never in doubt. In Richmond he

secured 36,693 votes, over 27,000 more than his closest rival and a couple of hundred more than his previous tally in 2017. Nationally, the Tories had gone from being the largest party in a hung parliament to an overall majority of eighty seats.

That Sunday, Sunak was back on the *Marr* programme, hailing the breakthrough in the north. 'My own constituency borders places like Darlington, Bishop Auckland, Stockton, and so I am familiar with it ... We want to make sure that opportunity is spread throughout the country. So better infrastructure, better education – that's how people will build better lives, wherever they happen to live.'

This was the usual sort of rhetoric from politicians following election victories. Sunak would soon be in a powerful position to determine whether the grand vision turned into anything more than an aspiration.

CHAPTER 15

BABY CHINO

When Rishi Sunak relaxes, there is nothing he likes better than watching *Star Wars* movies.

By his own admission, he is a huge fan – so much so that he's been known to queue for midnight showings, has read all the books and has filled his house with *Star Wars* paraphernalia: lightsabers, toys, Lego. As a child, his ambition was not to be a doctor like his father but to become a Jedi knight.

So when Sajid Javid got his hands on tickets to a special screening of *Star Wars: The Rise of Skywalker* at the IMAX cinema in London's Waterloo just before Christmas 2019, he knew whom to invite.

Together with Javid's young son and a special adviser, the Chancellor and the Chief Secretary made a proper evening of it, enjoying a meal together at an American diner before heading to the cinema, where they settled into some of the best seats in the house. This was Sunak's idea of heaven and a rare chance to switch off from a work schedule that was only getting more intense.

Christmas was five days away, but Sunak was still toiling away in London. Preparatory work for the Spring Budget had ground to a halt during the election campaign and though it was still a few months away, time was tight. Moreover, there was a lot of thinking to do about priorities. Downing Street had made clear that the package of measures should be driven by the levelling-up agenda, a principle Sunak fully supported. However, both he and Javid believed it had to be done without jeopardising the party's hard-won reputation for caution with the public finances. No. 10 was pushing for big expensive pledges, and tricky negotiations lay ahead. Before the House of Commons shut up shop for the holidays, Javid handed Johnson a twenty-page letter setting out his ideas for how to achieve the party's political objective while balancing the books.

Quite how much attention Johnson paid to this document is uncertain, because he had so much else on his mind, including personal matters. Unbeknown to all but close friends and family, his girlfriend Carrie Symonds was pregnant and the pair had become secretly engaged – happy news that would nonetheless require delicate handling, out of respect for his ex-wife Marina and their children.

Then there was Brexit. With a majority of eighty, the UK's departure from the EU was now assured, but Johnson would need to think carefully about how the occasion should be marked in a way that did not further divide the country. Beyond that, the Prime Minister would have to undertake a Cabinet reshuffle, something he had been putting off.

In the immediate aftermath of the election, he had decided not to change his ministerial line-up, on the basis that the House of Commons was about to rise for Christmas and it seemed to make more sense to wait until after Brexit. Nonetheless, he had let it be known that the shake-up would come in February – putting ministers on notice that they might not be in their jobs for long.

The state of the relationship between No. 10 and No. 11 was

another background concern. On the surface, this was healthy enough, certainly between Johnson and Javid personally. The difficulty was Javid's relationship with Dominic Cummings, the Prime Minister's chief adviser, which had deteriorated sharply since the summer. The problem had started back in August when Cummings began to suspect Javid's media aide Sonia Khan of briefing against Johnson's strategy for leaving the EU. The Chancellor had not supported Brexit during the referendum, and while he was no Europhile, he had never been part of Cummings's Vote Leave gang. At a point when Downing Street was under maximum pressure to honour the Prime Minister's pledge to leave the EU on 31 October, Cummings got it into his head that Javid's aide was undermining No. 10's efforts – culminating in Khan being summoned to Downing Street and summarily fired. She was marched out of the building under police escort.

Javid was livid. According to one source, during a heated exchange with Johnson, he suggested Cummings had concocted the allegations to damage him. As Khan launched industrial tribunal proceedings, the issue continued to fester.

Both sides made an effort to move on, but other differences between No. 10 and No. 11 were beginning to emerge. In particular, Cummings and Johnson were becoming frustrated by the Treasury's fiscal rules, which limited how fast they could raise public spending. By contrast, the Chancellor believed the restraints existed for a good reason and should not be tampered with.

Nor was Javid keen on possible new wealth taxes linked to property, which appealed to some of those in Johnson's inner circle. Exacting a levy on homes worth more than £2 million, an idea that had been kicking around since the early days of the coalition, was simply not Conservative, he felt, and would alienate many of the party's better-off supporters in London and the south-east. The measure was also fiercely opposed by Tory backbenchers. Behind the scenes, the Prime Minister's chief adviser was becoming frustrated that the Chancellor was not more pliable. As head of the Vote Leave campaign during the EU referendum, Cummings had famously coined the phrase 'Take Back Control' to encapsulate what the British public would be doing if they voted for Brexit. Now he wanted to do the same in respect of the relationship between No. 10 and the Treasury.

Down the ages, splits between these two great power bases had been the curse of many a premiership, but those involved generally accepted that some creative tension was in the public interest. A strong, independent Treasury acted as a healthy check on No. 10, helping to prevent political ambitions from imperilling the public finances. To Javid's dismay, Cummings had little truck with that, believing that Chancellors should know their place.

It had not escaped No. 10's notice that the young Chief Secretary to the Treasury was somewhat more receptive to their agenda, and Cummings began to cultivate Sunak in a way that could have become corrosive, had Sunak been less loyal to his boss. Westminster observers were beginning to pick up on this difficult dynamic, giving rise to mutterings that Javid was only keeping the seat warm for his talented young deputy.

'Everyone was constantly trying to make a story of the No. 10/No. 11 thing,' a former Treasury insider recalls.

Sometimes as a way of poking us, the No. 10 guys would big up Rishi a bit. Allies of Boris would hint that Rishi was being lined up to replace Saj. Diary pieces would appear about rumours that Boris wanted Rishi as Chancellor. There were people in No. 10 who were keen to have control of everything, who did like Rishi and wanted him as Chancellor, though I don't think it was coming from Boris. Anyway, for sure he was talked up a lot by certain people in No. 10, and he did get quite close to them. So I heard speculation on the other side, saying, are you sure you trust that Rishi guy, because he seems to be in cahoots with No. 10? But we definitely did trust him and disregarded that mischief-making.

Somewhere along the line, Javid acquired an unfortunate – and unfair – new nickname at Westminster: CHINO, meaning Chancellor in name only. This was not a description Javid had any intention of justifying. Nonetheless, by the time the election was called, he was beginning to feel uneasy about his position. He sought – and received – a public guarantee that his job was safe. At a CBI event in November, Johnson gave an 'absolutely categorical assurance' that the Chancellor would stay in post, adding, 'I think he's doing a fantastic job.'

In the weeks that followed, however, Javid's relationship with Cummings continued to deteriorate. There was a disagreement over who should succeed Mark Carney as Governor of the Bank of England and differences of opinion over the controversial high-speed rail scheme HS2. As the Budget approached, differences over fiscal policy also became an increasing source of tension. In a difficult meeting in mid-February, Javid argued that the fiscal rules Cummings disliked helped to concentrate minds on what was important and forced ministers to make sensible choices. Not everything could be a priority, the Chancellor said. He was deeply un-comfortable with excessive spending and borrowing. Johnson pushed back, and the matter was left unresolved.

None of this created anything like the bad blood that had characterised the relationship between Gordon Brown and Tony Blair – at least as far as Javid was concerned. He and Johnson remained on good terms, and as the Cabinet reshuf-fle approached in February, the Chancellor fully expected to remain in post.

What Javid did anticipate, however, was some attempt by Cummings to clip his wings. Shortly before the reshuffle, he had a conversation with some of his closest aides, during which at least one indicated a readiness to step down if that was re-quired to keep the Chancellor in his job. According to insiders, few at the Treasury really thought it would come to this.

Sunak, too, was expecting to stay put. While Downing Street now considered him more than capable of running his own department, it was not obvious where to move him. Johnson was happy with the line-up in the great offices of state, and in any case, Sunak loved what he was doing. Still relatively inexperienced, he preferred to stay where he was, albeit in the number two position, rather than take the top job in a less important ministry. No. 10 was aware of his feelings, and the plan was to keep him in place.

'Ahead of the reshuffle, Saj did say that he hoped Rishi would stay on for a while at the Treasury as there was a lot to do,' says a source familiar with the discussions that took place behind the scenes at the time.

It did seem like a good time to promote him, but the job he was doing as Chief Secretary was very good experience and exposure, and he was very well suited to it. The expectation was that the path he would take would be much like Saj's: he would do a couple of mid-ranking departments like Culture, Media and Sport before one of the big offices of state. He would have to earn his stripes. But at that reshuffle it wasn't clear that there would be any suitable departments coming up, so generally the view was that it would be best for him to stay on a bit at the Treasury.

Johnson's reshuffle began at 9 a.m. on 13 February amid reports that those in the firing line would be spared the 'walk of shame' past the waiting press on Downing Street; only those staying in post or being promoted could expect a meeting in No. 10. First to be sacked was Northern Ireland Secretary Julian Smith, followed by Business Secretary Andrea Leadsom. It was not until much later in the day that Javid was summoned to Downing Street, the location an encouraging sign that the meeting would be little more than a formality to confirm his reappointment. As he made his way into No. 10, the Chancellor's head was high.

Back at the Treasury, Sunak awaited the return of his boss, expecting him to reappear in fifteen or twenty minutes. But half an hour went by, then forty-five minutes, and still Javid did not emerge. What was going on? Javid's team was beginning to get twitchy.

Inside Downing Street, the Prime Minister had opened the meeting by lavishing the Chancellor with praise. Setting out his vision for levelling up the economy, Johnson told Javid he was 'the right man for the job'. There was just one catch: he would have to sack his entire team of advisers. Relations between the Treasury and No. 10 could not be allowed to deteriorate any further, the Prime Minister said, arguing that they had to work together in the way that Cameron and Osborne had during the coalition years. A new team of advisers would be a fresh start, he suggested.

This was an audacious power grab. For all their closeness, Cameron and Osborne had never shared special advisers. Shocked, Javid refused point-blank, telling Johnson that no self-respecting Cabinet minister would agree to these terms. He would not stay on if the Treasury was going to be 'neutered', he declared.

Taken aback by the strength of the Chancellor's reaction, Johnson suggested he think it over. Javid was ushered to a side room, where a senior Cabinet Office official reportedly talked him through plans for a new joint team of economic advisers based not in the Treasury but in Downing Street, doing his best to make the proposition sound reasonable.

Johnson's chief of staff Sir Eddie Lister and Chief Whip Mark Spencer are also said to have tried to talk him around, but Javid had made up his mind. Around an hour after the ill-fated meeting began, he left Downing Street and news of his resignation broke.

The Chancellor's sensational departure shocked Westminster and threw the reshuffle into disarray. Luckily, there was an obvious candidate for his replacement. In No. 10, there was never any doubt over who that should be: Rishi Sunak, the ferociously bright young Chief Secretary to the Treasury who had shown he was amenable to No. 10's fiscal agenda. Moments later, Sunak was on his way to Downing Street, where he accepted the Prime Minister's invitation to become Chancellor of the Exchequer. He was just thirty-nine years old.

The circumstances surrounding Javid's departure raised

serious questions over what kind of role the MP for Richmond had been so swift to embrace. Johnson had made clear that the traditional separation between the offices of the Chancellor and the Prime Minister would effectively cease to exist. The new Chancellor was expected to march in lockstep with his boss, and his special advisers would be appointed directly by No. 10.

In a series of media interviews after the reshuffle, Javid made no secret of his disdain for this arrangement, publicly declaring that it was not a price he personally had been willing to pay. 'A Chancellor, like all Cabinet ministers, has to be able to give candid advice to a Prime Minister so that he is speaking truth to power. I believe that the arrangement proposed would significantly inhibit that, and it would not have been in the national interest,' he would later tell the Commons.

If Javid wasn't prepared to remain in post under these conditions, what did it say about Sunak that he was? As the new Chancellor of the Exchequer made his way back to the Treasury, there were catcalls from the press pack outside. Would he just be a patsy – another Chancellor in name only – the media wanted to know?

Time would tell whether he would live up to this characterisation or an even more mischievous moniker that swiftly began doing the rounds: 'Baby Chino'. Sunak himself wasn't going to let any of that blow him off course. There was less than a month until the Budget, and its success or failure now rested on his shoulders.

CHAPTER 16

TRILLION-POUND TRADE-UP

Twenty-seven days after his unexpected elevation, Rishi Sunak stood at the despatch box to present the first Budget of Boris Johnson's Conservative majority government, and the first of a UK administration outside the European Union for forty-eight years. Even more notable was the fact that such a momentous statement was being delivered by a character still barely known outside Westminster. 'The story of this government has been the story of a national jobs miracle,' he told the House. 'And given the last few weeks that I've had, I'm all in favour of jobs miracles.'

The unforeseen change at the top of the Treasury had prompted rumours that the Budget might be postponed from the date originally announced by Sajid Javid in January, as the new Chancellor came to grips with his brief and considered new policy options. But on 18 February, Sunak provided clarity. 'Cracking on with preparations for my first Budget on 11 March,' he tweeted alongside a picture of himself, bespectacled and studious, surrounded by papers at his Treasury desk.

This left Sunak with less than four weeks to prepare for an event which would normally be months in the planning, and space had to be found in the diary. He decided not to attend the meeting of G20 Finance Ministers in Riyadh, Saudi Arabia, sending a senior official in his place and speaking to some of his opposite numbers by telephone.

The new Chancellor spent the days after his appointment 'just amassing information', according to a senior Treasury official. 'He's got a ferocious appetite for detailed information,' says the source. 'That first day we got to grips with how, tactically, we would run the private office for the next three weeks, how we were going to deliver a Budget in three weeks. Ultimately, you can't be overwhelmed.'

While he had his head down, the media had a chance to digest his appointment – not least in India, where it was major news. Sunak was already something of a celebrity in the country because of both his Indian heritage and the family he had married into. The *Times of India* noted that the British Cabinet now boasted four persons of Indian origin and the *Deccan Herald* was already mulling future prospects, head-lining its piece 'Rishi Sunak, NRN's son-in-law, and Britain's PM-in-waiting?' Some also considered what the appointment said about Britain itself. 'If post-Brexit UK wants to showcase itself as an opportunity society, it needs to merely look at Boris Johnson's cabinet,' wrote Swapan Dasgupta in the country's *Telegraph* newspaper, while observing that Sunak's promotion demonstrated 'more vividly than anything else that what really counts in contemporary Britain isn't colour but class. It is all about the ability to fit in and play the games according to the rules of the game.' Though of Indian heritage, 'in social terms he fits more into the traditional Tory groove than, say, Margaret Thatcher who had to – in another age – suffer con-descending jibes about being a grocer's daughter'.

Reporters in Britain also relished the advent of a new character in the nation's political drama, with sketch writers particularly enjoying Sunak's appearance at the first meeting of the post-reshuffle Cabinet on 14 February. Johnson opened the gathering by giving his senior colleagues a pep talk for the cameras. 'Congratulations to you all on achieving or indeed retaining the great offices of state that you hold,' he began, 'and that is no mean feat.' He reminded ministers that as 'the people's government, we have to get on with delivering the people's priorities ... We are going to cut crime, we're going to tackle homelessness, we're going to tackle waiting lists in our NHS.' The Prime Minister then launched into an unexpected round of call and response. 'How many hospitals are we going to build?' 'Forty!' chorused the Cabinet cheerfully. 'How many more police officers are we recruiting?' 'Twenty thousand!' 'How many more nurses are we recruiting?' 'Fifty thousand!' 'And how many more buses?' Some were less sure about this, but not Grant Shapps, the Transport Secretary. 'Four thousand!' This was correct, the PM affirmed. 'Four thousand beautiful bouncing British-built low-carbon buses.' Now was the time to repay the trust of the people and 'put the pedal to the metal', he concluded. 'In a low-carbon way.'

According to Quentin Letts in *The Times*, the new Chancellor 'was loving it. All shiny, his teeth a-gleam, he rocked with excitement. He had a rubbery bangle on his right wrist and seemed to be wearing a start-of-term suit. Matron may need to check that his mum sewed it with his name tapes.' *The Guardian's* Marina Hyde was similarly biting. 'The chancellor has been replaced by Rishi Sunak, whose entire aesthetic is that of an *Apprentice* candidate who's just drenched himself in Diesel's Only The Brave, and is willing to tear up his fiscal rules for the chance for Johnson to own 50% of his business,' she mused. 'Downing Street characterised its new working relationship with this chancellor as "hand in glove", an analogy that appears to cast Mr Sunak as a glove.'

Back at the Treasury, the new Chancellor had more important things to think about than his appearance. One of these was his own political position. On his departure, Sajid Javid had said that the Prime Minister's insistence that he sack all his political advisers left him with 'no option other than to resign', and that he did not believe that 'any self-respecting minister' would accept such conditions. Some took this to be a swipe at his successor, but this seems an unfair interpretation: it was not as though Sunak dismissed loyal staff to secure the post, as Javid had been asked to do. Javid himself also later dismissed the idea, telling the *FT* that he had urged Johnson not to replace him with a soft touch: 'I told the PM, "You need someone who is going to be straight with you and capable," and I said that had to be Rishi.'

But accepting the job did mean agreeing to a new joint economic unit based across the Treasury and No. 10, a plan first hatched between Johnson, Michael Gove and Dominic Cummings days after the EU referendum in 2016 in the expectation that the Boris premiership would begin in weeks rather than years. Sunak asked for the unit to be run by 33-year-old Liam Booth-Smith, described as 'razor-sharp' by insiders, who had served as deputy chief of staff to the PM since the previous July. Sunak knew him well from his days as a special adviser in the local government department, when the pair had taken themselves to Nando's every fortnight to catch up. One figure familiar with their working relationship says that while Booth-Smith was 'clearly close to Cummings and tied into the No. 10 operation', he was 'very much Rishi's adviser and Rishi's guy, giving him advice in his interests'.

Even so, there was no doubt that the centre would have an unprecedented degree of control over economic policy. 'His autonomy [was] clearly reduced compared to that of previous Chancellors,' says one expert observer of the Conservative Party,

> whether you look at the days of Treasury empire, Gordon Brown-style, trying to extend his power to outposts in other departments and trying to nobble what No. 10 was up to, or the kind of glumly defiant Philip Hammond's Treasury, where No. 10 wasn't strong enough to get its way so he just said, 'shan't, won't, shan't, won't'.

Still, it would be 'less compromising for a new Chancellor entering that role with his eyes open' than it would have been for Javid to stay but with new constraints.

The new set-up drew scorn from some commentators. Philip Collins, a Blair-era inhabitant of No. 10, felt Sunak had been 'promoted into the position of sacrificial lamb'. Though he would sit in the Treasury, 'it is not really worth calling him the chancellor of the exchequer', since officials would not take him seriously.

But to regard Sunak as a prime ministerial lapdog would be to misread the situation, according to an experienced observer on the Tory side. 'When he was first appointed, his position looked weak, but in fact it's the other way around. Having lost one Chancellor, Johnson would have taken a hit if he had to fire another.' In fact, the characterisation would actually be better directed elsewhere, according to another well-placed source: Sunak was 'not somebody you could accuse of being there purely because of his Boris-backing despite not being any good, which is a charge that could be levelled against some politicians who will remain nameless'.

Sunak himself later dismissed any concern that he was there simply to do what he was told, telling the *Sunday Telegraph* in a pre-Budget interview, 'They're all my team. And the relationship has been excellent.' He added, 'I come from a business background, and the idea that a finance director would be somewhat not working closely with the CEO of a company is very strange to anyone in the business world. I don't think it should be any different here.'

According to Richard Sharp, Sunak's old boss at Goldman Sachs, his approach will have been informed by his time with the firm. 'What made Goldman good was an ethos of teamwork. That will have impacted his thinking in terms of transforming the relationship between No. 10 and No. 11, against the forces that often push them apart.'

One figure who knows both Sunak and Cummings thought from the outset that the two would get along well personally. 'They're very different, *very* different sorts of people,' he says. 'Modestly confrontational, modestly not, to put it no more strongly than that. But both would approach things from a sort of intellectual, theoretical point of view – here's a problem to be solved, let's think about it.' There would be a level of mutual respect. 'Dom likes smart people, therefore, by definition, he'd like Rishi … Rishi would get on top of the subject very quickly. He'd ask the right questions and help shape the solution.'

More immediately pressing for Sunak than his place in the political firmament was the content of the Budget itself. Here, too, there were suggestions that the new tenant at No. 11 would be readier than his predecessor to do his neighbour's bidding. For some, this was because as a Leave campaigner in the 2016 referendum, a supporter of Johnson in the leadership race and a strong advocate of the PM's levelling-up agenda, he was on the same political wavelength. For the less sympathetic, he was simply more compliant and had no authority of his own.

Attention once again focused on the three fiscal rules that had appeared in the 2019 Conservative manifesto at Javid's insistence. These were, first, that the government would only borrow to invest, or that day-to-day spending on things like benefits and public services had to be matched by tax revenue; second, that public sector net investment would average no more than 3 per cent of GDP; and third, that if debt interest reached 6 per cent of revenue, the government would reassess its debt control plans – effectively a commitment that debt would be lower at the end of the parliament than at the beginning. Speculation began to mount that Sunak might loosen one or more of these strictures in order to accommodate the PM's spending ambitions. These included big increases for services including the NHS and social care, as well as major infrastructure investment, especially in the north of England. 'It wasn't a question of what they wanted to spend more money on,' one person close to the process remarked. 'It was more a question of whether there was anything they didn't want to spend more money on.'

But the idea of any significant difference in economic outlook between the incoming and outgoing Chancellors would be wrong, according to one insider who knows both men well. 'There is no ideological difference between Javid and Sunak worth noting,' he says. 'It's all about circumstance. Saj was the guardian of the rules and the financial orthodoxy, because he was Chancellor. Rishi will start from exactly the same place. The difference is that he's not tied personally to Saj's rules.'

Indeed, there was no reason to see Sunak as a free-spending fiscal expansionist. In a Budget debate in July 2015, two months after he was first elected to Parliament, the new MP for Richmond picked out the plan to balance the books as the single most commendable part of George Osborne's economic programme. 'I have spent my career in business,' he told the House.

> Every company I have been involved in sets a budget, as indeed does every household in this nation, and when they do, they operate with these basic principles: first, 'How much is coming in?' and only then, 'How much can I spend?' For too long, governments have got that back to front, spending first, ignoring how much is coming in, then letting borrowing endlessly make up the difference.

He noted:

> Since 1955, tax receipts, with limited variation and remarkable consistency, have averaged 36 per cent to 38 per cent of GDP. In spite of the vast differences between Labour and Conservative Members in our approach to setting tax rates, the average tax take has been remarkably similar under governments of both parties. There appears to be a natural ceiling to what any government can extract from the pockets of its hard-working taxpayers. That to me suggests a simple conclusion: in normal times, public spending should not exceed 37 per cent of GDP. That is the best estimate of our income as a government and therefore the best guide to what we can afford to spend.

Five years later, serving in a newly elected government whose manifesto committed it to significant extra spending, pragmatism would have to come to the fore.

As a former No. 10 operative puts it:

Rishi was happier to see which way the wind was blowing, and that if that's what the First Lord of the Treasury [the PM] wants the Treasury to do then that's what the Treasury really ought to do, particularly when the First Lord of the Treasury has just won a healthy majority. All things being equal, I think any Conservative Chancellor would want to reduce the amount the state does and cut taxes, but that's not the economic and political climate we were in.

As another unsentimental source notes, 'The question is, do you want to be Chancellor or not? And he's obviously made his mind up.'

There was no doubt that the Budget would be the biggest spending event since before the Conservatives returned to government in 2010. City analysts took the change of Chancellors as a clear signal that the expansion would go further than they had previously expected. This raised the inevitable question of where the money was coming from. Once the media had been safely cleared out, Sunak used his first Cabinet as Chancellor to remind his colleagues to find savings of 5 per cent in their departmental budgets, a demand first levelled by Javid the previous month. However, the funds freed up by such an exercise would clearly not cover the scale of the Prime Minister's ambitions or be anything like enough to prove that the age of austerity was over.

One school of thought, favoured by those prepared to relax the fiscal rules, was that with interest rates at historically low levels – the base rate had been at 0.75 per cent since August 2018, and had been below 1 per cent for more than a decade – there had never been a better time to borrow. This policy had already been pursued by Javid and his immediate predecessors, and support for scaling it up was to be found in some unexpected quarters. 'Borrowing a bit more today at very low rates of interest to undertake the Prime Minister's infrastructure revolution is fine,' declared John Redwood, an outspoken figure on the Tory right. 'Spending a bit more on crucial public services is desirable and affordable.'

But revenue would also need to be raised. The idea of a mansion tax on the most valuable homes, which Javid had resisted, continued to circulate. Another suggestion was to cut tax relief on pension contributions for higher earners from 45 or 40 per cent to the basic rate of 20 per cent, potentially raising £10 billion a year, or to scrap the provision under which retirees can take up to a quarter of their pension pot as a tax-free lump sum. Both proposals triggered outrage from Conservative MPs when they were floated in the weeks before the Budget. 'We are beginning to think like socialists,' Iain Duncan Smith complained to *The Times*. 'It's a tax on aspiration.'

A Treasury adviser says Sunak was taken aback by what he found in the Budget plans he inherited.

On the very first day we had the first meeting about the Budget, and his view right from the beginning, before anyone else spoke, was: 'This thing is just too big and unwieldy. We have to thin it down, we have to take out the stuff that doesn't really keep to the government's themes.'

These included some ideas that would have been politically explosive, according to the source.

> There had been a mansion tax mooted, alongside a full council tax revaluation which would have seen 8 or 9 million people seeing significant council tax rises. There was some discussion of it being on homes between £1 million and £2 million. We hadn't got elected on a pledge to do that. The problem is that it doesn't tell a story. There was just a lot of stuff that didn't really hang together. It was very woolly, it lacked definition. Even if it's the norm, it's a bad way of doing politics. What you want to do is start at the end point, what it is you're seeking to achieve, and work your way back. They'd done it in reverse.

Sunak's task, then, was to deliver on his party's manifesto promises, find the money for a big uplift in both day-to-day spending and long-term investment, and cement the Conservatives' relationship with their diverse new coalition of voters – while at the same time keeping the public finances in good order, satisfying Tory MPs, readying the economy for a new trading relationship with the EU, and stamping his own authority on the job.

If only that were all he would have to contend with. On 30 January, the World Health Organization declared the outbreak of coronavirus that had begun in China at the turn of the year to be a global public health emergency. By this stage only two people in the UK had tested positive for Covid-19, but Public Health England raised the risk level from low to moderate and the government launched a public health campaign, encouraging people to wash their hands regularly and use tissues to catch coughs and sneezes. The Foreign Office advised against all but essential travel to mainland China.

Only eight cases had been confirmed in Britain by the time of Sunak's appointment as Chancellor on 13 February, but the signs from around the world were that the country needed to prepare for a crisis. More than 65,000 cases and 1,400 deaths had been recorded globally.

On 28 February, the authorities documented the first case of Covid-19 being transmitted within the UK, and the first British death from the disease was confirmed. The day also brought to a close the worst week for global stock markets since the financial crash of 2008: around $5 trillion was wiped off the value of equities around the world, including more than £200 billion in the UK. By the following week, the virus had reached eighty-one countries, with more than 90,000 cases and 3,000 deaths worldwide. Italy, the epicentre of the outbreak in Europe, had recorded 100 deaths, closed all schools and universities, and announced measures to quarantine its entire 60 million population.

Inside the Treasury, it soon became clear that the Budget would have to be completely reshaped. After some thorough reading on the unfolding situation, one senior adviser recalls sitting down with Sunak and saying, 'This Budget is not going to be the thing that people think it's going to be. It's going to be the coronavirus Budget. And that's going to be it.' The Chancellor 'took a minute digesting that'.

On 3 March, the week before the Budget, Boris Johnson set out the government's contingency plans in the event of a widespread outbreak in the UK. The Coronavirus Action Plan envisaged asking people to work from home, quarantining the families of those who fell ill, closing schools and introducing a range of social distancing measures, including a ban on large gatherings. The government warned of an increase in deaths, especially among vulnerable groups and the elderly, and anticipated that up to one fifth of employees might be too ill to work.

While the message from the government at this stage was to keep calm and carry on, it was clear that the Budget would have to include provision for both heavy extra demands on the NHS and major economic disruption. In what now seems a rosily optimistic assessment, the Centre for Economic and Business Research, a respected consultancy, warned that a month-long lockdown of London could cost the economy £10 billion in lost output.

At the very least, the economic outlook – already unclear with the nature of the future relationship with the EU still to be determined – was now very much more uncertain. Short-term economic forecasts had become little more than guesswork.

* * *

'It gives me great pleasure to call, to deliver his Budget statement, Mr Chancellor of the Exchequer.' A cheer erupted from the packed Conservative benches as, on 11 March, not quite a month after his appointment and less than five years after entering Parliament, Sunak rose from the front bench, with perhaps just the hint of a stoop under the burden he carried. 'Madam Deputy Speaker, I want to get straight to the issue most on everyone's mind: coronavirus Covid-19. I know how worried people are – worried about their health, the health of their loved ones, their jobs, their income, their businesses, their financial security.'

With what now seems acute understatement, Sunak predicted 'a temporary disruption to our economy', both on the supply side, with people off work and supply chains interrupted, and on the demand side as consumer spending fell. But 'people will return to work. Supply chains will return to normal. Life will return to normal. For a period, it is going to be tough, but I am confident that our economic performance will recover.' None of this could be avoided – people were 'following doctors' orders to stay at home' – but the government could respond by providing security and support for those who became ill or could not work, and by offering 'a bridge for businesses to ensure that what is a temporary impact on our productive capacity does not become permanent'.

Support would come in three parts. 'First, whatever extra resources our NHS needs to cope with coronavirus, it will get … whatever it needs, whatever it costs.' Next was an expansion in statutory sick pay and changes to other benefits, together with a hardship fund for local authorities to support people in their area, totalling over £1 billion. Third came support for businesses, including a commitment to pay statutory sick pay in full for staff off work due to coronavirus in companies with up to 250 employees; extra time to pay tax bills; the scrapping of business rates for retail, leisure and hospitality businesses with a rateable value below £51,000, meaning nearly half of all business properties in England would pay no rates in the following twelve months; and £3,000 cash grants to the smallest businesses. Sunak also unveiled the coronavirus business interruption loan scheme (CBILS). An emergency interest rate cut to just 0.25 per cent, announced by the Bank of England earlier in the day, would help support cash flows and consumer confidence. Together with a £5 billion emergency response fund for the NHS and other public services, Sunak's coronavirus support package would total £12 billion. Alongside 'additional fiscal loosening', this amounted to £30 billion to support 'British people, British jobs and British businesses through this moment'.

Sunak noted that the Office for Budget Responsibility (OBR) had downgraded its growth forecast for the economy and that it was now clear that the spread of coronavirus would have a bigger impact than the watchdog had been able to account for when making its projections. This Budget would provide for security today, he said, and lay the foundations for prosperity tomorrow – but anyone looking at the list of spending commitments he went on to unveil would be forgiven for thinking the good times must be rolling already. In all, there would be £640 billion spent on infrastructure over the following five years, and day-to-day spending on public services would rise by £100 billion in cash terms by the end of the parliament. These, said the Chancellor, were the hallmarks of a government that 'gets things done'.

Most of the extra investment would be paid for by borrowing, and the Budget would add £125 billion to public debt by 2025, according to the OBR. Nevertheless, and despite the speculation, the Chancellor declared that it would be delivered 'not just within the fiscal rules in our manifesto but with room to spare'. But if these rules were still intact for the time being, the same could not be said for Sunak's previous dictum that public spending should not exceed 37 per cent of GDP. According to the OBR, the state spent 39.8 per cent of national income in 2019/20; this would rise above 40 per cent the following year and be closer to 41 per cent by the end of the parliament, more than at any time between the mid-1980s and the financial crisis of 2008 – and this was before the emergency measures that would follow. During this parliament, government spending would, for the first time, exceed £1 trillion a year.

Yet far from being reticent about this, Sunak revelled in it. His Budget represented 'the largest sustained fiscal boost for nearly thirty years'. As well as the infrastructure bonanza, departmental spending would grow 'at the fastest rate in fifteen years', and 'twice as fast as the economy'. We were, Sunak concluded, 'at the beginning of a new era in this country'. He spoke truer than he knew.

*   *   *

The reception for Sunak's debut was more than he could have wished for. 'Dr Feelgood to the rescue!' blared the front page of the *Daily Mail* on 12 March. Praise for the new Chancellor's performance was effusive. For Westminster commentators – not an easy bunch to please – Sunak was 'passionate, articulate, confident', 'neither nervous nor arrogant', and with 'a voice as light and clear as a confidently blown euphonium'. Some mused on whether they had just seen the next Prime Minister in action.

If Sunak's delivery was applauded, so, in most cases, was the programme he presented. *The Guardian*'s editorial took a tone of rejoicing over a repentant sinner ('a refreshing change for the better … we are all Keynesians now'), while in the *FT* Robert Shrimsley noted sardonically that this administration was

in no way to be confused with any other recent Conservative government in which almost all its leading lights were quite happy to serve. The Boris Johnson, Michael Gove and Rishi Sunak who held ministerial jobs over the past five years? You never saw them and they were three other blokes.

Whether expressed grudgingly or with admiration, the consensus was that by reversing austerity the Tory Party had once again demonstrated the ruthless capacity for adaptation that had made it such a formidable election-winning force. The party clearly had no intention of relinquishing the very different coalition of voters that had returned it to power. But, as Paul Goodman of ConservativeHome pointed out, the explanation was straightforward: Red Wall voters had backed not just the Tories but Brexit, and all that that implied. 'A People's Budget from a People's Government,' the Chancellor perorated. The voice may have been Sunak's, but the hands were those of Vote Leave.

There were no complaints about the billions to help the country through what was then hoped to be the short-term effect of coronavirus, but there were concerns about the wider package. One of these was that without significant reform, much of the extra spending on public services might be wasted. There had been no attempt to tackle social care, the cost of pensions, or inefficiencies in the NHS – nor any suggestion that any such reforms were on the way.

But the biggest worry for the warier observers was the wisdom of racking up such huge debts, even with servicing costs as low as they then were. These sceptics took their lead from Robert Chote, the outgoing head of the OBR, who told reporters that the new direction of policy had made the public finances 'much more vulnerable to nasty inflation and interest-rate surprises than they were'. Paul Johnson of the Institute for

Fiscal Studies pointed out that 'all the economic forecasts on which the core Budget was based were put together before any significant effect of the coronavirus was accounted for, and were therefore out of date at the moment of publication'.

Some of Sunak's colleagues raised similar concerns. Sajid Javid, while supporting his successor's statement, told the House that 'interest rates are incredibly volatile, and no government should rely on interest rates remaining low for an incredibly long time'. Theresa May cautioned that 'although spending a lot of money may be popular and may seem the natural thing to do', it was 'necessary to ensure that we have that restraint and caution that enables us to make the public finances continue to be strong into the future'.

Putting together a new Budget against the backdrop of a growing crisis had taken its toll on the Chancellor's team, but the work had been worthwhile. For now, Sunak had passed his first test as Chancellor in spectacular fashion, surpassing expectations, impressing colleagues and commentators and putting himself at the forefront of the new government. But it was clear to Sunak and his team that things were just beginning. 'I remember coming in on the Friday morning, and things were moving in Europe, with different finance ministries,' says a senior Treasury source. 'I was saying, "We're going to have to do more, it's not going to be enough." And he said, "Yeah, I know." And we had another of those quiet moments where he took that in.'

CHAPTER 17

A BIGGER BAZOOKA

Behind the podium in the Downing Street briefing room on 12 March, the day after the Budget, Boris Johnson's tone was grave. 'We've done what can be done to contain this disease,' he told the press conference which would soon become a daily event at No. 10. The aim now, he said, would be to delay its spread. 'We've all got to be clear; this is the worst public health crisis for a generation.' He added: 'I must level with you, level with the British public: many more families are going to lose loved ones before their time.'

Flanked by Professor Chris Whitty, the chief medical officer, and Sir Patrick Vallance, the government's chief scientific adviser, Johnson explained the plan to reduce the peak of coronavirus infections. Or, as he put it, 'squash the sombrero'. Anyone with a new cough or fever was to stay at home for at least seven days. Overseas school trips should be cancelled. And those aged seventy or more must avoid cruise ships. Everyone should stay at least two metres from vulnerable relatives. More stringent measures such as closing schools, banning mass gatherings or imposing compulsory social distancing were rejected at that time. Vallance said that while the number of confirmed cases in the UK was 596, the actual number infected was probably between 5,000 and 10,000. The peak of the pandemic in Britain was thought to be ten to fourteen weeks away.

In Washington, President Trump banned travel to America from all border-free Schengen countries of mainland Europe, plus Britain and Ireland. Coinciding with the WHO's decision to reclassify the outbreak from a public health emergency to a pandemic, the London and New York stock exchanges saw their biggest falls since 1987, with markets in France and Germany also plunging. The EU complained that America's action had been taken without consultation, but within days many of its member countries had closed their own borders.

As the week wore on, the virus began to impinge on more and more areas of life. Premier League football and the London Marathon were postponed. Retailers were forced to warn the public against panic buying and even imposed limits on how many items customers could take as toilet rolls, dried pasta, tinned vegetables, thermometers, paracetamol, hand sanitiser and soap vanished from supermarket shelves. Local elections, including that for the London mayoralty, due to be held on 7 May, were postponed for a year.

By 16 March, the number of Covid-19 deaths in Britain had risen to fifty-five and 1,543 people had tested positive for the virus, with the actual number of cases estimated at up to 50,000. That evening, Johnson reinforced the government's approach. 'Now is the time for everyone to stop non-essential contact with others and to stop all unnecessary travel,' he declared. 'We need people to start working from home where they possibly can. And you should avoid pubs, clubs, theatres and other such social venues.' Whitty warned these measures would need to be in place for some time: 'We should not be under any illusions that "if we just do this for a couple of weeks" that is sufficient,' he said.

Public health topped the agenda, but it was clear that the

economic cost of the virus would go well beyond early expectations. Millions of livelihoods in almost every sector were at risk. The Confederation of British Industry said businesses under stress would 'need a step change in support from the government in the coming days'.

Suddenly, Sunak's first Budget, hailed as a substantial response to the economic threat of the coronavirus, appeared insufficient. A global recession was on the cards. Analysts predicted the economy would fall further and faster than during the 2008 financial crisis, when US Treasury Secretary Hank Paulson – once Sunak's ultimate boss at Goldman Sachs – had described the federal war chest needed to deal with the crash as a 'bazooka'. Sunak's first weapon in 2020 was beginning to resemble a popgun.

Initially, civil servants struggled to grasp the implications of the situation. 'In those first few days there was a little bit of resistance from Treasury officials when it became clear we were going to have to do more,' says an adviser who worked with Sunak at the time.

I remember sitting in his No. 11 study, and he and I talked about how we had to move faster than anyone thought was possible. He bought that immediately. He brought all the senior officials in and said, 'You guys need to remove all limiting assumptions about what's possible.' In fairness, they got it right away. That was the Permanent Secretary, Tom Scholar, and all the DGs. To a person, all of them understood intuitively what he was saying, which was 'You have to stop thinking about this in any kind of traditional sense – we're going to have to do things we've never done before.'

Six days after delivering the Budget, Sunak announced an even bigger jolt to the public finances. The pandemic was not just a public health emergency, he said, but an economic one. 'We have never, in peacetime, faced an economic fight like this one.' The struggle would be won by a national effort 'underpinned by government interventions in the economy on a scale unimaginable only a few weeks ago. This is not a time for ideology and orthodoxy.' The government would support jobs, incomes, businesses, 'and we will help you protect your loved ones. We will do whatever it takes.' He unveiled a vast programme which would normally have taken months to develop but which had been drawn up in a few days. Indeed, Sunak's statement was still being printed moments before he left the Treasury to walk to Downing Street and deliver it. There would be £330 billion of government-backed and guaranteed loans – the equivalent of more than one third of annual state spending and 15 per cent of the country's entire GDP. If demand was greater than that, he said, 'I will go further and provide as much capacity as is required. I said whatever it takes, and I meant it.' Retail, hospitality and leisure businesses with a rateable value up to £51,000 would receive a cash grant of up to £25,000, on top of the twelve-month relief from business rates that had been unveiled in the Budget. Grants to the smallest businesses would be increased to £10,000, from the £3,000 announced the previous week. Lenders would offer a mortgage holiday of at least three months for those in difficulty due to coronavirus. These, said Sunak, were 'only the first steps'. He would work with unions and business groups to protect jobs and incomes.

Sunak's statement underlined how rapidly the situation had escalated. It also illustrated the magnitude of what he was up against, and the extent of the responsibility that had landed on his shoulders barely a month into his new job and less than five years into his parliamentary career. The total £350 billion package far outweighed what was offered during the 2008 banking collapse. With the OBR's blessing, it would be funded by borrowing. The CBI's director general, Carolyn Fairbairn, applauded Sunak's decisiveness.

Yet there were worries that this gargantuan first step did not go far enough, especially when it came to individual employees at risk of being laid off, not to mention self-employed and freelance workers. The point was restated repeatedly when Sunak reported his plans to Parliament. MPs from all parties urged him to do more, even asking the government to pay a proportion of workers' wages directly – a principle Sunak accepted. Conservatives joined in, pleading the case for every conceivable mainstream firm, from coach operators to craft breweries. Nobody asked about the extra debt that would be incurred – or the cost to taxpayers.

Three days later, at the end of a week which had seen interest rates cut to just 0.1 per cent, schools throughout the country were closed until further notice and GCSEs and A-levels cancelled. Airlines grounded their fleets and major companies including Jaguar Land Rover suspended production at UK plants. Train services were slashed and all public events abandoned. Health Secretary Matt Hancock called on doctors and nurses who had recently left the NHS to return. The number of coronavirus deaths in the UK rose to 177, an increase of forty in twenty-four hours.

At the Downing Street press conference, Johnson announced that pubs, restaurants and other venues would have to close. Sunak introduced what would become the cornerstone of the government's efforts to protect jobs and incomes during the crisis. 'For the first time in our history,' he declared, 'the government is going to step in and help to pay people's wages.' Under the coronavirus job retention scheme, any employer in the country would be able to apply to HM Revenue and Customs (HMRC) for grants covering 80 per cent of the wages, up to a maximum of £2,500 a month, of staff who were not working but kept on the payroll. They would be 'furloughed'. This Americanism, perhaps reflecting the amount of time Sunak had spent in the US, instantly became an everyday word in Britain. The scheme would be backdated to 1 March and would be open for at least three months.

The aim was to have the first grants paid by the end of April. In a continuation of the 'whatever it takes' theme first heard in the Budget, Sunak said he was placing no limit on the amount of funding available for the scheme. 'We will pay grants to support as many jobs as necessary.' There was more: CBILS, the loans to businesses, would be interest-free for twelve months rather than six, and VAT payments for the next quarter would be deferred to the end of the financial year – effectively a cash injection of £30 billion. Changes to Universal Credit and the Working Tax Credit would bring £7 billion of extra support, and the next tax payments for the self-employed were deferred until January 2021. There was nearly £1 billion in extra support for renters, increasing the proportion of local market rent that could be claimed through housing benefit and Universal Credit.

'Now, more than any time in our recent history, we will be judged by our capacity for compassion,' Sunak concluded.

Our ability to come through this won't just be down to what government or business can do, but by the individual acts of kindness we show one another ... When this is over, and it will be over, we want to look back at this moment and remember the many small acts of kindness done by us and to us. We want to look back at this time and remember how we thought first of others and acted with decency.

A Treasury adviser says the furlough plan was worked out 'at breakneck speed. It just wasn't possible to consult across Cabinet. In the country, panic was about to set in. Redundancy notices were about to be issued.' Discussing the launch, Sunak felt the tone would be as important as the content. 'I remember he and I having a chat about what we needed to do with the statement,' says the source.

> We came to the conclusion that although there's a bunch of policy that needs to be announced, this was more about the mood. As a country, we were bridging into panic mode. People needed to hear that they had some agency – this wasn't a moment that was going to get done to them. The whole point was to try and explain to people, even if this gets mad and you're not going to be able to go to work, you have a role to play in this. It was a unique political moment. As the speech was being finished, he was moving things around in the draft, minutes before he spoke.

The avalanche of cash inspired praise from most employers and trade unions. Even Len McCluskey, the hard-left general secretary of Unite, complimented Sunak's actions as 'historic, bold and very much necessary'. Sunak won another unlikely endorsement on the left from Bernie Sanders, the Democratic presidential primary candidate in the US, who told his

supporters, 'What is going on in the UK is the proper approach
… That is the direction we should have gone here.'

For the state to offer unlimited sums to save hundreds of
thousands or even millions of jobs was the clearest indication
yet of how bad things were expected to become.

On 23 March, Britain officially went into full lockdown.
The following day Sunak was back in Parliament answering
questions on his plans to support jobs. He admitted that 'we
will not be able to protect every single job or save every single
business' and that there were 'genuine practical and princi-
pled reasons why it is incredibly complicated' to design an
equivalent of the job retention scheme for Britain's 5 million
self-employed people: any assessment of their income would
often have to be made on the basis of tax returns more than
a year old, which was not the case for employees paying tax
through PAYE, and there was no immediate way to identify
those affected by the crisis.

Nevertheless, he said, the government was determined to
help.

Three days later, Sunak was at the familiar Downing Street
podium – now emblazoned with the slogan 'Stay Home, Protect
the NHS, Save Lives' – to announce that the government would
pay self-employed people affected by the coronavirus a taxable
grant worth 80 per cent of their average monthly profits over
the previous three years, up to £2,500 a month, as with employees. To make it 'deliverable and fair', the scheme would only be
open to those with an income up to £50,000 and would require
proof of status. The scheme would initially be open for three
months and was expected to cost about £3 billion a month.

Understandably, it was not all plain sailing. HMRC were
working on the system urgently but did not expect the first

grants to be paid by the beginning of June. Though changes to the welfare system meant the self-employed were now eligible for Universal Credit, the prospect of such a long wait was met with dismay. And to the anger of some Tory MPs, Sunak also warned that the National Insurance rate of 9 per cent paid by the self-employed, compared with 12 per cent for employees, might not be sustainable. Other glitches emerged. Some banks lending to small businesses under the CBILS scheme were charging interest rates of up to 12 per cent and asking for personal guarantees which owners were reluctant to give, often not knowing how much they needed to borrow or when they could repay. High street businesses outside the leisure, retail and hospitality sectors had been ordered to close under the lockdown rules but did not qualify for the Chancellor's business rate relief. And some firms were too big for the government's small business loan guarantees but too small to seek the investment-grade rating needed to access corporate finance through the Bank of England.

'There were a couple of moments during the worst period when it wasn't clear what the right answer was,' says a senior adviser at the Treasury. 'And in those moments you could sense the frustration on [Sunak's] part that the answer wasn't just immediately available. The realisation that the stuff he was dealing with in this job is harder than anything he's done before has forced him to go up a gear.'

Despite these bumps, and the appalling outlook for the British economy, Sunak was flying high. While pointing out occasional holes in his programme, economic commentators and analysts welcomed his actions. His performances even continued to impress the often-jaded Westminster press corps, whose members had long abandoned their talk of the Chancellor as a poodle of No. 10. Now they praised his calm authority and wrote of him as a possible Prime Minister-in-waiting.

A senior Treasury colleague says:

> When it gets to the crunch, Rishi wants to get on top of the detail. He's normally quite easy-going and jovial, but when he's focused in, the smile goes. The up and down in the voice starts to go; he becomes super-serious. It's really about him trying to get as much information in as possible so he can deal with the problem. Then it's a question of gaming all these different scenarios about how this was going to play out.

The polls were favourable as well. On 22 March, YouGov found 60 per cent of people had a positive view of Sunak, while just 11 per cent said the opposite: a remarkable score of +49, well above Boris Johnson on +20, or any other member of the Cabinet.

There was evidence that this popularity might not relate merely to perceived competence: Sunak had come to be known by some as 'Dishy Rishi'. Under such headlines as 'I fancy Rishi Sunak', female columnists in glossy magazines wrote of the 'spectacled hunk' whose 'bright eyes twinkling with sincerity' reminded them of 'the medic you had a crush on' at university. One *Guardian* columnist, Hannah Jane Parkinson, tweeted a montage of pictures of Sunak and wrote: 'For the avoidance of doubt this is *not* political approval but, sorry, he's clearly fit. [I] will be taking zero (0) questions.'

How did Sunak react to his newfound status as a heart-throb? One senior colleague says it didn't go to his head, 'partly because of the horror' he knew was coming.

CHAPTER 18

SANTA OR SCROOGE?

A s spring 2020 progressed, it became obvious that the epidemic was not just a health crisis but a potential economic catastrophe. Throughout March and April, companies announced plans to furlough huge numbers of staff, including 36,000 at British Airways and 43,000 at the JD Wetherspoon pub chain. Surveys from business groups found sales and confidence plummeting. Projections for unemployment began to spiral, especially in rural areas dependent on hospitality and tourism – including Sunak's Richmond constituency. One report by the Office for Budget Responsibility envisaged the deepest recession for 300 years.

Sunak did not try to play down these threats. He encouraged honesty with the public, saying, 'These are tough times – and there will be more to come. As I've said before, we can't protect every business and every household.' The government, though, was 'not just going to stand by and watch this happen. Our planned economic response is protecting millions of jobs, businesses, self-employed people, charities and households.'

But complaints had begun to mount that while help was at hand, getting hold of it in practice was another matter. By 3 April, banks had received over 130,000 enquiries about the small business loan scheme, yet fewer than 1,000 had been approved. Many interest-free loan requests were rejected outright. There was also anger at banks' apparent slowness to implement loans.

Business loan schemes were not the only aspects of Sunak's rescue package to be criticised. The Institute for Employment Studies estimated that about 100,000 workers had recently started a new job and been laid off because of the pandemic but did not qualify for furlough because they had not been included in a PAYE return by 19 March. A further half a million people who according to usual trends would have expected to begin a new job in April might have been left in limbo. Those who had left a previous job but not yet taken up their new one were encouraged to ask their old employer to rehire them, making them eligible to be furloughed. And those who fell through the cracks of the job retention scheme would have to rely on state benefits.

In the hard-hit hospitality sector, which had seen 80 per cent of staff furloughed by early April, waiting staff complained they were being short-changed. Government guidance said that tronc – an arrangement used by employers to distribute tips and gratuities – could not be taken into account when calculating earnings for the purposes of the furlough scheme, even though employees can rely on such service charges for two fifths of their income.

There was also consternation that employers had to choose whether to furlough workers completely or not at all. Groups including the Federation of Small Businesses and the Institute of Directors called for changes to allow staff to be compensated for reduced hours, which would help companies to keep functioning at a lower level and gradually ramp up operations as things returned to normal.

And the Institute for Fiscal Studies calculated that around

675,000 people who earned most of their income from self-employment would miss out on help because their profits were more than £50,000 a year or because they started their businesses after April 2019.

A sense of injustice was also felt by the owners of small firms who paid themselves in dividends rather than by a regular salary – often because revenue is irregular or seasonal and they need to keep money in the business to pay suppliers and staff. Though technically company directors, they included hundreds of thousands of bricklayers, plumbers and other tradesmen, as well as the owners of building firms, hair salons and other entrepreneurs.

One observer thought at the time that many of the points of criticism were not oversights on Sunak's part but were put in place for good reasons. They believed he was not just focused on what to do at the time but on the economy's state when it emerged from the crisis, saying:

> That's the basis of the loans. He really did want loans rather than grants. The £300 billion is an impressive figure but it's less generous than it sounds, because the Treasury expects to get most of it back. He has been very reluctant to ease the conditions of the loans. He doesn't want to see the Treasury bankrupted.

Only weeks after pledging unprecedented sums to help the country through the crisis, Sunak was back with more. On 8 April, he announced £750 million to support charities, many of which had suffered a huge loss of income during the pandemic. The following week, he launched the large business interruption loan scheme, an extension of the original CBILS initiative, which would offer loans of up to £25 million to companies which were too big for the small business scheme but not big enough to access corporate finance from the Bank of England. At the same time, he announced changes to the initial scheme, including making the loans available to all businesses affected by the coronavirus, not just those unable to secure regular commercial funding. He also banned lenders from seeking personal guarantees for loans up to £250,000 and prevented them from requesting directors' primary homes as collateral for bigger loans.

Further Sunak statements followed. The job retention scheme would be extended to the end of June; extra funding for local councils would be doubled to £3.2 billion; and a further £617 million in grants would be made to small firms who missed out on business rate relief because they worked in shared spaces. Under a £1.25 billion 'innovation support package', government loans would be converted into equity if they could not be repaid. Bizarrely, one beneficiary was Killing Kittens, a firm which *The Guardian* has described bluntly as a 'members-only sex club'. The company borrowed £170,000 and taxpayers ultimately ended up owning a small percentage stake in it.

Many of Sunak's actions, then, were designed to plug gaps in, or address criticism of, programmes which had been launched only weeks earlier. In no case was this truer than in the launch of 'Bounce Back' loans, yet another scheme to help smaller businesses. Using a seven-question online form, smaller firms could apply for loans of up to a quarter of their annual turnover, to a maximum of £50,000. No repayments were due in the first twelve months, and the government paid the first year's interest, which was to be capped at 2.5 per cent.

Crucially, the state also guaranteed 100 per cent of the value of the loan.

This represented a partial retreat by Sunak in the face of calls from MPs, business groups, three former Chancellors and even the Governor of the Bank of England, who argued that a full guarantee would be the fastest way to get credit flowing. Sunak had initially resisted such a move, fearing that underwriting entire loans would allow irresponsible lending and land the government with a big bill. Though he eventually conceded on loans to smaller companies, Sunak continued to reject the idea of fully underwriting the larger business loans. He had to balance 'the risk to the taxpayer with the need to support our smallest businesses', he argued. 'We should not ask ordinary taxpayers of today and tomorrow to bear the entire risk of lending almost unlimited sums to businesses that in some cases may have very little prospect of paying those loans back, and not necessarily because of the impact of the coronavirus.' However, he introduced technical changes aimed at speeding things up, including a change to the rules so that lenders had to decide if a firm had been a going concern before the pandemic, not whether it was viable during the crisis.

Though bankers privately admitted that fully guaranteeing their loans would accelerate the lending process, some were nervous about the implications. 'We don't want anyone coming back at us in two years, when the world looks very different from today, complaining we should never have lent these people the money,' said one.

Despite the relentlessly poor economic news, Sunak's personal standing continued to soar. 'He's really done three or even four Budgets since 11 March,' one well-connected observer noted at the height of the crisis. 'If any other Chancellor had had to introduce four Budgets in six weeks, I think by now his reputation would be quite damaged. He has been in a big fight with backbenchers over business loans, but his reputation has held up astonishingly well.' In part, this was surely because most people did not envy the giant size of the task. 'Journalists like him because he looks like he's in charge,' said a senior banker. 'He radiates self-confidence more than, say, Raab, but without the cockiness of Matt Hancock. He has a pleasing manner.'

TUC leader Frances O'Grady commended him after days of negotiations over the job protection programme. 'He is smart, he's energetic and he listens, which is important,' she told the *FT*. 'It's a lot of responsibility on young shoulders. What I would say is that he does have emotional intelligence. It's a different style, without that sense of superiority that some have.'

For Sunak's admirers, part of his appeal was that he came across as a technocrat rather than an ideologue. 'He doesn't have an agenda, he's a problem solver,' as a fellow minister put it. 'He's more of a businessman than a politician in that respect.' Another insider noted his ability to absorb huge volumes of detail, saying that he always 'takes the long brief instead of the short one'.

Though journalists were sometimes critical of the various rescue schemes, Sunak himself generally continued to enjoy positive write-ups in the media. *The Sun* pictured him in cowboy garb, complete with Stetson, pistol, holster and horse, to declare him 'the loan arranger'. The *Daily Telegraph* wrote that while it was too early to judge the success of Sunak's actions, 'it can at least be said that he generally strikes the right tone … His calmness is itself calming.'

In late April, Sunak even featured on the BBC Comic Relief

and Children in Need show *Big Night In*. Between home-recorded skits by comedians and celebrities he delivered a message from his book-lined study. 'Hi, everyone,' he began.

> I know these are difficult times. Look, we're all worried, worried about our health, our friends, our family. But I also think we will look back and remember that at this time of crisis, we came together as a country. We were there for each other and that's what the *Big Night In* is all about. I am so grateful to everyone who has donated tonight, and don't forget that the government has pledged to match every pound you donate, so please do give generously. After all, what better way to mark four weeks of staying in and watching TV than, well... staying in and watching TV. Enjoy the rest of the show and stay safe.

No previous Chancellor of the Exchequer had shown such ease in front of a TV camera – even in positive times – and, perhaps responding to his solid media performances, the polls continued to be kind. Though his ratings dipped from the stratospheric levels recorded by YouGov at the end of March, his net approval rating still outstripped that of Boris Johnson or any other member of the Cabinet. In the Conservative-Home Cabinet League Table, based on surveys of Tory members, Sunak received record net satisfaction scores of +94.8 in April and +93.2 in May (the previous holder being Theresa May, with a short-lived rating of +92.6 in the summer of 2016).

If it was some comfort that his efforts were appreciated, there was no doubt he was conscious of the burden. 'Rishi is feeling the weight of the world on his shoulders,' said one colleague in early April. 'He knows there is an enormous responsibility on him, and he's been working eighteen hours a day for weeks now. He's physically and psychologically exhausted. But he's always the one who says to people, "Come on, on to the next job."'

This ability to lead and motivate his team was crucial to his Chancellorship, according to a senior Treasury source.

He places a massive emphasis on courtesy. He also has this thing called the commitment to excellence – he just wants everything he does to be better than anyone else, and he expects that of everyone else. But he's so nice and considerate, he can get away with being incredibly demanding.

An adviser who spent many hours with the Chancellor during the crisis says, 'I've never seen him snap or lose his rag with anyone. If he does feel pissed off, he just goes quiet. And then you just go out of the room and give him a bit of space.'

William Hague agrees that Sunak copes well with pressure.

I haven't ever seen him lose his temper or use a swear word or look anxious in the sense of being overcome by worry. He has always quite methodically sorted out his thoughts in his head anyway, and quite quickly and clearly comes to a strategy. If he gets depressed or angry, he doesn't really show that, even to people he speaks privately to.

Though he really was as calm and confident as he seemed, Hague felt,

he's not self-assured in the sense that he thinks he just knows the answer, because it's a very strong attribute of his that he asks for opinion and advice. It's the same thing about going to learn about the milking in the constituency. He calls people up. He's very good at keeping in touch with people he thinks he can discuss things with.

Nor does he fret. 'Once he's decided what his strategy is, he doesn't keep going over it all again.'

Another Tory with long experience of advising Cabinet ministers says Sunak deals with the strains of office better than most. 'Hague was like the ice monster; I've never seen anything like it,' he says. 'Cameron could become irritable. George most of the time was buoyant, enjoying the ludicrousness of this moment in history. With Rishi you can feel the strain, it's all quite intense. But quietly so.'

In fact, Sunak was working so intensely during this time that staff became worried for his health. 'The day before he announced the furlough scheme, one of our economic advisers put a sandwich on his desk and said, "You must eat," because he just wasn't eating,' says a Treasury source. 'He was looking thin and faint.' Another adviser observed that he had to be told almost every day to eat. 'Otherwise he'll just work and work.' Another insider later revealed that Sunak sometimes goes without food deliberately, fasting on selected days from sunrise to sunset – not for religious reasons, but to 're-set after the weekend'.

Sunak himself said of this time that what he missed most, apart from his family, was the gym. He compensated for the absence of his usual fitness regime by buying a state-of-the-art exercise bike worth £2,000.

He admitted he was tired, but acknowledged he was far from alone, saying magnanimously:

Lots of people, not just in government but up and down the country in all their different ways, have been working around the clock ... people on the front line through to the Prime Minister himself. We're all dealing with something we haven't had to deal with before, it's hit us at extraordinary speed and severity, and everyone in their different ways is trying to do the best they can. That often requires just working very hard and it's stressful because it's very uncertain. And the decisions you make have wide-ranging impact and that weighs heavily on you, but you just try and give it everything you can.

CHAPTER 19

LOCKDOWN SHOWDOWN

On the evening of Thursday 26 March, Rishi Sunak stood in Downing Street with his neighbour, Boris Johnson, to take part in the first 'Clap for Carers'. The initiative, proposed by Annemarie Plas, a Dutch yoga teacher living in south London, saw millions of people around the country applauding and banging kitchen implements from doorsteps and balconies in appreciation for NHS staff and other workers helping Britain through the crisis. The gesture would be repeated for ten consecutive weeks.

The next morning, Johnson confirmed that he had come down with Covid-19 and had gone into self-isolation, transforming the story of the government's pandemic response from a national political drama to a personal one, while also confirming everybody's vulnerability to the virus. Rumours circulated that he was more seriously ill than officials dared acknowledge, and on 5 April he was admitted to St Thomas's Hospital – the same Sunday, as it happened, that the Queen made a rare TV address, calling on the nation to 'take comfort that while we may have more still to endure, better days will return: we will be with our friends again; we will be with our families again; we will meet again'.

Downing Street claimed Johnson's admission to hospital was a 'precautionary step' and insisted he would remain in charge of the government. Dominic Raab, as First Secretary of State and Foreign Secretary, would lead the next day's meeting of the Covid-19 'war cabinet' – which also included Sunak, Matt Hancock and Michael Gove – but Johnson would stay in touch with ministers and civil servants. Just under twenty-four hours later, Johnson was moved to intensive care. Raab had to take charge without seeming to overstep the mark. The circumstances of Johnson's absence – a critical illness at a time of national crisis – only added to the administrative and emotional pressure on those assuming extra responsibility.

After three nights, Johnson left intensive care, but he would need time to recover. With other senior figures including Michael Gove also indisposed through self-isolation, insiders fretted about the ongoing 'political vacuum' in Downing Street.

Tension also existed because, while ministers were united on the actions taken so far, the speed and direction of the next steps were more contentious. Under its emergency legislation, the government was obliged to review the lockdown after three weeks. Nobody expected any easing of the restrictions at that stage, and Raab's announcement on 16 April that they would stay in place was a formality. But even before Johnson became unwell, reports began to circulate of a Cabinet battle over when Britons would be allowed to go back to work.

'Rishi Sunak's war with Matt Hancock', trumpeted the *Mail on Sunday* eight days after Johnson's disclosure that he had the virus. Sunak was reported to have made 'robust representations on the importance of finding a path out of the lockdown soon and what that path looks like'.

The two denied any such rift. Hancock told Sky News the same day that he and Sunak were 'working very closely together', that Sunak was doing an 'absolutely brilliant' job and had been 'lauded around the world for the first-class economic response'. The answer to the lockdown was to 'resolve as a nation to follow those rules so we can get out of it as fast as possible,' he said.

Despite this show of unity, other reports surfaced suggesting the Cabinet was divided between 'hawks' who wanted the lockdown lifted within weeks and 'doves' who wanted to keep restrictions in place for longer. As well as hawk leader Sunak, those wanting to ease the rules faster included Home Secretary Priti Patel, who was concerned about an increase of nearly one third in reports of domestic violence; Education Secretary Gavin Williamson, worried about the effects on children of an extended break from school; and Work and Pensions Secretary Thérèse Coffey, whose department had received 1 million new Universal Credit claims – nine times the usual rate – in the fortnight after social distancing measures were introduced. Communities Secretary Robert Jenrick was also said to favour an early return to normal. 'There are social housing properties lying empty,' an insider said. 'If you're Jenrick, you know there are a whole load of people sitting in hostels who can't move into a house, people cooped up in homes where kids have bad lives, families with an abusive parent.' Transport Secretary Grant Shapps, Business Secretary Alok Sharma, Scottish Secretary Alister Jack, International Trade Secretary Liz Truss, Chief Whip Mark Spencer, and Leader of the Commons Jacob Rees-Mogg, were also said to take the hawkish view.

Their concerns were understood by Hancock, a dove, but his priority was to prevent a rise in cases that could overwhelm the NHS. Michael Gove, the Cabinet Office minister responsible for leading the wider public sector response to the crisis, was also said to be circumspect about any early change of approach.

A source familiar with top-level discussions emphasises that disagreements between ministers were about policy rather than personality, and that individuals were 'institutionally representing the interests of their departments'.

'Matt Hancock says, "They can't have an NHS collapse on my watch," and Rishi says, "There won't be an economic collapse on mine, and by the way, if there is, the NHS goes with it."' Although he was pushing hard to go as fast as possible, Sunak was arguing for a strategy, rather than an immediate lifting of controls. 'Before Boris went into hospital, he wasn't saying "end the lockdown", but he was saying "you've got to have a plan".'

A senior Treasury figure confirms that Sunak consistently reminded colleagues of the consequences of keeping the economy closed. 'The state told people they couldn't leave their homes; it was a recession caused by decisions to protect people from the virus,' says the source. 'Rishi has always been the person in the room who is aware of the difficult times ahead. So when people are getting carried away about the success of one or other scheme, he's usually not. He thinks: tough times.'

Another adviser says that Sunak and Hancock communicated regularly 'to make sure they had calibrated their messages properly for an internal audience. Both were concerned about the health side and the economy.' At the same time, says the source,

there were tensions. Not that one was being prioritised over the other, but things were not moving so fast at that time and we were working with incomplete information. Rishi found it frustrating that wider Whitehall departments just didn't seem to have the necessary grip one would expect in that moment. It wasn't a reflection on Matt but the structure that [former Health Secretary Andrew] Lansley built. It was very hard to get any control. The first few months were very difficult, trying to establish base-level facts on what was going on – the securing of PPE and ventilators, for example. We took the decision very early on that we should just process health requests at a moment's notice: no arbitrary spending cap, we should just throw the kitchen sink at it. Part of what you would expect in return for being that flexible was that the information would be available to justify that.

According to William Hague, Sunak's colleagues will have been left in no doubt as to his position. 'While he doesn't get angry and swear at people, he's wholly capable of expressing himself clearly and firmly,' he says, and from the beginning of the lockdown was worried

about how long it would go on. I think he's been very frustrated with the performance of the health department, and the Treasury ... had to do a lot of the thinking for other parts of the government in the absence of those parts doing the thinking, particularly about how to exit the lockdown. So there will have been some sharp exchanges.

Sunak regularly insisted that there was no simple trade-off between tackling the disease and saving jobs. 'The single most important thing we can do for the health of our economy is to protect the health of our people,' he told the daily news

conference on 14 April, after the OBR published a report suggesting the economy could shrink by more than a third, with
unemployment doubling, in the three months to June.

On 12 April, Easter Sunday, Johnson left hospital. Aides
were told that his chances of survival had been fifty-fifty. As
he recuperated at Chequers, the lockdown debate continued.
Many MPs became increasingly nervous about its effects in
their constituencies and ever more vocal about their concerns
for the future of the wider economy.

Part of the problem, some argued, was the slogan 'Stay
Home, Protect the NHS, Save Lives'. Ironically, it had worked
too well, summing up in seven words not just what people had
to do, but why they had to do it. Policymakers were startled
by the degree of public obedience. Those devising the plan
had expected far more people to continue working and using
schools and public transport.

Sunak feared the public had over-interpreted the rules so
that, rather than carrying on as normal unless their sector had
been shut down, they believed they should not work unless
they had key worker status. In Cabinet discussions, he argued
that the economy should gradually be reopened. There was
no shortage of evidence to help him make his case. When the
job retention scheme opened on 20 April, more than a million people were enrolled on the first day. The OBR assessed
the price of the Treasury's rescue schemes at £105 billion for
2020/21, while the Centre for Policy Studies estimated that
coronavirus had cost an extra £246 billion in terms of bailouts,
other spending and lower tax revenue, taking borrowing for
the year to £300 billion. The National Institute of Economic
and Social Research said unemployment could rise to 6 million, or 20 per cent of the workforce.

Business groups warned of catastrophic consequences from an extended lockdown. The OBR's public finance data for April showed tax receipts down 42 per cent and government spending up by more than half, taking borrowing to £62 billion for the month – more than had been forecast for the full year.

By early May, more than half of British adults were being paid by the state – whether via the furlough scheme, social security or as public sector workers or pensioners. Yet it was thought important not to talk about relaxing restrictions too soon, to avoid confusing the public. Any easing of the lockdown had to be timed to avoid a second wave of infections.

Professor Neil Ferguson of Imperial College, a government adviser whose modelling on the spread of coronavirus had prompted the tightening of restrictions in March, told the BBC on 5 April:

> I'm very conscious that people are suffering in this country right now … We all want it to be over as quickly as possible. But there's no point having done this and hopefully suppressed transmission unless we can find a strategy which allows us to exit from it but at the same time keeps transmissions low.

Throughout the crisis, the government had insisted it was guided by the science. Yet there were three problems with this. First, in epidemiology – especially with a virus which had never been seen before – precise predictions or solutions were not available. Ministers and officials came to see this branch of science as being akin to economics, with its assumptions and variables, not the least of which was human behaviour.

A second problem was that there was no such thing as 'the' science. Ferguson's work was not universally accepted as

definitive. Sceptics pointed out that the professor's dire estimates of the potential number of deaths from swine flu, bird
flu and BSE had proved overly pessimistic. Questions were
also raised about the Imperial coronavirus model itself. Professor John Ioannidis of Stanford University said that while he
did not doubt the modellers' competence, 'some of the major
assumptions and estimates that are built in the calculations
seem to be substantially inflated'. He compared the social and
economic consequences of lockdown to an elephant being
attacked by a house cat and jumping off a cliff. Others, like
Professor Carl Heneghan of Oxford University, argued that
the peak had already passed and that lockdown could do
more harm than the virus. Though lockdown sceptics were
in a minority among scientists in Britain, measures varied between countries. Famously, Sweden decided against the kind
of lockdown seen in most of Europe – and its policymakers
also argued this approach was informed by the science.

One minister complained that members of the government's Scientific Advisory Group for Emergencies, or Sage,
often disagreed with one another. 'They bicker. And we talk
about following "the science" as if there's one opinion and not
at least seven.' Another was shocked to discover that 'scientists
are as bitchy as a bunch of lawyers'.

The third problem with the science-led approach was the
fear that, when it came to easing restrictions, medical advisers
would focus on minimising the number of Covid-19 cases at
the expense of other considerations and might err too far on
the side of caution. It was argued that talk of 'beating the virus'
was futile without a vaccine or a cure; ways would need to be
found to adapt to something closer to normality while accepting that the risk of infection could not be eliminated.

For all these reasons, it was becoming clear that the questions of how and when to leave the lockdown could not just be a matter of science. Ministers would have to balance competing demands and priorities. Political decisions were crucial. The government, not its advisers, would ultimately be accountable to the public.

On this front, things had begun to heat up. Despite initially adopting a fairly bipartisan tone, Sir Keir Starmer, who had recently been elected Labour leader, called for the government to publish its exit strategy, including 'when the restrictions might be lifted and what the plan is for economic recovery'. Nicola Sturgeon added to the pressure by publishing a framework for easing lockdown in Scotland, including plans for reopening schools and businesses, saying she wanted a 'grown-up' conversation with voters about how the country could return to a 'semblance of normality'. The move stoked discontent in the Conservative ranks, with former leader Sir Iain Duncan Smith saying, 'We must trust the British public to understand how this will happen. The Scottish administration is right. I want the UK government to be doing the same.'

The pressure only grew as Johnson's recovery continued. Former Chancellor Philip Hammond argued at a Chatham House event that the economy must be revived, saying, 'I think the sensible compromise is to reopen it around a set of conditions which assume that, for the time being, we are co-existing with this virus rather than conquering it. This is a £2 trillion economy. You can't spin it up overnight from nothing.'

Conservative Party donors, including financier Michael Spencer, former construction tycoon Steve Morgan and mobile phone entrepreneur John Caudwell, added to the calls, with Morgan saying:

We're actually in danger that the medicine – if you can call the lockdown that – is more harmful than the cure. I'm strongly in favour of getting the country back to work. This is not about profit; this is about saving the country from going bankrupt, from mass unemployment, from business-es going bust, people losing their livelihoods and homes.

At the same time, Bank of England Governor Andrew Bailey warned against a 'false start', arguing that ending restrictions too early could backfire.

In public, ministers held the line. Sunak, still spoken of as the hawks' standard bearer, insisted there was no simple trade-off between health and the economy. 'We absolutely need a thriving economy, not least because it provides people with their jobs, their incomes, and pays for our public services,' he told the BBC. 'But the best way in the long term to ensure that is to get control of the virus now.' Refining the restrictions 'will be a process, it will not be a binary event where suddenly everything is back to normal. That would be unrealistic.'

Behind closed doors, however, discussions became more feverish. One insider complained that keeping the lockdown going was 'against the interests of every department apart from Health'.

Matt Hancock argued that the priority should be to ensure the NHS did not collapse under the weight of new cases, and Chris Whitty reminded ministers of the risk of a second wave if restrictions were eased too soon. Officials were also said to be split. Sir Mark Sedwill, the Cabinet Secretary, was reported to be among the hawks, while Dominic Cummings, armed with papers on the 1918 Spanish flu, argued that a cautious approach could protect lives and jobs more effectively.

So far, the public had been supportive of the actions to tackle the crisis. Approval of the government itself had risen initially, and 93 per cent of Britons backed the lockdown when it was introduced. Despite the clamour from some in politics and business, the public seemingly remained cautious about easing restrictions, despite – or perhaps because of – some high-profile lapses. Notoriously, Neil Ferguson resigned as a government adviser after it was revealed that he had allowed his married lover to visit him at home, travelling across London from her own house, in breach of social distancing rules. His media nickname changed overnight from Professor Lockdown to the Bonking Boffin.

The number of coronavirus deaths in the UK passed 30,000 on 6 May. The death toll, though falling, still averaged more than 500 a day. Public confidence seemed a long way off.

Policymakers worried that while protecting lives was rightly people's chief concern, one of the reasons the public were so ready to support the lockdown was the furlough scheme and other bailouts that went with it. These could not be sustained indefinitely, or even in the medium term. Health would remain people's top priority, at least until the number of infections and deaths fell dramatically, but there were fears that sentiment could turn quickly if those being bankrolled by the state began to worry about their own livelihoods.

By now, Johnson was contemplating his return. His dilemma was acute. Prolonging the lockdown meant keeping businesses closed at huge cost while risking long-term damage to the economy. Opening up meant the virus circulating and carried the danger of a second peak of infections and more deaths, which could prompt more economically damaging restrictions. Questions formed as to how Johnson's own brush with coronavirus had affected him. Those who saw him at close quarters believed his time in intensive care had indeed coloured his judgement. One observed that before he contracted the virus, 'Boris wasn't so much a hawk about lifting the lockdown; he was the Cabinet's golden eagle.' That was no longer the case. Colleagues said he seemed 'quite frightened'.

He returned to the office on 27 April and on 10 May he addressed the nation. Recognising that there were 'millions of people who are both fearful of this terrible disease and at the same time also fearful of what this long period of enforced inactivity will do to their livelihoods and their mental and physical wellbeing', he would provide 'the shape of a plan' to beat the virus and 'provide the first sketch of a road map for reopening society'.

A change of emphasis was evident: 'We said that you should work from home if you can, and only go to work if you must. We now need to stress that anyone who can't work from home, for instance those in construction or manufacturing, should be actively encouraged to go to work.' He urged people to take more outdoor exercise. And, if conditions allowed, schools would start to reopen after 1 June, and parts of the hospitality industry could begin to operate in early July. For now, he cautioned, 'we must stay alert, control the virus and save lives'. Perhaps inevitably, this partial end to lockdown was a recipe for confusion.

CHAPTER 20

CAPTAIN SENSIBLE

On 20 May, Johnson promised a 'world-beating' test-and-trace system in which individuals who had been in contact with those found to have the virus would be identified and advised to self-isolate. The launch was beset with problems, with reports of websites crashing and underprepared staff. Another key part of the government's test-and-trace plans, the development of a bespoke app for smartphones, was abandoned after three months when Matt Hancock announced the government would instead focus on technology developed by Apple and Google.

Good news occasionally made its way through, though. An antibody test for the virus was approved; the number of coronavirus cases fell; human trials of a potential vaccine were announced; the Covid-19 alert level was moved from Level 4 to Level 3, meaning the epidemic was still in general circulation but transmission was no longer high or rising exponentially; and the overall number of deaths had returned to normal for the first time since the middle of March.

All this prompted further easing of the lockdown. From early June, people from different households were allowed to meet outside in groups of up to six, and two weeks later non-essential shops were opened and single adults were allowed to spend the night in another house in a 'support bubble'.

But these chinks of light seemed slight when set against the growing evidence that Britain had suffered one of the highest coronavirus death rates in the world. The government's defenders argued that international comparisons could not be made until full data was available at the end of the pandemic, and that countries did not all record figures in the same way.

Still, there was no question that with over 60,000 excess deaths by late May, the impact on the UK had been catastrophic. Some scientists claimed that thousands of lives could have been saved if the lockdown had been implemented sooner. In fact, minutes from the Sage committee support the government's claim that it had followed scientific advice when making its decisions. Yet the suggestion that earlier action might have saved thousands only eroded public faith in the government's ability to manage the situation.

The government's reputation took a further battering at the end of May when Dominic Cummings was accused of having broken lockdown rules by driving his family from London to his parents' house in County Durham so that his son could be looked after while he and his wife were ill. Johnson defended his chief adviser, yet there was widespread anger. Forty-six Conservative MPs even called for Cummings to be sacked. Sunak supported him, loyally tweeting: 'Taking care of your wife and young child is justifiable and reasonable, trying to score political points over it isn't.'

The relentless pressure of the crisis caused political nerves to fray. One source claimed to the *Mail on Sunday* that Hancock was on 'borrowed time' and that Johnson had upbraided him on his department's performance. With Sir Keir Starmer providing a sharper opposition, greater scrutiny was inevitable.

Starmer focused on competence. Having called for an exit strategy, he told *The Guardian*:

> What we appear to have got is an exit without a strategy. We want to see society reopen, we want to see more children back at school, obviously people want to see their families and we want to see businesses open. But like many people across the country, there is a growing concern the government is now winging it.

Amid the pressure, Simon Case, private secretary to the Duke of Cambridge, was seconded to take up a new post as Permanent Secretary at No. 10 to co-ordinate the government's handling of the crisis. The previous structure of a daily Covid-19 meeting and four ministerial implementation groups was replaced by a strategy committee, CS, chaired by Johnson, and an operations committee, CO, chaired by Gove, with the intention of bringing a more cohesive approach to the government's handling of the pandemic. Sunak would sit on both committees.

Although this period was bedevilled by internal government rows, Sunak, with the exception of his intervention over the Cummings affair, appeared largely detached from all arguments that found their way into the public domain.

However, in early June he took what was for him the unusual step of speaking out about his experience of racism. The death of an unarmed black man, George Floyd, at the hands of police in Minneapolis had led to protests in America which spread to Britain under the banner of Black Lives Matter. Some of these turned violent. Police were attacked and public monuments were vandalised, including the Cenotaph and a statue of Winston Churchill in Parliament Square. Sunak tweeted:

As a British Asian of course I know that racism exists in this country. And I know people are angry and frustrated. They want to see, and feel, change. But a better society doesn't happen overnight – like all great acts of creation, it happens slowly, and depends on the cooperation of each of us toward that common goal. The truth is we have inherited a country far more inclusive and fairer than at any point in its history. Does this mean our story is over? No, but we shouldn't ignore the hard work of the many generations who came before us. To the small minority who committed acts of violence and vandalism last weekend, not only were your actions criminal, but they also perpetuate a dangerous lie: that the temporary excitement of destruction is the same thing as change. You are, and always will be, wrong. But to the vast majority who seek only peaceful protest within the law and a better future for themselves and their children: whilst our progress feels slow, I promise you it is permanent.

Yet the grim economic outlook meant Sunak had plenty more to worry about. Despite early expectations that there would be a V-shaped recovery, with growth returning quickly once lockdown was lifted, later projections were more pessimistic. Leaked analysis from the Treasury in early May, marked 'Official – Market sensitive', concluded that a U-shaped trajectory was the most likely scenario, meaning a 'prolonged recovery and some permanent damage to the economy'. An L-shaped economic decline was not ruled out.

Andy Haldane, chief economist at the Bank of England,

warned that unemployment levels not seen since the 1980s, when the jobless total peaked at over 3 million, were in prospect. Research by the Chartered Institute of Personnel and Development found companies' hiring intentions were the lowest on record. A survey from the Federation of Small Businesses suggested one in three small company owners forced to close because of the pandemic may never reopen.

On 12 May, Sunak's fortieth birthday, he told the BBC:

> We already know that many people have lost their jobs and it breaks my heart, we've seen what's happening with Universal Credit claims already. This is not something we're going to wait to see – it's already happening. There are already businesses that are shutting, there are already people who have lost their jobs. And as I said, that's heart-breaking to me and that's why I'm working night and day to limit the amount of job losses.

When official figures the next day showed the economy had shrunk by 5.8 per cent in March, the biggest month-on-month fall since records began, Institute for Fiscal Studies director Paul Johnson said Britain was heading for 'a recession to end all recessions, in terms of its scale'. The following month's figures showed the economy had contracted by a further 20.4 per cent in April, shattering the record again. Sunak did not shy away from the truth. Giving evidence to the House of Lords Economic Affairs Committee on 19 May, he said the country was 'likely to face a severe recession, the likes of which we have not seen'.

He echoed the OBR's assessment, saying, 'It is not obvious that there will be an immediate bounce-back,' but adding:

The question that occupies my mind and in the long term is probably more relevant is: what is the degree of long-term scarring of the economy as a result of this recession? What is the loss of productive capacity? Ultimately, once we recover from this crisis – by the nature of it, I believe it will be temporary, and we will suppress the virus and progressively lift the restrictions – the question is: what do we return to? On that question, the jury is out.

This left him on the horns of a dilemma. The government was committed to doing 'whatever it took' to help the country through the crisis, yet the Treasury's support could not last for ever. The complication was not simply that the £14 billion per month spending involved was unsustainable but that there would come a point when state subsidies actually prevented the economy from adjusting to the new reality. Saving people's jobs by paying their wages during an enforced break from work was one thing; financing jobs which had effectively ceased to exist was another.

Sunak's challenge was to wean Britain off his lavish programmes without triggering a wave of redundancies. These thoughts governed his approach to the job retention scheme. Unveiling it in March, he said it would be open for three months but that he would extend it if necessary. This he did on 12 May in a statement to the House of Commons. He said it would be run down gradually and would close in October.

Shortly afterwards, it was revealed that one beneficiary of the job retention scheme had been Infosys, the global IT company set up by Sunak's father-in-law, Narayana Murthy, which furloughed 3 per cent of its estimated 10,000 UK workforce. What was not reported at the time was that there was another bailout beneficiary even closer to home, namely Akshata Murthy, Sunak's wife.

In an interest that was not made public in Sunak's declaration of interests under the Ministerial Code but which did appear in the first edition of this book, Ms Murthy is a director of the holding company for an exclusive gentlemen's outfitter which sells £2,500 silk dressing gowns. The luxury menswear company is called New & Lingwood, an English brand that investors hope might catch on in America. Its flagship London store is in Jermyn Street and it is headquartered in Eton, where it is an official outfitter to Eton College.

In 2020, New & Lingwood developed a range of luxury silk face masks retailing at £30 each – a snip relative to the price of their range of nightwear. Designed for clientele keen to make a statement in the bedroom, the company's flamboyant silk housecoats retail at between £1,250 and £2,500. Those who really want to push the boat out could select an 'antique shawl lined' blue, red and purple dressing gown which, at £2,750, must be among the most expensive in the world.

Whether Sunak has ever possessed any of these items is unclear, but he had been silent about his wife's links to the firm. Under the Ministerial Code, ministers have a responsibility to list 'interests of [a] spouse, partner or close family member' which might reasonably be perceived to be directly relevant to the minister's public duties. The minister must decide how far his responsibility extends, but, given the width of those duties, it would surely have been prudent for a Chancellor of the Exchequer, particularly one at the heart of handing out money to save the economy, to take the broadest view of what needs to be disclosed. Sunak's entry to the register made no mention of his wife's role as one of six directors of N&L Acquisitions, the holding company of which New & Lingwood International is a subsidiary.

According to Companies House records, she was appointed to the position in June 2017, around eighteen months after the tailoring company was sold to New York-based investors Pop Capital. A customer who dropped into the London store in June 2020 was told that staff had been furloughed during the lockdown, suggesting the company benefited directly from the Chancellor's job support scheme.

Even before the pandemic, New & Lingwood was struggling. According to publicly available accounts, in 2018 it had just £202,000 in the bank, a figure that fell to £63,000 the following year. At the time of writing, this part of the company – which has a complex structure involving at least two holding entities – had a negative value of around -£1 million, relative to -£58,000 the previous year. The furlough scheme would, one imagines, have been a considerable relief to the directors, including Sunak's wife.

In the register of ministerial interests, Sunak does declare his wife's ownership of Catamaran Ventures, which he describes as a 'venture capital investment company'. However, he did not list her directorship of another business, Digme Fitness, a fitness chain with which she has been formally involved since spring 2017. Though it has gyms in Oxford, Ealing and Richmond, it caters primarily to young professionals in central London, with branches in Moorgate, Bank and Fitzrovia. Businesses in these parts of the capital were among the hardest hit in the country by coronavirus. Just days before the government announced the reopening of gyms in July, directors of Digme Fitness held a crisis meeting over the impact of coronavirus on the business, according to a senior source at the company. For the same reason, Sunak ought to have also registered his wife's interest in this company.

In a third undeclared interest, along with her brother Rohan, Akshata is a director of a software development company called Soroco. It boasts of having a 'global presence', with offices in London, Bangalore, Boston, Seattle and New York. The majority of staff appear to be based in India. According to Companies House, Akshata and her brother both became directors of the business in October 2014. His occupation at that time is listed as 'computer scientist', while hers is listed as 'none'. The most recent set of accounts suggest that this company too is haemorrhaging cash: it appears to be more than $5 million in the red.

Omitting to declare one spousal interest is unfortunate; omitting to declare several borders on the careless. One explanation for this unsatisfactory state of affairs could be that Sunak did disclose all the relevant information to the Permanent Secretary at the Treasury, as is permitted under the Ministerial Code, who decided that it was not necessary to enter it on the public register. Alternatively, the so-called Propriety and Ethics team at the Cabinet Office, which has the final say on what appears on the register, may have been made aware of the directorships but did not see fit to disclose them. However, this would seem inconsistent with the 'safety first' approach that has clearly been adopted in relation to other government ministers. In the section on relevant interests of a spouse, partner or close family member, many disclose interests that seem very tangential indeed to their brief.

What can be said with certainty is that Sunak had bigger fish to fry. This would certainly be an explanation for what seemed an uncharacteristic oversight or misjudgement.

* * *

Another reason Sunak seemed immune from the political venom during the later stages of lockdown was that many Conservative MPs saw him as an ally in the battle to persuade Downing Street to return society to pre-pandemic normality. During a conference call in late May, he told backbenchers he was frustrated that the economy remained largely shut, according to colleagues who took part. 'Somehow Greece and Italy are opening up,' he reportedly said. 'This country can't be the only place in the world where people can't go and have a drink in the pub.' Another MP stated, 'Rishi said the scientists on Sage were very cautious and that if we believed in opening up the tourism sector, we had to make the case for it.' Some detected a difference in approach from that of Johnson, who had continued to emphasise that the government would 'advance with maximum caution'. Sunak was 'signalling not very subtly where he was in this argument', another MP concluded.

The focal point of Tory discontent was the government's two-metre social distancing rule – more than was in place in most other countries, and an impossible constraint for many businesses, especially in the hospitality sector.

Conservative MPs were delighted when Sunak backed their cause at a meeting of the 1922 Committee, arguing that cutting the rule to one metre would allow three quarters of pubs to reopen, compared with only a quarter if it stayed as it was. He also said changing the rule would help to reopen schools, a point he underlined the same day in an interview with Sky News. 'I personally think that every day our children are not at school is a tragedy,' he said, subtly distancing himself from the recently announced dropping of plans to get all children back to the classroom before September, and aligning himself with sentiment on the Tory benches. The slow progress on school reopening had been a major source of frustration in the Treasury, where the return of primary-age children in particular was seen as crucial to allowing parents to return to work. Officials came in for more criticism on this front than the Education Secretary, Gavin Williamson. 'To be completely honest, Jonathan Slater [then the Permanent Secretary in the education department] just didn't have a grip,' says a source.

I got the sense, in the meetings I was in, that those guys didn't even really want to do any work. They were quite happy to let this thing rumble on. In fairness to Gavin, you rely so much on the Perm Sec to do the back-channelling with the unions, but it became very apparent that it just wasn't happening.

According to insiders, Sunak's campaign to champion jobs and the economy inside Downing Street had begun to pay off. In early June, he and Alok Sharma, the Business Secretary, took Johnson through a 45-minute presentation on the prospects for the economy, which included the warning that if pubs, bars and restaurants were not allowed to open in time for the summer season, 3.5 million hospitality jobs could be lost. Johnson's reaction was succinct: 'Christ!' he is said to have blurted. A senior minister said afterwards that No. 10 was now 'absolutely obsessed' with unemployment. 'Everything is being framed in terms of what it can do for jobs. Infrastructure, the green agenda – it's all being seen through the prism of job creation.'

Together with Gove, Jenrick, Shapps and Culture Secretary

Oliver Dowden, who were also pushing for changes to allow the economy to get back to work, Sunak and Sharma comprised a cabal calling itself the 'Save Summer Six'. They were tasked by Johnson with drawing up detailed adjustments to the rules to save seasonal industries and allow normality to return as far as possible.

A senior Treasury source recalls that Sunak 'pulled together a gaggle of ministers' in the early summer.

> Those guys worked pretty intently for a couple of months with the unions to ensure that when we could open stuff up we could do it safely and fast. The internal struggles over the summer were really about how much we should or shouldn't lean in to easing restrictions in certain industries where we thought it was safe. Rishi would have them on Zoom meetings three times a week. What regulations can we change? What flexibility can we provide? Who do we need to get onside?

A veteran Conservative MP said the continued presence of the two-metre rule contributed to the 'febrile, bordering on rebellious' mood on the Tory benches, where it was seen as an example of 'gold-plated' regulation resulting from overcautious scientific advice. Sunak himself emphasised that these decisions would ultimately be down to politicians who were accountable to the public, telling the BBC on 14 June:

> It's for ministers, whether it's me, the Prime Minister, the Health Secretary and others, you know, we're the people that are elected to make decisions in this country. People should hold us responsible and accountable for

making those decisions, but I think people are comforted and have confidence in those decisions if they know that we are taking advice from our scientists on what is ultimately a health crisis.

The public were far from gung-ho about further easing: 58 per cent told YouGov on 11 June that they thought the two-metre instruction should stay, more than twice the proportion who wanted it halved. Nevertheless, Sunak made no secret of his desire to change the rule. On 14 June, he publicly trailed a review, telling Sky News that scrapping it would be 'the difference between three quarters and maybe a third of pubs opening. So it is important that we look at it.' He added that this measure would be crucial to keeping employment as high as possible.

The campaign came to fruition on 23 June when Johnson announced to Parliament that 'our long national hibernation' was coming to an end. From 4 July, pubs, restaurants, cinemas, hotels, campsites, places of worship, museums, outdoor playgrounds and hairdressers could reopen, with specific guidelines for each sector. Two households would be allowed to meet indoors. The two-metre rule would be replaced with 'one-metre plus', meaning that the reduced distance was acceptable alongside other measures to reduce the likelihood of transmission.

Sunak continued to top the ConservativeHome Cabinet League Table, not suffering the decline in scores awarded by party members to his senior colleagues – especially Johnson, who fell to fourth place. Commentators began to draw a contrast between Sunak and other members of the Cabinet. *The Sun* observed that 'for all the other accusations levelled at the

Government during the Covid crisis, few critics can fault the Chancellor's efforts to keep us afloat. His bailouts have saved millions of jobs.' The television presenter Piers Morgan tweeted a picture of Sunak with the message 'I wish this guy was Prime Minister. Smart, confident, authoritative, empathetic, realistic & with a great grasp of detail. He's in a totally different league to Boris Johnson or any other Govt minister.'

Insiders also began to compare the Chancellor with his boss. 'He's Captain Sensible while Boris is blundering,' said one minister. Though Downing Street and Treasury sources insisted the two were in 'lockstep', the potential for conflict at the top was obvious. 'You've got to ask whether this is a Cameron–Osborne sofa government,' the minister added, 'or we could be in for a Blair–Brown shitshow.'

CHAPTER 21

REBUILDING

On the riverside terrace of a Chiswick pub, Sunak rhapsodised about Spanish cuisine. 'Broccolini, amazing grilled lamb chops, chorizo, patatas bravas, manchego with the honey and the almonds, Padrón peppers,' he enthused before talking about the restaurant he and his wife would be visiting that evening. 'It is literally our favourite place – we get the same stuff every single time. We're very excited.' This paean to tapas, given in an interview with *The Times*, was part of an effort to promote 'Super Saturday', 4 July 2020, on which hospitality venues would reopen to customers. Sunak's intention was not just to whet the appetite of readers but to instil a sense of obligation. 'We need to relearn what it's like to go out again,' he said.

> I'm worried about a generation that is scarred by coronavirus – we don't want to lose that generation … For me this is really about social justice. I look at the situation, and I'm desperate for all those people to go back to the jobs that they had at the beginning of all this.

This had long been a concern in the Treasury. When the furlough scheme was launched, 'it became really clear that this was going to turn into an employment crisis at some point in the year', says a senior adviser.

It wasn't just going to burn out. I remember walking into his office with a bunch of labour market evaluations I'd seen. I had a whole stack of them. And I said, 'This is going to turn, at some point in the next six months, into something else. And you need to think about what sort of interventions you're going to do.'

The drive to get Britons eating out again was also the focus of Sunak's latest multi-billion-pound package, unveiled in the Commons on 8 July. VAT on eat-in or hot takeaway food, accommodation and attractions like cinemas and theme parks would be cut from 20 per cent to 5 per cent for six months. On top of that, 'to get customers back into restaurants, cafés and pubs, and protect the 1.8 million people who work in them', he announced the Eat Out to Help Out discount: 50 per cent off meals eaten at any business that registered with the scheme, up to a maximum of £10, from Monday to Wednesday throughout August.

The new measures were designed to protect employment, but Sunak resisted calls from unions and business groups for a further extension to the job retention scheme: 'If I say the scheme must end in October, critics will say it should end in November. If I say it should end in November, critics will just say December,' he said. Leaving the scheme open too long would give people 'false hope that it will always be possible to return to the jobs they had before. And the longer people are on furlough, the more likely it is their skills could fade, and they will find it harder to get new opportunities.' Instead, a new job retention bonus of £1,000 would be available to employers for every staff member employed until January – a cost to the government of £9 billion if all 9 million furloughed workers returned.

Yet these plans might never have made it out of the Treasury. Jim Harra, the Permanent Secretary of HMRC, wrote to Sunak the day before the statement expressing concern that the job retention bonus and the Eat Out to Help Out discount might not represent value for public money and asking for a 'written instruction' to proceed. Sunak replied the same day that 'there are broader issues that I am able to weigh in my decision' that an independent civil servant was not able to consider. Though the Treasury insisted this was a normal part of government business, it turned the decision into a major judgement call for which Sunak had taken personal responsibility.

'"Eat Out to Help Out" was absolutely his idea,' says a Treasury figure.

> He wanted to do it through Visa, but there simply weren't enough cards – they have about 10 or 15 million in a vault somewhere at any one time, but they just couldn't do it. So we had to go back to the drawing board. We were worried it would have been susceptible to fraud – phantom businesses setting up and just claiming the receipts. You could have had the proprietor getting three receipts to get three lots of £10 off. In the end we just had to do a kind of 'trust people not to defraud the system'.

The exchange of letters between Harra and Sunak was one of several similar incidents that took place during the crisis, with Whitehall sources saying there was no time 'to do the value-for-money stuff that the Treasury would normally do'. Sunak saw that this was the only way to operate in the circumstances. 'His policy has always been don't overcomplicate it, make it user-friendly, make it generous but time-limited, make it work.'

Sunak also announced a new Kickstart scheme that would directly pay employers to hire 16–24-year-olds at risk of long-term unemployment. The government would pay firms to create new apprenticeships – a plan inspired by the Future Jobs Fund introduced by Labour in 2009 but scrapped by the coalition government. A Green Homes Grant of up to £10,000 would also be given to homeowners and landlords to make their properties more energy efficient, and stamp duty would be scrapped on transactions up to £500,000 for the following nine months. Two days earlier, Sunak had announced £1.5 billion of grants and loans for theatres, music venues, museums, galleries, heritage sites and independent cinemas to help boost the struggling arts and culture sector.

The Sun welcomed this attempt to 'to convince a public still alarmingly content to hide at home from even the tiniest risk of Covid'. Tory MPs were equally enamoured. 'We take it as read that everyone thinks you're brilliant,' said Sir Graham Brady after Sunak was greeted with thunderous desk-banging as he arrived at a meeting of the 1922 Committee after delivering his statement. MPs said they were grateful for a sense of direction out of lockdown rather than going round and round in circles.

Details of Sunak's jobs programme had been so tightly guarded, even the Cabinet was not briefed in advance on the meal discount or job retention schemes. That is not to say the package went without scrutiny. On the Monday evening before the announcement, Sunak was grilled by a 'murder board' – an idea originating in the military in which a team tests a plan's robustness by looking for flaws and potential problems. The session, which included senior aides and Treasury ministers, lasted nearly three hours.

Harra's warnings over value for money had underlined criticism from Labour and some commentators that the schemes
involved large 'deadweight' costs, where the state would
be paying to incentivise things that would have happened
anyway. Sunak acknowledged that some of this would be una-
voidable but felt it a price worth paying. Data from the Office
for National Statistics (ONS) showed that more than 600,000
jobs had been lost in April and May, while benefit claims had
more than doubled to 2.8 million. Sunak's team knew this
could only be the tip of the iceberg – many furloughed workers would have no job to go back to when the scheme came to
an end, and only then would the full impact of the crisis on
employment become clear.

The Bank of England's Andy Haldane struck an upbeat
note in a presentation on 30 June, saying the economy was
already two months into its recovery and that real-time data
on things like payments, traffic and energy use suggested a
swift bounce-back.

Yet other evidence was less encouraging. In the days before
and after Sunak unveiled his jobs plan, nearly 20,000 redundancies were announced by firms including Airbus, EasyJet,
Arcadia, Harrods, Boots and Burger King. While retail and
transport bore the brunt, thousands of white-collar positions
were cut at management consultancy firms and banks. The
week after the statement, official figures showed the economy
had grown just 1.8 per cent in May – well below forecasters'
expectations – and was nearly one quarter smaller than it had
been before the pandemic. The OBR predicted that 1.3 million
furloughed workers would lose their jobs when the scheme
ended, and the Organisation for Economic Co-operation and
Development warned that Britain's unemployment rate could

reach 5 million, or 15 per cent of the workforce, in the event of a second wave of the virus. The ONS found that job vacancies were scarcer than at any time since their surveys began, and well under the previous low recorded in 2009.

*　　*　　*

While the aim of the first phase of the government's economic response to the pandemic had been to sustain businesses and incomes during the lockdown, Sunak said this second phase was to 'protect, support and create jobs'. Its success, however, would depend not just on the size of the Treasury's stimulus but on people's willingness to resume their pre-pandemic lives.

Sunak put himself at the forefront of the drive to persuade people to spend. At each stage of lockdown easing he had appeared at markets and shops to highlight the steps businesses had taken to keep customers safe. After his Commons performance, Sunak even revived a previous career by popping up as a waiter at a London branch of the Asian restaurant chain Wagamama.

The discount dining schemes could claim some success. More than 72,000 venues had signed up to Eat Out to Help Out by the time it opened in August, including forty Michelin-starred restaurants and ninety chains such as McDonald's and Costa Coffee. Newspapers carried pictures of bustling restaurants, and many outlets reported their busiest Monday of the year.

Wetherspoon's announced new price cuts with posters hailing 'Dishi Rishi, Legend', and a Newcastle hotel group added a 'Low VAT! Low fat! Delishy Dishy Rishi Burger' to its menu. If the idea of a Chancellor of the Exchequer being celebrated in the form of a chargrilled chicken breast in a bun was unusual, so was the policy that gave rise to the tribute. More than 10.5 million discount meals were served in the first week, and more than 100 million during the whole of August.

More broadly, though, the public remained hesitant about taking advantage of this newfound liberty. Spending on Super Saturday was only about half the level of the comparable day the previous year. Retail industry figures showed that while online business had grown strongly in June, in-store sales were down dramatically on 2019, and YouGov found only just over half of people saying they felt comfortable going into non-essential shops.

This reluctance was probably unsurprising, as the government's instruction to go forth and spend was only one half of its message. Some scientists and ministers were at pains to point out that the virus had not gone away. As pubs and restaurants prepared to open on Super Saturday, Chris Whitty said at a Downing Street press conference, 'None of us believe, and I'm sure nobody watching this believes, this is a risk-free next step. It's absolutely not, that is why we have to be really serious about it.' As Whitty explained, this was 'an attempt to balance, as best we can, in a way that makes it possible for society to be as close as possible to normal, whilst living alongside this virus – which we will have to continue to do'. The government's apparently mixed messaging may have been understandable, but so, arguably, was the public's apprehension about resuming life as it had been. To heed the call, the people would not only have to be confident that the risk of contracting the virus was lower; they also needed to know that the NHS was prepared for any surge in cases.

Such confidence was hard to come by. The government was

able to track localised outbreaks well enough to be able to order a local lockdown in Leicester and to take targeted action in over a hundred other hotspots each week by July. However, the national track and trace system was far from fully effective by the summer. The revelation that Public Health England had been routinely overstating the number of Covid deaths by including anyone who had tested positive and subsequently died – even if they recovered and were hit by a bus three months later – did nothing to reassure people that the authorities knew what they were doing.

Neither did a muddle over the rules for wearing face masks in shops. Michael Gove told the BBC on 12 July that he did not think masks should be mandatory, but it was 'basic good manners' to wear one in a shop. Two days later, the government announced that masks would be compulsory in shops from 24 July, and Gove was pictured in a branch of Pret A Manger without one.

There was further confusion over official advice on working from home. At his final 'People's PMQs' session before the summer break, Johnson said:

It's very important that people should be going back to work if they can, now. I think everybody's taken the 'stay at home if you can'. I think now we should say 'go back to work if you can'. Because I think it's very important that people should try to live their lives more normally and I want to see more people feeling confident to use the shops, use the restaurants, get back to work.

Yet days later, Sir Patrick Vallance told the House of Commons Science and Technology Committee that social distancing remained important and that 'for many companies working from home remains a perfectly good option, because it's easy to do. A number of companies think it's not detrimental to productivity and in that situation [there is] absolutely no reason I can see to change it.'

The delay to normality was not just down to confused communication, however. A resurgence of cases in Europe was under way, and ONS data showed the number of UK infections on the rise again. The government was ready to issue new restrictions at short notice, including local 'stay at home' orders. At the end of July, those displaying symptoms were ordered to self-isolate for ten days rather than seven. Johnson announced it was time to 'squeeze the brake pedal' on the planned next stage of lockdown easing, including allowing wedding receptions, indoor theatre and concert performances, and the opening of bowling alleys and casinos (activities that were eventually allowed from 15 August, two weeks after initially intended). The requirement to wear a face covering was extended beyond shops to include indoor settings such as cinemas. A sombre Chris Whitty claimed the data showed the limit of what could be done in terms of opening up society had been reached. 'The idea that we can open up everything and keep the virus under control is clearly wrong,' he said.

A fortnight earlier, Johnson had spoken of a 'significant return to normality' by Christmas. Now the accent was again on caution and preventing a second wave over the winter. By September, the rise in cases was significant enough to prompt new restrictions. Social gatherings of more than six people were banned both indoors and outdoors. Having paid people to eat out only weeks earlier, the government ordered pubs and restaurants to close at 10 p.m.

Efforts to persuade people to return to the office were reversed as ministers once again urged people to work from
home, and many expected further new rules to follow. Any
return to normality was months away, at best. Yet according to
one senior MP, a full two-week national lockdown would have
been imposed had Sunak not persuaded Johnson that it would
be an economic disaster.

* * *

As Sunak told Parliament in his Summer Statement, supporting incomes during lockdown and attempting to protect jobs
after furlough ended would be followed by 'a third phase,
where we will rebuild'.

Planning for the longer-term economic recovery had been
under way for some time. As early as May, details emerged
of Project Birch, under which the state would step in to save
strategically important companies such as steelmakers and car
manufacturers whose failure would disproportionately harm
the economy. Help would take the form of loans which could
be converted into equity in certain circumstances, though
lending arrangements with taxpayers at the top of the hierarchy of creditors were the preferred option. Sunak told Bloom-
berg TV there would be an 'exceptionally high' bar for bailouts:
'This is not my money. It's not the government's money. This
is taxpayers' money. I shouldn't be sitting here trying to pick
winners.' He evidently viewed the plan as a necessary, if temporary, evil: 'It's not something that's an attractive, long-term
feature of the economy and if we're in a situation like that,
one would obviously expect financial investors and creditors
to significantly share in the burden.'

Sunak promised that more details of the government's economic plan would be unveiled in an Autumn Budget and Comprehensive Spending Review. But these set-piece events could surely not simply amount to yet another splurge of borrowed money. Some had compared his Summer Statement to the film *Brewster's Millions*, noting that whereas the film's hero is challenged to spend $30 million in thirty days, Sunak had managed to dispose of £30 billion in thirty minutes. The OBR said that, as a result, government borrowing would rise to £372 billion for the year, more than six times its March forecast, and that savings of £60 billion would need to be made every decade to make the deficit manageable in the years to come.

'In practice, no government could allow net debt to persist for long on these explosive paths,' said Robert Chote, the OBR's outgoing chair. The point was not lost on Sunak, who had spoken in his Summer Statement of the need to put the public finances back on a 'sustainable footing' over the medium term.

This was in fact a bigger concern for Sunak than he was able to reveal in public. Asked what most worried the Chancellor during the crisis, a senior Treasury source said it was 'the markets'.

> We make too many slack decisions. The size of the borrowing now is such that if the markets were to move, it would make such a big difference. Lots of people are saying 'keep on borrowing', and that might be right for the time being, but he has to be the one conveying to the markets that he has a plan to bring everything under control. If the markets were to decide in the fullness of time that we are not serious about getting spending under control, and decided that they didn't want to invest in the UK any more…

Sunak's options were already limited. Johnson had repeatedly and publicly ruled out a return to 'what people call austerity'. But nor was he keen to raise taxes – the government would not be 'launching some punitive raid on the wealth creators'. This sentiment was loudly echoed on the Conservative benches and by right-leaning think tanks, which warned that such policies could make matters worse.

Various ideas were floated to help narrow the gulf between revenue and spending. One potential target was the 'triple lock' policy under which pensions rise by average earnings, inflation or 2.5 per cent, whichever is greatest. Though this was a Conservative manifesto commitment at the 2019 election, many argued it was no longer affordable, especially since the number of people returning from furlough pay to their full salary could result in an earnings-related bonanza for pensioners which could not have been foreseen when the promise was made. One Westminster figure recalls Sunak telling him as long ago as 2017 that renewing the triple lock commitment was a bad idea. However, Johnson apparently vetoed Sunak's attempts to amend the policy.

The launch of a review of capital gains tax in July led to speculation that the government was gearing up to cut allowances or remove exemptions, perhaps including financial gains made on the sale of a main home. The Treasury also launched a consultation on business rates, which included a proposal for a new online sales tax to help high streets compete and go some way to balancing the government's books. The idea immediately divided senior Tories, as did later talk that a plot was afoot to increase corporation tax, fuel duty and National Insurance contributions for self-employed people.

'No. 10 don't like it,' says a senior Treasury source. 'They don't like the idea of the Tory Party raising taxes. There's a debate to be had about timing.' But unpalatable decisions would have to be made.

The day after announcing above-inflation pay rises for nearly 900,000 public sector workers, Sunak began the formal Comprehensive Spending Review process by writing to Cabinet ministers warning of 'tough choices' ahead, prompting unions to complain that rises of 3.1 per cent for teachers and 2.8 per cent for doctors and dentists were simply a smokescreen for what was to follow. Departments would need to find ways to 'reprioritise and deliver savings' to help pay for new spending, consider asset sales and propose plans to relocate offices out of London. Due to 'unprecedented uncertainty', Sunak declined to set an overall spending target but said it would grow in real terms, retreating from a pledge in March to raise departmental budgets by 9 per cent by 2024.

The call for savings from departments reflected a longstanding bugbear of Sunak. Sources revealed that he had become 'increasingly irritated' with parts of the state machine for what he considered their insufficiently detailed spending proposals and lax approach to administering expensive programmes. He viewed the health; education; and culture, media and sport departments as particular offenders. From early on in the crisis, he had been taken aback by other ministers' seemingly limitless appetite for cash, according to one familiar with the workings of government. Colleagues confirmed this frustration at the time. 'Rishi fundamentally believes other people in politics think we can carry on borrowing because the moment demands it, and the markets won't be upset about it,' says a senior Treasury source. 'But he thinks the longer that goes on, it's a gamble. And that's not a gamble he wants to take.'

Yet getting the economy back into shape would take more than just counting the pennies more carefully in Whitehall. Ideas were also in train for an overhaul of planning laws to boost growth and speed up infrastructure development, and to introduce freeports, in which towns, cities or regions would be legally outside the country's customs territory, with goods imported, manufactured or re-exported without incurring tariffs or import VAT until they entered the rest of the country. The aim was to establish them as international hubs for manufacturing and innovation. There was also a proposal for a national infrastructure bank to provide new funding for capital projects. He also had more immediate problems to battle, notably how to avoid mass unemployment.

The summer break brought the inevitable news that Britain was officially in recession. The economy had shrunk by a record 20.4 per cent in the three months to June, the biggest quarterly contraction of any large state. More positively, the collapse had happened entirely over two months and growth had begun again in May, but Sunak did not take the risk of trying to look on the bright side. 'Today's figures confirm that hard times are here,' he said. 'Hundreds of thousands of people have already lost their jobs, and sadly in the coming months many more will. But while there are difficult choices to be made ahead, we will get through this, and I can assure people that nobody will be left without hope or opportunity.'

As the end of the furlough scheme loomed, and with policy once again aimed at restricting rather than promoting normal life, people began to ask what form this hope and opportunity would take. Sunak's answer came on 24 September when, having scrapped plans for an Autumn Budget owing to the continued economic uncertainty, he unveiled his Winter Economy Plan.

He stuck to his guns on ending the job retention scheme: 'It is fundamentally wrong to hold people in jobs that only exist inside the furlough,' he told Parliament. 'I cannot save every business. I cannot save every job. No Chancellor could.' However, for six months from November, the government would subsidise wages so that businesses had the option of keeping employees on shorter hours rather than making them redundant. Staff working at least a third of their normal hours would be paid by their employer; for the hours employees could not work, the government and the employer would each cover one third of the lost pay. Sunak also gave businesses longer to repay Bounce Back loans, further deferred tax bills, and announced that the reduced 5 per cent VAT rate on hospitality and tourism would remain until March rather than January.

Concluding in a way that some took to indicate where he stood in the lockdown debate, he said:

> Our lives can no longer be put on hold. Since May, we have taken steps to liberate our economy and society. We did these things because life means more than simply existing. We find meaning and hope through our friends and family, through our work, through our community ... It would be dishonest to say there is now some risk-free solution. Or that we can mandate behaviour to such an extent we lose any sense of personal responsibility ... We must learn to live with it and live without fear.

Again, Sunak's measures were widely welcomed. On the day of the announcement, he even persuaded the TUC's Frances O'Grady and the CBI's Carolyn Fairbairn to join him for a photocall outside No. 11. But impending job cuts and the looming battle over the public finances would surely soon begin to erode his stratospheric reputation – wouldn't they?

CHAPTER 22

'HUNGRY YOUNG LION'

One person who was not present when Sunak unveiled his multi-billion-pound Winter Economy Plan in the House of Commons was Boris Johnson. In what was widely considered a surprising decision, the Prime Minister chose instead to make an official visit to a police station in Northampton, where he posed for press photographers in a new Interceptor squad car and watched a first-aid demonstration in a sports hall. Many Westminster observers struggled to understand why this should have taken precedence over supporting the Chancellor's latest strategy for steering the nation through the crisis. Coming just a few weeks after Sunak had been quizzed by a Times Radio interviewer about his prime ministerial ambitions (Sunak had answered, 'Oh gosh, I don't have that desire'), an idea began to take hold that Johnson's nose might have been put out of joint by the amount of attention being paid to his younger colleague. The men's very different personalities did nothing to contain this growing perception of disharmony, particularly among more mischievous-minded journalists.

When Johnson was asked by a Sky News reporter who had followed him to Northampton to justify his absence from London, his characteristic blather was very much in evidence. 'Of course I fully support the package of measures that we've jointly drawn up,' he said. 'What I'm doing today is setting out the vital corollary of those measures ... What the Chancellor is saying today – we're continuing to do everything we can to support the workforce, jobs and livelihoods throughout the crisis and again some very creative and imaginative proposals from the Chancellor.'

This unconvincing account only prompted more queries about what lay behind the supposed snub. And when a Downing Street spokesman positively dismissed rumours of a rift between Johnson and Sunak later that day, insisting that there was 'absolutely not' a problem, Otto von Bismarck's quip that one should never believe anything until it has been officially denied sprang to the minds of certain lobby correspondents.

In fact, one figure who worked in Downing Street in 2020 says there was an innocent explanation.

I remember everyone thinking Boris missing the Winter Economy Plan was a conspiracy, but it wasn't. Sunak's diary would be shared with No. 10 in advance. Not unwisely, Boris knew that if something was difficult, a distraction could be useful. The Winter Economy Plan was all about how to get through the winter, the tricky times ahead, and Boris wanted to say, 'Look over here, we're investing in the police' type of thing.

Be that as it may, by the autumn of 2020, the Johnson–Sunak alliance had begun to fluctuate. Those who worked with and around Johnson are certain that of the two of them, he had the more complicated character traits which contributed to the breakdown in their relationship. It was not unusual for the then Prime Minister, famously intolerant of rivals, to convince himself that others wanted to undermine him. One who ended up in the firing line was Sunak.

'On a personal level, Rishi and Boris got on well,' says a source who worked closely with Sunak when he was Chancellor.

> Boris is a fascinating character in a way. Depending on who's in the room, he'll hold court and he's the jester and he's looking for reaction from people. Rishi is one of the jolliest and most upbeat people you can imagine when he's not stressed about something to do with work. And they would have a laugh about things. But Boris has always got his eye on something. And because he's got ulterior motives, he thinks everybody else does as well.

A former No. 10 source is blunter.

> Boris could be paranoid. He respected Rishi's ability and intellect and he never forgot that Rishi backed his leadership bid in the summer of 2019, which was pivotal. But I remember saying to Boris after furlough had been completed by Rishi, 'It's nice to have a hungry young lion sitting round the Cabinet table,' and Boris replied, 'I don't want hungry young lions round the Cabinet table, I want tired old lions.' He hated the competition.

Aside from Johnson's brooding disposition, two other factors further muddied his association with Sunak. The first was his then girlfriend, Carrie Symonds. In 2016, two years before she became romantically involved with Johnson, she had worked briefly as a special adviser to Sajid Javid when he was the Secretary of State for Housing, Communities and Local

Government. She and Javid were close and she is said to have been 'furious' when he was forced to resign as Chancellor of the Exchequer and succeeded by Sunak. 'Carrie associated Rishi with Dominic Cummings, who'd orchestrated Javid's downfall,' says the former No. 10 source.

> She saw Rishi as part of that axis, even though he really wasn't part of it, and she worked hard to get Cummings out. So she had no qualms about stoking tensions. I remember once Rishi came into No. 10 and Boris and Carrie were standing in a corridor. Rishi shared with them some personal plans he had and the next thing he knew a story about it ended up in *The Sun*. This sort of thing eroded trust very quickly.

The second complicating factor was the seemingly relentless push of Sunak's personal 'brand'. A team of publicity experts had been hired to curate his social media profile so that, whether he was chairing a high-level government meeting, enjoying himself at a Yorkshire agricultural show or involved in a family water fight on a lush lawn, his Instagram account depicted him as what one admiring journalist described as 'the Disney Prince version of a Tory MP'. Official literature also bore Sunak's signature above the word 'CHANCELLOR', like a stamp of quality assurance.

These professional touches are said to have made Johnson highly suspicious. They were the work of Cass Horowitz, son of the author Anthony Horowitz, who, aged twenty-nine, had been appointed Sunak's media special adviser in spring 2020. Horowitz had co-founded The Clerkenwell Brothers, a creative agency specialising in 'brand strategy, identity, packaging, content and digital advertising'. He was recruited on the recommendation of Allegra Stratton, a former political journalist who had worked for *The Guardian*, the BBC and ITV News and whom Sunak had chosen to be his communications chief at about the same time.

Horowitz and Stratton worked hard to ensure that their boss appeared in the best possible light and for the most part they were successful. There were occasional slip-ups, notably the occasion when Sunak was photographed working at his Treasury desk while using a £180 Ember travel mug – a Bluetooth-enabled flask which allows drinkers to control the temperature of their coffee from an app on their phone. Owning an expensive gadget was not exactly a crime, but it was not likely to boost his image as a man of the people either, and he was much mocked for it.

In the main, however, Horowitz and Stratton were key players in bringing to life the multitude of announcements that flowed from the Treasury. Horowitz coined the term 'Bounce Back' loans for the fully guaranteed lending programme for small businesses, while Stratton dreamed up the phrase 'Eat Out to Help Out'. The unit in which they worked included a photographer and video crew to ensure suitable moments were captured for social media-driven posterity. When asked about 'Brand Rishi', Sunak made no secret of his belief that it was his responsibility to use every tool available to him to transmit the government's message to the public, telling the BBC, 'If [it] means they poke some fun at me in the process, so be it if it means they're talking about what we're doing and debating it and trying to figure out if they agree with it or not and challenge me on it; that's all for the good.' It was no wonder he rivalled Johnson as the most prominent politician in Britain.

His efforts went beyond the general public, though. He had also contacted every living former Chancellor of the Exchequer seeking their counsel, notably Gordon Brown, who had overseen Britain's response to the global crash of 2008–09 and with whom Sunak had several lengthy conversations. And he was assiduous in cultivating his parliamentary colleagues. He did not try to curry favour in the traditional manner of the political climber by hanging around the Tea Room, however. Instead, he made sure that he was available to explain his decisions, answer questions and listen.

Philip Davies, a backbencher since 2005 whose voting record suggests he is among the most rebellious Conservative MPs in the Commons, praises Sunak's willingness to confer before making big decisions. These qualities were particularly obvious when he realised lockdown was being imposed without any cost–benefit analysis.

'Rishi would consult people when he was Chancellor, in contrast to any of his predecessors,' says Davies.

I can remember two times he rang me out of the blue to hear my opinion on something. I've always got on well with him, but I was very surprised to receive these calls. The first call came during the first lockdown just after the furlough scheme was announced. It was about providing the same financial support for self-employed people. Because he thought lockdown was a terrible idea from an economic perspective, he said to me, 'We're going to be haemorrhaging money,' and he asked what I thought. I said, 'If you're telling people they've got to close their business then you'll have to extend furlough to the self-employed. These are our people.' The second time he rang was to ask advice on state help with rising energy bills, before his last Budget. He asked if I thought he should just focus on people receiving benefits and I said, 'Absolutely not. People on all incomes are struggling, so everyone needs help. That money must be spread out.' I'm sure I wasn't the only MP he consulted.

Whatever combination of character, intellect, professional discipline and political ability brought it about, Sunak's smooth and efficient marketing strategy was the talk of Westminster, where he inspired a certain fascination and was often considered the most successful element of the government's uneven response to the crisis. Inevitably, Johnson was dismissive of any suggestion of rivalry. 'I'm intensely relaxed about anybody in the Conservative Party being popular,' he claimed to the *Evening Standard*. As for whether Sunak might eventually succeed him, he produced the sort of vague answer people had come to expect of him, saying, 'I wouldn't want to blight anybody's career by offering that kind of study.'

By contrast, Dominic Cummings, Johnson's vexatious chief adviser for most of 2020, always made a very obvious show of the esteem in which he held Sunak and how closely they worked together. For Sunak, this was not necessarily beneficial. 'The more Boris's relationship with Dom worsened, the more paranoid Boris became about Rishi,' says a former No. 10 source.

This well-placed source believes that the first significant crack in their relationship can be traced back to July 2020, when Johnson decided he was going to poach Allegra Stratton from Sunak's team to fill a new post, that of Downing Street press secretary. This £100,000-a-year job, whose creation had been overseen by Johnson's then communications chief,

Lee Cain, was intended to open up lobby briefings to greater transparency via daily White House-style press conferences. There had been no shortage of applicants when it was first advertised that month on the Conservative Party's LinkedIn page, where it was described as a chance to 'communicate with the nation on behalf of the Prime Minister'. Johnson, however, upended the selection process Cain had put in place. Before all the interviews had been completed among the shortlisted candidates, he hosted a dinner at Chequers attended by his then girlfriend and now wife, Carrie Symonds, along with Stratton, Sunak and their spouses, at which he implied that Stratton had already got the job – despite the fact that she had not been interviewed for it. Whether his primary motive in making this unexpected announcement was to wrong-foot Sunak or whether, as some have claimed, he was merely carrying out the wishes of Carrie Symonds remains an open question, but the result was the same: by telling Stratton in public that she would be working for him, he put Sunak in an invidious position.

As Johnson knew full well, not only was Stratton a key member of Sunak's team but, as mentioned in Chapter 5, she is also the wife of Sunak's best friend, James Forsyth, who was then political editor of *The Spectator*. Even if, as has been suggested, Stratton did not particularly enjoy working in the Treasury and was looking for a way out, Johnson's intervention had the effect of diminishing Sunak's status. Furthermore, that it took place in a social setting meant that Sunak could not remonstrate with his boss. There is no doubt Sunak was upset. 'Boris said to Allegra something like, "I hear you're going to be my new press secretary,"' recalls somebody who was privy to what took place at the dinner. 'Rishi was completely blindsided. His team is very loyal to him, so he wasn't used to this. It was a power grab, a way of Boris marking his turf, and it was a definite flashpoint in their relationship.' Ironically, although Stratton held the post of Downing Street press secretary for six months, she was never required to give a single briefing because Johnson soon jettisoned the idea of having a press secretary. From April 2021, Stratton became a spokeswoman for the United Nations Climate Change Conference (COP26) President, Alok Sharma.

Further evidence of differences of opinion at the top of government in the autumn of 2020 comes from Matt Hancock, who was then Health Secretary. He reports in his diaries that on 25 September, the day after Sunak's statement, tensions between Johnson and Sunak were palpable. 'Meanwhile public finances are a horror show,' Hancock writes.

> According to official figures released today, the government borrowed £35.9 billion in August, up by £30.5 billion in a year. From April to August, the figure was £173.7 billion, six and a half times the figure for last year. Rishi has clearly been using these figures to freak out the PM, but the fact is there's no trade-off: the only sustainable way to get the economy back on track is to defeat the virus, not pretend it's gone away. We've got to suppress it until the vaccine can do its work.

Hancock's priorities in his capacity as Health Secretary were known to be distinct from Sunak's, as a fiscally prudent Chancellor whose job was to protect the economy, and Sunak never hid his concerns about the effects of lockdown. For instance, when the Scientific Advisory Group for Emergencies (Sage) called for a two-week 'circuit breaker' national lockdown on 21 September 2020, he successfully opposed the measure on economic grounds. Similarly, his strong disapproval of public information posters of Covid patients on ventilators had prompted him to deliver the line in his Winter Economy Plan statement about learning to 'live without fear'. Sunak's utterance of these words is said to have upset the Cabinet Office, which was ultimately in charge of the poster campaigns, a great deal.

His general attitude to lockdowns is now known to have been one of immense frustration. He felt it was dishonest of the state not to inform the public as clearly as possible that the many compromises being made at that time would haunt the nation's future, particularly school closures and the cancellation of NHS appointments. He did share his anxieties with Johnson in private, but, just like everybody else, he found his scepticism was suppressed. 'I wasn't allowed to talk about the trade-off', he said in August 2022. No. 10 gave ministers strict briefings on how to answer questions about the side-effects of lockdown. 'The script was not to ever acknowledge them. The script was "Oh, there's no trade-off, because doing this for our health is good for the economy."'

What perhaps troubled Sunak most about the first year of the Covid crisis is that, according to the then Chancellor, the lockdown policy was based purely on the suppositions of Sage's independent academics. Yet he felt that many of their projections would not have passed the type of test the Treasury would have set before embarking on a measure as drastic as closing the economy or restricting the rights of individuals. In the early days of lockdown, Sunak did find a way of exposing Sage's shortcomings and internal disagreements, however. Unbeknown to Sage scientists, a Treasury mole was able to listen to every conference call they held. The mole's notes of these meetings showed that dissenting voices were being edited out of the 'clean' version of the minutes which were later circulated around government. This meant that Sunak had extra information that others did not. As he later commented, 'If you empower all these independent people, you're screwed.'

'Rishi is a details man,' says one admirer who worked closely with him at the time.

> He was always brilliantly briefed going into meetings. He would stay up late into the night reading every single document he'd been given. I remember he read something on epidemiology including footnotes. The doctors couldn't believe how much he knew. That's why Treasury civil servants loved him. He knew so much and he wanted to learn more. He's also generous when it comes to praising his team. Boris was totally different. He was never prepared, but he was so clever he thought he could bluff his way through.

What concerned many backbench Conservative MPs in the autumn of 2020 was that after Johnson's near-death experience in April, he seemed to move closer to Hancock's bevy of doves and further away from Sunak's cast of hawks, losing touch, they feared, with socio-economic realities in the process. Their doubts were soon common knowledge. Sections of the press that were usually politically close to Johnson began to ask uncomfortable questions of him. This included *The Spectator*. Its edition published during the week of Sunak's Winter Economy Plan statement featured a withering analysis of Johnson's premiership, trailed on its front cover under the headline 'Where's Boris?' Conservative MPs, the magazine ventured, were wondering, 'What's happened to Boris? Where is the man we thought we voted for?' The article, written by *The Spectator*'s editor Fraser Nelson, opined that 'the effervescent, bombastic, energising leader who has deft political judgment and specialises in rallying cries' appeared to have undergone a personality change; it accused him of 'a conspicuous – and baffling – lack of leadership', adding that he seemed 'exhausted, broken' and that his inconsistent Covid strategy was a 'mystery'.

This journalistic missile was hurled just four weeks after another wounding incident that had raised questions about Johnson's political future. That August, it was reported that Sir Humphry Wakefield, the father-in-law of Dominic Cummings, had told a holidaymaker visiting Chillingham Castle, Sir Humphry's home in Northumberland, that Johnson intended to quit within six months because he was struggling with the physical effects of Covid-19. To Johnson's considerable irritation, this prediction found its way into the pages of *The Times*, which claimed that Sir Humphry, a keen horseman, had also said, 'If you put a horse back to work when it's injured, it will never recover.' There is no doubt that Johnson's outlook changed after his hospitalisation, according to a source who worked in Downing Street at the time. 'Boris got Covid because he was overweight. After he got it, he was much more sympathetic to the health side of the argument and much more cautious.' (Sunak, incidentally, has never tested positive for Covid.) While confidence in Johnson seemed to be running dry, Sunak, whose rise Johnson had facilitated, was prospering.

Coincidentally, and quite unknown to Sunak, within hours

of his Winter Economy Plan statement being delivered on 24 September, a new Twitter account was quietly activated. It was called 'Ready For Rishi' and it described itself as a 'grassroots campaign to propel Rishi Sunak to Number 10'. It was little noticed at the time, and indeed to this day it has barely more than 300 followers, but those three words – Ready For Rishi – would in the months ahead take on a far greater significance than anybody realised that autumn. All this was the background to the Johnson–Sunak connection, which would falter throughout 2021 and unravel entirely in 2022, failing.

*   *   *

By October 2020, Sunak was well aware that frequent talk of his popularity was fuelling speculation in the media about his own leadership ambitions, and his instinct was to dampen it. Quite apart from being unhelpful to Johnson, to whom he strove to be loyal in spite of the Chequers episode, he also knew that the impression of being held in such high regard could become a distraction from the business of running the Treasury. Moreover, friends insist that he knew he was involved in an emergency, not a popularity contest. In that sense, he felt it was vital to remind the public that he was not a benign magician who could simply conjure up billions of pounds to give away to individuals and businesses but was instead using taxpayers' money to prop up an economy which had been deliberately switched off, a measure he found increasingly troublesome.

One friend says:

He was never depressed during that period. That's not who he is. He is someone who just keeps going. He's not someone who sits in their tent and sulks. With Covid, he felt a big responsibility. He was very aware that it was his job to reassure lots of people in the country that everything was going to be OK. But something that's quite telling about him is that he was clear from the beginning that this was going to have to be paid for.

A source who worked with Sunak at the time also recalls how he kept up a phenomenal work rate, often putting in sixteen hours a day, without showing any sign of stinting.

Autumn 2020 was a time when we still didn't know what was going to happen with the virus. Rishi was incredibly con- cerned about lots of things – how much we were spending, how much we were borrowing, unemployment levels. In his mind he thought that a third of the population could end up unemployed if we kept locking down. And we'd opened up that summer, we'd just produced a major plan to protect jobs, especially for young people via the Kickstart scheme, which Rishi launched to help those on Universal Credit. So that autumn was quite fraught. Understandably, Boris was getting grief from parts of the press who were saying, 'Don't you dare lock down again.' But he was also feeling pressure from the scientists who were saying, 'You have to lock down again.' Rishi was reticent about lockdowns because of the economic consequences and because he wanted to protect Boris from the wrath of some Tory MPs who were deeply opposed to them.

Fortunately, the perfect forum for clarifying his position on both fronts presented itself in the form of the annual

Conservative Party conference. On 5 October, an interview Sunak had given to *The Sun* was published ahead of his speech to the party faithful. In it, he expressed his sympathy over public anger at the 10 p.m. pub curfew Johnson had announced two weeks previously. 'Everyone is very frustrated and exhausted and tired about all of this,' he told the paper in solidarity with lockdown sceptics everywhere. He also defended the Eat Out to Help Out scheme, which some had accused of fuelling a second wave of coronavirus. Yet he balanced these words by using a portion of his conference speech that day to lavish praise on Johnson. As that year's conference was held online only, he was free to speak without the interruptions and applause of enthusiastic activists, allowing him to send an unequivocal message about who was in charge.

'I've seen up close the burden the Prime Minister carries,' Sunak said during the ten-minute address.

We all know he has an ability to connect with people in a way few politicians manage. It is a special and rare quality. But what the commentators don't see, the thing I see, is the concern and care he feels, every day, for the wellbeing of the people of our country. Yes, it's been difficult, challenges are part of the job, but on the big calls, in the big moments, Boris Johnson has got it right and we need that leadership.

Elsewhere in his speech, he warned party members that the bill for the government's various spending schemes was in the post, as it were, as he mentioned the need to 'balance the books'. He asked, 'If we argue there is no limit on what we can spend, that we can simply borrow our way out of any hole, what is the point in us? I have never pretended there is some

easy, cost-free answer.' Since Johnson's economic philosophy
of 'boosterism' positively rejected a return to the days of austerity, the implication of Sunak's words seemed to be that tax
rises might follow.

Afterwards, Sunak gave a press conference in which he
repeated how well he and Johnson got on. He revealed that
Johnson called him 'Rish', while he preferred to keep things
professional, saying, 'I call him Prime Minister. He keeps
trying to tell me to call him other things, but I just stick with
"PM". We have a close personal friendship which then spreads
through the teams, where there's an enormous amount of
mutual trust.' Sunak even claimed that his two daughters' 'favourite thing in the world' was spending time with Johnson's
dog, Dilyn. 'Our families are very joined at that moment,' he
added, rather cloyingly. When pressed as to whether he eventually wanted to be Prime Minister, he said, 'No, definitely not,
seeing what the Prime Minister has to deal with.' He added
that being Chancellor is 'hard enough for me to do'.

Those who know both men are certain that Sunak meant
every word he spoke that day, and it does seem that their very
different personalities and skills remained complementary at
this point. However much Johnson cared about the misery
inflicted on Britain by Covid, he had little interest in drill-
ing down into the detail of how the various Covid schemes
worked. By contrast, Sunak relished solving every Covid-
inspired problem that confronted him and, it is easy to forget,
had already overseen a furlough system that ran smoothly
when so many big government IT projects do not. Despite
Johnson's occasionally perplexing behaviour, he did his best to
maintain their relationship. 'They used to have Sunday night
supper in each other's flats,' says a source.

ABOVE LEFT Rishi Sunak's childhood home, 21 Spindlewood Close, in the Southampton suburb of Bassett. His family formed lifelong friendships with neighbours in the cul-de-sac. © Simon Czapp/Solent News & Photo Agency

ABOVE RIGHT The chemist at the top of Hill Lane in Southampton run by Sunak's mother, Usha, from 1995 to 2014. Sunak helped with the accounts and, because his father was a GP, he has often spoken of growing up in an 'NHS family'. © Simon Czapp/Solent News & Photo Agency

ABOVE Sunak (pictured centre) attended Stroud, a prep school near Romsey, between 1989 and 1993. He was a keen sportsman but failed to secure an academic scholarship to his senior school, Winchester College, where he was head boy. © Gillman & Soame

LEFT Sunak's parents, Usha and Yashvir, with Usha's father, Raghubir Berry. Sunak's grandparents crossed continents to build better lives for their families. © Daily Echo/Solent News & Photo Agency

Kuti Miah, owner of the Sunaks' favourite Southampton restaurant. Sunak waited tables there as a student in the late 1990s and is remembered by Miah as 'charismatic and kind'.

© Ewan Galvin/Solent News & Photo Agency

Sunak aged twenty-two, soon after taking a first in PPE from Lincoln College, Oxford. He had recently begun the Goldman Sachs graduate training scheme and, separately, taken part in the BBC documentary *Middle Classes: Their Rise and Sprawl*. His contribution would come back to haunt him twenty years later.

© Solent News & Photo Agency

Sunak and his future wife, Akshata Murthy, at Stanford University in California, where they met as MBA students. He was a Fulbright scholar and graduated in 2006. On campus, they were seen as something of a 'power couple'.

NR Narayana Murthy, Sunak's billionaire father in law. In 1981, he co-founded Infosys, one of India's most successful IT firms, and is sometimes called 'India's Bill Gates'. Murthy is credited with encouraging Sunak to pursue his political ambitions.

© Namas Bhojani/Bloomberg via Getty Images

ABOVE LEFT The Sunaks' wedding in Bangalore in 2009. Society magazines were disappointed the event was not more ostentatious, but friends of the couple point out that neither of them was born into great wealth and they are more modest than is assumed. © BCCL *Times of India*

ABOVE RIGHT The Sunaks with their daughters Anoushka (born 2013) and Krishna (born 2011). Sunak speaks freely about his fatherly concerns, including worries that his children will be targeted by adverts for vaping products.

RIGHT Sunak getting into the spirit of a constituency occasion in Richmond, Yorkshire.

BELOW The Sunaks sporting Father Christmas outfits for the annual Santa Run charity fundraiser in Richmond. Constituents say he is always happy to join in locally.

Sunak representing the Conservative Party in a seven-way BBC debate during the 2019 general election campaign. His presence was a sure sign he would soon be promoted to the Cabinet. © Hannah McKay/Pool/AFP via Getty Images

Sunak stepping out of 10 Downing Street soon after being appointed Chancellor of the Exchequer in February 2020. Seven months earlier, he had been an obscure local government minister.
© Peter Summers/Getty Images

Sunak in 2020 attending his first Cabinet meeting. He and Boris Johnson then got on well personally, having supper in Downing Street on most Sundays. Professionally, Sunak found his boss 'chaotic'. One ally says, 'He could have meetings with Boris where something was agreed and in the next meeting Boris would say the opposite, but Rishi was very careful not to plot against Boris.'
© Matt Dunham/WPA/Pool/Getty Images

Sunak leading a coronavirus press conference. At the height of the pandemic, he worked so hard he had to be reminded to eat. Behind the scenes, he grew sceptical of lockdowns and convinced Boris Johnson not to impose another one when the Omicron strain reared its head in December 2021. © Andrew Parsons/10 Downing Street

Sunak serving customers at a branch of Wagamama in July 2020 to publicise his Eat Out to Help Out scheme. The initiative was suspected of fuelling a second wave of coronavirus – a charge Sunak denied.
© Simon Walker/HM Treasury

Boris Johnson and Sunak during Johnson's notorious lockdown birthday party in June 2020. In April 2022, police fined them £50 each for breaching Covid-19 regulations. Sue Gray, the civil servant who investigated the party's circumstances, concluded that the teetotal Sunak had arrived early for a meeting and had no 'advance knowledge' of the event.
© UK government via Getty Images

The

INDEPENDENT

Cold War Truss declares 'age of engagement with Russia is over'

Harry Cockburn
Why today's energy
strategy will fail

Rebecca Thomas
Bullying and racism
revealed in the NHS

Cathy Newman
MPs lag behind the
public on climate

Mark Critchley
Luis Diaz pays off
for Liverpool

The chancellor with his partner, whose family business is estimated to be worth around £3.5bn

Sunak's wife avoids tax through non-dom status

Akshata Murthy may have saved millions on foreign earnings

EXCLUSIVE
ANNA ISAAC
ECONOMICS EDITOR

Rishi Sunak's wife has claimed
non-domicile status in order to
save on her tax bill, *The
Independent* understands.
Akshata Murthy, whose family

business is estimated to be
worth £3.5bn, has continued
to use the status even after Mr
Sunak was put in charge of
setting taxes for the country in
February 2020, according to
two people familiar with her
financial arrangements. It
could have saved her millions

in tax over several years, claim
sources. A representative of
Mr Sunak did not respond to
requests for comment. In a
statement issued after
publication, a spokesperson for
Ms Murthy said she had to use
non-dom status because of her
Indian citizenship.

The April 2022 *Independent* scoop disclosing that Akshata Murthy was a 'non-dom' who did not pay UK tax on
her foreign earnings. Although legal, the revelation was hugely damaging. Other than Sunak, only three people
with government connections officially knew about Murthy's tax affairs. Who leaked the story? © *The Independent*

Sunak and Liz Truss during the first Tory leadership contest of 2022. One of Sunak's allies says that during the campaign 'she was very frosty towards him and didn't talk to him much, if at all'. Her victory was not the landslide that had been predicted. She quit 10 Downing Street after six weeks, leading to his premiership. It's understood they haven't spoken since November 2022.
© Jacob King/PA Images/Alamy Stock Photo

Sunak making his first speech as Prime Minister on 25 October 2022. He said his government would have 'integrity, professionalism and accountability at every level'. These words were used against him repeatedly as he dealt with Cabinet resignations and sackings during his first months in charge.
© Leon Neal/Getty Images

In October 2022, President Joe Biden hailed the arrival of a British Asian to No. 10, saying it was a 'groundbreaking milestone'. He then blundered by calling the new Prime Minister 'Rashid Sanook'. Sunak has continued to court him anyway. © Niall Carson/Pool/Getty Images

Sunak met Volodymyr Zelenskyy twice during his first six months in Downing Street. Under his premiership, Britain's support for Ukraine has been stronger than that of any other western nation in providing weapons to take on Russia. © Ukrainian presidency/Anadolu Agency via Getty Images

King Charles III had met Sunak – the second Prime Minister of his reign – before succeeding his mother as monarch in September 2022. They are said to get on well. © Jonathan Brady/Pool/AFP via Getty Images

It would be just the two of them. It happened regularly the whole way through Boris's premiership. And the first time Boris got Covid and was very ill, he worked in Rishi's No. 11 study because he could come down from his flat and go straight into Rishi's study without coming into contact with anyone else. Allowing someone to take over your study is surely indicative of a functional relationship on Rishi's part. In terms of the pace and scale of decision-making, this was the most pressure any government had faced since the Second World War and that was an inherently bonding experience for Boris and Rishi.

The hardest decision facing Johnson was what steps should be taken next to deal with the public health crisis, and by early October it was clear that he thought things would get worse before they got better as far as infection rates were concerned. He used a BBC interview to indicate that the approaching winter was going to be demanding. Then, on the evening of 31 October, he announced that there would be a second national lockdown to prevent a 'medical and moral disaster' for the NHS. Subject to a parliamentary vote, it would begin on 5 November and expire on 2 December, after which further lockdowns would be implemented on a local and regional basis according to data and trends. The government won the lockdown vote by 516 votes to thirty-eight, but what must have bothered Johnson was that thirty-four of the thirty-eight MPs who opposed it were Conservatives. Sunak backed it, but he did so reluctantly, having warned publicly on 14 October against 'rushing to another lockdown'. In March 2023, the *Daily Telegraph* published a leaked cache of 100,000 Covid-19 era WhatsApp messages from Matt Hancock's telephone. In one, Hancock speculated that Sunak took this position as a way of 'showing ankle to the hard right'. This form of words not only emphasises the men's very different attitudes to the crisis but also shows that those, like Sunak, who went against the political orthodoxy of the time risked being thought of even by their own colleagues as extremists.

As it turned out, the second lockdown period was a time of great upheaval for Johnson, but not for reasons he could have necessarily anticipated. In the space of three days that November, his two senior aides, Dominic Cummings and Lee Cain, resigned from Downing Street. Cummings had already told Johnson over the summer of his intention to quit on 18 December, meaning he walked out five weeks early, but Cain's exit came as a shock. They attributed their decisions to what they saw as the meddlesome behaviour and destructive scheming of Johnson's partner, Carrie. Johnson begged Cain to stay on, but he refused. It all made for the sort of plotline upon which the press thrives.

Sunak stayed well away from such drama, busying himself with his forthcoming Spending Review, which was to be delivered to the House of Commons on 25 November. In late October, the Treasury had won an arm wrestle with No. 10 which forced the cancellation of the customary three-year Spending Review in favour of just a one-year settlement. This decision blew a hole in Johnson's well-publicised plan to 'level up' the nation via a series of New Deal-type infrastructure projects costing £100 billion. As Sunak saw it, the Covid crisis meant Britain could not afford to set departmental budgets and devolved area grants so far into the future. This conclusion was reached as it was revealed that government borrowing for the first half of the financial year had ballooned to a mind-boggling £208.5 billion. Johnson was forced to accept the situation and, to Sunak's relief, many of the PM's pet projects, including an eccentric plan to build a bridge between Northern Ireland and Scotland, went up in smoke. After fifty Tory MPs in northern seats set up a pressure group called the Northern Research Group, however, Sunak did agree to make exceptions for 'signature' manifesto commitments in order to avoid risking a north–south schism within the parliamentary party.

Three days before he delivered his Spending Review, Sunak gave an interview to the *Sunday Times* which shed further light on the very different economic philosophies of himself and his leader. Although the article spelled out that his priorities as Chancellor were to protect as many jobs as possible, to spend money on combating the virus, and to focus on regional levelling-up funding, he again indicated that spending cuts and tax rises were on the horizon. It was put to him that achieving this would not be straightforward given that Johnson had just overruled him in three areas: a new defence settlement that would see spending increase by £16.5 billion over four years; extending the furlough scheme; and maintaining the pensions 'triple lock'. Johnson's insistence on the implementation of these schemes prompted one senior Tory MP to tell the *Daily Telegraph*, 'The man's gone mad. Along with Hancock and Gove, they're behaving like drunks on a Friday night. It's like Monopoly money. There are a great many Tories taking Rishi aside and saying: "This has got to stop."' Sunak appeared to have taken the MPs' pleas on board, for in an unguarded moment he joked to the *Sunday Times*, 'Maybe I should take [Johnson's] credit card away.' Not everyone thought he was speaking in jest.

When it came to the Spending Review itself, Sunak did not try to mask the scale of the situation. During his twenty-five minutes at the despatch box, he said the government was providing £280 billion in 2020 alone to get the country through the coronavirus crisis. He revealed that the economy would likely contract by 11.3 per cent – the largest fall in output for more than 300 years. And to add salt to the wound, he estimated that borrowing could reach an extraordinary £394 billion, equivalent to 19 per cent of GDP and the highest level in peacetime history. Yet in a move which delighted Red Wall Tories but angered others in the party, notably former Prime Ministers Sir John Major and David Cameron, he said that the overseas aid budget would be cut from 0.7 per cent of GDP to 0.5 per cent. This £4 billion saving was to be spent on the levelling-up fund, including road and rail projects in northern England. Sunak also designated £55 billion to deal with Covid during the following year, ensuring job support would carry on until April 2021.

While there was no detailed talk of tax rises, 1.3 million public sector workers were told that they faced a pay freeze the following year. An exception was made for NHS doctors and nurses, while the 2.1 million public sector workers who were paid less than the median wage of £24,000 would also receive a £250 pay rise. And a UK infrastructure bank to finance major new projects was to be established in the north of England. Sunak said that total government department spending in 2021 would be £540 billion, with day-to-day departmental spending rising by 3.8 per cent in real terms. Some might have felt that Christmas had come early, but Sunak was determined that nobody should be lulled into a false sense of security. 'Our health emergency is not yet over,' he said gravely. 'And our economic emergency has only just begun. This situation is clearly unsustainable over the medium term.' Again, the warning sign of tax rises was hard to miss.

Sunak had recently told the *Yorkshire Post* how 'lonely' he found his work 'because your job is to say no a lot'. Yet it would turn out to be Johnson, whose reputation for profligacy suggested he had little conception of the word 'no' when it came to public spending, who presented a major obstacle to Sunak's plans for nursing the economy back to health. As a Chancellor who was in favour of low taxes rather than high spending, Sunak was about to find out that his biggest political tests were still to come.

CHAPTER 23

HIGHS AND LOWS

Christmas 2020 should have been a time of joy and optimism. On 2 December, just three days before the official end of the second national lockdown, Boris Johnson announced that a mass immunisation programme would begin imminently after Britain had become the first country to approve an anti-Covid vaccine. No other single piece of news could have provided such light in the gloom of that winter and on 8 December, Margaret Keenan, a ninety-year-old from Coventry, became the first person in the world to receive the Pfizer Covid-19 jab. Although Britain was not out of the woods, and Sunak had just been obliged to extend the furlough scheme until 30 April 2021, things were looking up. Then a fresh blow was delivered. On 18 December, Johnson called an emergency meeting of the Covid-O Cabinet sub-committee. Sunak, Michael Gove and Matt Hancock were among the attendees who were told by government scientists Chris Whitty and Patrick Vallance that a previously unknown coronavirus strain had been detected. It was thought to be 70 per cent more transmissible and was already responsible for most new infections in London and the south-east. Fearing a large wave of deaths, Johnson declared at a press conference on 19 December that he must impose an immediate two-week lockdown in these areas. For one third of the population, Christmas was cancelled.

Apart from crushing the nation's collective spirit at such an important time of the year, this unwelcome development put Sunak under renewed pressure. Thousands of businesses, especially those in the hospitality sector which depended on Christmas trade, would face extra financial burdens and so, by extension, would the Chancellor, who would have to sanction bailing them out. It had been pointed out to him by a journalist just a few days previously that he had borrowed more money during his ten months in the Treasury than his famously high-spending Labour predecessor Gordon Brown had done in the space of nine years. Now, despite the public debt exceeding 100 per cent of GDP after the seemingly endless rounds of business loans and job retention programmes – to say nothing of the suspension of tax collection – more money would be required.

In fact, immediately before Johnson's shock announcement of the Christmas lockdown, Sunak had been sufficiently unhappy about the general economic picture that he had agreed to give an interview to *The Spectator*'s editor, Fraser Nelson, in his Downing Street office. There, he was able to show off the portraits of three of his political heroes: the 1950s Labour Chancellor Hugh Gaitskell, who, like Sunak, was a Eurosceptic alumnus of Winchester College; William Gladstone, who served four times as a Liberal Chancellor in the nineteenth century and whose fiscal conservatism Sunak praised; and Nigel Lawson, the tax-reforming Tory Chancellor of the 1980s, whose economic assessments Sunak still reads. In between expressing his admiration for this trio, he spoke about the problems facing Britain. 'It is clearly not sustainable to borrow at these levels,' he said. 'I don't think morally, economically or politically it would be right.' He also emphasised his belief that it would be foolhardy for the government to rely on the 0.3 per cent interest rate it was paying to service its vast borrowings remaining so low. At this time, many economists around the world took the view that low interest rates were here to stay. Yet Sunak went against the grain and warned – presciently, as it would turn out – that rates might easily rise, triggered by a nasty bout of inflation. 'Are you or anyone else going to guarantee me that, for the duration of this parliament, rates might not go back to 1 per cent?' he asked.

> There is this very large QE thing that's going on. No one has done that before. There are plenty of smart investors who are also thinking about the risks of inflation over the next twelve months. Because we are now so levered, small changes have huge cash implications. If I have to come up with £10–£20 billion a year in a few years' time because things have changed – well, that's a lot of money.

In his view, interest rates might easily rise. This point went to the core of his credo as a politician who is inherently cautious, and he spoke of the consequences of long-term borrowing and rising debt. 'If we think borrowing is the answer to everything, that debt rising is fine, then there's not much difference between us and the Labour Party,' he added. 'I worry about what that means for us politically down the line.'

Aside from the debt mountain, there was more bad news. On 4 January 2021, Johnson announced a third lockdown in England. It would last until 8 March. Businesses in the retail, hospitality and leisure sectors were closed in order to help control the virus, requiring Sunak to sign off £4.6 billion in new grants to help support them during the spring. A similar sum for these sectors followed in late February, when Johnson unveiled the government's 'roadmap' to ease lockdown restrictions in England by June. The previous autumn, Johnson had ruled out any tax rises, but, as we shall see, that didn't mean he wouldn't expect Sunak to help him endow further public sector projects in 2021.

Throughout the early weeks of the new year, Sunak's principal preoccupation was his Budget, which was to be delivered on 3 March. When Johnson and Sunak 'agreed' that the triple tax lock should be maintained in keeping with the 2019 Conservative Party manifesto, freezing rates of income tax, National Insurance and VAT, some Treasury officials saw this as surrender on Sunak's part, and used the decision to brief journalists that all was not well at the top of government. The *Financial Times* reported that a government insider had told colleagues on a conference call that 'not for the first or last time, the tensions are real' between 10 and 11 Downing Street. The consequence of the decision was that business taxes might have to rise instead, and rumours of further tax hikes swirled. Separate pleas urging the government not to increase any taxes straight away were made by a range of figures including David Cameron and Sir Keir Starmer. Resistance also came from Tory MPs inside and outside the Cabinet. Yet six months of polling and focus group research had gone into this set-piece financial statement, together with the input of more than 100 backbenchers whom Sunak had consulted. Through all this, he had concluded that what the public wanted most of all was frankness about the status quo – a sentiment that chimed with his own inclinations.

One person who worked with Sunak at the time recalls:

That was a Budget we were building up to psychologically for months because we knew we were going to have to do some hard stuff on tax, we knew it was going to be difficult for the party. We'd done a lot of work in terms of laying the ground. Rishi had been warning publicly that raising tax was on the cards.

Two days before he stood at the despatch box, a five-minute film was released by the Treasury telling the story of Sunak's extraordinary first year as Chancellor. As Johnson scarcely featured in the video, it was written off by his admirers as just another piece of self-publicity from the thrusting Young Turk in No. 11 who wanted to become Prime Minister. But those who watched it closely noted that, at the end of the film, Sunak repeated the mantra the focus groups had generated: 'At the heart of this Budget will be honesty and fairness.' And those familiar with the way Sunak's hero William Gladstone approached his stewardship of the economy were aware that one of the principles of 'sound finance' required Chancellors to be transparent so that Parliament and the people knew of the revenue obligation and the levels of taxation needed to fund it.

Just as Britain had been the first country in the world to embark on a vaccine programme, so Sunak's Budget made him the first Finance Minister of any major global economy to announce a plan to fix the nation's battered economy following its worst downturn for more than 300 years. 'Coronavirus has caused one of the largest, most comprehensive and sustained economic shocks this country has ever faced,' he told a sparsely attended, socially distanced House of Commons. He said that the well-run vaccine rollout had allowed the Office for Budget Responsibility to predict that the economy would recover by mid-2022, six months sooner than it had previously forecast. Unemployment was also expected to be lower than feared, though he did confirm that the furlough scheme would be extended again, until September 2021, some eighteen months after it had been introduced. Fuel and alcohol duty would be frozen. The minimum wage would rise to £8.91 per hour. And grants and tax breaks were promised to a wide range of struggling firms. The measures to support the economy that he announced that day amounted to £65 billion over the next two years, taking the total government support to a staggering £407 billion at a time when output was down by almost 10 per cent. With the triple tax lock unaffected and millions of jobs protected, this Budget – in which government expenditure was forecast to exceed £1 trillion – was immediately rated as being the most generous in Britain's peacetime history.

Ever the pragmatist, however, Sunak sounded the alarm again about the effects of future interest rate rises, using his doubts to justify raising the corporation tax rate from 19 per cent to 25 per cent from April 2023 and freezing the basic income tax threshold at £12,500 and the higher rate at £50,000. This £21 billion tax raid meant that another 1.3 million people would be paying tax by 2026, with 1 million more becoming higher-rate taxpayers. Such bitter pills could not be sweetened, but, as Sunak noted, a 1 per cent rise in interest rates would add more than £20 billion to Britain's debt bill within a few years. These were the biggest tax rises in Britain for thirty years, forcing rates up to their highest levels since the 1960s. So-called Middle England would be hit hard, as critical commentators were quick to point out, but Sunak believed he had no choice.

After he had finished speaking, he took the unprecedented step for a Chancellor of holding a live post-Budget press conference. Confronting any criticism about the tax rises head-on, he repeated the key message generated by the focus groups: 'I know the British people don't like tax rises, nor do I. But I also know they dislike dishonesty even more. That's why I've been honest with you about the problem we have and our plan to fix it.' Such unusual candour went down well with the taxpaying public: the first post-Budget poll to be published two days later gave the Tories a thirteen-point lead over Labour, up four points in a week. The same YouGov poll for *The Times* also found that more people preferred the idea of Sunak as Prime Minister than favoured Boris Johnson, by a margin of 28 per cent to 26 per cent. Sunak's desire to connect with the public by whatever means, which he had discussed with the BBC the previous year, seemed to have paid off. Indeed, the day after the Budget, it was reported that he had even become a pin-up of the experimental artists Gilbert & George, who revealed they had four images of him on a wall of their east London studio.

'We got through the Budget well enough, the country seemed to accept it, and the party was similarly accepting,' says a former adviser.

He picked two taxes to raise that were the least unpopular with the public to fill the Covid black hole to try to put the finances on a steadier footing. That Budget landed pretty well because corporation tax doesn't affect 90 per cent of businesses, only the really big companies which had had a lot of help during the pandemic anyway. Rishi thought, 'If we're wise for the next couple of years, we can cut taxes at the end of the parliament.' He believed that Budget was finished business.

There was to be no such luck, however. The government was soon criticised for not addressing funding problems in the social care sector, with many pensioners still being forced to sell their home or use their life savings to afford the help they needed. Those familiar with the often threadbare services that were in place for the elderly were not shy about amplifying their feelings, particularly as it was estimated at that time that up to 30,000 people had died in care homes as a result of Covid-19. Campaigners said that a combination of Britain's ageing population and public spending cuts over the previous decade had created a time bomb, pushing increasing numbers of vulnerable people towards hospitals, where they could become stranded for months on end.

As part of the BBC's post-Budget scrutiny, it was pointed out to Sunak in a Radio 4 *Today* programme interview that in Johnson's first ever speech as Prime Minister, in July 2019, he had declared, 'I am announcing now – on the steps of Downing Street – that we will fix the crisis in social care once and for all with a clear plan we have prepared to give every older person the dignity and security they deserve.' This commitment had also featured in the Conservative Party manifesto in 2019. Knowing how little time Johnson had devoted to this subject since he had uttered those words, and that no public funding was immediately available to tackle a problem which would require in excess of £10 billion each year, there was nothing for Sunak to say other than that proposals were still being worked on and that 'obviously right now our focus is the pandemic'.

Suddenly, Johnson had a political problem to solve, and he would require Sunak's help to find a solution. This acted as a prompt for the issue to be addressed and costed, but it would reveal some important differences between them that would fundamentally alter Sunak's relationship with Johnson.

*   *   *

Two weeks later, Sunak had an uncharacteristic brush with trouble. A multi-million-pound financial services firm called Greensill Capital, run by Australian businessman Lex Greensill, went into administration. This was newsworthy because it transpired that David Cameron, a paid adviser to this company with a personal stake in it once valued at £70 million, had spent four months of 2020 informally lobbying members of the government and civil servants. Cameron hoped this might lead to official rules being changed so that Greensill Capital could qualify for the Covid Corporate Financing Facility (CCFF), a taxpayer-backed loan scheme. One of those he had tapped for help was Sunak. Ultimately, these efforts were in vain after Greensill Capital was turned down for CCFF funding. That did not stop journalists and opposition MPs wanting to find out more about the former Prime Minister's attempts at persuasion.

In early April 2021, shortly after Sunak's name emerged in newspaper reports in connection with Cameron's lobbying activities, Sunak opted for openness and published his replies to text messages Cameron had sent him. The most compromising message read: 'I think the proposals in the end did require a change to the market notice but I have pushed the team to explore an alternative with the Bank that might work.

No guarantees, but the Bank are currently looking at it and Charles [Roxburgh] should be in touch. Best, Rishi.' It was hardly the stick of dynamite for which the scandal-seekers had been hoping.

Nevertheless, three separate inquiries into the wider Greensill Capital matter were set in motion, including one by MPs on the Treasury Select Committee, who demanded that Sunak give evidence to them. When he duly appeared on 26 May, he was able to cope easily with dozens of questions about his handling of Cameron's approach to him, what happened as a result of it, and whether Cameron's links to Greensill Capital meant that his concerns were given priority over those of other firms. None of this fazed Sunak. Indeed, if anything, it was Cameron who was compromised by Sunak's evidence session, as Sunak expressed his puzzlement at having been contacted by the former Prime Minister in the first place. 'I don't know David Cameron very well at all,' Sunak told the committee bluntly. 'I don't think I have spoken to him since I was a backbench MP and he was PM, so it was a surprise to receive the message.' He could have added that Cameron's lobbying was not brilliantly timed, given he was often working sixteen hours a day to save the British economy.

Sunak faced no further scrutiny over Greensill Capital and Cameron was eventually cleared of having acted inappropriately or unlawfully by all three inquiries. Yet with the benefit of hindsight, it could be argued that the Greensill Capital affair showed Sunak to his advantage, strengthening his reputation as a man of probity who would not abuse his position, even when a former Prime Minister in need of a favour came calling. It was soon apparent that such integrity was not confined to Sunak's link to a past occupant of 10 Downing Street. For while the Greensill Capital story was running hot, an unconnected financial irregularity involving Boris Johnson known as 'Wallpapergate' was also unearthed. It had a similarly benign effect on Sunak's reputation.

Wallpapergate centred on the question of how a £112,000 refurbishment of Johnson's Downing Street flat had been funded. The answer was convoluted. Eventually it came to light that initially a Conservative Party donor, Lord Brownlow, had secretly paid for the work. As half of Brownlow's gift had been routed through the Conservative Party at the same time as he made an unrelated £15,000 payment and the Tories had not declared the full value of the donation, however, the Electoral Commission issued a £17,800 fine. The story dragged on for months and was held up as a prime example of Johnson's haywire approach to matters of transparency. It was certainly an unhelpful distraction for the government and personally embarrassing for Johnson – but not for Sunak.

At an early stage, Bridget Phillipson, the shadow Chief Secretary to the Treasury, tabled a parliamentary question asking whether any refurbishments or redecorations had been requested for Sunak's official residences since he became Chancellor. The Labour Party hoped this would uncover a similarly unconventional set of arrangements to Johnson's, but it turned out that Sunak had funded the refurbishment of his Downing Street flat, where he lived with his wife and two daughters, personally, whereas one former and one serving Conservative Prime Minister were exposed in short order for what was taken as dishonourable conduct.

The negative attention that Johnson's administration received courtesy of both matters that spring was bruising. So, too, was a BBC report from the same period alleging that

Johnson had assured the businessman Sir James Dyson by text message that his employees would not have to pay extra tax if they came to the UK to make ventilators during the pandemic. Sunak was thought by No. 10 to have been involved in leaking Dyson's message, but one person who is familiar with the matter strongly denies this was the case. The cumulative effect of these stories began to make some senior Conservative Party figures nervous of sleaze accusations. Surprisingly, however, 6 May 2021 marked something of a high point for the governing party – perhaps the last it truly enjoyed under Johnson.

On that day, elections for local councils were held in England, for the London Assembly and Mayor, in the Scottish and Welsh Parliaments, for seven 'metro mayors' and for police and crime commissioners. There was also a Westminster by-election in Hartlepool. In England, the Conservative Party performed best, gaining eleven additional councils and 234 new councillors, while Labour lost control of ten councils and lost 326 councillors. And remarkably, after fifty-seven years as a Labour-held constituency, Hartlepool turned blue, with the Tories securing more than 50 per cent of the vote and a sixteen-point swing. It was only the second time since 1982 that the governing party had gained a seat in a by-election. With the Labour Party under Sir Keir Starmer apparently going backwards, Johnson's aides and colleagues began briefing the press that he was confident of spending at least a decade in power. Amid the euphoria, some of them even suggested that he might serve for longer than the eleven and a half years achieved by Margaret Thatcher, if he so desired. In the immediate aftermath of these undoubtedly handsome victories, which crowned the eighty-seat majority secured by the Conservatives almost eighteen months earlier, Johnson himself stated that he was to pursue the 'massive project' of 'levelling up' Britain, indicating that this was something which his predecessors had tried and failed to do. This policy, which had featured in the 2019 manifesto, apparently included social care reform.

Two weeks earlier it had been reported that Johnson and Sunak had met to discuss the social care issue which had proved so problematic straight after the Budget. It was claimed that Johnson was considering reheating an old idea that would cap at £45,000 the amount an individual must contribute towards their own care, with the state footing the remainder of the bill. No definitive costing existed, however. And, more to the point, Sunak was sceptical of how any of this could be paid for given the dire state of the public finances. With an eye on long-term implications, he also knew that the demographic data suggested social care would become more expensive over time, not less, because of Britain's ageing population. He was opposed to a tax rise, which left a spending cut or further borrowing as the only alternatives. He favoured neither option.

Others would not let the matter drop, adding to the pressure. On 11 May, Parliament gathered for the Queen's Speech, in which the government's legislative priorities for the new session were set out. In the ensuing parliamentary debate, Johnson was challenged by Theresa May, who pointed out that there had been no mention of how to address Britain's social care problems. The monarch's speech had included only nine words on the subject: 'Proposals on social care reform will be brought forward.' Behind the scenes, the twitchiness between Johnson and Sunak on this topic alone was growing.

'I remember it getting very difficult in the spring of 2021, when Boris started talking about social care,' says one who had a ringside seat.

Boris wanted to announce his social care plan in July. He basically said, 'I made a pledge on the steps of No. 10 to fix it, and fixing it could be something good for my legacy.' But there was no real thought behind it and it was absolutely the wrong time to do it because the pandemic had cost the nation £400 billion. Boris just wanted to make a speech and have something to talk about, but he didn't care whether it stood up to scrutiny. That was when it really became clear that Johnson's motivations were not what they should be for someone who was leading the country.

According to this source, Sunak told Johnson:

You're the PM; if you think this policy is right, I'll back it. But as your Chancellor I'm telling you that you can't borrow £10 billion a year – and even more down the line – because we can't afford it. If we're not cutting anything, the only way to fund it is to put up National Insurance contributions (NICs).

It seems likely that he was reflecting the orthodox view of the Treasury as much as expressing his own feelings, yet Sunak did not want to put taxes up, and he made this plain. For one thing, raising NICs would break a manifesto pledge. He thought Johnson would understand this, but apparently he didn't. The source goes on:

Boris wanted the policy but did not think through the implication of the tax rise. He just wanted to announce the plan to coincide with the second anniversary of his arrival in Downing Street. He wanted to do it around that time. That was a motivating factor in the July deadline.

Another friend says:

> Boris wasn't interested in the cost of things and suddenly
> here was someone laying out the cost and the economic im-
> plications. Boris thought, 'Why do we have to pay for it? Let's
> just say we've done it and tick the box. The policy will get us
> through the day.' Rishi thought that in fifteen or twenty years'
> time, this policy will have become cripplingly expensive and
> you can't just keep borrowing the money. Rishi is the kind
> of person who likes to be covered for eventualities. He is not
> comfortable putting himself in the position where one bad
> day can blow you off course and leave you unable to pay your
> bills. Interest rates globally were very low at this point. Boris
> was very seduced by the argument that was gaining traction,
> especially among economists on the right, that interest rates
> globally are going to be lower for longer, so we should be
> much more relaxed about borrowing, it would almost be
> rude not to and so on. Rishi said the reasons that rates have
> been so low are disappearing ... He was aware of all the var-
> ious complicated factors that were in play at the time. This is
> why they ended up increasing National Insurance.

While this argument played out, Johnson had other difficulties
to face. On 26 May, his former chief aide Dominic Cummings
appeared in front of the House of Commons Health and Science Committees. During a seven-hour session, he lambasted
Johnson, accusing him of being 'unfit' for office for failing to
take the pandemic seriously enough. He also claimed that the
Prime Minister was obsessed with the media and so indecisive
that he resembled a 'shopping trolley smashing from one side
of the aisle to the other'. Matt Hancock, the Health Secretary,

was also subjected to a verbal pummelling, with Cummings alleging he had lied to the public and to ministers and was guilty of 'criminal' behaviour. Sunak, however, received nothing but praise, as Cummings acknowledged his hard work and competence. Cummings did, however, lob a grenade by suggesting that Sunak and Johnson did not get on. 'Like lots of us, he [Sunak] was completely at his wits' end about the shopping trolley,' Cummings agitated. When Sunak was asked by the *Mail on Sunday* a few days later if he really did have reservations about Johnson's leadership, he said, 'The PM's got an exceptionally hard job which I see up close every day.' As supportive statements go, it was not exactly ebullient.

Although Sunak's working relationship with Johnson was under strain by this point, he had been enjoying a far more harmonious rapport with politicians internationally, notably the American Treasury Secretary, Janet Yellen. Having established a consensus among EU countries that multinational digital firms including Amazon and Google should pay tax in every country in which they operated, rather than where they booked profits, he used his diplomatic skills to sell this idea to the American government. It had opposed the plan, which had been debated for almost a decade, but, thanks in part to Sunak's lobbying, Washington agreed to the idea in principle in return for the setting of a global corporation tax rate of at least 15 per cent for the biggest companies, which would take effect from 2023.

During the first weekend in June 2021, Sunak hosted the G7 Finance Ministers' meeting in London, where both planks of this mooted deal were announced. It was hailed as a 'historic' step towards tax becoming fairer. From Sunak's perspective, his reputation as a man who could get things done was similarly enhanced. Coming so soon after Cummings's attempted political assassination of Johnson, the stars certainly seemed to have aligned for the Chancellor once again.

Johnson then swung into action as host of the G7 summit in Cornwall, telling world leaders in his opening speech that, post-Covid, he wanted to 'build back better, greener, fairer and in a more gender-neutral and perhaps a more feminine way'. Nobody knew what this would mean in practice, but he did champion his personal commitment to working towards decarbonising Britain by 2050. He also used the occasion to peddle an environmental Marshall Plan in which poorer nations would receive funding from richer ones to tackle global warming. The idea was based on the Marshall Plan of the 1940s, in which America helped to rebuild European economies that had been shattered by the Second World War. Significantly, the Treasury let it be known that Sunak had not been consulted over this proposal, again emphasising a grow-ing distance between the two men.

Soon after, there was a further setback for the nation when Johnson announced that the plan to end Covid restrictions in England on 21 June, so-called 'Freedom Day', had been axed. Instead, the government said the measures would remain in place until at least 19 July because of concern over rising cases and the fast-spreading Delta variant. The vaccine roll-out had been hugely successful, with almost 80 per cent of the adult population having received at least one shot by this point. This provided Johnson with grounds for optimism, but he remained realistic. 'We cannot simply eliminate Covid,' he said at a press conference. 'We must learn to live with it.' It did not go unnoticed that this was an echo of Sunak's line about learning to 'live without fear' some nine months previously. Within days, Sunak told reporters that he was looking forward to not having to wear a face mask 'as soon as possible'. He also ramped up pressure on Johnson by declaring his belief that 'Freedom Day' would not be postponed again. 'It was a specific extension for a specific purpose, which was to get some more jabs into more people's arms,' he said. 'We're accomplishing that, so it just shouldn't be necessary to delay any further.'

In mid-June, a new television channel, GB News, was launched under the chairmanship of Andrew Neil, who doubled up as its lead presenter. Interest in the enterprise was considerable, and Sunak was the first front-rank politician Neil interviewed during its opening week on air. If this was a tribute to Sunak's high standing in British politics, Neil did not show him any further deference as he grilled him over vast government spending and the true cost of Boris Johnson's green agenda. On the former point, Sunak backed the government's pensions triple lock, which guaranteed the state pension would rise by whichever was the highest out of wage growth, inflation or 2.5 per cent. Yet he appeared to do so through gritted teeth, for wages had increased by an average of 8.4 per cent thanks to the artificial inflation created by Covid, meaning the pension bill would rocket by £7 billion. Johnson was known to be opposed to upsetting the over-65s, a key group of Tory voters, though Sunak was privately keen to scrap the pledge for the good of the economy. Neither did Sunak have a firm response to Neil's charge that Johnson's pledge to decarbonise Britain by 2050 would cost an estimated £1 trillion. He appeared to take a cautious approach to the net zero policy in general and, unlike other politicians, did not advocate households switch from gas boilers to heat pumps. He was not alone in being unable to defend a policy whose financial cost was seemingly incalculable.

If there was any doubt by this stage of the increasingly divergent views held by Johnson and Sunak when it came to economic matters, Neil arguably did Sunak a favour by inviting him to confirm this fact. He asked if he would describe himself as a 'big government Conservative' like Johnson or a 'fiscal Conservative'. Sunak replied, 'Of course I'm a fiscal Conservative. It's not my money, it is other people's money and I take my responsibility for that very seriously.'

This remark was particularly pertinent at the time because another source of friction was building between the pair, in this instance over Johnson's desire to commission a new royal yacht. The price of this pet project – for which there was no great clamour – was estimated at £200 million, plus tens of millions annually in running costs. In the context of Covid these might have been considered small sums, but the idea had been mentioned publicly without any discussion with the Treasury about funding, to Sunak's profound irritation. The Cabinet Office and the Department for International Trade also thought it a non-starter. One of Sunak's allies recalls:

> It's so indicative of Boris that he pushed to have the new royal yacht. The *Daily Telegraph* wrote about it endlessly. Everyone thought it was crazy, but nobody put up a fight. We all thought Boris was doing it because he wanted the *Telegraph* and *The Sun* to talk about how wonderful Boris is. It was a classic example of Boris doing a project to get some nice headlines.

In Johnson's defence, he may have thought some positive coverage about a 'fun' project was desirable, especially after the diabolical result of the Chesham and Amersham by-election, held on 17 June following the death of the veteran MP Dame Cheryl Gillan. This traditionally Conservative-voting seat, which had been held in 2019 with a majority of 16,000 votes, was lost to the Liberal Democrats in a result that stunned Westminster and alarmed Tory strategists. Reaction against local planning reforms and moves to build hundreds of houses in the area played a major role in the upset. Even so, it showed the governing party to be woefully out of touch with its core vote. Further by-election disappointment followed two weeks later, on 1 July, when the Labour Party held the West Yorkshire constituency of Batley and Spen following the resignation of Tracy Brabin. Although the Conservatives had been tipped to take the seat following their recent success in Hartlepool, they fell short by 323 votes. Far worse electoral outcomes would have to be endured by the Tories before Christmas.

Just before Parliament rose for the summer, Johnson and Sunak met to finalise and then announce the plan they had devised for the contentious social care reforms that had dominated the previous few months. After Matt Hancock was forced to resign as Health Secretary in late June for being caught on camera in an extra-marital clinch with his colleague Gina Coladangelo – breaking lockdown rules in the process – Johnson had intended to unveil the scheme with Sunak and the new Health Secretary, Sajid Javid. On 17 July, however, fate intervened. Javid tested positive for Covid and was required to self-isolate, as were Johnson and Sunak. There was no choice but to delay the announcement until Parliament returned in September.

From a political perspective, this turn of events did not work in Johnson's favour. Although 'Freedom Day' was duly marked on 19 July, unleashing a wave of elation, a Cabinet revolt had been fermenting over Johnson's rumoured acceptance that social care reform could be funded by an increase in National Insurance contributions. This new tax, Johnson trusted, would raise the £10 billion or so a year that was needed. But, egged on by the International Trade Secretary, Liz Truss, dissent spilled onto the airwaves. Kwasi Kwarteng, the Business Secretary, gave an interview to Sky News on 22 July pouring cold water on the idea as he pointed out that the Conservative manifesto had promised National Insurance would be frozen for the duration of the parliament. And the electorate, who would have to pay for the social care reform scheme via this extra tax, appeared to be of a similar cast of mind. The policy, or perhaps the row that surrounded it, may have contributed to the Tories' falling poll lead – down from thirteen points to four according to a survey for *The Times* published on 24 July.

The general sense of disarray at the heart of government leeched into August, compounding the erosion of trust between Johnson and Sunak. This was most evident when a letter Sunak had written to his Downing Street neighbour in late July urging him to ease coronavirus travel restrictions was leaked to the press. In the letter, Sunak warned Johnson that the UK was 'out of step' with EU countries and raised concerns that overly zealous border controls were damaging the economy. Astonishingly, Johnson did not read the letter. The first he heard of it was when it was splashed on the front page of the *Sunday Times* several days later. He is said to have been so angry about the leak that he told twelve colleagues who had gathered for a meeting that he had been thinking of demoting Sunak to Health Secretary, hinting that he might now do so. Even if he was not being entirely serious, his assumption that Sunak was behind the briefing spoke volumes about where things stood between them. In fact, it was wide of the mark. For Sunak's letter had also been copied to the Department for Transport, and it soon became known that one of its staff, rather than anybody on Sunak's side, had passed it to a reporter. 'Johnson obviously thought we'd leaked it,' a Treasury figure recalls. 'We hadn't. But such a misunderstanding clearly exacerbated the breakdown of his and Rishi's relationship.'

Kevin Hollinrake, the Conservative MP for Thirsk and Malton, whose seat borders Sunak's, recalls the occasion well. He and his wife were having dinner with the Sunaks that night at the Star Inn at Harome, on the edge of the North Yorkshire Moors. 'Rishi was on the phone to Boris for over an hour,' Hollinrake says.

> You could tell the situation was tense, but Rishi stayed very calm. We were in a private dining area. He just sat at the table while this conversation took place and the rest of us sat there and chatted away and just carried on. So we heard his side of the conversation. It was obviously a pretty difficult conversation, but he didn't lose his temper. Rishi is very passionate and committed. When something happens that doesn't fit with his plans, he can get a bit short-tempered and stroppy. I was impressed in that situation that he didn't get into an argument. He just stated his side of the story. Otherwise he wouldn't have been able to stay in the restaurant. People would have heard.

There have been tensions between almost every Chancellor and Prime Minister in modern political history, of course, but the difference in this context was that whereas Sunak was eager to tackle Britain's national debt, which stood at a record high of more than £2 trillion, Johnson appeared to be less attuned to the concepts of discipline and sacrifice involved in improving the country's fiscal position. His goals of 'levelling up', decarbonising Britain and introducing social care reforms would all cost vast sums of money that did not exist. Sunak's priority was to refire the economy, yet, for the sake of pursuing Johnson's policies, he was being asked to spend increasing amounts of his time working out how to pay for new schemes – without harming the Conservatives' reputation for low taxation. It was an unenviable – indeed, an impossible – balancing act for an instinctively small-state politician like Sunak and it took its toll. Johnson had assumed that Sunak would be biddable. He was very much mistaken.

One ally who worked with Sunak at the time says:

One of the difficult things about Boris is that he likes chaos around him, and that presented itself not just in his staff and those who worked around him but also in the way he governed. One minute there'd be a disaster here; the next a disaster over there. And there was not one iota of discipline. If Rishi hadn't been Boris's Chancellor, and Boris had had a yes man as Chancellor instead, Boris's administration would have ended up going the same way as Liz Truss's. Boris would have happily borrowed to finance things like social care and defence spending here, there and everywhere. There was a whole ream of stuff that he was pushing to do and Rishi resisted it. With Boris, everything is surface-level, short-term. He would ask, 'What headlines am I going to get and will this be good for my legacy?' He never stopped to ask, 'What's the best thing for the country, and what does this mean for the long term?'

Two stories that related to Sunak's personal, rather than political, life also cropped up in August. As a man who is generally protective of his family, this attention was certainly unwanted, even if it was not unexpected for a sitting politician. The first concerned two businesses in which his wife owned shares going into administration, owing a total of £623,000 to HMRC. One was a private members' club called Lava Mayfair Club Limited, which collapsed owing £43.7 million to creditors; the other was an education company called Mrs Wordsmith, which had debts of £16.3 million despite having received a £1.3 million loan from the government's Future Fund. The size of Murthy's investments – and losses – was not revealed. Separately, and more trivially, it emerged that the Sunaks had obtained permission from Hambleton District Council to build a gym, a swimming pool and a tennis court in the grounds of their house in Yorkshire, at a projected cost of £400,000. Sunak had already declared himself in a newspaper interview to be the owner of a Peloton bike and he was known to be a fan of partaking in early morning workouts under the instruction of American fitness coach Cody Rigsby.

While Sunak's supporters were able to bat away these stories, saying they had nothing to do with his job, there is no doubt that they generated further unwelcome interest in his family's financial arrangements – both inside the government and outside it – among the public. As shall become clear, one member of Johnson's inner circle would go on to cast a particularly keen eye over the Sunaks' private affairs. A question mark remains over whether that person acted illegally in doing so.

CHAPTER 24

TAXMAN

It was perhaps inevitable that some of the shine would come off Rishi Sunak's halo sooner or later, and that moment arguably arrived during the first week of September 2021. By then, amid great secrecy, plans for the health and social care levy had been agreed between him, Boris Johnson and Sajid Javid. There would be a 1.25 per cent rise in National Insurance contributions from April 2022 and from April 2023 this charge would become a separate income tax which would appear on employees' payslips as a health and social care tariff. In a last-minute agreement, it was decided that the 1.25 per cent rise would be applicable to dividends from shareholdings as well. Most of the £36 billion this was expected to raise over three years would be used to clear an NHS patient backlog which had mushroomed to 5.5 million during the pandemic, with a remaining £5.4 billion being targeted at social care spending in England. As this plan broke a Tory manifesto pledge not to raise National Insurance, income tax or VAT, it posed fundamental questions about whether the Conservatives had abandoned their status as a low-tax party. When taken in conjunction with the tax rises of the latest Budget, it would leave millions of Britons grappling with a tax burden that had not been higher since the 1970s. This was a defining moment in Johnson's premiership and most of his Cabinet colleagues did not support it. As Sunak was inextricably linked with the scheme, he would have to take some of the flak. One of his most trenchant critics was Liz Truss, who believed that borrowing, rather than taxing, was the way to pay for these new spending commitments. She and Sunak had never been close.

'Rishi didn't want to raise taxes,' reasserts someone who worked for Sunak at the time.

> He could have resigned. I'm sure those close to Boris would spin this differently, but Rishi took the view that if he was working for the PM, and social care reform was something the PM really wanted to do, he would have to go along with it even though his advice was not to do it just at that point. Rishi had told Boris, 'We can't borrow, so it will have to be funded by a tax rise.'

Johnson seemingly called his bluff. When news of the tax rise began to filter out among the Cabinet and further afield, the central criticism voiced was that it would have the biggest financial impact on those with low and middle incomes, while higher earners would be less affected. Sir John Major was one senior figure to intervene, calling the National Insurance increase 'regressive'. Three former Conservative Chancellors – Norman Lamont, Ken Clarke and Philip Hammond – also expressed their dissatisfaction. The only victory Sunak could claim was that a cap of £86,000 would be imposed on the amount an individual would have to spend on care over their lifetime. Johnson had wanted the cap to be set at £50,000, but Sunak successfully held out for the higher figure, reckoning it would save the Treasury £1 billion per year.

Opposition to the 1.25 per cent tax rise was hammered home

on 5 September when an anonymous member of the Cabinet briefed the *Sunday Telegraph* that they thought Johnson and Sunak were 'morally, economically and politically wrong' in seeking to impose it. This stinging attack, which demolished the idea of Cabinet collective responsibility, appeared on page 1 of the newspaper under the headline 'Tories at war over "idiotic" tax increase'. Again, its economic inequalities were cited as a particular concern. 'It makes a total mockery of the levelling-up agenda and Red Wallers will be up in arms,' the briefer went on. 'That's before you even get to the fact that a couple of years ago we promised not to do it.' These were known to be the same opinions as those held by Liz Truss, but influential backbenchers including Steve Baker and Sir Iain Duncan Smith were happy to vent spleen on the record when asked by the newspaper for their opinion. Duncan Smith said, 'If we start raising substantial sums of money without a proper solution, we end up, if we're not careful, as a high-tax, high-spend party and the problem not solved.'

A parliamentary vote would be required to enact the tax rise. When Downing Street put the word out that Johnson might hold a Cabinet reshuffle imminently, this was seen as being not a coincidence but an old trick used to bring recalcitrant MPs to heel. It would prove highly effective.

By 6 September, every Tory-supporting newspaper in the country had condemned the levy. The *Daily Mail* reflected the growing sense of mutiny when it quoted one Cabinet minister who claimed, 'I've seen it reported that five Cabinet ministers are opposed to the idea. The truth is you would struggle to find five of us who are in favour.' That evening, Johnson and Sunak attended a drinks reception in Westminster for the 1922 Committee of backbench MPs. Johnson said nothing about social care directly at the event, instead dwelling on the 'great triumphs' of the summer, including Great Britain's sporting success at the Olympics. Sunak, however, used the occasion to call for MPs to back Johnson. 'I, like all of you, take our lead from the Prime Minister – the leader of our party and the country,' he told the gathering. 'We owe him our support and loyalty. It's fair to say that we've got a tough autumn ahead. That doesn't mean there won't be disagreements, there always are, but we should never lose sight of the central fact that we are a team.'

The first Cabinet meeting of the autumn was held on 7 September. Truss had been expected to offer her thoughts with the same force the anonymous comments in the *Sunday Telegraph* had carried. In the event, she was uncharacteristically restrained, carefully listing the reasons she thought the policy was a mistake but not in such a way as to suggest she might resign. The fire of injustice that had burned in her so brightly over previous days was smouldering. Still, it was noted by those present that her opinions were aimed directly at Sunak. She even turned to face him when speaking. Jacob Rees-Mogg also queried the decision to raise tax, asking why the government couldn't borrow more money instead. To this, Sunak replied that borrowing would break the party's pledge to voters to be fiscally responsible. His stance should not have come as a surprise. After all, in the second speech he ever gave in the Commons in 2015, he had said, 'Whether one is a Thatcherite or a Trotskyite, the rules of budgeting are the same: one cannot sustainably spend more than one earns.'

One person who was present at the meeting recalls:

I remember lots of people who didn't approve of the National Insurance rise didn't say anything. Quite a number were called, but Liz Truss was the first person to say it was a bad idea. She said the Conservatives never win elections by raising taxes and that it was un-Conservative to do so. Jacob and David Frost said something similar. Rishi got pretty shirty, saying he couldn't believe that Conservatives were advocating higher debt. In a Cabinet meeting it was unusual for him to get cross, though he can be quite irritable. He's not somebody who is always good at engaging in a constructive discussion about a policy or about ideas. He can be quite brittle and defensive.

Johnson said he agreed with Truss's points but that he had 'no choice' in how to fund the reform and signalled his intention to press on. In retrospect, who can discount the possibility that personal feelings played some part in his pursuit of this policy? His 79-year-old mother, Charlotte, was frail and would die unexpectedly the following week after being admitted to hospital.

Hours after the Cabinet meeting ended, Johnson was in the Commons announcing the mooted tax rise. Sir Keir Starmer taunted him with the words, 'Read my lips – the Tories can never again claim to be the party of low tax.' This charge was amplified when another manifesto pledge – the pensions triple lock formula – was also compromised that day. In a move that was expected to save up to £5 billion, it was suspended for a year because of the unprecedented rise in earnings after the pandemic.

Johnson, Sunak and Javid, the joint architects of the new health levy, attended a press conference that afternoon to field questions. During it, Johnson justified the tax rise by saying the 'global pandemic was in no one's manifesto'. However, it was left to Sunak to acknowledge that the Tories were now prepared to adopt policies more traditionally associated with the Labour Party – even though, ironically, Labour did not back the idea, believing it would not solve the social care problem and it was wrong to fund it via a tax on jobs. 'Today we have created an expanded safety net,' Sunak said.

> Instead of individuals having to bear the financial risks of catastrophic care costs themselves, we as a country are deciding to share more of that risk collectively. This is a permanent new role for the government. And, as such, we need a permanent new way to fund it. The only alternative would be to borrow more indefinitely. But that would be ir-responsible, at a time when our national debt is already the highest it has been in peacetime, and it would be dishonest. Borrowing more today just means higher taxes tomorrow.

Despite these public proclamations, Sunak's loyalty to Johnson had worn thin by this point, according to one insider. For one thing, he had serious doubts about the effectiveness of inject-ing large sums of cash into the NHS without solid evidence of how it would improve the system or, more importantly, patients' experience. Johnson's desire to throw money at the situation went entirely against Sunak's managerial instincts to analyse, consult and then find a solution.

'Rishi went through with it and he stood up there with Saj and Boris knowing that he was going to be pinned for the tax rises, which isn't something a Conservative Chancellor wants to be pinned for,' says this source.

> And I think in a way he probably regretted it. He didn't

believe the plan was the right thing anyway and he thought there were a lot of other things we should do before we start trying to change this massive system. This was in contrast to Boris, who just wanted to be able to say things about social care for a few weeks.

Another ally says the problems surrounding the social care levy, and the fact that it generated such a significant backlash, represented a wider moment of awakening for Sunak.

This was when Rishi thought, 'Boris isn't listening and he doesn't really care, he just wants to stand up and make a speech.' Boris didn't even understand some of the details of the social care plan. Had he been quizzed in depth, he'd have struggled. You have to remember: until then Rishi's experience of working in close proximity to Boris was just about fire-fighting and dealing with unprecedented crises courtesy of Covid. The social care plan was when he had exposure to the post-fire-fighting stage, and there was all this chaos. It opened Rishi's eyes. He realised this was who Boris really was and how he actually operated.

Conservative MP Kevin Hollinrake echoes these thoughts.

I was aware that their relationship had become increasingly strained. Rishi did talk to me about it. Everyone likes Boris. He's so likeable. But one of the things that was so controversial was the health and social care levy. Boris wanted to spend the money to tackle the social care problem. I don't think, if it had been Rishi's call, that he'd have done the social care reforms. He realised the money that would cost.

He was never the one pushing to spend £12 billion a year on social care. It was Boris who'd committed to that, so he wanted to fund a solution. That was a bone of contention between them. Those kinds of things, Rishi found increasingly difficult to deal with. I think at the time there was just a complete difference in styles that made things impossible. Rishi knows what he wants, but we'd sit down and talk.

The Tory rebellion over the levy which had been on the cards never materialised and the ensuing parliamentary vote was won by 319 to 248. Five Tory MPs voted against the tax rise, while three dozen others abstained. Despite the victory, concerns were growing that what had been passed amounted to a Red Wall tax which would ultimately benefit the Labour Party. Having secured the parliamentary backing he needed, Johnson went ahead with the rumoured reshuffle. It has been suggested that he toyed with the idea of removing Sunak from his post at this time, perhaps feeling under threat from his younger colleague. Little did he know that, as mentioned above by one of his allies, Sunak had briefly considered quitting.

From Sunak's perspective, the moves of two colleagues in the reshuffle were noteworthy. Simon Clarke, the Middlesbrough MP whose seat borders Sunak's, returned to the government as Chief Secretary to the Treasury. Ostensibly his role was to ensure appropriate levels of investment reached the north of England as part of the commitments made to Red Wall seats, but it was clear he could also act as Johnson's eyes and ears in the Treasury. 'This was a classic move by No. 10,' recalls a source who knows Clarke.

It's happened before. If No. 10 is becoming frustrated with

the Chancellor, they appoint a Chief Secretary whose primary loyalty is to No. 10, not the Treasury. Simon was very close to Dan Rosenfield, Boris's then chief of staff. All No. 10s become convinced the Treasury is withholding information or money and Simon's job was to find it.

There was even a suggestion that Johnson assigned Clarke (height: 6ft 5in.) to the Treasury because it tickled him to see him standing beside the 5ft 6in. Sunak.

The most striking appointment, though, was Liz Truss's elevation to Foreign Secretary. This was believed to serve several purposes as far as Johnson was concerned. First, it was seen as a reward for Truss's agreement not to lead a revolt over the social care levy. Second, by giving her one of the four great offices of state, alongside Sunak, Johnson hoped to create some tension between the pair. It was no coincidence that Truss had topped a recent ConservativeHome poll of party activists with a positive approval rating of eighty-five out of 100, compared with seventy-four for Sunak, who was slipping down the rankings. And third, Johnson hoped that Truss might act as an obstacle to Sunak's putative ambitions, thereby safeguarding his own position.

This presupposes that Sunak really was scheming for the top job at this point, as Johnson suspected. Was he? Not according to his friend Kevin Hollinrake, who says his obvious talents did not equate to back-room plotting. 'The first day I met Rishi, I could just see he could be party leader,' Hollinrake says.

Why else would someone of his calibre come into this business? It was obvious he was going to rise to the top.

I remember telling him very early on that it was obvious he was going to the top. Everybody could see it. Most MPs claim publicly that they don't want to go to the top. Rishi just said, 'Let's see what happens.' But it's absolute nonsense that he was trying to get rid of Boris. I'd be the first to know about it if that sort of thing had been happening because I'm very close to Rishi and we talk about the future. I didn't see any of that. Of course he's ambitious. I remember when the first tranche of our intake were made PPSs and he wasn't among them. He was so crestfallen! But he wasn't plotting.

Another friend of both Johnson and Sunak agrees. 'It doesn't pass the logic test,' says this person.

Rishi became Chancellor at the age of thirty-nine. Boris is more than fifteen years older than him. You don't need to be a political genius to work out that the safest thing for Rishi to have done would have been to tuck himself in behind Boris and let Boris praise him as the heir apparent. I always thought Boris's plan was to fight an election in 2023, maybe do a year or two after that, and then go off to make some money. This would have allowed Rishi to get some experience and maybe there would have been an orderly transition sometime around 2024. If you were playing the purely political game, that's what you'd have done. Temperamentally, they're two different characters. They're both products of the job they did before. Boris approached his job as a newspaper columnist would. He liked an idea because he liked it, but there wasn't any logic behind those decisions. Rishi would look at problems from the perspective of an investment manager. Boris found it frustrating that there was someone who'd ask, 'What's the cost; what are we cutting; or if you don't want to cut we must raise a tax – but by the way that's not a Conservative thing to do.' I think those feelings on Boris's part drove a lot of the tensions between them.

Whatever lay behind Johnson's political insecurities would soon become academic, in any case. For even he could not have anticipated that, ten months later, Sunak and Truss would be locked in exactly the same argument they had just finished about borrowing versus taxing – this time in the entirely different context of a contest to succeed him as Conservative Party leader and Prime Minister.

* * *

By the time the Tories gathered for their annual conference in Manchester during the first weekend in October, there appeared to be much for the party to celebrate. The curtain had just come down on the furlough scheme; the Labour Party under Sir Keir Starmer had shown little sign of a sustained revival; the economy was predicted to grow; and unemployment was not as high as had been feared.

Beneath this calm exterior, however, problems were mounting. In late September, Sunak had been forced to remind ministers to 'control' the public finances after government borrowing rose to £20.5 billion in the month of August, taking the UK's debt mountain to £2.2 trillion, the highest relative to GDP for sixty years. The Bank of England had also issued an alert that inflation was predicted to reach 4 per cent by December, which was twice its official target. And, in common with every major economy in the world, energy prices in

Britain were rocketing, particularly that of natural gas. To add to these troubles, there was a shortage of workers, hitting food and fuel supply chains. Pictures of empty supermarket shelves and snaking queues at petrol stations peppered television news bulletins. And the term 'cost-of-living crisis' was being used with increasing regularity. All this came just six months before the unpopular National Insurance rise was due to kick in. Kwasi Kwarteng, the Business Secretary, did not help the government's cause by arguing publicly that 'higher tax is basically a tax on economic activity ... I don't believe we can tax our way to wealth.' Neither did his Cabinet colleague Jacob Rees-Mogg, the Leader of the House of Commons, who said the UK was already 'taxed as highly as the country can afford' and suggested that wealthy people would move their assets abroad if they were unhappy with Britain's tax regime.

Directly or otherwise, all of these difficulties were a legacy of the pandemic. Although it was reported in the *Sunday Times* on the eve of the conference that Sunak had persuaded Johnson to agree to cut taxes before the next general election in exchange for fiscal restraint, the challenge for the government was how to explain to activists that it could 'level up' poorer communities while at the same time increasing the tax burden of the people who lived in those communities. Many watched to see how much of the approaching storm would be acknowledged in Sunak's speech, his first – and what would turn out to be last – as Chancellor in this forum.

Lamenting the fact that the previous year's conference had been cancelled because of Covid, Sunak began with a joke at his own expense, saying, 'That is why these last few days have been such a joy. Meeting you all face to face and hearing so many of you say to me, "Wow, you're even shorter in real life!"'

No doubt with the forthcoming Spending Review and Budget in mind, he then turned his attention to the serious matters of economics, returning to his familiar theme of morality. 'I believe in fiscal responsibility,' he said. 'Just borrowing more money and stacking up bills for future generations to pay is not just economically irresponsible. It's immoral. Because it's not the state's money, it's your money.' Whether Sunak spoke these words as much to box in Johnson as to appeal to his core supporters is debatable, but he did emphasise his desire for lower taxes. 'I know tax rises are unpopular … I want tax cuts. But in order to do that, our public finances must be put back on a sustainable footing,' he said, cautioning that public debt was now nearly 100 per cent of GDP.

Plenty of people were convinced that Brexit had worsened Britain's economic plight in the post-Covid age. Sunak had an answer for them, too, as he cemented his commitment to Britain's departure from the bloc. He said that 'optimism' and an 'unshakeable belief that the future can be different and better' were also at the heart of Brexit. And he made clear that even when he was warned that voting for the Leave side might damage his career prospects, he stuck to his principles. Many interpreted this as a jibe at the new Foreign Secretary, Liz Truss, who had backed Remain in 2016 but converted to the Brexit cause under Johnson's administration.

Sunak's twenty-minute speech resulted in a standing ovation from the packed conference hall. Yet it was hard to escape the feeling that he had ducked some of the hardest questions facing the country. Johnson, who was sitting at the front of the room, was among the first to take to his feet and applaud him. Evidence was accumulating that their professional relationship was not exactly in rude health, however.

Among the tough questions that went unanswered was one relating to the energy crisis. The week after Sunak's speech, on 10 October, Kwasi Kwarteng gave an interview to the BBC that ultimately underlined the discord between Johnson and his Chancellor. Kwarteng said he was in talks with Sunak about companies that were on the brink of collapse because of the energy crisis receiving a state bailout. Tussles between the Department for Business and the Treasury are not untypical. Very unusually, however, on this occasion Kwarteng's declaration resulted in a 'Treasury source' issuing a strong rebuke which seemed designed to humiliate him. 'This is not the first time the [Business] Secretary has made things up in interviews,' the Treasury source told the BBC. 'To be crystal clear, the Treasury are not involved in any talks.' Sunak, who was known to be keen to shoot down the pandemic-inspired idea that the state would be on hand to support any struggling business, was suspected of condoning this extraordinary statement. Suddenly the government appeared to be split on one of the biggest issues of the day. Johnson was on holiday in Spain at the time, but he soon contacted London to make clear via a Downing Street statement that he was on Kwarteng's side, as he confirmed that Treasury officials had in fact been involved in discussions with Kwarteng. Such a weighty counter-punch, delivered from afar, did nothing to quell ill feeling between Sunak and Johnson.

More evidence of unease followed. Shortly before the Autumn Budget, Johnson published some proposals outlining how Britain would decarbonise by the year 2050. Coming just a week before the United Nations Climate Change Conference, COP26, which was held in Glasgow and at which Johnson would be the star turn, the Treasury was swift to call to the public's attention that achieving net zero would cost an estimated £1 trillion and that much of this virtually incomprehensible expense would have to be met by taxpayers. Sunak, who would also address the COP26 summit, had been frustrated for many months by Johnson's environmental fixation, largely because he felt that he was never honest with the public about its true cost. As with the royal yacht and social care reform, Johnson wanted the policy but never gave much thought to how it would be funded.

Sunak also had misgivings about the business implications of taking Britain down the net zero path. Confidential Treasury documents predicting that the policy might make Britain uncompetitive had been leaked to *The Observer* and were published shortly before Johnson's own paper. The leaked documents stated, 'Climate action in the UK can lead to economic activity moving abroad if it directly leads to costs increasing and it is more profitable to produce in countries with less stringent climate policies.' Friends of Sunak say that, while he is environmentally conscious, he is not a 'hair-shirt green'. Instead, he thinks about the issue in terms of green technology, believing that a lot of the answers that will enable people to carry on living as they do now while reducing emissions lie in mechanical and computer-led advances. 'He will often say we've already managed to grow the economy and reduce carbon. He says Britain has a really good track record in this regard and we shouldn't beat ourselves up about it,' explains one ally.

By 27 October, the day of Sunak's Autumn Budget and Spending Review, so much of its contents had been announced in the press via a series of off-the-record briefings that Sunak was admonished by Dame Eleanor Laing, the Deputy Speaker of the House of Commons. She told him that 'important policy announcements should be made first to Parliament'. Sunak was suitably contrite. In fact, this parliamentary event had been almost overshadowed not by media leaks about what it contained but by the far more trivial matter of some official photographs of Sunak working at his desk as he put the finishing touches to his Budget. He was wearing white socks and a pair of £95 sliders from the fashion brand Palm Angels. This was a look favoured by some young Americans, but, now aged forty-one, he was teased mercilessly for dressing like a teenager. It was certainly difficult to imagine any of his predecessors being photographed at work in anything other than a business suit. One friend jokes, 'I am always amused at his lack of sophistication.'

The Budget itself guaranteed an increase in public spending of £150 billion by the end of the parliament – the biggest for half a century. According to the Resolution Foundation think tank, the average household would have to pay £3,000 per year more in tax to fund this commitment. There was no shortage of disapproving commentary around an approach to the economy that would saddle voters with the highest taxes since the days of Clement Attlee, even if it was generally recognised that Sunak had to somehow both stimulate the economy and repair the public finances after a seismic shock to the system.

Some who reread his Budget speech soon saw the apparent contradiction that existed within it. Sunak had declared that the impressive recovery from the previous winter's lockdown meant that the economy was expected to grow by 6.5 per cent rather than the 4 per cent the Office for Budget Responsibility had predicted. This had contributed to an unexpected £35 billion windfall to the public purse. It soon became clear that

Sunak had wanted to put this money aside for future tax cuts, but Johnson had forced him to plough most of it into public services instead. Sunak had used his speech to justify with some pride the vast spending promises the Budget contained as a necessary step in a post-pandemic age. A few minutes later, however, his closing remarks betrayed an attitude that could be taken as something closer to Thatcherite. Having acknowledged that the pandemic had forced the government to 'put aside questions of ideology and orthodoxy', he said that the state had grown to be over half the size of the total economy and taxes had risen to their highest level as a percentage of GDP since the 1950s. 'I don't like it, but I cannot apologise for it,' he said. 'But now, we have a choice. Do we want to live in a country where the response to every question is: "What is the government going to do about it?" ... or do we choose to recognise that government has limits?' He went on to emphasise the importance of 'family, community, and personal responsibility' and said, 'My goal is to reduce taxes. By the end of this parliament, I want taxes to be going down, not up.'

In a subsequent BBC interview, Simon Clarke said that public spending was rising because the government's policy priorities meant a bigger role for the state. This was in sharp contrast to the previous decade, when David Cameron and George Osborne had pursued a policy of austerity. If this was what could be called 'Johnsonism', some notable Tory figures were distinctly unimpressed. 'This is certainly not Conservative philosophy,' Michael Portillo, who had held Clarke's job in the early 1990s, told Times Radio. 'This is something quite different. This is what Conservatives absolutely do not believe in. The Conservatives do not believe that these policies could possibly be successful. And yet they've just been announced by the Chancellor. So it is, I think, a bit of an identity crisis for the Conservative Party.'

On the basis that all Budgets are compromises between Prime Ministers and Chancellors, it is fair to say that, privately, Sunak probably agreed with some of Portillo's analysis. For evidence, we need look no further than one of Sunak's earliest parliamentary speeches as a backbencher, in July 2015. In it, he revealed that tax receipts since 1955 had at that point averaged 36 per cent to 38 per cent of GDP under Conservative and Labour governments. This prompted his aforementioned belief that 'public spending should not exceed 37 per cent of GDP'. The circumstances of the pandemic and the Prime Minister's wishes meant that practical politics had taken precedence over Sunak's stated principles as a small-state conservative.

After a successful party conference and a generally well-received COP26 summit, some saw Sunak's flexibility that autumn as further proof that Johnson's position as Prime Minister and First Lord of the Treasury was rock-solid. And perhaps it was. This makes it all the more remarkable that what has become known as the 'Tory death spiral' was about to begin.

CHAPTER 25

OMICRON AND THE
DEATH SPIRAL

The day before Sunak delivered his Autumn Budget in
October 2021, Owen Paterson, a Conservative former
Cabinet minister who had retired to the back benches, was
found guilty by the Parliamentary Commissioner for Standards, Kathryn Stone, of breaching lobbying rules. His misde-
meanour was considered so serious that he faced a thirty-day
suspension from the House of Commons, a punishment that
might easily lead to a by-election in his North Shropshire
constituency. Initially, Johnson signalled his intention to help
Paterson by sanctioning a parliamentary vote whose outcome
was designed to block the suspension and change the rules
so that Paterson could appeal the commissioner's findings. A
three-line whip was even imposed on Tory MPs to ensure that
this highly unusual move was successful. Ultimately, however,
the intervention provoked such a strong reaction from politicians of all parties and the public that the rescue attempt was
ditched. Paterson resigned his seat on 4 November, triggering
a by-election which would be held the following month. The
damage to the Conservative Party and to Johnson was significant. The so-called Tory death spiral, a series of incidents and
episodes which led to Johnson's defenestration just months
later, had begun.

When Sunak was asked about the Paterson debacle soon afterwards during an interview, it was noticeable from the little he did say that he was in no mood to defend what had happened. Conveniently, he had been speaking at the COP26 summit in Glasgow when the vote to save the erring MP had taken place, so he was not part of the process that had left some of his colleagues feeling sullied. 'Reflecting over recent events, I think for us as a government, it's fair to say that we need to do better than we did last week, and we know that,' he commented. Privately, he regarded the entire affair with dismay. Not only did it represent the kind of slippage that harmed public trust in politicians; he also knew that the Conservatives had inflicted a wound upon themselves and there would be a price to pay. As well as headlines about 'Tory sleaze', the most immediate penalty was a slump in the polls.

The next item in the catalogue of errors that helped form the backdrop to Johnson's eventual downfall followed on 22 November. That day, he gave a speech to the Confederation of British Industry, the group representing Britain's biggest firms. He turned up to the venue at the Port of Tyne near South Shields apparently unprepared and then spoke in a 'rambling' fashion about the virtues of the children's theme park Peppa Pig World. He also compared himself to Moses and imitated the noise of an accelerating car. Finally, he lost his place for twenty seconds, repeatedly muttering 'forgive me' as he frantically searched through his notes. The roomful of business leaders looked on, unimpressed and confused.

Hours later, the BBC's political editor, Laura Kuenssberg, reported that a 'No. 10 source' had admitted to her that deep unease existed about Johnson's future. 'There is a lot of concern inside the building about the PM,' the source said. 'It's just not working. Cabinet needs to wake up and demand serious changes, otherwise it'll keep getting worse. If they don't insist, he just won't do anything about it.' Johnson's aides were said to be staggered by the directness of this verbal attack. When the BBC website later changed the status of the unnamed briefer from a 'No. 10 source' to a 'Downing Street source', Johnson's staffers made clear their suspicion that whoever had spoken to Kuenssberg worked on Sunak's team. This incident helped to expose wider divisions in the Downing Street operation.

When Sunak had succeeded Sajid Javid as Chancellor in February 2020, he had inherited a retinue of advisers that had been assembled by Dominic Cummings, then Johnson's chief aide. Together with Johnson's own staff, these advisers formed what was known as the Joint Economic Unit. Its purpose was to work across 10 and 11 Downing Street in order to give Cummings and Johnson greater control over the Treasury. This was the power grab that had prompted Javid to quit. By late 2021, however, a year after Cummings's departure, Sunak had effectively taken control of the unit himself, in part because Cummings had moved on but also because of the loyalty and respect he commanded as Chancellor. In this way, Sunak consolidated his power base, leaving Johnson to rely on forty civil servants to run the No. 10 Delivery Unit. If this was a measure of how far and how fast Sunak had risen in less than two years, it also reinstated the line of division between 10 and 11 Downing Street.

The co-head of the Joint Economic Unit and Sunak's de facto chief of staff was Liam Booth-Smith, who was in his early thirties. It was known that he was not Johnson's greatest fan and Johnson's team claimed publicly that it was he who had spoken to Kuenssberg, though this was never proved. This spat did nothing to improve matters between Johnson and Sunak. Even Sir Keir Starmer latched on to the idea of their fraying relationship, jeering at Prime Minister's Questions two days later, 'The Prime Minister's routine is falling flat. His Chancellor is worried that people are getting wise, his backbenchers say it's embarrassing … and senior people in Downing Street tell the BBC, "It's just not working." Is everything OK, Prime Minister?'

Everything was not OK, as it turned out. It was reported on 27 November that a WhatsApp messaging group called 'Liz for Leader' had been set up by some backbench Tory MPs as part of a plan to install Liz Truss as Johnson's replacement. The most immediate threat to Johnson's leadership now appeared to come from his new Foreign Secretary and not from Sunak, as Johnson had long assumed. That same afternoon, Johnson called a Downing Street press conference after two cases of the Omicron variant of coronavirus were detected in Britain, a strain about which little was known at the time. He cautioned that restrictions would have to be reintroduced, including the mandatory wearing of face masks in shops and on public transport in England for at least three weeks. Self-isolation requirements were also brought back. Both measures were subject to a parliamentary vote on 30 November and were reinstated, though twenty Tory MPs voted against the reintroduction of face masks and thirty-two Tory MPs voted against the return of self-isolation. Johnson could not ignore the fact that significant opposition to him was growing within his party.

As big a blow as introducing new Covid restrictions undoubtedly was, however, the night of 30 November brought questions of a very different nature for Johnson – ones that would have far greater ramifications. The *Daily Mirror* was preparing a front-page story headlined 'Boris Johnson "broke Covid lockdown rules" with Downing Street parties at Xmas'. The central allegation was that parties and gatherings had been held at No. 10 on 18 December 2020, when large swathes of the country were in lockdown. 'Officials knocked back glasses of wine during a Christmas quiz and a Secret Santa while the rest of the country was forced to stay at home,' the *Mirror* reported. Downing Street did not deny the claims. Instead, a spokesman said, 'Covid rules have been followed at all times.' These words committed Johnson to a position even though no proper investigation had been carried out to establish any facts.

It was by no means the end of the matter, but Johnson must have felt some relief, at least, that the *Mirror*'s revelation had had no definitive bearing on the outcome of the by-election in the constituency of Old Bexley and Sidcup on 2 December 2021, following the death of Tory MP James Brokenshire. The seat was held, albeit with a swing away from the Conservatives of 13 per cent. On 3 December 2021, the Labour MP Barry Gardiner wrote to the Metropolitan Police asking them to investigate the truth surrounding the *Mirror*'s story. The Met declined, saying it did not routinely look into 'retrospective breaches of the Covid-19 regulations'.

The following week, the scent of scandal returned to Downing Street after a compromising video of Allegra Stratton, the government's COP26 spokesman, was unearthed by ITV News. At the time the footage had been filmed twelve months previously, Stratton still officially occupied the soon-to-be-redundant post of Downing Street press secretary and she was seen in the video at a mock press conference joking about a party having been hosted at Downing Street in December

2020. On 8 December 2021, Sir Keir Starmer mentioned the Stratton video at Prime Minister's Questions, asking if Johnson had the 'moral authority' to lead the country. Johnson said he was 'furious to see that clip' and had asked the Cabinet Secretary Simon Case to 'establish all the facts and to report back as soon as possible'. Case would have to excuse himself from the role of chief inquisitor nine days later after being accused of attending one of the parties he was tasked with investigating; he was replaced by a senior civil servant, Sue Gray.

At that same session of PMQs, another Labour MP, Catherine West, asked Johnson if there had been a party in Downing Street on a separate occasion, giving the date of 13 November 2020. To this, Johnson replied, 'No, but I am sure that whatever happened, the guidance was followed and the rules were followed at all times.' Again, he unwisely committed himself to what sounded like a specific position. Three hours later, Stratton resigned. As she had not been at the party she had joked about, many in Downing Street felt that, in an environment with a rapidly rising temperature, she was a convenient scapegoat. That day, the Metropolitan Police confirmed that, despite receiving a significant number of complaints about potential Covid law-breaking at 10 Downing Street in November and December 2020, it would still not investigate.

Over the next few days there flowed a spate of separate allegations that many public servants had been present at events in official buildings during 2020, thereby breaching Covid regulations. This unethical behaviour was to become known in the press as 'Partygate'. Those involved included Johnson's communications chief, Jack Doyle; two dozen Treasury staff; Johnson himself, who was accused of taking part in a 'virtual Christmas quiz' on 15 December 2020; Department for

Work and Pensions staff, who apparently drank alcohol late at night in a work building; and Shaun Bailey, the Conservative London Assembly member, who had apparently gone to a party at Conservative Campaign Headquarters when he was the party's London mayoral candidate.

Just as the Partygate fire started, on 8 December 2021, Johnson decided to call another Covid press conference, this time to tell the nation he intended to introduce 'Plan B' measures to curb the spread of Omicron. He asked people to work from home again; he extended mandatory face mask wearing to most large public indoor venues; and he made the NHS Covid pass mandatory for entry into nightclubs and other large venues. On 14 December, these mooted measures were put to Parliament. Ninety-nine Conservative MPs voted against the introduction of the NHS Covid pass, including Louie French, who had only been an MP for twelve days following his election at Old Bexley and Sidcup. It was the largest rebellion of Johnson's premiership and meant that he had to rely on opposition parties to get the legislation through. Coming on the second anniversary of Johnson's eighty-seat election win, this result would have been unimaginable only months earlier.

On 15 December, Johnson held yet another press conference. Flanking him was Professor Chris Whitty, who asked people to stop socialising in the run-up to Christmas Day and warned that a higher number of Covid hospitalisations was 'nailed on' after new UK Covid cases rose to a record daily high of 78,610. 'I'm afraid we have to be realistic that records will be broken a lot over the next few weeks,' Whitty said, adding that Britain was being hit by 'two epidemics on top of each other', as Delta variant cases remained high but stable while Omicron cases were rapidly growing.

This lockdown in all but name prompted angry business leaders to enquire after Sunak's whereabouts, as they sought compensation or financial support. Baroness McGregor-Smith, the British Chambers of Commerce president, complained that there had been 'no news of any new financial support measures coming from government to help those businesses and others badly affected by the current restrictions'. And Conservative MP Anne Marie Morris was one of several parliamentarians who took a similar view. 'If we're effectively telling people not to visit hospitality venues this Christmas, then this needs to be accompanied by immediate sector-specific financial support from the Treasury,' she said.

In fact, Sunak was thousands of miles away in California, on a long-planned trip to meet the bosses of tech and investment firms. He had intended to stay on there and spend the Christmas holidays with his wife and two children at their flat in Santa Monica, but that plan was soon scotched. Sensing an opportunity, the Labour Party issued a statement saying that his absence from the UK was 'an insult to British businesses and workers'. Having held crisis talks with some struggling UK firms by video call on 16 December, Sunak cut short his trip and, leaving his family to enjoy Christmas in California without him, flew back to London that night so he could draw up an emergency £1 billion rescue package. By the time he boarded the plane, government scientists had concluded that without another lockdown, between 600 and 6,000 Covid-related deaths could be recorded in Britain every day. A source who worked with Sunak at the time says his doubts about the lethality of Omicron meant that he was sceptical that a further lockdown would be necessary, however. His return to London would ultimately prove to be to the nation's benefit, as he was able to show the type of cool-headed leadership that seemed to be lacking in No. 10 at the time.

'California was the first and only trip outside of Europe that he took as Chancellor because of Covid,' says this source.

> He did go to Italy, Paris and Berlin that autumn in the space of few days, but the US trip was all about tech investment, basically selling the UK as a great place to invest. Even before he left, some of us thought he was going to have to return because all the No. 10 people were saying, 'Lockdown is inevitable.' He'd been in to see Boris before he left and he'd told him, 'They're selling you nonsense here. Look at the data from South Africa. There are doctors in South Africa saying this is a mild version of the virus, don't worry, we're not getting pushed into this again.' He had to come back because Boris felt the pressure from all sides and couldn't make up his own mind. Rishi gave him some of the best advice he ever received during his three-year term over Omicron.

Johnson could have been forgiven for being at sixes and sevens on 17 December, the morning of Sunak's return to the Treasury. The Tory Party was licking its wounds, having lost the North Shropshire by-election the night before in spectacular style. Owen Paterson's 23,000-strong majority had been overturned by the Liberal Democrats on a swing against the Tories of 34 per cent. Now Sage seemed determined that a second successive Christmas should be cancelled, a move which would cast Johnson as the nation's killjoy.

Sunak got down to work, tapping into his own network, which included academics from Stanford University. He was also on the JP Morgan research email list. He saw immediately that the bank had used South African data on Omicron and had concluded that, contrary to Sage's frightening predictions, no lockdown in Britain would be necessary. Sunak and Johnson spoke privately. Sunak urged the Prime Minister to consult Cabinet colleagues rather than simply informing them of the decision that had been reached, as had happened on previous occasions. 'Boris was worried about the scientists and Rishi said to him, "Get collective agreement, get all your Cabinet ministers round the table," recalls this source.

> Boris called the Cabinet meeting for Monday 20 December, told them that we shouldn't lock down, the Cabinet all agreed and Rishi's point to Boris was he could then go to the backbenchers and tell them that Cabinet had decided we're not going to lock down. His advice to Boris was instrumental. Rishi got him out of that scrape. If he had locked down, the party wouldn't have forgiven him. And if he had locked down and everyone had realised a month later that it had been completely unnecessary for him to lock down because Omicron was not as threatening as Boris had been told, he'd have been out of a job even sooner than he was. So if Rishi really had been scheming, he could have allowed Boris to make that wrong decision and pay the penalty. And, of course, he didn't. He encouraged Boris to make a braver decision in which ultimately Boris was proved right and which undoubtedly benefited him.

At the time it was Johnson, and not Sunak, who was credited with saving Christmas in England by defying the scientific experts whose gloomy prognosis turned out to be so woefully off-beam. Their forecast of up to 6,000 Covid-related deaths per day was wrong by a factor of twenty. Yet in an interview with *The Spectator* in August 2022, Sunak did cast modesty aside to acknowledge the key role he had played in averting another lockdown, saying that he had 'used the closest formulation of words that I could' to make clear to Johnson that he regarded this as a resignation issue without actually threatening to quit. 'Everything I did was seen through the prism of: "You're trying to be difficult, trying to be leader,"' he told the magazine. Yet he insisted that his actions had nothing to do with a leadership bid and everything to do with sparing the nation from another economic shutdown. Sunak recalled, 'I remember telling him: "Have the Cabinet meeting. You'll see. Everyone will be completely behind you … You don't have to worry. I will be standing next to you, as will every other member of the Cabinet, bar probably Michael [Gove] and Saj [Javid]."' He was right. By and large, the Cabinet did stand with Johnson.

Showing some political nous, Sunak said that as well as keeping his conversations with Johnson strictly private, he was also careful not to write anything down in case any of his opinions, ideas or thoughts were leaked or used against him by opponents. Sunak may not quite have threatened to resign at that time, believing that to do so would undermine the government, but Johnson was absorbing news of another high-profile deserter that weekend. The *Mail on Sunday* revealed that Lord Frost, the Brexit Minister, had stepped down in protest at the introduction of vaccine passports, tax rises and the cost of net zero environmental policies.

* * *

January 2022 was a grim month for the government in general and for Johnson in particular. It began with the press being tipped off that Jacob Rees-Mogg had used the first Cabinet meeting of the year to stoke tensions again over the forthcoming National Insurance contributions rise, due in April, arguing that people's burdens should be eased as life's necessities became more costly. Sunak was quizzed about this intervention and, ultimately, forced to publicly defend a policy that, as we have seen, he didn't wholly believe in himself but had backed as the only option available. 'It is always easy to duck difficult decisions, but I don't think that is the responsible thing to do,' he told a Sky News journalist.

A few days later, there was another leak, this time of an email written by Johnson's principal private secretary, Martin Reynolds, on 20 May 2020 – at the height of lockdown – inviting 100 Downing Street staff to a gathering in the No. 10 garden. This leak followed separate allegations from ITV News about another event in the garden which had taken place five days earlier in May 2020 and which was brought to life by a photograph of Johnson and his wife, Carrie, sitting with No. 10 staff on the terrace with a bottle of wine and some cheese. As a handful of Tory MPs called for Johnson to resign, Labour pulled further ahead in the polls, achieving 40 per cent for the first time since July 2018. That was before yet more Partygate details were trumpeted by the *Daily Telegraph*, this time of two functions having been held in Downing Street the night before Prince Philip's funeral in April 2021, when such social contact remained banned. Given that the Queen had been pictured sitting alone and masked at her husband's funeral at St George's Chapel in Windsor Castle, a vision of personal sacrifice, this story delivered yet another nasty knock to Johnson.

On 19 January, Christian Wakeford, the Conservative MP for Bury South, defected to the Labour Party minutes before Prime Minister's Questions began. As if that were not enough, the veteran MP David Davis used the same session to call for Johnson to step down, quoting another Conservative politician, Leo Amery, who famously said to then Prime Minister Neville Chamberlain during the Norway debate of May 1940, 'In the name of God, go!' On 24 January, the Business Minister, Lord Agnew, did just that. Dramatically, he resigned his post from the despatch box in the House of Lords, citing the government's 'lamentable' record of tackling more than £4 billion of fraud in the Covid business schemes as his chief reason for leaving. The Labour Party argued that this reflected poorly on Sunak and demanded an explanation.

The next day, it was announced that the Metropolitan Police had launched a criminal investigation into whether the law had been broken in Downing Street by parties having been held there. It was given the codename Operation Hillman. This move had been deemed necessary after Scotland Yard received evidence from Sue Gray's inquiry into alleged parties being held there and elsewhere during November and December 2020. At the same time, it was also reported that a small surprise party to mark Johnson's fifty-sixth birthday had been held in a Downing Street stateroom during the afternoon of 19 June 2020. About thirty guests were said to have been there to enjoy a piece of cake and a drink. It transpired that Sunak, a teetotaller whose only known weakness when it comes to beverages is for extra-sweet Mexican Coca-Cola, was one of them. His spokesman said that he had not been invited but had instead turned up to the room a few minutes early for a work meeting. Nonetheless, a photograph of him in attendance was later published, linking him to Partygate, fairly or otherwise.

On 29 January, Anna Isaac, a journalist writing for *The Independent*, reported that Sunak was 'putting the finishing touches to a PR-led leadership campaign after telling allies he believes Partygate could be "unsurvivable"' for Johnson. It was claimed his efforts included setting up a website and sounding out officials and MPs about his chances of winning a leadership contest. How Isaac got the story is not clear; its accuracy is also moot, but it was flatly denied by Sunak's team.

One former aide to Sunak says the pressure had taken its toll on Johnson's Downing Street operation by this point, as it became convinced that Sunak was lining up support among MPs. 'The press had written up a lot of stuff about Rishi versus Liz Truss and created the impression of the two of them vying to be the next leader and the truth is Liz was involved in various leadership manoeuvres and Rishi wasn't,' recalls this source.

> I think that soured the relationship with No. 10 because they were only ever really worried about one person – Rishi – and he wasn't doing any of these things. I remember you could see the paranoia in No. 10. There was one *Sunday Times* story where they mentioned his PPS Claire Coutinho as someone running these leadership engagements for Rishi and they talked about her standing in the corridor outside his office, which was next to the PM's office in Parliament, welcoming MPs. In fact, the meetings were cost-of-living meetings with MPs that Rishi had been asked to host by No. 10. So we'd carry out the work as per the instruction and still have the paranoia from No. 10.

On 31 January, Johnson went to the Commons to make a statement about Sue Gray's report. She had finished her investigation but, because the Met Police had begun its own inquiry,
the full disclosure of Gray's findings was put on hold and a
short 'update' had been published instead. Johnson apologised
to the House, but when he and Starmer then began to debate,
Johnson counter-attacked, lambasting Starmer over his five-
year record as Director of Public Prosecutions in charge of
the Crown Prosecution Service (CPS) by saying he had spent
'more time prosecuting journalists and failing to prosecute
Jimmy Savile'.

This was a gift to any anti-Johnson individual or institution,
and numerous MPs, newspapers and broadcasters piled in to
declare that the accusation he had levelled against Starmer
about arguably Britain's most notorious sex offender was both
baseless and offensive. In fact, insiders say that taking Starmer
to task over the CPS's failure to prosecute Savile was an idea
that Conservative Party figures had been working on for some
time. The plan was to deploy this weapon at a later date as
part of a carefully orchestrated attempt to discredit the Labour
leader. Yet, perhaps acting in panic or in anger, Johnson blurted it out early in a haphazard way, effectively killing off the
scheme.

After three days, he 'clarified' his remark, explaining,
'I was making a point about his responsibility for [the
CPS] as a whole.' Not everybody thought this modified
U-turn was sufficient. To Johnson's dismay, his longstanding policy chief, Munira Mirza, used his Savile comment
as a reason for her resignation on 3 February. This overshadowed Sunak's announcement that day of £350 assis-
tance to poorer households, to be paid via council tax

discounts as part of a £9 billion package designed to 'take the sting' out of rising energy bills. Shortly afterwards, three more of Johnson's aides departed: Dan Rosenfield, his chief of staff; Martin Reynolds, his principal private secretary; and Jack Doyle, his director of communications. All three had been implicated in Partygate; Doyle is said to have told staff that 'recent weeks have taken a terrible toll on my family life'.

The only positive news Johnson received that day was itself borne of tragedy. A by-election took place at Southend West following the murder of the veteran backbench MP Sir David Amess. Opposition parties decided not to contest it out of respect to Sir David, and the Tories held the seat. When Sunak was asked about the Savile remark at a press conference that afternoon, he was categorical. 'Being honest, I wouldn't have said it and I'm glad that the Prime Minister clarified what he meant.' Whereas previously Sunak had kept his counsel whenever he was invited to criticise Johnson, this time he did not. His words undoubtedly pricked the Prime Minister's ego and cemented his certainty that Sunak intended to stand for the leadership himself.

In fact, it can be argued that Sunak may have taken this opportunity to jump on the bandwagon and put some distance between himself and Johnson a little too enthusiastically. If one subscribes to the view that the head of any organisation must be accountable for the way it functions, there is a logic to Johnson's point, for while Starmer says he was not personally responsible for the decision not to prosecute Savile, there is no doubt that the failure occurred on his watch.

Four days later, Johnson's opinion of Sunak was tested when he visited the Kent Oncology Centre at Maidstone Hospital. When asked by a journalist if he ever worried that Sunak had designs on his job, he replied, 'I think that what we're doing is working together across the whole of government to fix the Covid backlogs, which, believe me, is a massive priority for us, for everybody in the country.' He was then asked if he doubted Sunak's loyalty. 'Absolutely not,' he replied. He added:

What I would say is that it's thanks to the investment that we're able to put in, thanks to the sound management of the economy, everything that we did, if you think about it, all the looking after business throughout the pandemic, that's enabled our economy to bounce back so well, that in turn enables us to put the investment that we need now in the NHS.

Over a period of a little more than 100 days, Johnson's administration had been pummelled not just by the unearthing of scandals, improprieties and mishaps but also by its reaction to them – all with the approaching menace of another public health crisis on the horizon. This left little room for the business of government to carry on, though of course it had to, albeit not, perhaps, in a way that Sunak could have predicted.

On 8 February, Johnson carried out a Cabinet reshuffle in which his chief cheerleader, Jacob Rees-Mogg, was given a powerful new role as the Minister for Brexit Opportunities. Guto Harri, who had been drafted in three days earlier to replace Jack Doyle as Johnson's director of communications, has recalled that Johnson had by this point become deeply frustrated by what he saw as the Establishment's sneering hatred of Brexit and Brexit voters. Rees-Mogg's mission was to rid the statute book of thousands of EU regulations. He approached this task with relish and, according to Harri, began by alerting Johnson to his belief that Sunak was one of those who was effectively acting as a block on Brexit's progress, even going so far as to say he had 'gone native'. In June 2023, Harri remembered:

> Boris asked him to give it all a massive kick. Jacob Rees-Mogg warned then that he would have to tread on some big toes. 'Actually, little toes,' he added patronisingly with a sort of dig at Rishi Sunak's size. And Boris, after a little chuckle, gave him carte blanche to be a pain in the backside for the Treasury and for Rishi Sunak. His words were quite simply: 'Go ahead.'

Rees-Mogg obeyed, starting with the EU Reform Bill, by which he hoped to reassert the sovereignty of Parliament.

On 24 February, Sunak was scheduled to deliver the prestigious Mais Lecture at the Bayes Business School in London. He went ahead with his planned speech, which centred on the theme of a new culture of enterprise, but the event was eclipsed by Russia's invasion of Ukraine that morning. Sunak prefaced his address by telling the audience of City grandees that sanctions against Russia were to be brought forward. He explained that he had spoken to the Governor of the Bank of England, Andrew Bailey, in order to help monitor Britain's financial stability. And he said that he would keep a 'careful watch' on the energy markets, with volatility in wholesale gas prices expected. Soon after, it was confirmed that the average dual fuel bill in Britain would rise by £700 per year.

On the same day, Sunak received a Partygate questionnaire from the Metropolitan Police. At least fifty such forms were sent to people under Operation Hillman, which was looking into a dozen reported gatherings. The clear inference was that Sunak, like Johnson, was under suspicion of breaking coronavirus regulations, a situation that did nothing to add to the Conservative Party's ambitions at the Birmingham Erdington by-election on 3 March. Labour held the seat convincingly. All this was the unwelcome prelude to Sunak's final Spring Statement as Chancellor, which was delivered on 23 March.

Shortly before he was due to speak in the Commons, the Office for National Statistics released figures showing that inflation had hit a new thirty-year high of 6.2 per cent as pressure on household budgets intensified. This was 0.2 per cent more than expected and economists feared it was bound to go higher still. Having steered Britain through the pandemic, Sunak was scrambling to deal with a situation that was spinning beyond his control thanks, partly, to a foreign war which was having a profound effect on energy prices.

The general reaction to the Spring Statement was one of confusion, some of which was laced with hostility. One headline measure he introduced that day was a temporary 5p cut in fuel duty. Being the largest such cut ever made, this was welcomed. Another key policy he announced was to increase the threshold at which people pay National Insurance by £3,000 per year. In one sense this, too, was well received. Yet in slashing the number of people who would be affected by the controversial 1.25 per cent National Insurance rise that was to be introduced the following month, the irony was lost on nobody that Sunak was the Chancellor who had instituted it in the first place. Another promise was to deliver a 1p cut in the basic rate of income tax ahead of a 2024 general election. Again, however, some considered this to be disingenuous. How could he be sure that he would be in office by then to oversee such a cut? Almost every think tank and newspaper reacted negatively to what had been billed as a tax-cutting statement, but the normally supportive *Daily Mail* was among the most damning in its conclusions. Its editorial comment, headlined 'Don't tax our patience with Budget illusions', thundered, 'While Rishi Sunak poses as a low-tax Chancellor, the Institute for Fiscal Studies says he is set to rake in a mind-blowing £1 trillion in a year – £42,000 per household.'

Seemingly, few were prepared to believe any longer that Sunak was a Chancellor who wished to keep taxes low. Yet one insider explains:

One reason he announced this tax cut so far in advance is that he wanted to be able to say to colleagues, 'If you want to spend money on X, you're going to lose the tax cut. If you want to keep that tax cut, you've got to hold the line.' He is not an instinctive big-state, high-tax politician.

This apparently went over most people's heads at the time, and prompted the *Daily Mail* to ask why he had not used an unexpected £50 billion of revenue which had been generated by Britain's near-full employment to cut some taxes immediately.

Such questions preoccupied many of Sunak's colleagues in the parliamentary party too. Among them was Philip Davies. 'I wasn't personally aware of tensions between him and Boris,' Davies says.

And Rishi's not the type of person who'd say anything

anyway. He's a team player. In my opinion, he was too much of a team player under Boris. He'd get the blame for all sorts of things and instead of letting it be known it had nothing to do with him, he'd take it on the chin. We got to the highest tax rises in history and Johnson's team were briefing out left, right and centre that this was Sunak and that Boris was a low-tax Conservative. Rishi would take it on the chin. I never saw any retaliation in the media. The only time I ever became aware of a tension in the ranks – and even then it wasn't overt – was very late on in his time as Chancellor. He came to a meeting of the No Turning Back group, which John Redwood chairs. It was a small meeting in John's office. There were about eight of us. We're free-market libertarians. Our concern was about taxes being too high. We wanted to convey that to Rishi. He's a very polite guy, but you could see an underlying frustration because he was copping it as a high-tax Chancellor. He basically said, 'If you start making sure that we spend less money, I'm quite happy to tax less, but unfortunately what's not possible is to keep spending money as if it's going out of fashion and for that not to be paid for somehow.' He said that's the problem: we're spending too much. He wasn't talking about Covid; he was talking in general terms. He never blamed Boris for that, but it was obvious that he was hugely frustrated that the government was wanting to spend money and he was taking the blame by trying to be fiscally responsible and not borrowing more and more.

Who would have envied Sunak his post as Chancellor – especially when the MailOnline reported with some glee after the statement that he had not used his own car for the purposes of a photo opportunity at a London petrol station to publicise the 5p fuel cut but had instead borrowed a Kia Rio from a Sainsbury's worker? The website further noted that when he had tried to speak to two members of the public at the garage, he had been given a 'right earful' over the 'pathetic' support package in his statement. He had also given credence to the notion that he was out of touch with 'ordinary' people by apparently struggling to pay for the petrol via a contactless payment system, at one point presenting his credit card to a barcode reader instead.

Questions of far greater personal significance were circling Sunak, however, one of which could not have been closer to home. On 25 March, he gave an interview to Sky News in which he was challenged over his wife's 0.91 per cent share-holding in his father-in-law's multinational IT company, Info-sys. Her stake had recently been valued at £690 million. Two weeks previously, in the light of Russia's invasion of Ukraine, Sunak had made a statement 'urging firms to think very care-fully about their investments in Russia and how they may aid the Putin regime'. Yet Infosys had an office in Moscow which had not at that point closed down. Was he giving advice to others that was not being followed by his father-in-law's com-pany, asked journalist Jayne Secker? Looking uncomfortable, Sunak replied, 'I'm an elected politician and I'm here to talk to you about what I'm responsible for. My wife is not.' When pressed on whether his family could be benefiting from Pu-tin's regime, Sunak said, 'No, I really don't think that's the case. And as I said, the operations of all companies are up to them. We've put in place significant sanctions and all the companies that we're responsible for are following those as they rightly should, sending a very strong message to Putin's aggression.'

He added that he had 'absolutely no idea' what Infosys's reaction had been to countries introducing sanctions on Russia, as he had 'nothing to do with that company'.

Sunak's answers may have been sufficient to convince Sky News that day not to push him on this topic, but others, operating in the shadows, were already sharpening their knives in preparation for the next line of attack.

CHAPTER 26

DIRTY TRICKS

In the immediate aftermath of his Spring Statement, Sunak felt bruised. He had been labelled a high-tax Chancellor even though he had tried to present himself as the opposite; he had been made to look foolish by the most widely read English-language news website in the world, MailOnline; and questions which he felt were unwarranted were being asked about his wife's financial affairs, with the *Daily Telegraph* reporting that she had received £12 million of dividend payments from her stake in her father's IT company, Infosys. He had also been forced to defend his statement while giving evidence to the Treasury Select Committee after MPs accused him of not doing enough to help those on welfare in a time of surging inflation. After the pandemic, and because of the war in Ukraine, it was hardly surprising that prices were rising. Still, he needed to restore some balance and Laura Kuenssberg, the outgoing BBC political editor, was able to provide the perfect platform for him via Newscast, a BBC podcast for which she conducted interviews.

Kuenssberg's conversation with Sunak was broadcast on 31 March and offered valuable insights into his state of mind. 'You know, I think it's totally fine for people to take shots at me,' he said.

It's fair game. I'm the one sitting here and that's what I

signed up for. It's very upsetting and, I think, wrong for people to try and come at my wife and beyond that actually, with regard to my father-in-law, for whom I have nothing but enormous pride and admiration for everything that he's achieved. No amount of attempted smearing is going to make me change that because he's wonderful and has achieved a huge amount, as I said, I'm enormously proud of him.

Friends of Sunak observe that for him to say he is 'proud' of his father-in-law is something of an understatement. More accurately, he credits Narayana Murthy with giving him the courage to embark on a political career because of the positive impact he could have on people's lives. He also tried to make light of the situation by telling Kuenssberg that he had not behaved like Will Smith, the Hollywood actor, who had slapped fellow actor Chris Rock at the Oscars ceremony a few days previously for a perceived slight against his wife, Jada Pinkett Smith. 'I feel, on reflection, both Will Smith and me having our wives attacked – at least I didn't get up and slap anybody, which is good.' It was a contemporary, if slightly puzzling, parallel to draw.

As far as the economy was concerned, Sunak told Kuenssberg that he was content with the government's response to the cost-of-living crisis while conceding that some of the measures, such as the rise in National Insurance, were unpopular. Yet again, his aversion to debt shone through. 'I'm confident in what we've done,' he said.

I know it's tough for people. We're facing a very difficult situation with the price of things going up and I want to do

what we can to ameliorate some of that, but I'm also honest
with people that we can't ameliorate all of it, sadly. That's
difficult for people to hear and the toughest part of this job
is not being able to do everything that people would like
you to do because we're already borrowing quite a large
amount of money, and I don't think borrowing lots more
would be sensible. Actually, it has the risk of making the
problem worse when you've got inflation and interest rates
going up. Some of these things are difficult. They're certainly unpopular. But they're responsible and will help us in the
long-term and I'm not going to deviate from that just for
some short-term popularity gain.

After the interview, Kuenssberg gave her own summary view.
'I think he was trying to find a way of saying, "I've had a tough
time but actually now let me explain all the things that are
really important,"' she commented. 'What he said very clearly
was: "We've just got to stop borrowing as much as a country."'
Not unreasonably, she wondered why he hadn't used such
straightforward language during his statement speech. To
have done so might have helped him to avoid so many negative headlines. These were compounded soon after it was delivered by analysis from the Office for Budget Responsibility,
which concluded that the tax burden had risen to the highest
level since the 1940s and predicted that the UK would see 'the
biggest fall in living standards on record'.

Around the same time, those of a conspiratorial disposition began to wonder whether dark forces might be working
against Sunak. There was certainly a belief that Boris Johnson's
band of loyalists might be dripping poison about him to
the media. Stories about him preparing for a holiday to

California and wearing trainers costing £335 popped up un-expectedly. More consequentially, following the statement, No. 10 also briefed journalists that Sunak was refusing to bankroll a £1 billion scheme that would increase the energy efficiency of homes, cutting domestic bills at a moment of hardship. All seemed designed to portray him as rich, uncar-ing and out of touch. Perhaps it worked. On 4 April, Conserv-ativeHome published a survey of Tory members and activists which showed that Sunak's popularity among that group had dropped like a stone. Whereas once he had been the most popular member of the Cabinet, now he was in thirtieth place, third from the bottom. His Spring Statement was said to be the chief reason he had slipped so far down the rankings.

The next day, along came another awkward story that was widely picked up. Sam Coates, the deputy political editor of Sky News, reported that since at least 2014 Sunak had donated more than £100,000 to Winchester College. He had 'contin-ued to give money to the school, where he was head boy, since becoming Chancellor', according to Coates. His wife had also been a donor. The money was to be used to fund bursaries for children whose parents would otherwise not be able to afford to send them there. This information had been fished out of the school magazine, the *Wykeham Journal*, where the Sunaks were listed as Wykeham Benefactors, those 'whose total do-nations to Winchester College (including pledges) are greater than £100,000'.

While many people would commend such generosity, politicians in the modern era tend to tread extremely care-fully when it comes to private education. Sunak is different, though. He has always been refreshingly honest about the fact that his parents worked hard and chose to put much of their income towards his school fees to ensure he had the best start in life. He is also the first to say that his schooling experience made him the person he is today. Indeed, not long before Sky's story broke, he had given the same broadcaster an interview in which he said of his time at Winchester:

> I was really lucky to have that opportunity. It was something that was really extraordinary, it certainly put my life on a different trajectory … It's part of the reason I'm sitting here … It's helped make me who I am as a person, and it helps me do the job in the way that I do it. And it confirms to me that education is one of the best tools at our disposal in politics to spread opportunity.

Inevitably, the Labour Party regarded news of his donations as a free hit against a politician willing to defend a system that it believes is steeped in unfairness. Coming hot on the heels of the other negative stories, some on Sunak's team wondered why Sky News had chosen this particular moment to run such an item about him. Others saw the irony that Coates, the journalist who broke the story, was himself the beneficiary of a private education, having attended King's College School in Wimbledon before earning a place at the University of Cambridge.

Far more problematic revelations came the next day, 6 April. Anna Isaac, the journalist who, as noted in the previous chapter, had claimed in January that Sunak was 'putting the finishing touches to a PR-led leadership campaign', had an exclusive story in *The Independent* about his wife's tax affairs. Headlined 'Rishi Sunak's millionaire wife avoids tax through non-dom status', the report stated unequivocally that she was treated as non-domiciled for UK tax purposes, meaning that she paid UK tax only on her UK earnings. *The Independent* acknowledged that while this arrangement is legal, unnamed sources it had spoken to estimated she had saved up to £4.4 million in UK taxes, though she would have had to pay tax on any overseas income in the relevant countries. A spokesperson for Murthy confirmed to *The Independent* that she is an Indian national and that because India forbids its citizens from holding dual citizenship, she had had to assume non-domiciled status. Significantly, however, this confirmation came only after the article had been published. This strongly suggests that Anna Isaac and *The Independent* had obtained verification elsewhere that their information was completely accurate.

This was the worst kind of publicity imaginable for Sunak, whose image had been crafted so carefully over the previous two years. He had no control over what was being said about him; it was obviously politically toxic for the wife of a tax-raising Chancellor to be accused of avoiding UK taxes herself; and it was personally wounding. Whoever leaked the story did so with the express intention of putting a lasting dent in his political career. 'It was a deeply unpleasant period for him,' says a friend. 'One could debate the politics of it, but his wife being dragged into this is different. You can take a lot of criticism yourself personally, but when your job is getting your family criticised, that's a different calculus.' Sunak's immediate reaction was to give an interview to *The Sun* in which he defended his wife's tax affairs robustly, saying that she paid a £30,000 annual levy to be non-domiciled in Britain. 'She's a private citizen, and of course I support my wife's choices. She's not her husband's possession,' he said. He also indicated that he thought the Labour Party was responsible for the 'unpleasant smears'. Not everybody in the Conservative Party subscribed to this theory, however.

Within two days of *The Independent*'s story appearing, Sky News reported that Sunak had held a Green Card, which allowed him permanent residency in America, until the autumn of 2021. This meant that he had had to file a US tax return annually. Again, while not illegal, this set-up was certainly unorthodox for the politician in charge of Britain's economy and it raised further questions. Sunak later admitted that he had relinquished the Green Card after taking advice from civil servants. Having recruited her own PR adviser, the former *Evening Standard* editor Sarah Sands, Murthy then sought to kill off the row about her tax affairs altogether by volunteering to pay full UK taxes on her worldwide earnings with immediate effect. She said she didn't want the issue 'to be a distraction for my husband'. Yet the damage was done. There was widespread speculation that the episode could be at least as poisonous for Sunak as Partygate was for Johnson, despite the fact that no laws had been broken and every regulation had been honoured. The question is: how did the story come to light?

A benign explanation might be that media interest in Murthy's wealth, and that of her family, had been building. Not only had the *Daily Telegraph* reported on 26 March that she had received a £12 million dividend but *Private Eye* magazine had at the same time pointed out that Murthy was 'eminently eligible' for non-domiciled status. It had not gone any further, however, presumably because it could not prove anything and because it was aware that confirmation of such confidential information would be almost impossible to obtain. Did Anna Isaac simply act like any enterprising journalist would and reach a conclusion which on the surface seemed to be highly likely, even if not provable? Those with an intimate knowledge of this affair struggle to believe it. For one thing, *The Independent* – which opted out of printing newspapers in 2016 for financial reasons – is not in the habit of breaking risky stories which might have consequences. For another, the title's owner, Lord Lebedev, who is a close friend of Boris Johnson, is not keen on the expense of complicated legal trials. Isaac's article stated that it had relied on information provided by 'two people familiar with [Murthy's] financial arrangements'. Who were they and how was Isaac so sure of her facts?

Sunak had disclosed his wife's tax status in January 2018, when he was appointed to government as a junior Housing minister. Although it was not at that time strictly necessary for a minister to reveal such information about a spouse, he did so in order to put himself beyond reproach. This declaration was lodged in the List of Ministers' Interests, which is kept in an office in Whitehall in hard copy only. Exhaustive enquiries for the purposes of this book have determined that, other than Murthy, only four people with government connections are believed to have known officially about her tax affairs at the time of the leak. They were Rishi Sunak; Tom Scholar, the Permanent Secretary to the Treasury; Helen MacNamara, the Director General for Propriety and Ethics in the Cabinet Office and the civil servant to whom Sunak made the declaration in 2018; and Elizabeth Perelman, who was then Sunak's principal private secretary. No one believes that any of these four individuals was responsible for the leak.

A source who worked in Downing Street at the time says:

In April 2022, nobody else knew. Boris Johnson would

only have known if he'd requested an update on ministers' financial interests, which the PM can do at any time for any reason. So he would have had to ask for that. Remember, Rishi didn't declare this at a time when Boris was PM; he'd declared it a long time before Boris became PM. There is no way of knowing whether Boris did ask to see the register.

How this story ended up in *The Independent* remains a mystery, and the matter of whether any laws were broken when the records were leaked was obscured by the frenzied media reaction to it. Yet those who have taken a close interest in this part of Sunak's political career remain convinced that, contrary to what Sunak said at the time, the Labour Party had nothing to do with the leak. Instead, they believe, a member of Johnson's inner circle had the right connections and sufficient knowledge of these explosive facts to arrange for the story to be placed in the public domain without Johnson's fingerprints being near it. The motive for this piece of skulduggery was simple. With Johnson's future hanging in the balance, his acolytes thought Sunak posed the only serious threat to his leadership. Compromising him would probably stabilise Johnson. And, for a time, it worked.

A source familiar with the episode says:

Anna Isaac suddenly turned up with this scoop and people were suspicious of its origin. You can count on the fingers of one hand the number of people who were aware of Rishi's personal interests. Only a tiny number of people would have had access to them and for security reasons that access would only have been available in hard copy in an envelope that would have had a pen mark over the seal, making it impossible to open and reseal the envelope without any-body knowing.

In whose interests would it have been to try to weaken Sunak? And who would have been able to obtain the information about Murthy's tax status and then plant the story in *The Independent* safe in the knowledge that it could be published without Murthy having to personally confirm to the online newspaper her tax status? Amid a flurry of articles across every newspaper that weekend questioning whether Sunak really had the political judgement to become Prime Minister one day, the *Sunday Times* claimed that a Whitehall investigation to find the source was under way. It was made clear that a criminal prosecution might even be launched because it is against the law to leak someone's tax status. No concrete findings from this investigation have ever been made public because, as far as I have been able to ascertain, it never took flight in any meaningful way. Through my own inquiries, however, I believe that I have established the identi-ty of the culprit. I have chosen not to name him or her for the time being, but suffice it to say they are extremely lucky not to have faced wider scrutiny so far. For how long their high-profile status will allow them to remain distanced from this dirty trick is anybody's guess.

The controversy acted as an invitation to others to pore over the Sunaks' prosperity. Before long, Sunak's name was includ-ed in the *Sunday Times* Rich List, making him the first front-line politician to appear in the annual wealth ranking since its inception in 1989. His career in finance combined with his wife's 0.91 per cent stake in Infosys allowed the list's compilers to estimate their joint wealth at £730 million, placing them in equal 222nd place among Britain's 1,000 richest people. 'The

Infosys holding should have delivered at least £54 million in dividends over the past seven and a half years – including £11 million in 2021,' the *Sunday Times* noted. 'Without non-dom status [Murthy] would have been liable for £20.6 million of UK tax on those Infosys dividends.'

Even if Sunak had wanted to find out for himself who had hacked into his wife's personal tax affairs, thereby potentially breaking the law, he did not have long to catch his breath. He spent the weekend of the row overseeing the move of his wife and two daughters out of the glare of Downing Street and back to their mews house in Kensington. It was claimed publicly that the decision to return there had been planned all along because his eldest daughter was in her final term at a London day school before taking up a place as a boarder at Wycombe Abbey in Buckinghamshire. He also asked that Lord Geidt, the independent adviser on ministerial interests, examine whether his various declarations of interest had been properly stated. Geidt cleared him of any wrongdoing within two weeks.

Then, on the afternoon of 12 April, Downing Street confirmed that Sunak and Johnson were among fifty people who had received a £50 fixed penalty notice from the Metropolitan Police for attending Johnson's surprise birthday party in No. 10 on 19 June 2020. Bafflingly, Simon Case, the Cabinet Secretary, who was also photographed at the impromptu gathering – and who had attended a second illegal gathering in December 2020 – did not receive a fine. At the very least, this suggested a lack of consistency on the part of the police.

'Rishi was very shocked to get the fixed penalty notice,' remembers one friend. 'He hadn't been waiting around nervously for it. He had other problems to deal with at the time, but that wasn't one that he'd even considered.' Another friend echoes this, saying:

> He was very upset about it. You have to understand, getting into trouble is simply not something he'd ever done before. He'd never had so much as a speeding ticket, so it's obviously ironic that he'd had to enter the government to get a fixed penalty notice. That just isn't him at all.

Yet some Conservative MPs, including backbencher Philip Davies, felt that the fixed penalty notice represented a legitimate escape route for a Chancellor who not only found himself at loggerheads with his Prime Minister but saw his own political future now at risk of being tarnished by his association with Johnson. Davies thought Sunak could turn the situation to his advantage. 'I rang him and said it's a travesty, but you've got a massive opportunity here to re-establish your popularity in the country,' remembers Davies.

> I told him that if he said, 'I accept I'm in the wrong and I'm resigning because it's the honourable thing to do,' he would be massively respected and popular around the country for making that decision. He said to me, 'When I got the fixed penalty notice, I was crestfallen, and my first instinct was to resign because I knew it would be the honourable thing to do, but I've spoken to other people and I've thought about it and if I were to resign, I would put Boris in an impossible position. In effect, I would be saying that he should resign as well.' I told him he could resign but make it clear that Boris must stay, but he said, 'That wouldn't work.' He told me he didn't want Boris to resign. He said, 'If it was just me,

I'd fall on my sword, but it would put Boris in a position that I don't want to put him in.' I put the phone down and thought, 'Here he is taking one for the team again.' I was frustrated by it. But when people say he was always scheming to get rid of Boris, I know that's nonsense. That's not a matter of opinion, it's fact. This was the best opportunity he had if he was scheming against Boris.

One of those who had influenced Sunak's thinking by the time Davies rang him was fellow Conservative MP Kevin Hollinrake.

I spoke to Rishi that day on the phone and he said he was going to resign on principle. I said, 'I understand why you'd do that, but that's going to isolate Boris, and that's unhelpful on several levels.' And he got that, and that's the reason he didn't resign. He could've easily tried to bring down Boris under that pretext, expose Boris and put him under huge pressure, but he didn't.

Hollinrake adds rhetorically, 'If his plan all along was to bring Boris down, why didn't he do it?'

Soon after 8 p.m., having agonised for hours about his political future, Sunak released a statement in which he made 'an unreserved apology' but made clear that he would remain in post. It concluded, 'Like the Prime Minister, I am focused on delivering for the British people at this challenging time.' He could have had no idea that he was shortly to resign from the government for other reasons altogether; would then fight and lose a leadership contest; but would become Prime Minister unopposed in chaotic circumstances all within the ensuing six months.

CHAPTER 27

THE LAST SUPPER

It was to be expected that opposition politicians would call on Boris Johnson to resign for receiving a fixed penalty notice. As the first sitting Prime Minister in history to have been found to have broken the law – a law he had introduced – it would have been strange if this suggestion had not been made. But Johnson had no difficulty in shrugging off the demand. For one thing, he was now cast in some eyes as a war leader through his unwavering support for Ukraine following Russia's invasion and he hoped that an international crisis would obscure what he considered to be a little local difficulty. By comparison, criticism of Sunak's law-breaking was more muted. Aside from the fact that he wasn't the occupant of 10 Downing Street, there was some sympathy for what most people regarded as this teetotaller's purely technical breach of the rules. Furthermore, having just been comprehensively humbled over a period of less than three weeks, some wondered if Sunak may have already achieved his political peak. Johnson was among them. During an official trip to India in mid-April, he even told journalists that in the event of a possible Cabinet reshuffle he would be happy for Sunak to remain as his Chancellor, perhaps implying outwardly that he did not see Sunak as a threat at this stage.

Other threats to Johnson still loomed large, however. The

most immediate difficulty came from those voting in the local elections on 5 May. A drubbing at the polls would trigger fresh questions about his leadership, which had in any case been further weakened on 21 April by the launch of an inquiry by the House of Commons Privileges Committee into whether he had misled Parliament over Partygate allegations. Johnson's colleagues in the Parliamentary Conservative Party represented another danger. Also on 21 April, former minister Steve Baker called on Johnson to quit, telling the Commons in damning tones, 'The Prime Minister should just know the gig's up.' Other MPs had already decided that he had lost whatever moral authority he could previously have claimed to possess and concluded they did not want him to lead them into the next general election. Under party rules, once 15 per cent of Tory MPs moved against him he would face a confidence vote. The clock was ticking on his future, even in the absence of an obvious alternative leadership candidate.

With the cost-of-living crisis firmly lodged at the top of the news agenda, Sunak's chief political vulnerability lay in the question of taxes. As well as continued pressure to scrap the hated National Insurance rise, in late April 2022 it became known that during a Cabinet meeting he had been urged by the Policing Minister, Kit Malthouse, a staunch ally of Johnson, to cut other taxes in order to help families who were struggling with rising food and energy bills. Sunak's response was that such cuts would have to wait until the Autumn Budget, when the economic picture was clearer. Given the country's tax receipts were one quarter higher than they had been a year before, with HMRC figures showing it had collected £718.2 billion in the previous twelve months, his attitude caused no small amount of frustration. David Davis, the former Brexit

Secretary, was one senior figure willing to criticise his approach publicly. 'This yet again demonstrates how totally unnecessary the National Insurance contributions increase is,' Davis said. 'Every single forecast has been over-pessimistic. The one thing that will make the tax take go down is tax increases. Yet again, we have evidence the Treasury does not understand dynamic taxes.'

Sunak did make clear in an interview with the Mumsnet website, however, that a windfall tax on energy companies, which were making multi-billion-pound profits because of price rises, remained a possibility. This policy had first been advanced by the Labour Party, but, with inflation predicted by the Bank of England to hit 10 per cent and a recession thought to be in the offing, appropriating it did not seem to worry this self-declared small-state conservative Chancellor. Average household energy bills were forecast to be £2,800 per year and all avenues had to be explored. Kwasi Kwarteng, the Business Secretary, was resistant to the idea of a windfall tax on energy firms, calling it 'a disincentive to invest'. He staged a meeting with energy firm executives on 29 April asking them to set out their plans for putting profits into North Sea and offshore wind farm investment that would ultimately cut bills.

Given the government's various woes, the local elections one week later did not prove to be the outright whitewash that some Conservatives had feared, even if the results were very poor. The party lost 487 seats, mainly in the south, but this thrashing was counter-balanced to some degree by Labour gaining only 108 seats and making little impression in northern areas. The Liberal Democrats performed best, picking up 224 seats. Labour did succeed in taking overall control of the most councils, including three in London – Wandsworth,

Westminster and Barnet – which were regarded as jewels in the Tory crown. Modelling by Sky News suggested that if the results were replicated in a general election, the Conservatives would lose their majority but would remain the largest party in a hung parliament, with 278 MPs to Labour's 271. Johnson's view was that the local election results flattered Starmer, who was himself under police investigation by this stage for an alleged breach of Covid laws during a work trip to Durham in April 2021 – an episode that became known as 'Beergate'. (He would later be cleared of wrongdoing.) Yet momentum against Johnson was quietly building in his own party, with many Tory MPs linking Partygate and tax rises with the substandard outcome at the ballot box.

Sunak was out of the blocks quickly the weekend after the local elections, writing in the *Mail on Sunday* of his desire to help hard-pressed Britons. 'I know many families are still struggling,' he said. 'We will look to do all we can to help people with their energy bills in the autumn when we know more about what prices will be then.' He further used the article to announce £1.3 billion in military and aid funding for Ukraine. This came on top of £1.5 billion of support which had already been given, taking Britain's military spending on a war to its highest level since the campaigns in Iraq and Afghanistan twenty years previously. 'While we do everything we can to ease the squeeze for families at home, we have also ensured cash is there to help the Ukrainian people defend themselves and bring this horrific conflict to an end,' he added.

Normally, Sunak did not stray from his domestic economic brief, but behind the scenes his feeling was that the government should have been honest with voters about the economic price of backing Ukraine from the outset of the war, as he revealed in a lengthy interview with *The Spectator* in August 2022. 'I remember saying at the beginning of this thing: "defending freedom is important, but you've got to tell people that it is likely the energy bills go up to £4,000 or £5,000 in the worst-case scenario…"' he said. 'I was like: "you need to go into it knowing that that is what might happen. You've got to prepare the country for it, make sure that everyone is on board with that."'

This was also the view he took when dealing with the Covid crisis. 'He always has the same concerns,' says one ally. 'He feels it's vital to be honest about the trade-offs you're making and vital you don't try to pretend there are no costs to what you're doing. Nearly all decisions in politics have knock-on effects – if you're going to do one thing, you can't do something else.'

On 25 May, Sue Gray's Partygate report was published. While some gatherings she covered in the sixty-page dossier were troubling, including late-night revelries in the very corridors of power where draconian Covid restrictions imposed on the rest of the nation had been conceived and ratified, Sunak was mentioned only once, in relation to Johnson's surprise birthday party in June 2020. Gray revealed that this now-infamous twenty-minute afternoon event had taken place in the Cabinet Room, which had been set up with 'sandwiches, snacks, soft drinks and cans of beer'. As well as Carrie Johnson, 'the Permanent Secretary for Covid and Pandemic Response, Simon Case, attended for a short period having arrived early for a meeting', the report stated. 'The Chancellor was also there briefly having also arrived early for the same meeting. He had no advance knowledge about what had been planned.' There were four photographs of the event in the report, and Sunak featured in them, leaving an indelible trace of his links to the controversial episode. Yet Gray's description of the gathering does once again prompt the question of why Sunak was fined £50 when Case, who was guilty of an identical breach, was not. One suggestion that has been made is that Gray felt it impossible to criminalise one politician for having been at the event but not another, meaning that if Johnson was to be fined, Sunak would have to be fined as well. Case may have escaped punishment thanks to his status as a civil servant.

In a desperate bid to make amends, that day Johnson delivered a statement to the House of Commons and appeared at a press conference. He also attended a meeting with his backbenchers. The thrust of his message was that the government had 'learned our lesson' after the 'appalling' behaviour came to light. When asked by a journalist if he ever considered resigning, Johnson responded:

> I overwhelmingly feel it is my job to get on and deliver. No matter how bitter and painful that the conclusions of this may be – and they are – and no matter how humbling they are, I have got to keep moving forward and the government has got to keep moving. And we are.

These were the words of a Prime Minister on borrowed time.

The next day, Sunak introduced what would prove to be his final significant policy as Chancellor. It would also provide a brief distraction from the fallout of Gray's report. To what extent this announcement was choreographed is unclear, but the outcome of it was that the government was to provide up to £15 billion of support for millions of struggling households, funded partly by what Sunak called an 'energy price levy' but which most people would call a windfall tax on energy companies. The size and scope of the levy took many industry commentators by surprise.

The key event that made up Sunak's mind is said to have been the admission three weeks earlier by Bernard Looney, the CEO of the oil giant BP, that the company would invest in Britain regardless of whether or not a windfall tax was imposed. This sentiment was expressed as BP revealed quarterly profits of $6.2 billion, the highest for fourteen years. It was hoped that the levy, which would be in place until December 2025, would raise £5 billion. Some 8 million households on means-tested benefits would receive a £650 payment, with a further £200 being given to all energy bill payers that would not have to be repaid.

Some Tory MPs were scathing, with Richard Drax accusing Sunak of 'throwing red meat to socialists' and Craig Mackinlay arguing, 'I'm disappointed, embarrassed and appalled that a Conservative Chancellor could come up with this tripe.' Yet it was not as though Sunak was the first Conservative Chancellor to go down this route. In 1981, Sir Geoffrey Howe had introduced a levy on banks. And in 2011, George Osborne acted similarly by increasing the surcharge on North Sea oil and gas producers above the usual corporation tax rate. One ally of Sunak says that despite the criticism he received from some colleagues in the parliamentary party, he knew exactly what he was doing.

Rishi's view was that the profits the energy firms were making were extremely high, so some kind of extra tax was not illegitimate, but he didn't want some kind of crude windfall tax which would deter investment. One of the other lessons of the war he learned is that you need to be as close to energy independence as possible, which is why he subsequently set up the new Department for Energy Security and Net Zero. This desire for energy independence is a big thing for him. He wanted to construct something that, through investment incentives, encourages people to continue to get oil and gas out of the North Sea but would also raise money. Part of the reason he did it was Bernard Looney saying a windfall tax wouldn't change BP's decisions about investments. Rishi thought, 'If I can bring the tax that will generate some extra revenue but will also boost that by incentivising these companies to get more oil and gas out of the North Sea then that is a sensible thing to do.' Also, the state was having to spend a huge amount of money unexpectedly because energy prices had gone so high, so he thought, 'If we can find a way to raise tax from the same people who are benefiting from the same thing that is causing the state to spend all this money, and construct it in such a way that we're not deterring investment, it makes sense.'

Sunak defended his position in the Commons, saying, 'What people want and what I am is to be a pragmatic Chancellor, to do the things that I believe are right for the country both in the short term and in the long term.' Yet one critic who was close to the decision says it arguably provides further evidence of the extent to which he had been seized by the Treasury. 'The Treasury is a very powerful organisation,' says this person.

It has 1,800 civil servants, a strong esprit de corps and a strong sense of its identity. And Rishi was hand in glove with those guys. It was a meeting of minds. Are they small-state people? No. They wouldn't say they are. I never knew and still don't know beyond the Treasury orthodoxy what he stands for. I would struggle to define what Sunakism is. He reflects the Treasury orthodoxy and I don't see any time that he's challenged it. He's never done anything which suggests to me he's a small-state conservative. There have been tweaks on things like capital allowances and super-deductions. But National Insurance and a windfall tax are not small-state conservative things. I don't see him as the architect of that, I see the officials as the architects, but he did the Treasury's bidding.

By the time the Queen's Platinum Jubilee celebrations began on 2 June, thirty Conservative MPs had said publicly that Boris Johnson should quit. Over the course of that weekend, Johnson received a call from Sir Graham Brady, the chairman of the 1922 Committee of backbench MPs, in which he was told that the requisite number of letters calling for a confidence vote – fifty-four – had been submitted by Conservative MPs. Under party rules the vote would have to take place as soon as was practicably possible. No time was wasted. The secret ballot was held on Monday 6 June. Johnson scraped home with 211 MPs backing him – 59 per cent of the parliamentary party – and 148 MPs voting against him. In theory, this was enough for him to hang on for a further twelve months unchallenged. In practice, the result meant that almost half his colleagues wanted to ditch him. No previous leader had survived such a situation. Whatever Johnson claimed publicly, there was no longer any doubt that he was, at best, stumbling on. History does not relate whether Sunak voted for Johnson that day. Close friends are coy when asked this question.

On 20 June, the Conservative Party held its annual summer fundraiser at the V&A in London. Sunak found time to attend, though he arrived late. Polling strategist Chris Bruni-Lowe was seated next to him and during the dinner observed that, unusually for a politician with an eye on the future, he made no attempt to ingratiate himself with the many wealthy donors who were there. He recalls,

We talked for a long time about various things. He remembered that we'd met once before and was extremely personable. And he was obsessed with how the public saw him. For example, he told me his team had advised him not to wear a tie all the time and asked me what I thought about that. And he told me about some YouTube videos he'd made and said he'd be interested to know what I thought of them. He also asked some really forensic questions about his approval rating – in particular how it matched up against Boris's. He said he knew he was being blamed for the cost-of-living crisis and clearly thought this was unfair. I gave him a detailed breakdown of why Boris at that time was not being blamed for it, explaining that because he'd sold Britain's support for Ukraine so well, people were prepared to take on higher bills and energy costs. I remember Rishi's reaction to that. It was clear at that dinner that he wasn't going to stick around as Chancellor, but I took it as read that he'd be off to California next.

Twin disasters followed on 23 June in the form of a pair of by-elections in seats the Tories had won at the 2019 general election. The first, at Wakefield, was held after the Conservative MP Imran Ahmad Khan had been forced to resign following a criminal conviction for child sexual assault. Labour took it convincingly. The second, in the previously solid Tory constituency of Tiverton and Honiton, was called after Neil Parish admitted to viewing pornography on his mobile phone in the House of Commons chamber. Parish's 24,239 majority was overturned by the Liberal Democrats in one of Westminster's biggest ever by-election upsets. Shortly before dawn on 24 June, Oliver Dowden, the Conservative Party chairman and a close political ally of Sunak, resigned, saying that he took responsibility for the dire results. Johnson and his team, who were in Rwanda at the Commonwealth Heads of Government Meeting, became convinced that Dowden's departure was part of an orchestrated attempt by Sunak to undermine the Prime Minister, although Sunak's camp have always strenuously denied this was the case.

Less than a week later, on 30 June, further disgrace was brought upon the Conservative Party after *The Sun* revealed that Chris Pincher, the Deputy Chief Whip, had resigned for allegedly groping two men at the Carlton Club in central London while drunk. Initially, Johnson's office claimed that he was unaware that Pincher was prone to such behaviour and said Johnson had not heard any allegations about Pincher before appointing him. On 3 July, however, six further claims against him came to light, all concerning unwanted advances towards male MPs. One complainant said he had told Downing Street in February about his experience with Pincher and had raised doubts then about his suitability for becoming a whip. In response, No. 10 said that Johnson was not aware of any 'specific allegations' about Pincher.

That evening, Johnson and Sunak had their customary Sunday night Downing Street supper together. It would be the last. They were supposed to be putting the final touches to a long-planned joint speech setting out their economic vision for the country. Nobody else was present at the supper, but it is known that in the midst of going over the speech they discussed the Pincher affair. Sunak had little to say when Johnson asked him what he thought about it. This neutral position is said to have unnerved Johnson.

In fact, Sunak was somewhat distracted himself. He had come to regard the joint speech with Johnson as a disastrous idea. Once again, it brought into sharp focus their difference in outlook on economic matters – a contrast which had until this point been disguised by the fact that they had planned to discuss separate areas of the economy when the speech was delivered. Moreover, it soon became obvious to Sunak that, for purely political reasons, Johnson's approach to this specific exercise was at odds with his preferred way of working through a problem. No sooner had they agreed something than Johnson would make a new set of demands based on his own agenda. Sunak found this method of working impossible. With Johnson fighting to save himself politically, he was said to be prepared to take ever greater risks with the economy, advocating tax cuts because the political circumstances dictated it rather than because the economic situation allowed it. 'Boris could see the way the political wind was blowing and was keen to show he wanted to cut taxes straight away,' says a source. 'This highlighted how different their positions were and it was getting worse and worse. Rishi could see it was a question of Boris saying to himself, "If we cut taxes now I can buy myself some more time."' By that Sunday evening, Sunak had concluded that his working relationship with Johnson was all but over.

As the Pincher affair escalated on Monday 4 July, No. 10 changed its story, admitting that Johnson knew of 'allegations that were either resolved or did not progress to a formal complaint' and adding that 'it was deemed not appropriate to stop an appointment simply because of unsubstantiated allegations'. While No. 10 attempted to put out that fire, the joint speech negotiations became even more problematic for Sunak. By the morning of 5 July, when a Cabinet meeting was held, he had made up his mind to resign and told close friends of his decision. Whether he decided before or after Lord McDonald, a former Foreign Office civil servant, came forward with what appeared to be incontrovertible evidence that Johnson had known about Pincher before appointing him to the Whips' Office is not clear. Yet McDonald, who had crossed swords with Johnson when he was Foreign Secretary, arguably hammered the decisive nail into the Prime Minister's political coffin. In a letter to the Parliamentary Standards Commissioner, Kathryn Stone, which he shared online, McDonald alleged that Downing Street had failed to tell the truth about the matter. He said that Johnson was briefed 'in person' about a 'formal complaint' into Pincher's conduct in a separate episode that had taken place in 2019. This had resulted in an investigation. The upshot of McDonald's letter that day was that Johnson was forced to admit that he could, after all, remember the 2019 briefing but did not 'recall this' when the latest allegations against Pincher emerged.

At 5 p.m., Johnson gave an emergency interview to the BBC saying he 'bitterly' regretted not acting on the information he had received about Pincher. It was too late. At 6.02 p.m., Sajid Javid, the Health Secretary, resigned. 'The British people rightly expect integrity from their government,' Javid wrote in his letter to Johnson. Nine minutes later, Sunak's resignation letter was also published. On one side of typed House of Commons headed paper, he spoke of his 'deep sadness' at quitting and said he had not taken the decision lightly. 'However,' he wrote, 'the public rightly expect government to be conducted properly, competently and seriously.' He carried on:

> Our country is facing immense challenges. We both want a low-tax, high-growth economy, and world class public services, but this can only be responsibly delivered if we are prepared to work hard, make sacrifices and take difficult decisions.
>
> I firmly believe the public are ready to hear that truth. Our people know that if something is too good to be true then it's not true. They need to know that whilst there is a path to a better future, it is not an easy one. In preparation for our proposed joint speech on the economy next week, it has become clear to me that our approaches are fundamentally too different.
>
> I am sad to be leaving Government but I have reluctantly come to the conclusion that we cannot continue like this.

It is clear that Sunak's departure tipped the balance as far as Johnson's premiership was concerned. Contrary to what some suggested at the time, however, friends of Sunak and Javid insist they did not conspire in the timing of their resignations to set in motion a coup to topple Johnson. Rather, independently of each other, both felt compelled to act because they regarded the status quo as untenable – in Sunak's case because his view of how to run the economy was so different to Johnson's. 'It wasn't easy,' says Claire Coutinho, who was

Sunak's parliamentary private secretary during his chancellorship. 'His letter set it out. He had been very worried about
inflation and not racking up too much debt and Boris was less
worried about that. But it was not co-ordinated between him
and Sajid.'

Another ally who was in regular contact with him at the
time says:

Rishi was very careful not to plot, not to get a campaign
ready. He did want to make his relationship with Boris work
in the early months of 2022 if he possibly could, but he came
to the view around the end of June that it was an unsustainable situation and that it was important for senior figures
to do something about it. The way the leadership election
turned out against Liz Truss, he'd probably have been better
off if he'd sat it out and not resigned himself, but that's not
the sort of person he is. He believes in doing something if
you can to rectify a situation. So he was not scheming up
until that point. The timing of his resignation was dictated
by the Chris Pincher scandal and the dissatisfaction it gave
rise to. Rishi was despairing about reaching a consensus
with Boris on economic policy and the growing tension
between them over financial discipline. Rishi was always on
the side of paying your debts and Boris was always saying,
'We can always come up with some more money.' There was
a really big gap between them in terms of how rigorous you
have to be about the economy and how rigorous you have
to be about decision-making. Rishi could never believe
how chaotic the decision-making was in Boris's Downing
Street. He could have meetings with Boris where something
was agreed and then in the next meeting Boris would say

the opposite. Agreements could not be nailed down with him and that's absolutely not how Rishi does business, as everyone can see. He goes through things methodically and concludes deals that everybody trusts. Rishi had never come across a situation in his life of somebody very senior like Boris who was just so varied in their thinking from one week to the next, or who went back on what had been agreed. It came to a head in June 2022 when everyone was asking after Covid, 'What is the growth strategy?' at the same time as repeated scandals were pushing Boris over the edge. He thought it was unsustainable.

Johnson is said to have been livid when he learned of Sunak's resignation, swearing repeatedly in front of aides about what he regarded as a personal betrayal. Not having time to pause for thought, he quickly gathered himself together to join a group of about fifty MPs to whom he was giving a long-promised drink thanking them for their support during the previous month's confidence vote. According to Sebastian Payne, who charted Johnson's decline in his book *The Fall of Boris Johnson*, he was greeted by cheers as he entered his parliamentary office, where the gathering was taking place. 'I want to thank everybody, everyone has done a fantastic job. We fight on,' he said. 'Those of you who champion free markets and tax cuts might find in light of the very recent news that we might be able to deliver some of those now.'

Many of those present that evening are said to have told Johnson by way of reassurance that they were glad to see the back of Sunak. However well-intentioned such remarks were, this sentiment was of little value. The next day, 6 July, a further three dozen members of the government quit in the space of twenty-four hours. By lunchtime on 7 July, Johnson had resigned. According to his spin doctor, Guto Harri, Johnson wanted to send a video to Sunak calling him a 'c*nt', but he resisted the urge. It would have made little difference in any case. By then, Sunak was hours away from officially launching his campaign to replace him.

CHAPTER 28

GETTING READY FOR RISHI

Rishi Sunak is often accused by his political enemies of having spent months carefully planning Boris Johnson's downfall so that he could trigger a leadership contest, convince a majority of MPs to back him, and then win over enough Conservative Party members to enter 10 Downing Street. Yet, as is well known, things did not work out that way in the summer of 2022. Looking at the outcome of that leadership race objectively, the fact that Sunak failed to clear the last of these hurdles and was instead beaten by the activists' choice, Liz Truss, is surely proof that, whatever the scale of his political ambitions, he could never have been certain of victory. Apart from anything else, he was widely criticised for being a tax-raising Chancellor; viewed with scepticism by many thanks to the leak about his wife's tax affairs; and knew he was actively disliked by thousands for – in their eyes – finishing off the frontline political career of Boris Johnson, who was still held in great affection by many party members.

'Rishi was fully prepared for the fact that resigning might mean the end of his own career and that he might not be the beneficiary of Johnson's fall,' says a friend who was in regular contact with Sunak throughout this period of time.

So in that sense his resignation was not a plot to become

Prime Minister. He thought the party would be better off with a different leader, but he was aware that things couldn't be controlled and votes could go in any direction. Had he just been thinking of his own interests, he wouldn't have resigned because it's a time-honoured tradition in the Conservative Party that the assassin doesn't get to wear the crown. Yes, he thought his resignation would probably bring Boris Johnson down, but he had no idea whether he was going to replace him.

Sunak had dozens of supporters in the parliamentary party, but insiders say his campaign was not as assured as his opponents claimed, and it began less smoothly than is perhaps realised. On 7 July, the day Johnson announced his intention to stand down as Prime Minister, Sunak and his closest advisers did not have an 'oven-ready' video to launch on various social media channels, as some thought. They did not even have a script that was in a fit state to record. Instead, they went looking for a quiet place in which to base themselves so that an agreed form of words could be worked on. That afternoon, a room was booked in the Conrad Hotel close to St James's Park Underground Station and a draft thrashed out before Sunak had his first stab at committing it to film. Having put in a solid few hours' work, he left to attend *The Spectator*'s nearby summer drinks party, an event so prominent in the Conservative Party social calendar that aides told him it would be unwise to miss it. By the time it began, his colleagues Suella Braverman and Tom Tugendhat had revealed their desire to stand for the leadership.

The following morning, the final touches were put to Sunak's pitch speech and two further takes were recorded at the hotel. Once finished, his team relocated to a small office in Dean Trench Street in Westminster that was owned by the PR firm Bridge F61 and shortly after 4 p.m., his leadership campaign launched officially on Twitter, making him the first major candidate to declare. 'I'm standing to be the next leader of the Conservative Party and your Prime Minister,' he tweeted. 'Let's restore trust, rebuild the economy and reunite the country. #Ready4Rishi'. Some reporters were surprised at the 'slickness' of the accompanying three-minute video, which was produced by Sunak's media adviser Cass Horowitz. They wondered how such an operation could have been launched so soon. The quicker-witted ones soon discovered that the name 'readyforrishi.com' had first been registered with the American domain name registrar GoDaddy on 23 December 2021, while 'ready4rishi.com' – the slogan used online by Sunak throughout the official campaign – was registered on 6 July 2022, the day after he resigned as Chancellor. As the former domain name these days redirects to the latter domain name, there was a suspicion about how long in the planning Sunak's campaign had been. Those who are close to him insist that he did not sanction the GoDaddy registration in December 2021, however.

The video itself was heavily dependent on photos from the Sunak family album and took a nostalgic look at his parents' arrival in Britain decades earlier and the opportunities their hard work had afforded him. Then, he turned his attention to the economy. To a generic piano soundtrack, Sunak said the country faced its most serious challenges for a generation. 'Do we confront this moment with honesty, seriousness and determination, or do we tell ourselves comforting fairy tales that might make us feel better in the moment but will leave our children worse off tomorrow?' he asked. In what appeared to be an oblique reference to the chaos of Johnson's administration, he added, 'Someone has to grip this moment and make the right decisions. That's why I'm standing to be the next leader of the Conservative Party and your Prime Minister.'

A snap opinion poll of 493 Conservative Party members carried out by Opinium for *Channel 4 News* made Sunak the favourite to become the next Prime Minister on 25 per cent, ahead of Liz Truss on 21 per cent. It would turn out to be one of very few polls that was favourable to Sunak. His priority, he said, was to kill the disease of inflation. Truss, who was at a G20 summit in Bali and had not declared yet, had already put the word out that, as the only candidate who could unite Red Wall voters in the north of England with traditional so-called Blue Wall Tory voters, she was Johnson's natural successor. The first Cabinet minister to back Sunak was Mark Spencer, the former Chief Whip, who rebutted rumours of financial scandals involving Sunak straight away. He told the BBC, 'There are no secrets to Rishi Sunak. There are no skeletons in that cupboard.' Yet Johnson's supporters swore revenge. One Cabinet minister who was loyal to him told the *Financial Times* that Friday afternoon of their plan to try to prevent Sunak from winning the leadership contest. 'Rishi will get everything he deserves for leading the charge in bringing down the Prime Minister,' the anonymous MP commented ominously.

Sunak and his team spent the weekend drumming up support among MPs and preparing for what they knew was likely to be an arduous campaign. Their efforts were not helped when a clip from a 2001 BBC TV series called *Middle Classes: Their Rise and Sprawl* surfaced. In it, a twenty-year-old Sunak, then an undergraduate, was seen discussing his social circle, saying, 'I have friends who are aristocrats, I have friends who are upper class, I have friends who are, you know, working class,' before correcting himself and saying:

> Well, not working class, but I mix and match, and then I go to see kids from an inner-city state school and tell them to apply to Oxford and talk to them about people like me and then I shock them at the end of chatting to them for half an hour and tell them I was at Winchester.

Inevitably, only the first half of this dialogue was widely shared on social media channels, casting him in the worst possible light. A 424-word 'dirty dossier' on Sunak was also circulated among Tory MPs via WhatsApp that weekend. Depicting him as the left-of-centre candidate, it accused him of 'a failed March 2022 budget that was a welter of contradictions, tax raises and sleights of hand that defied analysis, logic or comprehension' and alleged he had 'publicly lied not once but twice when seeking to explain his wife's "non-dom" tax status'. It also claimed he had 'launched his campaign for the leadership of the Conservative Party with a website domain registered in December 2021'. 'Getting "Ready for Rishi" means supporting a candidate who, like Boris, landed a Partygate fine from the police for breaking lockdown rules.' After doing some digging of its own, *The Times* confronted a PR consultant called Patrick Robertson, asking if it was true that he was linked with the damaging memo. Robertson would only admit to having shared it.

The process for the leadership election was approved by the 1922 Committee on 11 July. Each candidate would need to gain the support of at least twenty Conservative MPs to reach the first ballot. Any candidates who failed to secure thirty votes at the first ballot would have to drop out. Thereafter, the candidate with the fewest votes would be eliminated after subsequent ballots until only two MPs remained. A series of twelve public hustings would then be held around Britain over five weeks, during which Conservative Party members could cast their vote at any point, with the winner being declared in London on 5 September. Boris Johnson would remain in post until his successor was announced. Two debates between the candidates were televised either side of the final ballot of MPs. Multiple TV, radio and press interviews also took place throughout the contest. There was criticism that the race would stretch over a period of eight weeks, but with eight candidates to sift before the members had an opportunity to pick their preferred leader, this was the compromise that was reached after talks with the National Conservative Convention, the most senior body of the Conservative Party's voluntary wing. Alongside Sunak and Truss were Tom Tugendhat, Suella Braverman, Jeremy Hunt, Nadhim Zahawi, Kemi Badenoch and Penny Mordaunt.

On 13 July, the day of the first ballot, Truss received a major boost after two of Johnson's staunchest allies, Jacob Rees-Mogg and Nadine Dorries, backed her. Speaking to broadcasters in Downing Street as they left a Cabinet meeting, they said they favoured Truss because of her low-tax Euroscepticism (despite the fact that she voted Remain at the 2016 referendum). Given that they were speaking with Johnson's blessing, the clear implication was that Sunak was neither in favour of lower taxes nor sufficiently Eurosceptic. Allies of Sunak have described this episode as akin to a 'drive-by shooting' between rival gangs. Rees-Mogg followed it up with a *Daily Mail* article in which he said that Truss opposed Sunak 'raising the tax burden to the highest since the socialism of 1950s Labour'. When asked by Sky News if he considered Sunak a socialist, Rees-Mogg replied, 'Well, no, you're referring to things that may or may not have been said in Cabinet. I think as a Chancellor, he made decisions that were of the left rather than on the right, that he was a tax-increasing Chancellor. I didn't support the decisions he made.' And would he serve in a Sunak government? 'No, of course I wouldn't,' he shot back. 'I believe his behaviour towards Boris Johnson, his disloyalty, means that I could not possibly support him. And he wouldn't want me in his Cabinet anyway.' One well-placed Westminster figure says they can remember speaking to Rees-Mogg at this time and being taken aback at the way he targeted Sunak. 'I've known Jacob take people on before, but I've never known him brief against people in that sort of style,' says this source. 'But he did tell me in all seriousness that he would like to lead the party, so that may explain his behaviour.'

In the first round of voting, Jeremy Hunt and Nadhim Zahawi failed to attract thirty backers and were removed from the contest. The next day, Suella Braverman followed suit. Two weekend TV debates ensued. On 15 July, Channel 4 invited the remaining five candidates to be questioned en masse. Polling afterwards showed that Tom Tugendhat was considered to have done best, with 36 per cent of the public backing him, followed by Sunak on 25 per cent. Truss, who had done little by way of preparation, came out worst with only 6 per cent support. Then, on 17 July, ITV hosted the same group. This time, Truss performed more convincingly, attacking Sunak over his private education and his record on the economy. So piercing were her words that Sunak apparently turned to her afterwards to ask, 'Why are we doing this?'

Three subsequent rounds of voting over the following three days knocked out the remaining contenders, leaving only Truss and Sunak standing. Footage of Sunak celebrating this result by pumping his fist, hugging friends and shouting to his team, 'Guys, we totally smashed it, well done!' spread around social media. Many mocked him for what they considered to be David Brent-like behaviour. Yet given the capriciousness of the electorate he had just won over, he could probably be forgiven for feeling so pleased. He led in every round and showed steady progress throughout. By contrast, Truss only narrowly made it to the party members' vote stage, having lagged behind Penny Mordaunt until the fifth round of the MPs' ballot, when she leapfrogged her rival.

Winning over a sufficient number of colleagues in the parliamentary party was the easy bit for Sunak. His next task was to convince the 180,000 or so Tory members around Britain that he was best placed to succeed Johnson – and that he deserved to do so. At this point, his campaign team expanded, requiring a move to larger offices in Holborn. Nobody was surprised that he was willing to put in extremely long days, but others were expected to keep up. Alongside about thirty unpaid volunteers was a group of key players including Mel Stride, the Treasury Select Committee chairman who was his campaign manager; his special adviser, Liam Booth-Smith; Cass Horowitz; and former government whips Mark Spencer, Gavin Williamson and Mark Harper. This trio's knowledge of the parliamentary party was considered invaluable in ensuring Sunak made it onto the final shortlist. Sunak's senior parliamentary assistant, Lisa Lovering, was also a mainstay, accompanying him to every event during the campaign. Dominic Raab and Grant Shapps introduced Sunak at his in-person campaign launch. And further support came from MPs Kevin Hollinrake, Richard Holden, Craig Williams and Julian Smith. The consensus was that Sunak certainly had the most polished and professional campaigning machine among those who stood.

It is believed that each candidate was asked for £300,000 to meet the expense of hiring the venues. 'Tickets and merchandise covered some costs,' explains Peter Booth, chairman of the National Conservative Convention. Sponsorship also came from some broadcasters, including TalkTV and LBC, which broadcast the events. 'When the contest began, Rishi rang me within thirty-six hours to introduce himself,' adds Booth.

> He also rang the other five members of my team individually to introduce himself. This was extremely impressive. Liz Truss's team called us and we spoke to her a few days later. It was probably more difficult for her as Foreign Secretary fulfilling the duties of government and campaigning to be leader. Rishi Sunak definitely stole the initiative. Rishi also wrote a letter to me after the contest was finished to thank me for my involvement in helping to organise the hustings, being at every venue around the country. I was very impressed that he took the time to do this.

Things got off to a poor start for Sunak, however. Straight after the final round of MPs' voting, on 21 July, a YouGov poll of Tory members was published suggesting that Truss would beat him by 62 per cent to 38 per cent. This set the tone for the remainder of the campaign. In every members' poll taken from 11 July, Sunak came off second best. A friend who spoke to him throughout that time says:

It was clear once it went to the activists that Rishi was really up against it. They were looking for somebody who was new and who'd stood by Boris. Rishi lost because of that perception of betrayal. And Truss fought a good campaign and was better at campaigning than she was at governing, as it turned out. But fundamentally, Rishi had that one third of activists who would not countenance voting for the person who had precipitated the leadership election. He couldn't have quantified in advance that he was going to be cast as the Judas figure, but he knew he had been. It was very clear. It was a constant problem.

On 25 July, Sunak and Truss travelled to the Victoria Hall in Stoke-on-Trent for a head-to-head televised debate. The atmosphere was tense. Over the preceding three or four days, journalists had feasted on briefings and counter-briefings provided by each candidate's camp, cementing the idea that there was little love lost between them. A good example of how catty things became can be found in comments made by Nadine Dorries, who chose to criticise Sunak for wearing expensive clothes: '[Truss] will be travelling the country wearing her earrings which cost circa £4.50 from Claire Accessories. Meanwhile… Rishi visits Teeside [*sic*] in Prada shoes worth £450 and sported £3,500 bespoke suit as he prepared for crunch leadership vote.'

Whether sanctioned or not, Dorries's observations certainly chimed with Truss's own view that her route to victory would come by connecting with 'ordinary' Tory voters. As such, she portrayed herself as the plucky anti-Establishment candidate who favoured tax cuts, a role she slotted into easily. She believed the privately educated Sunak's personal wealth far removed him from most people's experiences. 'Liz thought then and still thinks now that in Britain, the corporate model and the City are more likely to believe in big government and higher taxes,' says one MP who supported her. 'The Tory voter base is with small business and people who are frustrated by the oligarchy. Big business, vast swathes of the civil service, the banks, the Treasury and the Office for Budget Responsibility are part of the Establishment. There's a groupthink about it all. She put Rishi in that camp.'

One Sunak associate says Truss made little attempt to disguise her personal dislike for him.

> Rishi found relations with Liz very difficult during the leadership election. She was very frosty towards him and didn't engage with him or talk to him much, if at all. Whereas it's quite normal in politics if you're running against somebody that you do have decent relations with them, she was very unfriendly, which was actually very short-sighted as she didn't even stop to think about the fact that they would in any case one day have to work together to win a general election. He found her very difficult on the campaign trail in that regard.

Although rumours about Truss's personal life were being swapped at the time, including one claim of an extra-marital affair and another that a sex tape of her existed, Sunak told his team that they were to have nothing to do with what he dismissed as grubby speculation. It should also be noted that during the campaign Truss never raised the issue of Sunak's wife's former tax status or of Sunak having had a Green Card.

During the first twelve minutes of the Stoke-on-Trent

debate, Sunak interrupted Truss so frequently that he was later publicly accused by a member of her team of 'aggressive mansplaining' and 'shouty behaviour'. When talk moved on to economic issues, Truss compared Sunak to Gordon Brown, saying his refusal to cut tax would drive Britain into a recession. Sunak hit back, declaring Truss's promise to borrow in order to fund tax cuts to be neither 'moral' nor 'conservative' and predicting it would 'tip millions of people into misery'. Citing a figure of £30 billion, he said, 'That is the country's credit card and it's our children and grandchildren, everyone here's kids will pick up the tab for that. There's nothing conservative about it.' Given subsequent events, some of the blows they traded that night on economic issues were eerily prescient. At one point, Sunak foretold that Truss's economic policy would force up mortgage rates. She said, 'This is scaremongering, this is Project Fear.' But Sunak used this accusation to remind people that, unlike her, he had voted for Brexit. He retorted, 'I remember the referendum campaign and there was only one of us who was on the side of Remain and Project Fear and it was you, not me.'

A poll of Conservative voters after the BBC debate conducted by Opinium found that Truss had performed better, though Sunak won narrowly among all voters. In many ways, this poll summarised perfectly how the rest of the campaign played out. There is a school of thought that says Truss emerged victorious because she was more effective in speaking directly to the constituency that mattered most for the purposes of the contest: Conservative Party activists. The same theory has it that Sunak lost in large part because his campaign was aimed towards the country as a whole, even though most of them were not Conservative Party activists and therefore did not have a vote. Yet even when Sunak tried to recast himself as a tax-cutter, it backfired. On 27 July, he put forward a proposal to slash VAT on energy bills – an idea he had rejected in February. It did no good, with Truss's close friend Kwasi Kwarteng accusing him of performing 'a screeching handbrake U-turn' and telling Sky News he was 'delighted to see that Rishi Sunak has now come late to the party and decided that tax cuts are a good idea and they're not a fairy tale'.

And yet, curiously for a leadership hopeful who accused her rival of being an Establishment man, it is clear that Truss was, arguably, the greater beneficiary of help from the Establishment. While Sunak managed to convince only one national newspaper – *The Times* – that he was the best-placed candidate to lead party and country, Truss, who had scraped onto the final ballot, was endorsed by the *Daily Mail*, *Daily Telegraph* and *Daily Express*. She also managed to attract £537,939 in cash and services donations – more than Sunak, who accepted £496,043. (Perhaps surprisingly, Sir Keir Starmer received more than either of them – just over £700,000 in cash and services – when he stood for the Labour leadership in 2020.) Her campaign was further bolstered by the fact that Boris Johnson invited her to a breakfast meeting in Downing Street on 29 July and to another meeting at Chequers a few weeks later, both times offering her advice on her campaign strategy.

A supporter of Sunak who was in touch with him during the campaign reflects:

The contest was remarkable. It's an odd thing to say about someone who won the MPs' round and who had been

Chancellor until just before it began, but in many ways he was so up against the machine. You had No. 10 allowing Nadine and Jacob to stand in Downing Street endorsing Truss. You had Cabinet ministers writing about Cabinet discussions that were designed to paint Rishi in the worst light on a range of issues. It was tough. Lots of people in his shoes would have rung Liz and said, 'I'm not dropping out but I'm just doing two events a week, call the dogs off.' But he said, 'I'm going to fight.'

The month of August was devoted to the dozen hustings in all four corners of the United Kingdom, where each candidate would make a ten-minute speech before fielding questions from the audience. Truss, who has never been considered a natural public speaker, seemed far happier operating in this environment than in a TV studio. Her confidence grew, thanks partly to having attracted the support of most of those MPs who had already been eliminated from the leadership con-test – Braverman, Mordaunt, Tugendhat and Zahawi – plus the backing of Javid. Only Hunt endorsed Sunak. Badenoch did not declare her hand. Worse for Sunak was that two of his backers, former Cabinet ministers Robert Buckland and Alun Cairns, defected to Truss's camp amid a blaze of publicity. He also had to endure repeated questions about his role in Boris Johnson's defenestration. Yet he never became depressed, ac-cording to friends, and he was greatly encouraged when his political hero Nigel Lawson, by then ninety years old, came out in his favour, praising him in the *Daily Telegraph* as the only candidate who understood Thatcherite economics and the principle of sound money while prophesying that Truss's economic plans could lead to ruin.

'It's very revealing that Rishi kept going – and at massive intensity,' says one ally.

Truss kept doubting the polling numbers. At one point she got YouGov to do another members' poll just for her because she kept thinking the published numbers must be wrong and she couldn't understand why he was still going at it with such vigour. She became very sceptical and wanted to know why he was arguing so hard. I think she realised that he didn't think it was a foregone conclusion. Rishi's view was that he wanted to say then all that he had to say about the economy. It's hard to get up on a Sunday morning and drive four hours to an event to give a series of speeches when a newspaper has a poll out that morning that you're going to lose, but he was arguing for stuff that he really believed in. He derived strength from his belief that what he was saying was right. When you're Chancellor, you're under the PM and can't say exactly what you think. Budgets are always a compromise. I think he really enjoyed being able to tell people what he thought. Having risen so quickly in politics, he'd never had a chance to do that.

Away from the hustings, Sunak's campaign sometimes misfired. For example, on 5 August, a recording made a week earlier was leaked to the *New Statesman* in which he was seen telling activists in Tunbridge Wells that as Chancellor he had diverted public funding from deprived areas. 'I managed to start changing the funding formulas, to make sure areas like this are getting the funding they deserve because we inherited a bunch of formulas from Labour that shoved all the funding into deprived urban areas and that needed to be undone,' he said. 'I started the work of undoing that.' He was lambasted by Conservatives including Jake Berry and Zac Goldsmith as well as by Labour MPs for what they said was at best an appalling blunder and at worst something close to pork barrel politics. Yet it was near-certain that his comments were taken out of context, as his spokesman explained that he had moved the money from inner-city areas to towns and poorer rural areas.

Other endeavours were more successful, such as when Dominic Raab, the Justice Secretary, who stuck by Sunak when other MPs deserted him, was persuaded to write an article for *The Times* in which he described Truss's tax-cutting plans as 'an electoral suicide note'. Sunak also gave a notable interview to GB News on 6 August in which he took a much tougher line on illegal immigration and grooming gangs than people might have expected from the supposedly left-of-centre candidate of Asian origin. He vowed to complete Brexit and fully 'take back control' of Britain's borders, even if that meant leaving the European Convention on Human Rights (ECHR). Of the cross-Channel migrant crisis, he said:

> It vexes me and was part of the reason I supported Brexit, even though I was told that it would be potentially damaging for my career. But I believed in it and one of the reasons was clearly making sure that we had proper control of our borders. We've got to change the definition of asylum. At the moment we use the ECHR, the European definition, and that is very broad. It's become broader. Over time, it's exploited by lefty lawyers for lots of spurious reasons to keep people here. So, I think we should move to a different definition, another international standard that the Australians and others use, which is much tighter and narrower, so that will help.

He also said countries needed

> to agree to take back all your failed asylum seekers ... I
> want everyone watching to be in absolutely no doubt I will
> grip this situation. The plan I've set out is radical. I will do
> whatever it takes including any legal changes to make the
> Rwanda [deportation] policy work, because we must have
> control over our borders.

On Asian grooming gangs, he blamed 'political correctness' on matters of race for the police's failure to tackle the problem. He pledged to introduce a new requirement for police forces to record the ethnicity of those involved in grooming and said he would create a new life tariff for sex gang members, with very little opportunity for parole.

During the leadership election, my own research, published in mid-August, helped explain why Truss managed to capture the imagination of Tories around the country. Most had clocked the big policy divide between them, namely their approach to tax and debt. In principle, many agreed with Sunak that the priority should be to rein in the deficit, but the feeling that people were struggling and needed help now meant that Truss's pledge of early tax cuts found a ready audience. As one woman asked of Sunak's commitment to fiscal prudence, 'I wonder if he would be saying the same thing if he was on my wage?'

The idea that Sunak's gilded lifestyle put him in a different world from most voters dominated their perceptions. Asked what word or phrase came to mind when they thought about each candidate, the most prominent answer for Sunak was 'rich'. This might have mattered less were it not combined with 'out of touch'. His family's wealth and his wife's former non-dom tax status were always among the first things spontaneously mentioned about him in focus groups. Some made disobliging references to his role in Johnson's downfall ('snake' and 'backstabber' were terms often heard) and many felt he had helped engineer it to further his own ambitions. With the pandemic receding, views about Sunak's record as Chancellor were by this point also decidedly mixed. There was praise for the furlough scheme and Sunak's calm authority but anger about wasted money, bungled PPE contracts and rising taxes. While Sunak was predicted by voters to be a competent premier if he won, and to have good judgement in a crisis, Truss was well ahead when it came to being honest with the public, behaving with personal integrity and caring about 'people like me' – all hangovers, however unfair, from stories of riches and tax-related chicanery.

Bitter off-the-record briefings remained a feature throughout the contest. At the hustings in Birmingham on 23 August, with Truss's victory all but assured, Sunak was asked whether he would vote for her emergency tax-cutting package. He refused to answer what he called a hypothetical question. The next day he was pushed for an answer to the same question on BBC Radio 4's *Today* programme. Again he refused, saying he was 'not going to engage in these things' while the leadership contest was under way. One of Truss's allies told reporters:

> Sunak is in a complete micro-world of his own, he's thrashing around all over the place like a wounded stoat. All he's doing is attacking her. At some point someone has to grab him by the scruff of the neck and say, 'What are you doing? Are you trying to destroy this party?'

Two days later, at the penultimate hustings at Norwich, both candidates were asked whether President Macron was 'friend or foe'. Sunak responded, 'Friend.' Truss said, 'The jury is out. But if I become PM, I'll hold him to deeds not words.' While Truss may have supplied the instant gratification of a populist answer, it should come as no surprise that, by late August, many Conservatives felt the contest had outlived its usefulness.

Previous chapters of this book have referred to a long interview Sunak gave to *The Spectator* during the final week of the contest. Headlined 'The lockdown files: Rishi Sunak on what we weren't told', it contained the most conspicuous and, arguably, the most important words he spoke that summer. As we have seen, he claimed that minutes from meetings attended by the government's scientific advisers edited out dissenting voices; said that 'empowering' independent scientists 'screwed' Britain; criticised the government for pumping out a 'fear narrative'; and lamented the fact that nobody ever considered the economic costs of lockdown proportionately. 'I wasn't allowed to talk about the trade-off', he revealed. Sunak said 'no one talked' about missed GP appointments, the growing NHS backlog or the damage done to children's education. He said that in one meeting

I was very emotional about it. I was like: 'Forget about the economy. Surely we can all agree that kids not being in school is a major nightmare' or something like that. There was a big silence afterwards. It was the first time someone had said it. I was so furious.

It is rare in politics that voters are able to compare what an

MP claimed after the event to have said with what they actually said via a contemporaneous record. Yet in March 2023, after the *Daily Telegraph* published a leaked cache of 100,000 pandemic-era WhatsApp messages from Matt Hancock's phone, it became possible to do just that – a test from which Sunak emerged positively. As one colleague says:

> The record shows that he was truthful. Other things can also be seen through that prism as well. He really did keep saying we must pay this money back. He was deeply uncomfortable with what was going on, how draconian things were, how decisions were taken, how little challenge there was to those decisions.

By the time of the final hustings at Wembley Arena on 31 August, it was obvious that Truss had won. Sunak gave a spirited speech in which he thanked his parents and wife, who were in attendance, and also, some might say rather more magnanimously, paid tribute to Truss. Michael Gove was singled out for praise as well. In his last campaign interview a few days earlier, Sunak had told the *Financial Times* that he 'struggled' to see how Truss's economic plans could work. He may have been proved right subsequently, but this view did not change enough minds at the time. Still, some detected that at Wembley he seemed to speak more naturally and fluently than he had done all summer. Whether he was certain that he would one day be proved right on economic matters or simply relieved that the contest was over is debatable. On 5 September, both candidates and their teams gathered at the Queen Elizabeth II Conference Centre in Westminster to hear the results. Of the votes cast, Sunak secured 60,399 (43 per cent), while 81,326 (57 per cent) backed Truss. Though she had won, it was not by the landslide that had been predicted. Sunak and Truss barely exchanged a word when they were told the outcome ten minutes before everybody else. They have spoken only once since, and that was when they greeted each other with a terse 'Hello' at the Remembrance Sunday service on 13 November 2022 under very different circumstances.

*   *   *

'Rishi was very pleased to break 40 per cent,' reports a colleague.

> That was important to him psychologically. The result was close enough. It gave him some satisfaction. And it meant something to him that people had stuck with him through the contest. He hadn't had much time off for more than two years. He planned to play cricket, spend time with his children, do things he hadn't done for so long. Later on, he also invited his team to his house for a few days so that they could spend some time together in a calmer environment.

Another ally says:

> The result was in line with what I'd predicted and he knew that for a month beforehand, but he kept going because having got that far he thought it was his duty to keep up the campaign and to tell the truth. This stood him in very good stead because who knew that only two months later everybody would be saying he was right? He wanted to win, but it wasn't going to be the end of the world to be out of

office and be able to speak his mind more and spend more time with his family. That was not unappealing to him. He was in a perfectly good mood about the whole thing, he enjoyed the campaign, and he was ready for either outcome. Any politician knows they want to lose with the biggest vote possible. That makes a big difference to what happens afterwards. So you still have that incentive to maximise your voice. It affects the atmosphere in the party afterwards, it affects if you can ever run again, and he knew all that was important. Most of us also thought at the time that if Truss was going to win, she would construct a Cabinet that would have to include at least some of his backers in it.

That assumption turned out to be wrong. Not a single Sunak supporter was invited to join Truss at the top table. 'One of the things that hadn't been anticipated was that she would exclude all of Rishi's supporters from the Cabinet and have this very narrowly based Cabinet, which turned out to be a disaster,' comments a senior politician.

So it was an assumption until Truss appointed her Cabinet that another reason for Rishi fighting on hard was to affect the balance of a future government. In all full Cabinet positions, Truss fired anybody who supported Rishi. This was one of the reasons her government blew up so quickly – she constructed a Cabinet from half the MPs, not all of them. So as soon as she was in trouble she didn't have that depth of support. It was very vengeful.

It may also have been politically naïve. Truss's allies still maintain that some of Sunak's supporters sought to chip away at the new administration from the word go. If that is true, her exclusionary policy can hardly have helped. 'I thought that once the contest was won, there would be some acceptance, but the Rishi campaign team didn't accept the result,' claims one MP who is close to Truss.

> They carried on campaigning and seeking to undermine Liz's government all the way through and they succeeded in unseating Liz. There was a general sense of entitlement about it. Even after Liz had won, Gove and Mel Stride and any number of others were actively trying to undermine what she was doing.

While Truss was en route to Balmoral to kiss hands with the Queen on the morning of 6 September, Sunak returned to work, taking part in a Westminster Hall debate that morning in which he spoke about the Friarage Hospital in Northallerton. The following afternoon he was in the Commons chamber speaking on the Financial Services and Markets Bill. Friends say this willingness to slip back into the role of a backbench MP is proof that Sunak wanted to remain in politics, even if that meant operating at a low level.

'We discussed what he wanted to do next and he was determined to stand again for Parliament,' remembers one friend. 'We agreed that his career wasn't over. He would be vindicated, though we didn't think it would happen so soon. He wanted to think about what policy areas he would specialise in.' Another recalls:

> His plan was to remain a loyal Conservative. He accepted that after the contest he would then have to shut up. He

wasn't planning to pop up and make speeches about Truss-onomics. He could then go back to being a constituency MP. People have this idea that he planned to get the first flight back to California, but he's much tougher than that.

In her first major act as Prime Minister, Truss announced on 8 September her government's plans to freeze energy bills at an average of £2,500 per year for two years. This measure was estimated to cost anything between £120 billion and £150 billion – money that would have to be borrowed. Truss believed it would reduce inflation and help to inspire growth and the markets welcomed it. As this package was introduced in the Commons, news filtered through of the Queen's death, throwing the rest of Truss's plans for her opening days in Downing Street off course while day-to-day politics was paused for ten days of mourning. A state funeral was held on 19 September, after which Truss's administration began to set out more policies. On 21 September, a scheme to freeze wholesale gas and electricity prices for businesses for six months was announced. The next day, it was confirmed that Sunak's hated 1.25 per cent rise in National Insurance contributions would be reversed. On the same day, the plan to introduce the health and social care levy was scrapped.

Then, on 23 September, Truss's Chancellor, Kwasi Kwarteng, delivered a statement to the Commons that would prove seismic. Officially called the Growth Plan, but better known as the mini-Budget, Kwarteng spoke of this being 'the beginning of a new era' as he announced a range of tax cuts. Among the most eye-catching were that the cap on bankers' bonuses would be scrapped; so too would Sunak's plan to increase corporation tax from 19 per cent to 25 per cent; the basic rate of income tax would be lowered by 1p; and the 45 per cent top rate of tax, which kicked in at earnings of £150,000, was to be abolished.

While some right-of-centre politicians and commentators initially applauded these plans, the markets soon took fright. A common view was that the levels of borrowing required to sustain the energy price cap plus the mini-Budget, together with the fact that no independent forecast by the Office for Budget Responsibility had been published, prompted sterling to go into free fall. By the end of that day, it had plunged by 3.5 cents to reach its lowest level against the US dollar since 1985, closing at $1.09. Worse was to come when the Asian markets opened on the next day of trading, as sterling's value slipped below $1.07. On 28 September, the International Monetary Fund waded into these troubled waters, urging a rethink of the mini-Budget.

Truss's political decline was soon felt to be inexorable, though everybody – including Sunak – was stunned at how swiftly she fell. The reasons for the economic turmoil that ensued are felt by some to be far more intricate than was suggested at the time. Be that as it may, the narrative that took hold was that a panic to sell UK government bonds began, forcing the Bank of England to intervene. Pension funds were reported to be close to going bust as a result of their use of liability-driven investments, and mortgage lenders began hiking rates and withdrawing mortgage offers overnight – all this before Truss's first Conservative Party conference as leader, which was held in Manchester between 2 and 5 October.

On 3 October, it was announced that the plan to axe the top rate of tax, perhaps the most controversial of the mini-Budget measures, would be junked. This move was insufficient. In a desperate bid to retain credibility, Truss fired Kwarteng on 14 October, making him the shortest-serving Chancellor since 1970, and replaced him with Jeremy Hunt, the fourth person to hold that brief in as many months. 'On the day I was sacked, Rishi called me,' remembers Kwarteng. 'I thought that was a really nice touch. He's very considerate. I like him. He's a very good guy.' The next day, in a highly unusual development, President Joe Biden's opinion on Britain's apparently precarious position was sought by reporters while he visited an ice cream parlour in Oregon. Notwithstanding the incongruousness of his surroundings, he took the very unusual step of criticising Truss's attempt at economic reform. 'I wasn't the only one that thought it was a mistake,' he said. 'I think that the idea of cutting taxes on the super-wealthy at a time when … I disagree with the policy, but it's up to Britain to make that judgement, not me.' By now, Truss's political standing was severely dented. A chaotic Commons vote followed on 19 October on whether fracking should be banned – an idea Truss opposed. The government won despite forty Tory MPs rebelling, but the game was up. Under extreme pressure and widely thought to be out of her depth, Truss quit the next day, saying she recognised that 'given the situation, I cannot deliver the mandate on which I was elected by the Conservative Party'. The 44-day fever dream was over. A new leader would have to be found and Sunak was the clear favourite.

'Rishi sat out the party conference in Yorkshire,' says a supporter.

I spoke to him that week. It still seemed some way off that Truss would resign. It wasn't possible to tell until the week of the fracking vote that the meltdown was going to happen so quickly. That was a surprise to Rishi. Suddenly there was a new leadership election on and he had to do a lot of thinking very quickly. He did not expect to be back in action so quickly. But he had no doubt at all that if she was going then he had to claim the leadership. I think he felt a sense of duty. I also think he knew that if he didn't take over in those circumstances, when would he? He'd been proved right, he'd got a good showing a few weeks before, and he would have well over half the MPs in his favour. So even though he knew he'd face this monumentally difficult challenge as PM, he had to go for it. It was duty and the chance wouldn't ever come again if he didn't take it at that time.

Backbench MP Philip Davies recalls:

When things were going very wrong for Liz Truss's administration, Rishi came back to Parliament having been up in Yorkshire for several weeks. His parliamentary office was three doors up from mine. I saw him in the corridor one day and said, 'Liz Truss is not going to last. Are you doing anything?' And he said, 'No, I can't be seen to be undermining the Prime Minister.' And I said, 'You need to be ready to go. And this time it's going to be a pure numbers game. You'll need to make sure that everyone who supported you last time will back you this time round, because if you get the most MPs, you'll win. You need to make sure all those people are onside.' We agreed his opponents would likely include Penny, Suella and Kemi. I told him I thought Jeremy Hunt was happy as Chancellor. I said I assumed he wouldn't move Jeremy given he was the fourth Chancellor we'd had in four months. He didn't say a word, but the look he gave me said it all. It said, 'Crikey, I hadn't even considered that I'd have to keep Jeremy.'

Sunak was with his daughters, who were enjoying a half-term break, eating lunch in a branch of TGI Friday's in Teesside when Truss announced her resignation on 20 October. 'He thought the people who were speculating that she was going to go were either overexcited or wrongly trying to make him feel better about having lost the leadership election,' remarks a friend.

> You can tell this because on the day she quit he was out with his kids. This is not someone who was sitting in Smith Square having borrowed some townhouse working out what they're going to do. And then she did resign. He went home and then drove back to London that night. He thought he was the best person to do the job, but he knew it wasn't going to be easy. A lot of people were telling him to go for it. One of the things that persuaded him was that people who hadn't backed him in the summer told him he was right and said they should have backed him then. Sajid backed him, and that was a big moment. In the summer, he'd said Rishi was wrong about the economy. Those things convinced him he could unite the party and would have the confidence of the Commons and could form a government.

As Sunak made his way south, the 1922 Committee was hastily redrafting its rules for the new leadership contest that was under way. Candidates would need the nominations of at least 100 MPs by 2 p.m. on Monday 24 October to proceed to the ballot, removing at a stroke all but the strongest claimants to the party's throne. If necessary, the final two candidates would take part in a televised hustings that week and party members would have the final say via an online vote. The result would be announced by Friday 28 October.

Penny Mordaunt was the first to announce her intention to stand, on Friday 21 October, and on the Saturday morning Sunak's team confirmed that he had already secured at least 100 backers among the parliamentary party, though he did not declare until the following day. Media speculation had been trained most keenly on Boris Johnson's plans. To the great pleasure of journalists, he provided them with more drama. He was on holiday in the Dominican Republic at the time of Truss's resignation, but he caught the first available plane back to London with his wife and children in the hope that he could muster sufficient support to take on Sunak. Having arrived at Gatwick at lunchtime on the Saturday, it came to light that he and Sunak were to have a private meeting at Millbank Tower that evening. Johnson claimed to have the support of at least 100 MPs, but when Sunak's team requested proof, none was forthcoming.

'The organisation of it was mafia-esque,' recalls one who was close to the action.

It sounds dramatic, but it was a bit like two mafia bosses meeting. They'd agreed a time, Rishi went along with a few staff, then Boris changed the time because he obviously hadn't got the numbers yet. He arrived with a few people. As for what was discussed in the meeting, only they know because only they were in the room and they agreed that nothing would be said outside of the room. The whole thing went on for just under an hour. They came out and there was a bit of joking. Boris said, 'Don't worry, guys, Rishi's agreed to be my Chancellor,' and then Rishi coolly turned around, slapped Boris on the shoulder and said, 'See you at the debate,' and walked out. It wasn't done aggressively; it was a jokey thing.

Another friend says:

> Boris suggested they form a dream ticket, with Boris as
> leader, and Rishi said no. Fundamentally, Rishi knew he
> wanted to do this on his own terms. He'd discovered that
> his view on the best thing for the economy was not the same
> as Boris's. He knew when he went into that meeting that if
> you try to get the band together again, the same creative dif-
> ferences that broke them up would emerge soon and they'd
> be back at square one.

By the Sunday afternoon, Johnson had contacted Mordaunt to
try to persuade her to drop out of the race and fall in behind
him. She, too, rejected the idea. Only fifty-six MPs had backed
him publicly by this point. Sunak then issued a statement confirming his intention to stand. He said he would fix the economy
and acknowledged that the crisis facing the UK was 'profound'.
In a statement, he said, 'I served as your Chancellor, helping to
steer our economy through the toughest of times. The challenges we face now are even greater. But the opportunities – if we
make the right choice – are phenomenal.' He added:

> There will be integrity, professionalism and accountability at
> every level of the government I lead and I will work day in,
> day out to get the job done. I am asking you for the opportu-
> nity to help fix our problems. To lead our party and country
> forwards towards the next general election, confident in our
> record, firm in our convictions and ready to lead again.

A few hours later, Johnson insisted that he had secured the
100 nominations needed to get onto the ballot paper, and that

if he had stood there was a 'very good chance' he would win. Yet he went on:

> In the course of the last days I have sadly come to the con-
> clusion that this would simply not be the right thing to do.
> You can't govern effectively unless you have a united party
> in Parliament. And though I have reached out to both Rishi
> and Penny – because I hoped that we could come together
> in the national interest – we have sadly not been able to
> work out a way of doing this. Therefore I am afraid the best
> thing is that I do not allow my nomination to go forward
> and commit my support to whoever succeeds.

Never one to close the door altogether, he added, 'I believe I have much to offer, but I am afraid that this is simply not the right time.'

It looked as though it would be a two-way race between Sunak, who had more than 120 public backers by the Sunday night, and Mordaunt, who had only twenty-four. Sunak's allies were in no doubt who would win. 'On the day Johnson withdrew, I discussed with Rishi how to get ready for being PM a few hours later,' says one confidant.

> I gave advice about how to make key appointments, the staff
> he would need based on things I've observed from previous
> Prime Ministers, the support they need, things they need to
> think about immediately, no doubt along with a lot of other
> people he was talking to. He wasn't nervous. He took it in
> his stride.

Another says:

I remember on the Monday morning when people thought Penny might have the numbers, he wasn't fretful about that. There were all sorts of people offering him unsolicited advice, saying if you offer her X, we can avoid a contest. His view was: 'If she gets the numbers, we'll have a contest and we can argue this publicly.' That prospect held no fears for him.

By lunchtime on Monday 24 October, Sunak had secured the public nominations of 193 MPs. They included Suella Braverman, Steve Baker and Kemi Badenoch, each of whom was considered, in different ways, important to have onside. Mordaunt's camp said privately that she had ninety nominations, though the number of those who backed her publicly was twenty-six. Two minutes before the 2 p.m. deadline, she announced on Twitter that she was pulling out of the contest, leaving Sunak as the last candidate standing. As had happened to Michael Howard in 2003, he would be crowned Conservative Party leader unopposed. In the middle of 2019, Sunak was an unknown junior minister; seven months later, he became Chancellor of the Exchequer; and now he had secured the highest office in the land. Aged forty-two, he was Britain's youngest Prime Minister for more than 200 years. Remarkably, he was also the fifth person to occupy the post since 2016.

His elevation had occurred on the same day that the important Indian festival of Diwali was celebrated that year. In view of the problems that had beset the government and the country over the preceding months, this feast day, in which candles and lamps represent the triumph of light over darkness and hope for the future, was considered by his supporters to be an entirely appropriate moment for Sunak to have achieved his aim of moving into 10 Downing Street.

CHAPTER 29

DUTY

It is difficult to overstate the immensity of the task that Rishi Sunak inherited when he succeeded Liz Truss as Prime Minister so unexpectedly. As well as the daily responsibilities that go with the top job, he had to assemble a Cabinet that would restore confidence within his party and around the country; grapple with a battered economy; confront an unprecedented NHS backlog; oversee Britain's support for Ukraine; address the political and trade uncertainties in Northern Ireland caused by Brexit; deal with the wave of strikes prompted by soaring inflation; and square up to the various problems created by cross-Channel illegal immigration. All this while taking the fight to a Labour Party that was surging in the polls and preparing for the next general election, desperate to deny the Tories an unprecedented fifth term in office.

Even in good times, tackling these matters would not have been straightforward, yet the underlying circumstances at this point were far from favourable – particularly within the Conservative Party. The unopposed manner of Sunak's arrival in 10 Downing Street meant that he was seen by many of the 180,000 Tory members and activists as having no mandate not just among the wider electorate but among a majority of them as well. He was, some said, merely the emergency choice of most of his party's MPs – a party whose brand appeared to have been wrecked by the actions of the short-lived Truss administration and which was so split that Sunak regarded it more as a coalition that could only function if he was prepared to compromise. This split encompassed both the difference in interests between northern Red Wall MPs and those representing traditional southern constituencies; the usual ideological divisions of One Nation Tories as against those on the right of the party; and Boris Johnson's supporters versus the rest. Sunak also had to contend with the potential difficulties of knowing that four previous party leaders were still sitting behind him in the Commons chamber – Sir Iain Duncan Smith, Theresa May, Johnson and Truss – three of whom had been Prime Minister. Add to this the stark reality that he had taken on the mantle when the Conservatives were considered jaded after spending more than twelve years in power, and it is easy to see why almost everybody agreed that he had accepted a deeply unappealing, and lonely, job.

Yet his neighbouring MP and friend Kevin Hollinrake believes recent history equipped him well for it. 'Rishi relishes the challenges of fixing problems,' Hollinrake says,

and he knows how to do it. Many people forget that the furlough scheme was delivered in record time exceptionally effectively. Others say, 'But there was fraud.' The fraud on the Covid loans of £80 billion was probably between £1 billion and £2 billion. Of course, that's £1 billion or £2 billion too much, but there's always going to be some of that. But the scheme was delivered in a way that was quite remarkable given the timescale. He's able to break down complex problems into smaller parts which he then fixes very effectively.

Another associate says:

> Things moved very quickly, but he's a very logical think-
> er, he does things in a sequence. It required rapid moving
> on, mentally speaking. He switched from being in exile for
> seven weeks to, from that Monday, preparing to become the
> PM. Normally, the outgoing PM departs on a Wednesday,
> so the initial assumption was there'd be a couple of days to
> get ready in terms of appointing a Cabinet, staff and sort-
> ing things out logistically. But Truss was so determined to
> get out the door that she made clear she was going on the
> Tuesday and not doing another PMQs. No PM has had to
> do PMQs on their first full day in office. That meant Rishi
> had this extraordinary first twenty-four hours as PM where
> he had to appoint a Cabinet and have all the other initial
> briefings that a PM has to have, such as those around secu-
> rity and the nuclear deterrent, and do PMQs on his first full
> day in office. I think he felt the pressure, but he took it in
> his stride. He made a list of the things he had to decide and
> everyone he must speak to and posts that must be filled. He
> didn't seem panicky in any way.

A handover timetable for Tuesday 25 October was drawn up
under which Truss would chair a final Cabinet meeting and
go to Buckingham Palace for an audience with King Charles.
Sunak would then meet the monarch to be asked to form a
government and would give a speech outside 10 Downing
Street shortly before midday. He had met the King before
and they were already known to get on well. Truss's relationship with the monarch had appeared less smooth. When she

attended their first – and what turned out to be last – weekly audience at Buckingham Palace, a TV microphone picked up him muttering as he greeted her, 'Back again? Dear, oh dear.'

Sir Keir Starmer was among those on Sunak's list to contact on his first day in the job so that they could swap personal contact details. And in a show of commitment to Ukraine, President Volodymyr Zelenskyy was the first foreign leader to receive a telephone call from Downing Street. President Joe Biden was one of the first world leaders to comment on Sunak's elevation that day. Speaking at a press conference, he called the arrival of a British Asian to No. 10 a 'groundbreaking milestone' for Britain and said, 'It matters.' These warm words immediately turned cold when he got Sunak's name wrong, calling him 'Rashid Sanook'. The journalist Mihir Bose was able to produce a more considered opinion of Sunak's remarkable rise. Writing in *The Guardian*, Bose observed that his arrival in Downing Street

is a more complex story than that of the first brown man to hold the highest office in the land advertising the diversity of our country. It is the result of a remarkable revolution in the Tory party's attitude to the Hindus, which illustrates the complex nature of postwar Asian migration to this country. It should also ring loud alarm bells for Labour. The Tory Hindu revolution has seen it convert from a party that, historically, hated Hindus – and that is not too strong a word – to one that has pivoted enough towards the Hindus for the community to lose its old fear of the Tories.

It is interesting, some might say reassuring, to note that by and large no great fuss was made about Sunak being Britain's first

Prime Minister of Asian heritage. Sunak himself had no desire to indulge in a game of identity politics, not least because English is his first language and he does not even speak Hindi fluently. And as the Conservative Party long ago broke new ground by providing Britain's first ethnically Jewish Prime Minister in Benjamin Disraeli in 1868 and Britain's first female Prime Minister, Margaret Thatcher, in 1979, it is equally unsurprising that it felt unfazed in 2022 that Sunak was Britain's first Hindu premier. That is not to say that others were averse to celebrating. Sanjay Chandarana, president of the Vedic Society Hindu Temple in Southampton, which was established by Sunak's grandfather Ram Dass Sunak in 1971, gave a short interview in which he said Sunak's ascent was Britain's 'Barack Obama moment'. Explaining that Sunak remains an active worshipper at the temple, Chandarana predicted he would 'unite the country, because he practises Hindu religion religiously and one of the key values we have is the whole world is our family and we believe in unity in that respect'. He added that because Sunak's promotion coincided with Diwali, 'we increased our firework time from fifteen minutes to twenty minutes. Also when we learned he was going to be Prime Minister we offered a special prayer and he will feature in my Diwali speech. It's going to be another festival within a festival, the icing on the cake.'

Amid the euphoria there was rancour, however. Nadia Whittome, a Labour MP of Asian heritage, put out a tweet claiming that Sunak's conquest 'isn't a win for Asian representation'. She then made critical comments about his wealth. More negativity flowed on Twitter from an SNP MP called Anum Qaisar, who wrote, 'Just because you share the same characteristics as someone, does not mean that you'll be supportive of that community.' And an academic called Dr Shola Mos-Shogbamimu explained that she would 'love to celebrate this moment but can't because of Rishi Sunak'. She added, 'In representation & substance he's the status quo of normalising systemic racism, anti-woke & culture war-mongering. Representation can't just be skin deep, substance matters.' Less factional observers deduced that Sunak simply wasn't interesting enough to excite the masses in the way Obama had done. In any case, he did show that he was not without steeliness, a quality that was in marked contrast to Boris Johnson, who often seemed allergic to the idea of upsetting his colleagues. On the day of Sunak's 'coronation', a crowd gathered outside Conservative Party Campaign Headquarters in Westminster to congratulate him. Among those wanting to shake his hand was Matt Hancock. In what appeared to be a calculated snub to the former Health Secretary that escaped nobody's attention, Sunak walked straight past him. A week later, he would remove the whip from Hancock for accepting an offer of £400,000 (minus his agent's fee) to be a contestant on the ITV reality programme *I'm A Celebrity… Get Me Out Of Here*. In early December 2022, Hancock confirmed that he would stand down as an MP at the next general election.

In Sunak's first speech as Prime Minister, he paid tribute to Truss and to Johnson. He spoke of the profound economic crisis facing Britain, vowed to 'place economic stability and confidence at the heart of this government's agenda' and promised to unite the country. 'This government will have integrity, professionalism and accountability at every level,' he said. 'Trust is earned. And I will earn yours.' He added that he felt sure Johnson would agree that the mandate the Conservative Party secured in 2019 'is not the sole property of any one individual; it is a mandate that belongs to and unites all of us. And the heart of that mandate is our manifesto. I will deliver on its promise.' He went on:

> I am not daunted. I know the high office I have accepted and I hope to live up to its demands. But when the opportunity to serve comes along, you cannot question the moment, only your willingness. So I stand here before you ready to lead our country into the future. To put your needs above politics. To reach out and build a government that represents the very best traditions of my party. Together we can achieve incredible things. We will create a future worthy of the sacrifices so many have made and fill tomorrow, and every day thereafter, with hope. Thank you.

By the close of play that day, sterling had rebounded against the US dollar. That Sunak's arrival had such a tangible effect meant that his most immediate aim, to steady the markets, had been carried out successfully. At the same time, this ability to right the ship did nothing to dampen the idea among some MPs that he was a creature of big corporate interests; a technocrat or manager rather than an instinctive politician with a natural ability to connect with the electorate. Some even believed that Truss had been ousted and Sunak installed in her place as part of a conspiracy involving senior civil servants, the World Economic Forum, the International Monetary Fund, elements of the mainstream media and other powerful players. Truss herself would hint at this sense of a coup d'état in February 2023 when she wrote in the *Sunday Telegraph*, 'I was not given a realistic chance to enact my policies by a very powerful economic establishment, coupled with a lack of political support ... I seriously underestimated the strength of the economic orthodoxy and its influence on the market.'

Over his first forty-eight hours in Downing Street, Sunak appointed a Cabinet that represented each wing of the parliamentary party. Notably, two MPs who had supported Truss that summer, James Cleverly and Ben Wallace, remained in post as Foreign Secretary and Defence Secretary respectively. Another Truss supporter, Suella Braverman, was reappointed as Home Secretary. This surprised many. Braverman had resigned from that brief six days earlier for breaching ministerial rules by sending a highly sensitive official document from her personal email account to fellow Conservative MP Sir John Hayes. It was speculated that her swift return was a reward for backing Sunak, and encouraging her supporters on the right of the party to do the same, during the October leadership contest. Jeremy Hunt, whom Sunak had inherited as Chancellor and who had backed him for the leadership three months previously, remained in 11 Downing Street. Nadhim Zahawi was made Conservative Party chairman. One staunch Sunak ally, Dominic Raab, was reappointed Justice Secretary and Deputy Prime Minister. Another, Michael Gove, who had been sacked by Boris Johnson three months previously, became Levelling Up Secretary in charge of intergovernmental relations. A third, Oliver Dowden, became Chancellor of the Duchy of Lancaster, in which role he was expected to be instrumental in helping Sunak to oversee government business. There was some surprise that Andrew Mitchell was made a Foreign Office minister, given he had organised a Tory rebellion over foreign aid cuts instituted by Sunak in 2021. Observers noted that the range of voices around Sunak's Cabinet table was in contrast to his predecessor's decision to appoint only those who had backed her leadership campaign.

Sunak's first session of PMQs was significant mainly for his reversal of Truss's decision to lift the ban on fracking. Sunak said he would stand by the 2019 manifesto, which had placed a moratorium on fracking in England following opposition from environmentalists. That day, it was also confirmed, however, that Sunak would accept some of Truss's policies. His own controversial 1.25 per cent National Insurance hike to pay for the social care levy would not be reinstated after Truss had scrapped it the previous month. Neither would Truss's decision to cancel stamp duty on properties priced below £250,000 be undone. Sunak was felt to have performed adequately that Wednesday lunchtime and, despite appearing at the despatch box at such short notice, he was comfortably considered to be Starmer's equal, accusing him of being 'soft on crime and in favour of unlimited immigration'. Starmer responded by reminding the House about the tax affairs of Sunak's wife. 'I do not need to explain to the Prime Minister how non-dom status works,' he goaded. Ms Murthy, incidentally, would soon appoint workmen, at personal expense, to strip out wallpaper and interiors in the Downing Street flat left behind by Boris and Carrie Johnson and replace them with blinds, curtains, window seats and sofas provided by her favourite furnishing company, Challis Interior of Richmond, North Yorkshire. She also vowed to open up the Downing Street staterooms, hosting more events involving a greater range of people, with a particular focus on education.

There was no shortage of turbulence for Sunak to navigate during these early days. Starmer had also raised at that first session of PMQs the matter of Braverman's reinstatement as Home Secretary so soon after she had quit that post under Truss, and a concerted effort was mounted by Labour and

Liberal Democrat Members to dislodge her. Two Tory MPs, Caroline Nokes and former party chairman Sir Jake Berry, added to the pressure, with Nokes even calling for an inquiry into Braverman's conduct and, by extension, Sunak's judgement. Sunak held his nerve, but any lingering doubts as to the sheer relentlessness of being Prime Minister were soon put aside, because there was more to come. On 3 November, one of his backbenchers, Andrew Bridgen, was suspended from the Commons for five days after being found guilty of breaching lobbying rules. Sunak himself was then criticised for performing his first U-turn when he announced that he would, after all, fly to Egypt to attend the COP27 climate change summit. On the day he left London, 6 November, the press reported that Gavin Williamson, a Sunak ally and his Minister without Portfolio, had sent 'bullying' messages to Wendy Morton while she had served as Chief Whip under Liz Truss. Sir Jake Berry had apparently warned Sunak during a private meeting before he had appointed Williamson that Morton had made a formal complaint against Williamson. 'What delicate flowers these MPs now are,' reflected the former Conservative backbencher Matthew Parris in a *Times* article. He said whips usually do the bullying, rather than the other way round, and contrasted Morton's complaint with an occasion in the 1980s when his own whip, Sir Spencer Le Marchant, shouted at him, 'Darling, why are you such a c***?' in front of some constituents. Williamson resigned on 8 November, denying wrongdoing but saying he did not wish to become a distraction to the new government.

Of course, each of these matters *did* intrude on the complicated job of getting the government machine up and running efficiently. 'The hardest thing as PM is just to get the system to work,' says one former Cabinet minister.

There are so many different departments, agencies and regulators. Tony Blair says the hardest thing he found in government was to get the system to be responsive to what he wanted. And that's even harder when you're a PM who comes in with only a couple of years of the parliamentary term left and you don't have the authority of having just won a general election. It's because there's been all this churn. You don't have people with experience who can drive the system. Many ministers just don't have that political heft and knowledge of how Whitehall works. Gove has it, but not many others do. If you haven't just won a general election, you have to re-earn your mandate before anyone takes notice of you.

In mid-November, an urgent task for Sunak was to set out his plans to deal with illegal immigration, a problem Boris Johnson and his Home Secretary, Priti Patel, had failed to crack. By this stage, regular reports were appearing of hotels around the country being block-booked in order to house hundreds of new arrivals, costing taxpayers upwards of £6 million per day in bed and board alone, and causing tensions in existing communities. Having announced a new £64 million deal with France to try to stop illicit Channel crossings by small boats, Sunak told reporters accompanying him to a G20 conference in Bali that he had held constructive talks with President Macron about the issue the previous week. Arguably, his decision not to suggest that Macron might be a 'foe', as Liz Truss had done during that summer's leadership contest, had paid off in so far as he and Macron at least appeared to have a functioning relationship. 'I made a commitment that I would grip [illegal immigration] in the summer and I can tell you all that

I've spent more time working on that than anything else, other than obviously the Autumn Statement, over the past couple of weeks,' Sunak said. This was no sop offered to the right of his party to keep them sweet, according to an insider, but an issue in which Sunak sees the need for principle as well as practicality. 'What people don't get about Rishi is how much he thinks in moral terms,' says this person.

> He has always thought it unfair that taxpayers have to pay for the small boats problem. He also thinks it crazy that genuine refugees are being pushed out because our system is overwhelmed. The same is true of inflation. It was never a technocratic exercise for him. He thinks if government isn't prepared to do the tough things to cut it out of the system, everyone is going to get poorer each year. It's the same for strikes. He always knew the simple thing to do would be to cave in, but he always thought that would be a mistake and we have to stop inflation becoming embedded in the system.

The Autumn Statement, which was in effect Jeremy Hunt's first Budget, was also the first set-piece event of Sunak's administration and its contents only added to a tally of bleak statistics. On 17 November, having just heard that inflation had hit 11.1 per cent, Hunt announced a plan to raise taxes by £25 billion, creating the highest level of taxation since the 1950s, as he and Sunak sought to balance the books in light of the £400 billion coronavirus bill and the costs of the war in Ukraine. On the same day, the Office for Budget Responsibility (OBR) stated that the UK had entered a recession, having experienced two successive quarters of a shrinking economy. The OBR further forecast that living standards would fall by 7 per cent over the following two years. Some £30 billion of public expenditure cuts were also pencilled in but would not be triggered immediately. One bright spot was Hunt's promise that state schools would receive an extra £2.3 billion per year for the following two years.

There is no doubt that Sunak was deeply involved in the decisions that led to this Budget. And yet only three months previously, during the summer leadership contest, he had undertaken to cut taxes 'at the fastest rate since Nigel Lawson and Margaret Thatcher' in the 1980s. Many wondered how he could square this circle. In fact, Sunak had paid Lawson a visit before he became Prime Minister, keen to learn from a former Chancellor whom he held in the highest regard but who waited until 1988, five years into his chancellorship, before cutting the top rate of income tax. 'Rishi was always a huge admirer of Nigel,' says an ally.

He went to see him at his flat in Sussex. People have forgotten two things about Thatcherism. First it destroyed inflation, then it set about cutting taxes. Thatcherism wasn't just about boldness and radicalism; it was also about the seriousness about governing. Nigel Lawson couldn't have achieved what he did without Mrs Thatcher's attention to detail. That's another thing Rishi feels – he has his vision for the country but to achieve that you've got to have focus and drive. Radicalism isn't just about moving on to the next thing; it's about doing what you said you would do.

If the collective response to Hunt's first Budget was best summarised by the *Financial Times* as 'muted', arguably that was because Britain's economic woes were not unique in the western world. Sunak knew that whoever was in charge of the economy was going to have to play a long game, just as Lawson had done.

From the moment he entered No. 10 as Prime Minister, Sunak was always acutely aware of the advantage of being on good terms with his own parliamentary party, particularly because of the so-called 'rogue elements' on the back benches. As one longstanding Conservative MP puts it:

> The Johnson people are his enemies. They're the reason he lost the July leadership election. They hate him. It's been pointed out to people like Jacob Rees-Mogg that Liz Truss was an unlikely person for him to back seeing as she was a former Lib Dem who wanted to abolish the monarchy and who voted Remain in the referendum, but people like Jacob rallied to Truss because they blamed Rishi for Boris being ousted. They'd have backed anyone but him for the leadership. If Jeremy Corbyn had been standing, they'd have backed him. They hated Rishi with a passion.

Partly to neutralise that threat, and partly to emphasise how different he is to Boris Johnson, Sunak made a considerable effort to get to know Members on his side of the House. 'He's been spending a lot of time with the MPs and the ministers and he's been quite exceptional by the standards of his predecessors,' says a former Cabinet minister.

> He's been working his way through the whole party, inviting MPs to No. 10 and Chequers and making sure they have a chance to get to know him. Some have criticised him for

not being in the media enough, but what he's been doing since October 2022 is making sure he really knows the MPs. He thinks that stability in the party brings better media coverage, as MPs push that positivity into the media themselves. That's how he's been trying to deal with these rogue elements on the back benches.

One MP to receive an invitation to Chequers soon after Sunak became Prime Minister was Philip Davies, who was accompanied by his wife and fellow Conservative MP Esther McVey. 'We went fairly early on,' recalls Davies.

It was a Saturday night. It was an eclectic bunch. David Davis was there, plus Maria Miller, Theresa May, Julian Smith and John Hayes. We had drinks and dinner followed by coffee upstairs in the library. It was a social event. There was no sales pitch, no political discussion, no hard sell on anything. He's also invited a lot of people round to No. 10.

Unsurprisingly, Sunak also placed hard work at the centre of his strategy as he took charge of a restless party in a shaky economic environment. 'Rishi is a workaholic,' says Davies.

His wife told me he's always working, whatever the hour of the day. I remember a group of about fifteen of us were chosen to go and talk to him about the small boats crisis and he and his advisers listened to our views about what should be done. And then he invited the same group back the morning he announced what they were going to do. Suella Braverman was there sitting beside him. Rishi said, 'Fixing this problem is my number one priority. I've seen

Suella more than I've seen Jeremy Hunt.' And Suella joked, 'I thought you were going to say you'd seen me more than you've seen your wife.' And Rishi said, 'Oh no, my wife's a long way down the list of people I've seen since I became Prime Minister!'

If socialising with his MPs offered much-needed respite from the pressures of work, he had to immerse himself in the problems that mattered to their constituents if he was going to thwart a future leadership challenge – an intention which, extraordinarily, remained attractive to some Tory MPs. In late November, the rather pathetically named Operation Get Tough was launched to reinforce to the party that Sunak shared its concerns over unparalleled levels of immigration – including more than 40,000 illegal immigrants who had crossed the Channel in small boats in the first ten months of the year – as well as the criminal acts of single-issue organisations like Just Stop Oil. Yet having been in office for barely a month, some colleagues were already beginning to drift away, announcing they would not stand at the next election. Chloe Smith, William Wragg and Dehenna Davison were three MPs who confirmed they would quit the Commons. Strikingly, each of them was aged forty or under. At least ten more joined them before Christmas.

At this time, my own polling revealed what voters thought of Sunak's abrupt transition to Downing Street. For wavering Tories, the overwhelming reaction was relief that a degree of professionalism and sanity had been restored. Acknowledging the huge task the latest new Prime Minister had on his hands, many said they were prepared to give him time before making up their minds about the next election – an important caveat to the headline polls indicating mass desertions among 2019 Conservatives. Sunak and Starmer were thought to be closely matched as potential Prime Ministers. But underlying attitudes were much more ominous for Sunak. Fewer than one in ten saw the Tories as competent – an essential attribute for a governing party – and Labour were more trusted on nearly all policy issues, including traditionally Tory territory like immigration and crime. Few expected the new government to succeed in any of its immediate challenges, such as bringing financial stability, controlling inflation or making a success of Brexit, let alone dealing with migrants crossing the Channel on small boats, or cutting NHS waiting lists.

Most serious of all was the pervasive feeling that even if progress could be made on these issues, the game was more or less up for the Conservatives. As with John Major's Tories in 1997 – when the governing party looked so exhausted, tainted and ill-disciplined that even a strongly recovering economy could not stave off defeat at the hands of a newly detoxified Labour opposition – the mood of the country was against them. Of all the political challenges Sunak faced on entering No. 10, overcoming the general perception of drift and decline was perhaps the most formidable.

In late November, an issue surfaced organically which not only allowed Sunak to brandish another principle but also put a clear line between the Conservatives and Labour, helping him to begin to create the sense that he was not afraid to engage in a political wrangle of the type that sometimes preoccupied Margaret Thatcher. The *Mail on Sunday* picked up on the fact that if the opposition won the next general election, private schools would be stripped of their charitable status, forcing them to add VAT of 20 per cent to fees. As it was calculated that hundreds of smaller establishments would go out of business if this policy ever materialised, causing unemployment and placing a huge strain on existing state schools, it became a talking point across the media for days. At PMQs, Starmer asked Sunak to defend a school like Winchester receiving this 'tax break', which, Labour believed, deprived the Exchequer of £1.7 billion annually. Ironically, Starmer had been the beneficiary of a private education at Reigate Grammar School in the 1970s, albeit courtesy of his local education authority, though Sunak said nothing about this. Instead, he reminded Starmer that the government had that month already increased the amount of public money going into state schools by £2.3 billion per year. He added:

> Whenever he attacks me about where I went to school, he is attacking the hard-working aspiration of millions of people in this country. He's attacking people like my parents. This is a country that believes in opportunity, not resentment. He doesn't understand that and that's why he's not fit to lead.

These words drew loud cheers from his benches as they welcomed not only his belief in choice but also an authenticity which they felt some of his predecessors, particularly David Cameron, had lacked. Sunak has never hidden the fact that his two daughters are privately educated. By contrast, Cameron let it be known once he was in office that his children would attend state schools. Having left Downing Street in 2016, however, at least two of Cameron's children were enrolled in private schools.

As Christmas came into view, bad news kept on coming. Labour's poll lead remained stubbornly high, averaging at least twenty points; Boris Johnson, whose supporters still had the potential to cause trouble, announced his intention to stand again as an MP at the next election; in by-elections, Labour held the seats of Chester and Stretford and Urmston, with swings away from the Conservatives of nearly 14 per cent and 11 per cent respectively; Tory MP Julian Knight had the whip removed after a complaint about his conduct was made to the police, cutting Sunak's majority to sixty-nine; and it became apparent that millions of workers planned prolonged winter strikes across the NHS, the civil service and the rail and postal sectors. The Royal College of Nursing said its members would strike on 15 and 20 December for the first time in its 106-year history. Each group said it was concerned that wages were not keeping pace with inflation. Sunak's view was that giving in to their demands would embed rather than elimi-nate inflation and in January 2023 his government introduced anti-strike legislation which would, once passed, force unions to provide minimum levels of service during industrial action. This measure appeared to have strong public backing, again allowing him to position himself as a leader whose youth did not mean he would hesitate.

He let none of this get in the way of his plan of attack. Shortly before Christmas, it was confirmed that he had hired his longstanding friend James Forsyth, at that time the polit-ical editor of *The Spectator*, as his political secretary. Forsyth would be paid out of party funds to act as a general fixer and problem-solver, with a particular focus on liaising with MPs. Isaac Levido, a protégée of Sir Lynton Crosby who had helped the Tories to victory at the 2019 election, was also recruited as a strategist. In interviews, Sunak made it clear that he would take three days off for Christmas and would then work on his blueprint for the first days of 2023, at the centre of which was Thatcher's dictum from 1980: 'No policy which puts at risk the defeat of inflation – however great its short-term attraction – can be right.'

One figure who operated under Thatcher in the 1980s and who also knows Sunak well sees a similarity in Sunak's insistence on prioritising work above all else. Yet if Thatcher's ability to regularly put in eighteen hours a day was often fortified by a large glass of whisky and soda, Sunak's approach to toiling for long hours is altogether more Californian. 'One of the things about Rishi is that he *likes* work,' according to this source.

So unless he has to go out to a dinner or something, he'll be sitting until ten at night working in No. 10. He's a very effective worker – someone who fires off memos and expects answers; who interrogates data. He enjoys all of that. It compensates to some degree for the sluggishness in the government system. He's like Mrs Thatcher in that respect. He knows that the way British government works depends on the energy and discipline of the one person in the middle of it all to make it work. He witnessed under Boris somebody who didn't make it work and didn't have the discipline to do so. So he is just naturally like Thatcher. He's also so disciplined in his personal habits – eating, drinking and exercising – that he can perform at a high level the whole time. That's how he's always operated and that's a very important thing about him because it means he is not somebody who easily gets tired. He doesn't drink alcohol, so he is never under the influence of that. So he really does work at a high rate of productivity. I think Mrs Thatcher would love that work ethic.

Furthermore, Sunak's formidable mother-in-law, Sudha Murthy, says that Sunak has adopted her family's habit of fasting every Thursday by restricting himself to eating just one meal. This keeps his weight down and his mind lively.

While most other people, including his family, enjoyed a holiday, Sunak was preparing his first major speech since succeeding Liz Truss. A small statue of the Hindu god Lord Ganesh, the bringer of success to any new enterprise, and a photograph of the football manager Lawrie McMenemy, who won the FA Cup with Southampton in 1976, were on his desk for company. The speech, delivered at the Queen Elizabeth Olympic Park in east London on 4 January 2023, outlined his five-point plan for the year: to halve inflation; grow the economy; reduce debt; cut NHS waiting lists; and pass laws to act against illegal immigration or, more directly, 'stop the boats' from crossing the English Channel. These five pledges, which allies say he chose not because he was certain of meeting them but because he regarded them as the most pressing matters facing the country, would be repeated by Sunak, almost like a chant, in most interviews he gave from that point. Looking at the bigger picture, he said that better education is the answer to most of life's problems. 'Improving education is the closest thing to a silver bullet there is,' he declared. 'It is the best economic policy, the best social policy, the best moral policy. And that's why it's this government's policy.' One plan he unveiled was that all school pupils will study maths until the age of eighteen.

By coincidence, Sir Keir Starmer delivered his New Year speech the next day at the same venue, offering commentators a chance to compare the two men directly. Coming out on the side of Starmer, the *Observer* columnist Andrew Rawnsley spoke for many as he pointed out, not unreasonably, that Sunak's principal challenge was 'how to pitch himself as the man with a plan to fix Britain when so many of the broken things about this country are of his own party's making'. Sunak's political inheritance after a dozen years of Tory rule was indeed meagre. Yet aides say he was convinced that the quickest route to success lay in offering solutions to a small number of issues that affect people's lives which he could then be judged on; and in concentrating on things he thought he could control as opposed to mopping up messes created by Boris Johnson. This sense of Sunak's pragmatism was also seen in the decision, announced on 5 January, not to sell Channel 4. Privatising this forty-year-old left-leaning broadcaster had been mooted by Boris Johnson's government. While a sale had obvious attractions – not least the ten-figure sum it would probably raise for the public purse – the view was taken that inviting bids at that point would be more trouble than it was worth. Many Conservatives were disappointed that Sunak had ducked this opportunity.

More evidence of his industriousness followed. On 7 January he hosted the country's top clinical leaders and health experts in Downing Street for the NHS Recovery Forum, a summit that took on extra relevance in the face of widespread strikes among health workers and ambulance drivers. Steve Barclay, the Health Secretary, was also present, but Sunak took personal charge of the session. It was clear that he had absorbed vast amounts of data in a personal effort to overcome the NHS's myriad problems. 'The churn of ministers means Rishi hasn't got many senior colleagues who've been in the departments a long time who can really carry a lot of the work of government fluently,' says one seasoned observer. 'What we've seen recently is that things can move in government – but only if Rishi really focuses on them himself.' One attendee at the event said that about forty people who were there had each submitted a report beforehand. Remarkably, Sunak had read every one and was clearly very well informed. And yet this hard work was undermined the next day by an interview he gave to the BBC. In it, he was asked if he was currently or had ever been registered with a private GP. Sunak was diffident and evasive, and it did not go down well. Not only did many Tories compare him unfavourably with Margaret Thatcher, who had spoken openly of her use of private healthcare during her premiership; it also handed Labour a chance to portray him, once again, as out of touch. It took another three days for him to reveal that he is registered with an NHS GP, having previously used private healthcare.

It is clear that Sunak wanted to restore order and competence to Downing Street after several years of havoc. And, bluntly, he wanted to be left alone to get on with the job. Yet acolytes of Boris Johnson remained determined to agitate. Some did so under the umbrella of the newly formed Conservative Democratic Organisation, a grassroots operation bankrolled by Lord Cruddas. Its ostensible aim was to give party members a greater say in choosing the party leader and parliamentary candidates, though its apparent, if unspoken, shorter-term goal was to return Johnson to the leadership. Three days after Sunak delivered his New Year speech in east London, Nadine Dorries wrote in the *Mail on Sunday* that the Conservatives had made a dreadful mistake in deposing Johnson six months previously. 'It's bring back Boris Johnson or die because the first priority of any Labour government will be to ensure that there will never be a majority Conservative government ever again,' Dorries warned. A few days later, a portrait of Johnson by Richard Stone was unveiled at the Carlton Club. In his address to the 100 or so people who had gathered, Johnson showed notional loyalty to Sunak as he urged, 'Never give in, keep fighting, keep backing the government – keep making the case for levelling up, for opportunities and for a dynamic, low-tax, global Britain. That is how we will win again … Thank you all very much and Happy New Year.' Yet in an apparent reference to the ongoing inquiry into Partygate being carried out by a parliamentary select committee, he quipped to a reporter on his way out, 'I was framed.' Some felt the joke was laced with resentment.

Sunak carried on, signing a new defence agreement in London with the Japanese Prime Minister Fumio Kishida that would allow each country to deploy forces on each other's soil in a bid to counter China's looming threat. He also agreed to send Challenger 2 tanks to Ukraine, making Britain the first western power to supply President Zelenskyy with main battle tanks which would be used to help train Ukrainian troops. On 12 January, he visited Scotland for talks with the then First Minister, Nicola Sturgeon. In doing so, he once again set himself apart from his predecessor, Liz Truss, who had memorably described Sturgeon during a leadership hustings as an 'attention seeker' who was best ignored. Sunak was at least willing to engage. More significantly, four days later, he used his power as British Prime Minister to block the SNP's controversial Gender Recognition Reform Bill, legislation which would have given anyone in Scotland over the age of sixteen the ability to change gender without a medical diagnosis, allowing biological males access to female-only spaces. He became the first Prime Minister in history to deploy this so-called 'nuclear option', made possible under Section 35 of the Scotland Act 1998. Involving himself in an issue that has proved to be so highly charged was seen by many in all political parties as an important and decisive step. Many felt his decision was vindicated just a few days later after a sex criminal called Isla Bryson, who had been convicted of raping two women when named Adam Graham, was sent to a women's prison in Scotland, sparking a political row which was thought to have been linked to Sturgeon's shock resignation less than a month later. A key question which Sir Keir Starmer will never have to answer in anything other than a hypothetical sense is whether he, too, would have blocked the Gender Recognition Reform Bill at that time. Many remember that in September 2021, Starmer refused to accept that 'only women have a cervix'; and in March 2022 he was asked repeatedly on LBC Radio whether 'a woman can have a penis' but he would not give a straight answer. In April 2023, Starmer eventually settled on the notion that '99.9 per cent of women haven't got a penis'.

Despite this apparent boost to his reputation as a determined leader, mid-January demonstrated the seemingly endless tightrope walk that was expected of Sunak. In the space of a few days, he had to give ground over the Online Safety Bill after fifty Tory MPs signalled they would rebel unless it was rewritten to ensure the heads of social media platforms would be penalised if children were not protected from online harm. He also had to confront anti-Brexit members of his own party who were determined to weaken legislation that would remove up to 4,000 Brussels regulations from the British statute book under the auspices of the Retained EU Law Bill. At the same time, supporters of Liz Truss held the first

Conservative Growth Group meeting, putting renewed pressure on Sunak to cut taxes.

As he edged closer to marking his first 100 days in Downing Street, there was more difficulty in store. On 21 January, he was fined £100 for not wearing a seatbelt in a moving car while filming a video in Lancashire to promote the government's levelling-up spending. A member of the public is believed to have contacted the police to complain after seeing the video online. Although not exactly a major transgression, it was the second time in nine months that he had received a fixed penalty notice. Aides said that he deeply regretted the blunder. More seriously, he had to sack Nadhim Zahawi, the party chairman, on 29 January for breaching the ministerial code in relation to his tax affairs. A sleaze scandal surrounding Zahawi and the mystery of why he had made a secret £5 million payment to HMRC had dragged on one way or another since the summer, before Sunak became Prime Minister. It was only resolved when Sunak asked his newly appointed ethics adviser, Sir Laurie Magnus, to investigate. Dominic Raab, Sunak's deputy, was also under investigation by this time for allegedly bullying civil servants at the Ministry of Justice. And the ghost of Boris Johnson's premiership was not far away either, this time in relation to questions being posed about the BBC chairman Richard Sharp. He had been appointed to that post in January 2021 by Johnson, but Sunak knew him independently, having worked with him at Goldman Sachs almost twenty years earlier. Before he was interviewed for the BBC chairmanship, Sharp was said to have had a hand in helping Johnson to facilitate an £800,000 loan, which had been guaranteed by Canadian businessman Sam Blyth. After the *Sunday Times* put the story on its front page in January 2023,

Labour's shadow Culture Secretary Lucy Powell wrote to the Commissioner for Public Appointments, William Shawcross, seeking clarification on whether this amounted to a conflict of interests, and an investigation was launched.

To mark his 100th day in office, Sunak agreed to give an interview to the TalkTV presenter Piers Morgan. During their wide-ranging conversation, he was asked why he had decided to try for a second time to be party leader and Prime Minister. He acknowledged that he found being in office onerous but explained the Hindu concept of dharma, which translates approximately as 'duty'. He said that he had been brought up to do the things that were expected of him. 'Even though [being Prime Minister] was going to be a nightmare job ... I felt that I could make a difference and was the best person to make a difference at that moment, especially given the challenges that people were facing and what they were seeing with their mortgages,' he said. 'And that's ultimately why I put myself forward to do it, knowing that it would be difficult and challenging but ultimately doing what I thought was my duty in that situation because I believe deeply in service and thought I could make a difference for the country.'

Few doubted Sunak's sincerity, but perhaps when all was said and done, the biggest challenge he faced was a lack of time. As Morgan – who admitted he was very impressed by Sunak – pointed out, he had about 500 days at most before the next general election must be held. Would that be long enough to convince voters he could make a difference to their lives?

CHAPTER 30

BETTING THE FARM

The sacking of Nadhim Zahawi presented Sunak with an opportunity to reshuffle his first Cabinet and on 7 February he took it. Three government departments were reorganised entirely, creating the new Department for Business and Trade, run by Kemi Badenoch; the new Department for Energy Security and Net Zero, headed by Grant Shapps; and the new Department for Science, Innovation and Technology, under Michelle Donelan. Perhaps the most interesting appointment was that of Lee Anderson as the party's deputy chairman. As a bluff-talking former Nottinghamshire coal miner and ex-Labour Party councillor, he and Sunak do not appear at first glance to have much in common. Yet Anderson was considered a useful Tory representative in the crucial Red Wall seats in the north of England and he and Sunak got on well – even if the Prime Minister did have to clarify forty-eight hours after Anderson's appointment that he, unlike Anderson, does not support reintroducing the death penalty.

Of the reshuffle in general and the creation of the new Department for Energy Security and Net Zero in particular, an insider explains:

Rishi believes one of the lessons of the war in Ukraine is that Britain needs to be as close to energy independence as possible. He knows he won't be the principal beneficiary of the government being set up in a much more logical way, but that one of his successors in the next decade will be. He will derive some benefit from it, but the real improvement will show over time.

Two days later, the Labour Party held the safe seat of West Lancashire in a by-election, its third such victory in the 106 days since Sunak had become Prime Minister. It did so with a ten-point swing in its favour, further concentrating minds in Downing Street as to the scale of the task facing the new administration, particularly while Boris Johnson's supporters were still scheming openly against Sunak. Jacob Rees-Mogg, by now doubling up as a presenter on GB News, had even told friends in private that he wanted to be the next Tory leader. 'Jacob always comes over as amenable and polite, but he clearly dislikes Rishi a lot,' says one source. 'He genuinely believes that he could lead the party. He's told me that.' By this point, however, Sunak was entrenched in another matter entirely. He had been quietly working away for weeks on a project that he hoped would break the continuing Brexit deadlock, help to build his reputation as a statesman and cast him as a master problem-solver and all-round fixer capable of an achievement denied to his predecessors.

Very shortly after taking office, he had turned his attention to the island of Ireland, becoming the first Prime Minister for fifteen years to attend the British–Irish Council summit, which was held in Blackpool. There, he had a meeting with the Taoiseach, Micheál Martin, which Martin described as 'significant'. Sunak's interest in Ireland was driven principally by the fact that the Northern Ireland Assembly at Stormont, which had been set up under the terms of the 1998 Belfast Agreement, had not functioned since February 2022 because of disagreements within the cross-community power-sharing parties over the Northern Ireland Protocol. This protocol, which had been struck between Boris Johnson and the EU and had been in force since January 2021, determined Northern Ireland's trading rules. Under its terms, the Irish land border remained open, but checks were made on all goods arriving from Britain at Northern Ireland's ports – even if those goods were staying in Northern Ireland rather than crossing into the Republic of Ireland. Businesses were being harmed by the bureaucracy this created, while unionists and Brexiteers were dismayed that EU law remained absolute in Northern Ireland, effectively leaving at least half its 1.9 million inhabitants in limbo. They believed the province had been reduced to the status of an EU colony, leading the Democratic Unionist Party (DUP) to boycott the Stormont Assembly.

Liz Truss had begun to address this issue in 2022 and Sunak picked up the baton, assisted by the Foreign Secretary James Cleverly and the Northern Ireland Secretary Chris Heaton-Harris. 'There was one meeting with [DUP leader] Sir Jeffrey Donaldson in London in December, another in Northern Ireland, and then another in London,' says a source. 'Rishi also met the leaders of the other Northern Ireland parties. He put a lot of time, intellectual effort and energy into it. The political culture in Northern Ireland demands that.' In mid-February, Sunak also visited Paris and Berlin for talks with EU leaders including President Macron and Ursula von der Leyen, the president of the European Commission.

The result of these efforts was the Windsor Framework, an agreement in principle between the UK and the EU

Commission, which was announced at the Windsor Guild-hall on 27 February. It was plain to see that relations between Sunak's government and those negotiating for the EU were considerably more positive than they had been under Theresa May, Boris Johnson or Liz Truss. Von der Leyen even referred to Sunak as 'dear Rishi' throughout the press conference. If Sunak, who is more than twenty years her junior, found this patronising, he did not say so. He regarded the deal as the decisive Brexit breakthrough that would allow the approaching twenty-fifth anniversary of the Belfast Agreement to be marked with renewed positivity, while the framework's architects believed it would honour the integrity of the UK and the EU single market while safeguarding the Belfast Agreement in matters relating to VAT, customs, food and medicines. It was announced that the cumbersome checks on goods being exported from mainland Britain to Northern Ireland would be speeded up via a 'green lane', while checks on goods destined for the Republic of Ireland would be subject to a 'red lane'. In order to guarantee that every community in Northern Ireland had a meaningful stake in the new structure, the 'Stormont Brake' would also be established. This mechanism was supposed to allow the Northern Ireland Assembly to object to changes to EU rules that applied in Northern Ireland if at least thirty Members of the Legislative Assembly requested it.

The plans, which were to be put to a Commons vote, were greeted with cautious optimism by commentators and politicians. Yet while Sir Jeffrey Donaldson said the framework represented 'significant progress', he did acknowledge there were still 'key issues of concern'. Others went further. In a speech at the Brand Finance Global Soft Power Summit in London on 2 March, Boris Johnson said:

I'm going to find it very difficult to vote for something like this myself, because I believed we should've done something very different ... I'm conscious I'm not going to be thanked for saying this, but I think it is my job to do so: we must be clear about what is really going on here. This is not about the UK taking back control, and although there are easements, this is really a version of the solution that was being offered last year to Liz Truss when she was Foreign Secretary. This is the EU graciously unbending to allow us to do what we want to do in our own country, not by our laws but by theirs.

The DUP MP Ian Paisley Jr was blunter still, saying the framework 'does not cut the mustard'.

The European Research Group (ERG), an organisation of Eurosceptic Tory MPs, commissioned an assessment of the plan. Its legal experts took an astonishing three weeks to decode its contents. On 21 March, its principal findings were that EU law would still be supreme in Northern Ireland; that the green lane would be ineffective; that the Stormont Brake was 'practically useless'; and that 'the framework itself has no exit other than through a highly complex legal process'. When the Windsor Framework agreement was put before the Commons on 22 March, however, it sailed through, with 515 MPs voting in favour and twenty-nine against. It came as little surprise to those who are well versed in the intricacies of Northern Ireland's politics that no DUP MPs endorsed it. Joining them in the 'No' lobby were twenty-two Tory MPs. They included three former leaders – Boris Johnson, Liz Truss and Sir Iain Duncan Smith – plus a band of hardline Brexiteers and Johnson loyalists. A further forty-six Tory MPs did not vote, either because they abstained or because they were otherwise indisposed. Downing Street had been braced for a substantial Tory rebellion organised by acolytes of Johnson and had even anticipated that the vote might only pass with Labour's help. That this turned out not to be the case was seen as a double victory for Sunak: it showed that the Windsor Framework was considered acceptable to the overwhelming majority of MPs and that opposition in his own party – and by extension support for Johnson – was quite limited.

Despite the Commons result, the DUP's opposition to the framework meant that Stormont remained an Assembly that could not function because of its dependence on power-sharing. Ian Paisley explains:

There aren't enough substantial changes between the Protocol and Windsor Framework. We can't say, 'Thanks, Rishi, as a Brexiteer and a unionist you've managed to square this circle,' because he hasn't. The trade frictions are still there, as are frictions around identity. The agrifood sector is Northern Ireland's biggest business. Thousands of Northern Irish farms feed millions of mouths in Britain. Yet our livestock traders still can't bring their livestock to another part of the United Kingdom without suffering six-month quarantine rules. When I put it to Rishi directly in the House that this is the same as him trying to move cattle from Yorkshire to Lancashire and being told those cattle would have to stay in Lancashire for six months if they went unsold, he was flummoxed. Many unionists feel they're still a place apart and subservient to EU rules and laws without any democratic accountability. Rishi's left us subjugated in that way. He is guilty of gross mis-selling.

One figure who is close to Sunak counters these complaints, saying:

Rishi, Chris Heaton-Harris and James Cleverly got a lot further than anyone expected at the beginning of the process. This is something that will make Brexit work for the whole of the UK. And the unfinished business of 2019 has been addressed. Rishi invested a lot of time in understanding what people in Northern Ireland felt and in getting to know Ursula von der Leyen, which helped because he could say to her, 'You want to protect the Good Friday Agreement and that's why you have the Northern Ireland Protocol, but the protocol is one of the reasons why the institutions set up by the Good Friday Agreement aren't functioning and we have to address that.' She was more prepared to engage on this question than the EU had been since 2016. Rishi went into huge and exhaustive detail to make sure every feature was covered. It was an intellectual exercise, but he also understood emotionally that he needed to persuade people that you could have a negotiation. He's tackled a problem that lots of people thought was intractable, including those who thought it should be put off for a couple of years.

Matters were not helped by suspicions among unionists that the framework was rushed through to coincide with the twenty-fifth anniversary of the Belfast Agreement in April 2023, an occasion which brought President Biden to the island of Ireland along with Bill and Hillary Clinton and Tony Blair. Ian Paisley adds, 'There was an awful lot of pressure facilitated by Biden and this was basically because he wanted to secure the Irish-American vote in the next US general election. This was extremely unhelpful. I don't know why Biden had to be indulged in this way.'

To compound the situation, Chris Heaton-Harris gave a speech during an event in Belfast to mark the anniversary in which he angered many unionists by praising two senior IRA figures, Gerry Adams and the late Martin McGuinness, saying, 'Martin McGuinness, along with Gerry Adams, will be remembered for the courage and leadership they showed' around the time of the Belfast Agreement. Then, speaking at Queen's University in Belfast shortly afterwards, Sunak appealed to the DUP. His words backfired. 'I urge you to work with us to get Stormont up and running again,' he said. 'That's the right thing to do on its own terms and I'm convinced it's also the right thing to do for our Union.' He added, 'Over the long term, [a non-functioning Stormont] will not bolster the cause of unionism,' before warning that they risked convincing people that a united Ireland might be their best option after all.

'The worst thing Rishi's done is try to leverage unionists into a position they don't want to be in,' says Paisley.

For a Tory PM whose party was kept in power by the DUP in 2017 to tell unionists there will be a united Ireland unless you do what I tell you is unacceptable. The prospect of him getting the Assembly back any time soon is more remote. Unionists are ultra-suspicious of the institutions created under the Belfast Agreement. If that's what the British government is saying publicly, what are they saying behind our backs? We're in difficult territory and I think Rishi's speech went too far. There's exhaustion and boredom with this on all sides. Most MPs in the Commons don't even understand what's going on. They believe the hype they've heard around the Windsor Framework but they don't read the detail. They're going to have to come back to this.

At the time of writing, it is anybody's guess how or when the situation will be resolved. A long-term solution enabling Stormont to operate again will only come about if arrangements that command the support of both communities in Northern Ireland are found, because the fundamental principle that underlies the Belfast Agreement is consent. DUP politicians say they are prepared to play a long game. They are also aware that if the next general election were to result in a hung parliament, their help in propping up the Conservatives may be called upon via a confidence and supply agreement, as was the case in 2017. Such a deal could depend on Sunak's willingness to amend the framework that he hopes will be seen as one of the diplomatic triumphs of his first year in Downing Street. It is also worth posing the question of how much British voters care about Northern Ireland's trade arrangements, and therefore whether the Windsor Framework will have any electoral benefits.

By coincidence, on the day of the Windsor Framework vote, Boris Johnson was subjected to several hours of questioning about Partygate by the Commons Privileges Committee. In April 2022, MPs had passed a motion tabled by Sir Keir Starmer calling for the then Prime Minister to be investigated over the serious charge of having potentially misled Parliament in statements he made about alleged breaches of lockdown rules in Downing Street. While Johnson endured this televised cross-examination, Sunak honoured a promise he had made in the autumn of 2022 by publishing three years of his personal tax returns. These showed that he earned £4.766 million between April 2019 and April 2022 and paid a total of £1.053 million in tax at an overall effective rate of 22 per cent. About £60,000 was taken off his tax bills for overseas liabilities. In each year, most of his income came from capital gains – profit derived from the sale of assets.

Although Sunak is self-made, his wealth had been regarded as a key line of attack for the Labour Party. Yet after an initial flurry of scrutiny, including criticism of the fact that he had benefited from the top rate of capital gains tax having been lowered to 20 per cent by the Conservatives in 2016, the declaration did little, if any, sustained damage – not least because news of Sunak's wealth will hardly have come as a revelation to many voters. Indeed, some of the brickbats hurled in his direction merely related to the idea that he had used Johnson's committee appearance as cover to slip out a tricky story. Even if this were true, it cannot be forgotten that his wife's finances, and his own, had only come under the public microscope a year previously because of a leak carried out by somebody operating in Johnson's Downing Street. If Johnson's predicament that afternoon was considered by Sunak to be an expedient moment to publish this financial information, few could have blamed him.

Moreover, at this time Sunak was being challenged over a very different and far more consequential financial matter which had featured in Jeremy Hunt's recent Budget, namely raising corporation tax from 19 per cent to 25 per cent. Sunak had first announced this measure in his March 2021 Budget, seeing it as a way to repair the hole torn in the public finances by the lockdown. It had always been planned to take effect from 1 April 2023, yet it had been so unpopular and, some economists thought, unattractive to investors that Kwasi Kwarteng had ditched the idea in September 2022. Hunt had reinstated it. Sunak and Hunt were often reminded of how contradictory this decision appeared in light of Hunt having stood for the Tory leadership in July 2022 on a promise to cut corporation tax to 15 per cent. The reinstation of the corporation tax policy was taken as proof of Sunak's intimate involvement in producing Hunt's Spring 2023 Budget, which aside from the corporation tax hike was widely considered to be acceptable to elements of the mainstream press, if not particularly radical. The *Daily Mail* praised it for advancing the traditional Tory values of 'rewarding aspiration and making work pay' via new low-tax investment zones, a fuel duty freeze, scrapping the lifetime cap on tax-free pension savings and introducing initiatives such as an expansion of free childcare to allow parents in England to return to the workplace. Ironically, this last measure soon proved difficult for Sunak after it emerged that his wife is a shareholder in a childcare agency called Koru Kids that stood to benefit from the new policy. An inquiry was launched by the Parliamentary Commissioner for Standards, Daniel Greenberg, though Sunak insisted the shareholding was properly declared.

Sunak's other key concern during the spring of 2023 related to the Illegal Migration Bill, which was introduced by Suella Braverman, the Home Secretary. If enacted, it would change the law so that anybody entering Britain illegally could be deported immediately to their home nation or to a safe state such as Rwanda, a country to which Britain had already paid £140 million for this purpose. Nobody could claim asylum using the Modern Slavery Act either. It was hoped that this policy would be a deterrent to those paying people-traffickers up to €5,000 each to enter Britain. Sir Keir Starmer and the Labour Party opposed the idea on moral grounds, but the Bill then received far wider coverage than most government policies after the BBC presenter Gary Lineker linked it to Nazism. He claimed that, when announcing it, Braverman had employed 'language that is not dissimilar to that used by Germany in the '30s'. Sunak was conspicuous among Conservative MPs for refusing to criticise Lineker's provocative interpretation, but he remained steadfast. With official forecasts predicting that at least 56,000 more people could cross the Channel illegally by the end of the year, he considered new legislation to be essential to untangling a knot which had been tightening for several years.

A major stumbling block was the European Court of Human Rights (ECtHR). In June 2022, shortly before Sunak quit as Chancellor, one of its judges had ordered the cancellation of the inaugural Rwanda-bound flight containing a small number of asylum seekers ninety minutes before it was due to take off. As this had happened at night, it was mockingly dubbed a 'pyjama injunction'. The fact that nobody was allowed to know the judge's name only added to the sense that post-Brexit Britain still had no proper control over its borders.

'When the small boats pledge came out in January 2023, I remember thinking, "Wow, that's pretty punchy," says former Conservative minister Mark Francois.

Rishi obviously took a decision to be emphatic, and the Illegal Migration Bill is emphatic, so it has to work. But this isn't about whether or not you've got clever spin or good whipping. Either the boats stop or they don't. And if we haven't got a bomb-proof system to stop them coming, they'll keep coming, so he's bet the farm on this. It's talked about a lot among backbenchers, it's raised with Rishi a lot, and it's a very live issue. But this could prove a hostage to fortune because the wording of his pledge, 'stop the boats', is so unequivocal. To stop people from making the crossings, you've got to have a system of rapid removal and that means keeping ECtHR judges out of it. Otherwise no plane will ever take off.

Not only did Sunak have to contend with various factions within his parliamentary party, with One Nation Conservatives keen to water down some measures and those on the right seeking to strengthen them; there were also differences of opinion between him and his Home Secretary. Braverman favoured exiting the European Convention on Human Rights altogether; he and his advisers did not. 'Rishi has always said he is prepared to do what's necessary to deal with this problem and he's confident you can deal with it within certain parameters,' says one source.

The reason this Bill didn't have its first reading in the Commons earlier than 7 March is that it's been through the wringer with the lawyers. His attitude is that we shouldn't break the glass in terms of breaking the law, but we should push our noses right up against the glass. He wants to go as far as he can and he is confident that via that approach we will secure more, but you won't see the benefits of the Bill in summer 2023 because it won't have been passed.

Another source says:

He's keen on international comparisons. He always wants to know what other countries are doing because it's a good way of testing whether what we're doing is right. When we started out on the illegal immigration stuff, there wasn't much to say about what other countries are doing. Now there's a lot more. It's a problem for every developed country. This isn't just a British problem – Italy and Germany are examining similar schemes to ours. Macron gets that and the co-operation is getting better.

In mid-April, Sunak gave an interview to the Conservative-Home website in which he appeared to change tack slightly, allowing a perception to form that his promise to 'stop the boats' may be in jeopardy. When asked by a member of the public if migrant crossings will be under control by the time of the next general election, he replied, 'I've always said that this is not something that is easy – it is a complicated problem, where there's no single, simple solution that will fix it. And I've also said that it won't happen overnight.' He added that it is 'hugely important' to him personally and to the public but that legal challenges might follow. 'We're taking an approach that is novel, that is untested, that's ambitious. I don't make any apologies for that,' he said. On 26 April, the Bill passed its third reading in the Commons by 289 votes to 230 and was sent to the House of Lords for scrutiny. Sunak's allies claimed that if peers sought to weaken the legislation, he would be prepared to force it through using the Parliament Act, which has been used only seven times since 1911.

An influential Tory backbencher who has also engaged with Sunak over the contentious question of immigration offers further insights into his thinking. 'Rishi knows he's got to make a major dent in the numbers crossing the Channel for us to have a hope at the election,' says this MP.

It's a make or break issue. There is this cynical suspicion among the opposition that he's intending to fail so that he can go into the next election saying we're going to pull out of the ECHR, therefore making it a Brexit-style election, but I don't believe that. He sees it as a problem which can be solved by intelligent people talking to each other. So he sees it differently to some voters – certainly Red Wall voters. I think he's done a really good job getting us to this point. He had to be pushed a bit, but that's because of pressure from within the party. There are people for whom anything that sounds anti-refugee is unacceptable and for whom ECHR membership and human rights law is more important than anything else. And the government legal service which reports to the Attorney General is part of the established way of doing things and it had to be dissuaded. He and Suella are respectful of each other. She campaigned to leave the ECHR, he's very much not in that space, and she accepts that.

The complication for Sunak is that illegal immigration, particularly via the English Channel, is escalating. It is never more prevalent than during the summer months, a fact that was no doubt on his mind in May 2023, when he used a Council of Europe summit in Iceland to urge the ECtHR to adjust its use of interim 'pyjama injunctions' to provide greater fairness and transparency. As a senior Tory backbencher observes:

This could drag on for a while, during which time tens of thousands more people could arrive. Already MPs are finding hotels in their constituencies are full of cross-Channel refugees, most of whom are young men, and their constituents are paying for it. I think privately many Labour MPs are concerned as well. You can imagine what Nigel Farage and Richard Tice of the Reform Party will do if this doesn't succeed. These are high stakes.

Yet at the same time as this legal battle raged, concerns grew about the vast increases in legal migration to Britain. Between June 2021 and June 2022, net migration – the difference between immigration and emigration – totalled a record 504,000 people after 1.1 million immigrants arrived in Britain and 560,000 departed. In May 2023, the Home Office produced figures showing that this record had itself been surpassed in 2022, with the net migration number reaching 606,000. Such statistics prompted questions which many felt were far more urgent than those surrounding the comparatively lower numbers of people entering Britain illegally. Those concerned included more than twenty MPs – among them the party's deputy chairman Lee Anderson – who in July 2023 launched a group calling itself the New Conservatives. They issued Sunak with a twelve-point plan to cut immigration to below 226,000, in keeping with the 2019 manifesto, piling pressure onto the Prime Minister.

During this period there were other attempts at undermining the sense of stability Sunak had brought back to his party and the government. On 6 April, the Labour Party began running a series of digital 'attack' adverts in which he was personally targeted as being soft on crime, in favour of council tax hikes and for his family being the beneficiaries of a 'tax loophole'. In each advert, his photograph and handwritten signature, which had formerly been used as a stamp of quality assurance during the Covid era, appeared prominently. The most tendentious advert read, 'Do you think adults convicted of sexually assaulting children should go to prison? Rishi Sunak doesn't.' In smaller type below were statistics claiming that under the Tories, 4,500 people convicted of sexually assaulting children 'served no prison time'. Opinion as to the effectiveness of this campaign was split. Colleagues said that Sunak himself was 'bemused' by it, as he felt it made little sense. Some Labour insiders claimed that anything that got people talking about the Labour Party was positive. Others, including those on the left, believed that American-style tactics were unacceptable in British politics. Many critics believed this attack ridiculous because Sunak was not even an MP when the sentencing guidelines were passed in 2012 – the year in which Starmer, then Director of Public Prosecutions, had sat on the sentencing council. Strikingly, an Opinium poll for *The Observer* published in mid-April found the advert claiming that Sunak did not believe that child sex abusers should go to prison made 12 per cent of voters feel less favourable towards the Labour Party. Still, shrugging off suggestions that he should tone down his personal rebukes of Sunak, Sir Keir Starmer wasted no opportunities that came his way during Prime Minister's Questions to refer to Sunak's wife's non-domiciled status – entirely misleadingly, in fact. Starmer told the Commons in April 2023 that Sunak 'refuses to scrap the status that benefits him and his family'. Yet Sunak's wife has not exercised her right not to pay UK tax on her overseas earnings since April 2022. Sunak's own view was dismissive. He told allies that Labour had resorted to attacking him personally in such an over-the-top fashion because it had no substantial political arguments in its locker.

On top of this came two resignations in quick succession, both of which caused further complications for Sunak. On 21

April, Dominic Raab stood down as Deputy Prime Minister and Justice Secretary after an independent inquiry conducted by Adam Tolley KC into allegations that he had bullied civil servants upheld two of eight complaints, concluding that Raab's management style 'involved an abuse or misuse of power in a way that undermines or humiliates'. These findings about one of Sunak's most loyal lieutenants placed Sunak in a difficult position. On the one hand, many felt that Raab had himself been treated harshly. On the other hand, Raab had personally requested this independent investigation in November 2022 when his supposed transgressions first surfaced and had promised to resign if he was found to have erred. As Sunak had agreed to Tolley being commissioned on that basis, he believed he could not stand in the way of Raab keeping his word, even though he was a close friend and was the third minister to quit his Cabinet since 8 November. Regrettably for both Sunak and Raab, Tolley had only been tasked with this inquiry in November 2022 because Sir Laurie Magnus had not yet been appointed as the Prime Minister's new independent adviser on ministers' interests. As a KC, Tolley's definition of bullying was entirely legalistic and therefore probably quite different to what Magnus's would have been had he been examining the case. Sunak was denounced in some quarters not only for allowing Raab to leave the political stage in these circumstances but also for giving in to what many saw as the baseless, trumped-up, politically motivated claims of certain unelected left-leaning bureaucrats memorably nicknamed 'the Blob' by Dominic Cummings.

Among the most urgent questions that cropped up was whether complaining civil servants had taken against Raab because he was an exacting minister who was routinely prepared to work fourteen-hour days – and who was a Brexiteer to boot. Many noted the steady stream of stories about Raab's alleged bullying trumpeted by the BBC and *The Guardian* during the five months that Tolley's investigation was in train and concluded that he was simply the victim of a political assassination. Senior backbencher Sir John Redwood was felt to speak for many Conservatives when he told the *Sunday Telegraph* that it was 'a great pity that the Prime Minister accepted Dominic Raab's resignation'. This sense of regret was exacerbated when Sunak appointed Raab's successors. Alex Chalk, a Remainer who has spoken in support of the eco-warrior protest group Extinction Rebellion, became the new Justice Secretary, while Sunak's close political ally Oliver Dowden – another Remainer – became Deputy Prime Minister. The *Daily Express* calculated that Chalk's elevation raised to twenty-one the number of Remainers who now attended Sunak's Cabinet, against only eight Brexiteers.

Where, some right-of-centre Tories worried, do Sunak's loyalties really lie? This question intensified after Chalk decided to scrap the bill of rights Raab had worked on for months in the hope that it would replace the Human Rights Act, which many Conservatives blame for compromising judges' ability to deport foreign criminals and illegal immigrants. It became more prominent still when the Business Secretary Kemi Badenoch announced in early May that the government was dropping much-publicised plans to scrap thousands of EU laws by the end of 2023 – not least because Sunak had pledged in the summer leadership election contest that during his first 100 days in power he would review or repeal 2,400 of them. Critics felt that either Sunak's government had meekly given in to 'the Blob' again or it was in fact more pro-EU than it dared to admit, an idea the ERG had already formed having examined the Windsor Framework agreement. Whichever explanation was correct, the retention of these EU laws made many Brexiteers angry.

The strength of Sunak's commitment to Brexit has long been questioned, but it is worth adding at this point the recollections of the lobby journalist David Maddox, the political editor of the *Sunday Express* at the time of the referendum in 2016. 'The first time I met Rishi was shortly before the referendum,' Maddox recalls.

> David Cameron was ringing backbenchers and asking for their loyalty and inviting them over to Downing Street. I met Rishi by arrangement for a cup of tea in Portcullis House and he said to me, 'I've just told Cameron that I'm not going over to No. 10 because I support Leave and there's no point in me wasting his time.' Despite what's been chucked at him, I'd say questioning his commitment to Brexit is unfair because clearly he was ambitious and wanted to get to the top but he wasn't willing to put aside his support for Brexit. From that first meeting I've always thought of him as a Brexiteer. He wasn't a Spartan, but he was always on board and fairly principled about it, as most of them were.

The second resignation in April 2023 that troubled Sunak was that of Richard Sharp as BBC chairman. As noted in the previous chapter, Sharp, who was once Sunak's boss at Goldman Sachs, had been accused of breaching the code of practice for government appointments by not revealing to the BBC panel that interviewed him his involvement in helping to secure an £800,000 loan for Boris Johnson in late 2020, immediately before he became BBC chairman. As all BBC chairmen are appointed on the advice of the Prime Minister, establishing the chain of events leading to Sharp's successful bid was clearly in the public interest. Following an inquiry, Sharp was found guilty of two 'potential perceived conflicts of interest'. First, he had told Johnson of his wish to apply to become the BBC chairman before he made his application in November 2020. Second, before he was interviewed, he had brokered a meeting between a businessman, Sam Blyth, who had volunteered to help Johnson with the personal loan, and the Cabinet Secretary, Simon Case. Despite Sharp's limited role in this affair, which even the KC who ran the inquiry said was not enough to 'invalidate' his appointment, he quit.

Sharp, who had previously donated £400,000 to the Conservatives, was thought by some to be merely the latest public figure to have fallen victim to a left-wing conspiracy thanks to his personal political leanings. That he felt forced to fall on his sword immediately before the May 2023 local elections in England was obviously unhelpful to Sunak, who was portrayed by opponents as presiding over the party of 'sleaze'. Yet his departure also piled on pressure from his own side. For even though the Sharp affair was a throwback to the Johnson era and had nothing to do with Sunak per se, the question of who should replace him was seen as a test of the Prime Minister's mettle. Sunak was urged to appoint another prominent Conservative as BBC chairman or risk surrendering to a clique of unelected agitators whose common aim was to bring down his government six months after it had been formed.

Sunak could still plausibly claim to have brought stability to British politics, however. For example, he could point to the deal struck in early March in which he and Jeremy Hunt had worked to salvage the UK arm of the troubled Silicon Valley Bank, which was sold to HSBC for £1, saving thousands of jobs and businesses in the tech sector; or to Britain's agreement to join the Comprehensive and Progressive Agreement for Trans-Pacific Partnership (CPTPP), a trade deal with countries including Canada, Australia, Japan and Mexico. He could also speak of the pay deal with more than 1 million NHS staff in England; of having launched a crackdown on anti-social behaviour; and of his efforts to restore the Conservatives' battered reputation as the party of business through hosting 200 leading chief executives at the Business Connect conference in London.

These accomplishments and others had allowed the Tories to begin eating into Labour's 500-day-long national poll lead in early spring, albeit that they remained fourteen points adrift. Yet for all Sunak's efforts, by 4 May, when voters went to cast their ballots in hundreds of England's district councils, metropolitan boroughs and unitary authorities, party advisers in CCHQ still said they were prepared for a night of grim results. They would not be proved wrong.

EPILOGUE

Shortly before the polls opened for the English local elections on 4 May 2023, Conservative spin doctors put the word out that, of the 8,000 seats being contested, the Tories expected to lose 1,000. This figure was almost certainly artificially inflated in order to create a 'good' news story if the final result was less catastrophic. In the event, it was worse. The party lost 1,061 council seats and relinquished control of forty-eight councils, both in the south, where it has traditionally performed best, and in the all-important Red Wall areas of the north. By contrast, Labour and the Liberal Democrats made substantial gains around the country, picking up 537 seats and 407 seats respectively. Labour won twenty-two new councils to succeed the Tories as the largest party in local government for the first time since 2002; the Liberal Democrat council tally swelled by twelve. Even though no elections took place in Wales or Scotland, nor in London or any other big cities, Sir Keir Starmer wasted no time in declaring what he thought the outcome meant. 'Make no mistake,' he said twelve hours after the polls closed. 'We are on course for a Labour majority at the next general election.' This forecast was at the time considered by analysts to be overly optimistic, but there was no disguising the fact that the Conservative Party had comprehensively failed its first major electoral test with Sunak at the helm.

The subsequent inquest into this unexpected drubbing generated theories from all sides of the political spectrum. Some Tory MPs blamed Sunak personally, pointing out that he had been in 10 and 11 Downing Street for most of the previous three years presiding over the highest tax levels since the 1950s. Others criticised a lacklustre campaign from a worn-out party entering its fourteenth year in office. A different group claimed that Boris Johnson's magnetic presence on the stump would have saved them. Attention also turned to the rise of tactical voting and Labour–LibDem pacts in some areas. Labour Party strategists, meanwhile, believed that their decision to portray Sunak as out of touch with everyday people had worked effectively.

There may be elements of truth in each of these explanations. On the other hand, one worthwhile question that also emerged concerned how many people had used their vote to protest against a mid-term Conservative government rather than positively backing the opposition parties. While that question may be impossible to answer definitively, a parallel can be drawn between this set of results and the 1989 European Parliament election. On that occasion, Labour won a national poll for the first time in fifteen years, but the bigger story was that the Green Party notched up 15 per cent of the vote. This was taken as a sign that, after a decade of Margaret Thatcher being in power, Britons had shifted to the left. The reality was that disgruntled Conservatives had registered a protest vote, not backed Labour, and they returned to the Tories in 1992, awarding them a fourth term in office. It is also worth remembering how fickle voters in local elections can be. The Conservatives did extremely well in the local elections of 2017, while Labour performed very badly. One month later, at the general election, the Tories lost their majority while Labour won thirty extra seats. A similar tale unfolded in 2019, when the Tories were crushed in the local elections but won an eighty-seat majority at the general election seven months later.

The respected political scientist Sir John Curtice extrapolated that if the 2023 local election results were replicated at a general election, there would be a hung parliament in which Labour held 312 seats – well short of the 326 needed. This interpretation must give Sunak a glimmer of hope that all is not lost and, indeed, that there is everything to play for. Some political observers think it remarkable that even though the Tories have been in power for thirteen years, Starmer did not do better.

In the weeks that followed, I conducted further polling to find out what, if anything, had really changed in the seven months since Sunak became Prime Minister. Nationally, the Conservatives' poll rating had recovered from the low 20s at the end of the brief Truss era to around 30 per cent – that is, from catastrophic to merely very bad indeed. My findings underlined that Sunak faced a race against time, on two fronts. Few former Conservative voters, let alone anyone else, thought Sunak had yet made much progress on his five self-imposed tests of controlling inflation, cutting NHS waiting lists, bringing down the debt, getting the economy growing and tackling small boat migration. But as well as dealing with Britain's multiple crises, he was running against voters' weariness with the Tories after their long spell in office. The proportion saying the Conservatives shared their values, were competent or would do what they say remained in single figures, while the seemingly unending parade of distraction and division – especially the continuing circus surrounding Boris Johnson – hardly helped to show a party with the focus and discipline needed to put the country back on its feet.

Many praised Sunak himself for calmly and diligently trying to tackle the country's problems ('a normal boring politician, in a good way – just what the country needs', as one participant put it), albeit with little help from his squabbling colleagues. While Starmer seemed competent and sensible compared to his predecessor Jeremy Corbyn, he was considered 'a bit of a wet fish' and few voters knew of any Labour plans to change things, even if they thought the party was instinctively more in touch with their concerns. But our analysis found that the ground Sunak had already recovered for the Tories was among voters who valued competence, wanted to make Brexit work and felt the PM was starting to get a grip. Those who remained adrift were of two distinct types. One comprised prosperous, liberal Remain voters who had only reluctantly voted for Johnson on the grounds that a Corbyn government would be even worse but now blamed the Conservatives for Britain's woes. The other, recognisable as part of the 'Red Wall', had believed in Brexit and Johnson but been bitterly disappointed by both. They were appalled by the Partygate revelations and felt that the change in their fortunes they had been promised in return for their first-time Tory votes had failed to materialise. Without the three factors that brought it together – Brexit deadlock, fear of Corbyn and the magnetism of pre-Partygate Boris – it was always going to be a struggle to hold together the 2019 Conservative-voting coalition, with its competing views and interests. In the economic and political circumstances facing Sunak in mid-2023, the task looked all the harder.

Sunak did not have time to reflect too deeply on the local election results. On the day they were declared, he was busy meeting dozens of world leaders who had come to London for the coronation of King Charles III. Yet he would have known that his party would have been far worse off if those elections had been fought at the height of the Truss era in October 2022. And he could take comfort from the fact that the parliamentary arithmetic was more favourable to the Tories than it might have seemed. Labour would have to gain an extra 129 more seats in the Commons in order to achieve a majority of just one. To put this in perspective, in 2010 David Cameron made a net gain of ninety-six seats and still fell short, forcing the Conservatives into coalition with the Liberal Democrats. For Labour under Starmer to pivot unassisted from opposition to majority government in one leap would be a monumental achievement. If a Labour-fronted pact were necessary, it would have to involve either the pro-EU Liberal Democrats or the Scottish independence-obsessed SNP. Both might demand a heavy price to enter into such a partnership. Part of Sunak's political mission will be to remind voters of the instability such arrangements could create.

Yet just as Starmer has a vast mountain to scale if he is to reach No. 10, the burden Sunak carries is equally daunting, and few people envy him the task he took on in the autumn of 2022. An allegation that is often levelled at Sunak by some Conservatives is that he plotted Boris Johnson's downfall as part of a plan to succeed him. Yet, as the later chapters of this book show, all the available evidence suggests that this idea is wide of the mark. Sunak always knew there was no guarantee that he would be chosen by party members to replace

Johnson in the event of the Prime Minister's downfall, and Sunak's failure to win them over in September 2022 is proof that
his instinct was right. Instead of walking away from politics,
however, he retired to the back benches, determined to make
a contribution to public life. When, surprisingly, the call came
to succeed Liz Truss just six weeks later, he did not hesitate to
respond. He has always been ambitious, but he maintains that
he acted out of duty even though others advised him not to do
so. As his friend and neighbouring MP Kevin Hollinrake says,
'Some people said to me, "Rishi's better off waiting. Let's lose
the next election, come back and he can be leader then." Rishi
would never have thought that's the right thing to do. He's in
this because he wants to sort problems out.' It is safe to add
that he is not in 10 Downing Street because he needs or wants
the £160,000 salary that goes with this all-consuming job.

If Sunak's sense of obligation is indicative of a fundamental
decency, his work rate is just as impressive. Claire Coutinho
MP, who was his parliamentary private secretary throughout
his chancellorship, remembers him as 'a machine' who could
'go through piles of information'. She says, 'We'd work from 7
a.m. until midnight. He's very good at getting through a vast
amount of detail.' And a Downing Street colleague adds, 'He
works at a phenomenal pace. If something goes round the
building, he will read it and absorb it and will come back with
questions very quickly. He cranks through a huge amount of
stuff.' Such a grasp of fine detail has contributed to some of his
biggest advances, particularly when negotiating with the EU.
After years in cold storage, it is noticeable that relations between Britain and figures in the bloc such as President Macron
have thawed while Sunak has been in No. 10.

Through being calm and methodical, he has so far shown

that he has the right temperament to be a leader. Some may miss the flamboyance or the showmanship of Boris Johnson, but the fact is that many of Sunak's MPs believe they are lucky that he is in charge. Indeed, the overwhelming majority of those interviewed for the purpose of this book are in no doubt that he represents their best chance of staying in power. As the backbench MP Philip Davies puts it:

Rishi Sunak is not the problem, it's the Conservative Party brand that's the problem. It's been completely trashed, first by Boris and then by Liz Truss. Our only hope of doing better than expected is for the next election to be Sunak versus Starmer. If it's Labour versus Conservative, it'll be even more difficult.

As British general elections have increasingly become presidential contests, Davies is not alone in his thinking. Few would deny that of the current crop of MPs, Sunak is deserving of his position as first among equals. He has thrown himself into the challenge of running the country with vigour. Those who know him best say that he has taken from his parents not just a strong work ethic but also a set of Hindu beliefs which are paramount in his approach to life. One friend says:

His parents felt they had to ensure their children should have a better life than them. Rishi uses that in politics. He wants the next generation of Britons to have a better life. Political-ly, it's easiest to borrow money and say, 'Someone else can worry about this later.' He takes a different view. The belief in hard work, public service and delayed gratification keep him going. Flag, faith and family are very important to him.

Not only has Sunak successfully begun the process of piecing together his party, ensuring that his MPs are more disciplined and united than they were in 2022, but, more urgently, he has also moved quickly to try to put the country on a better footing. His five pledges – to halve inflation; grow the economy; reduce debt; cut NHS waiting lists; and stop the boats – are at the core of his programme for 2023 and he has promised to be accountable if he fails to pass even one of these self-imposed challenges. Well-placed sources insist that he will stick to this course.

His opponents – even those on his own side – have tried to use his and his family's financial status against him, portraying him as unable to understand most voters' concerns because he was privately educated and is rich. Yet it is important to point out that his wife was not born into great wealth, nor did she grow up in a rarefied environment. Rather, she was raised in a middle-class household in India and inherited money in adulthood thanks to her father's business acumen. Is it justifiable to hold this against Sunak? Moreover, it is surprising – and perhaps a little depressing – that Sunak's life story is not more widely regarded in Britain first and foremost as being inspirational. His immigrant parents worked hard, they brought him up to do the same, and when he went out into the world he did so. His reward was to make his own fortune as a young man – something most senior politicians achieve once they have left office. That Sunak has done things the other way round is unusual, but it might be preferable. It certainly makes him as close to incorruptible as it is possible to be, for he is unlikely to have his head turned by the promise of a private financial deal while in elected office. Should his wealth exclude him from public life? Does it render him incapable of connecting with 'ordinary' voters? One close friend thinks not, saying:

He hasn't changed for thirty years. He goes to TGI Fridays with his daughters. That's who he is. He's pretty normal. His cultural tastes are very middle-brow. I always think it's amusing how ordinary his tastes are. He likes to eat chicken Kiev and watch *Emily in Paris*. And he has always been good at meeting a wide range of people. It's a world away from what many people might assume about him.

It is not as though Sunak is above criticism, however. In an interview recorded in early April 2023, his political hero Nigel Lawson said it was 'undesirable and unsatisfactory' that tax as a share of GDP had hit a seventy-year high. He observed that

the Conservatives have been in office for an unusually long time and I don't see that they're likely to be able to bring it down. Rishi, the new Prime Minister, is a good guy and I think in the circumstances he was the right choice as a successor to Boris, but I don't think that he's going to be known for his tax-cutting.

It is true that during his chancellorship and premiership, taxes have risen considerably, and many feel this has turned Britain into a low-growth, anti-business economy at a time of stubbornly high inflation. The upshot is that most people answering Ronald Reagan's vital question 'Are you better off than you were four years ago?' would do so with a resounding 'No.' Yet it is only fair to remember why taxes have gone up on Sunak's watch. He has been in office during an unusually stormy – and expensive – era and he never hid from the public what the consequences of this turbulence would be. While dealing with the £400 billion fallout of the Covid crisis, he warned repeatedly that the state's perceived generosity would in time have to be accounted for. Plus, as described in this book, he consistently sounded the alarm over inflation. He also had to serve in 11 Downing Street under Boris Johnson, a Prime Minister whose attitude to public spending was, notoriously, often driven by short-term self-interest rather than having any wider benefit. Who can forget his remark to a journalist in November 2020 that he wanted to 'take Johnson's credit card away'? Furthermore, Sunak's government has continued to pump billions of pounds of state support into half the population's bank accounts in order to tackle greater energy costs, exacerbated partly by the war in Ukraine.

His supporters would argue that events have prevented him from being able to put his own ideas into practice. Having spoken to those in politics who know him best, it is clear that he does still aspire to be a low-tax, small-state politician who, as he told the Commons weeks after first being elected an MP in 2015, believes that 'public spending should not exceed 37 per cent of GDP'.

Underlying everything, however, is the fact that he is a pragmatist. He has the ability to make unpopular decisions if necessary, and raising taxes was one of them. Sunak's friend William Hague pointed out straight after the local elections that while the quick fix of a tax cut might be tempting, it would be politically unwise, not least in the aftermath of the economic experiments carried out when Liz Truss was in 10 Downing Street. In any case, by the end of May 2023 UK debt exceeded the size of the economy for the first time since 1961, having reached £2.6 trillion, further compromising Sunak's options. He is well aware that he will have to make a decent offer to the electorate if he is to have a hope of remaining in power.

He will know that tax cuts – and tightly controlled spending – will form part of that offer, but he also knows that for the health of the economy he will have to bide his time. Allowing people to keep more of their earnings is critical, which is why he promised in January 2023 to reduce the burden of taxation on working people as soon as possible. Those who are close to him, however, say he believes the way to cut taxes sustainably is get inflation and spending under control first.

None of this is to suggest that the Sunak fan club is oversubscribed. One former government adviser comments:

> I wonder if Rishi gets lost in the weeds too much. And his political instincts are not as sharp as they might be. For example – how did he let Truss, a Remainer, outflank him? He's the guy who helped get us through Covid, yet he hasn't capitalised on the benefits of that at all. Boris wanted to win at all costs. Does Rishi? And while he has good people around him, where is his Peter Mandelson or Damian McBride figure? Truss ruined the Tory brand. She did a vast amount of damage. So did Johnson, to a lesser extent. And that's what's so hard for Rishi as their successor.

And a prominent Tory backbencher worries that, under Sunak, it may prove impossible to reassemble the 2019 coalition of Red Wall and true blue Conservative voters that led to the party's thumping victory.

> Rishi says more or less the right things on every topic: he's pro-Brexit, wants to stop the boats, wants to cut tax and on social conservative questions is sound. I just don't feel he walks the walk enough for it to matter what he says. The

danger for us is that he is seen to be too much part of the global tech-driven economy with no feel for the 2019 Red Wall voter, even though he voted for Brexit, is a good family man and his parents ran a small business. We need to do more to win the 2019 voters back.

Others who are well-placed believe he has kowtowed to civil servants more often than is desirable, which is why the civil service likes working with him so much. The refrain from several of his parliamentary colleagues that as Chancellor he was 'captured by the Treasury's orthodoxy' became familiar during research for this book. One said:

> He's a centrist. He's a technocrat. He's like a CFO. I don't see him as a right-winger. I can't define Sunakism and I think he's been thrust into this position ten years too soon. As Chancellor, he went along with what the officials wanted to do most of the time. But I do know he can be ruthless if he has to be.

Parts of his foreign policy were also called into question, not least by Liz Truss, who flew to Taiwan in May 2023 to deliver a speech in which she warned that the West 'can't believe a word' China says. Truss took the opportunity to remind her audience of Sunak's as yet unfulfilled vow, made during the summer 2022 leadership contest, to close down the thirty Confucius Institutes that operate in Britain. These colleges, which teach Chinese languages and are typically attached to universities, are entities of the Chinese state that have received millions of pounds of British government funding. In her speech, Truss said, 'Last summer, the new British Prime

Minister ... said that the Confucius Institutes should be closed. He was right and we need to see those policies enacted urgently.' Elsewhere in her speech, she added, 'Recently, there have been too many mixed messages from the free world. We need to end that ambiguity.' Truss is by no means alone in thinking that Sunak risks accusations of facing both ways on this key global issue. During the leadership race he said he would 'kick the CCP [Chinese Communist Party] out of our universities' and described China as 'the biggest long-term threat to Britain'. Yet after becoming Prime Minister, he tempered his language significantly, referring to China only as an 'epoch-defining challenge' rather than a 'threat'. Once in office, his administration promised to cease funding the Confucius Institutes, but it stopped short of closing them down.

What is more, there are doubts that he has the necessary steel to be a leader in the mould of, say, Thatcher precisely when such a figure is needed. Many Conservatives are increasingly concerned by the apparent indoctrination of schoolchildren on issues including sex, sexuality, gender, race and climate change. More generally, there is a perception that Britain is trapped in a left-wing chokehold, with law-abiding citizens regularly subjected to the actions of single-issue protest groups such as Just Stop Oil, or forced to suffer the inconvenience of public sector strikes. All this has, by accident or by design, combined to inhibit the smooth running of the country as its fragile economic recovery continues.

Yet one Conservative thinker who knows Sunak predicts that he will be prepared to act accordingly. 'He doesn't cross the road for a fight, but he stands his ground,' says this person.

He's not prepared to see people's lives disrupted. He's more socially conservative than people realise, not just in the way that he lives his own life because of his own upbringing, but also in relation to things like child sex education. His view as a parent is that it has got massively out of kilter.

Many Conservative voters will be watching closely to see if Sunak focuses on this area. Arguably, he has already shown his commitment to it through his decision to veto the SNP's Gender Recognition Reform Bill. Civil servants advised him not to become the first Prime Minister in history to use this power, but he stuck to his guns.

If the next general election, which must be held by 28 January 2025, really does become a contest of personalities in which Sunak is pitted against Starmer, rather than the Conservatives fighting Labour, the differences between the two men go deeper than the consequences of their near twenty-year age gap or the fact that Sunak is often thought to be a superior public speaker and more effective communicator than his opposite number. Sunak has consistently stated that a woman is 'an adult human female', whereas Starmer believes that only 99.9 per cent of women 'haven't got a penis'. Sunak is teetotal and says he has never taken drugs, but the same is not true of Starmer. Sunak represents a northern rural seat, while Starmer is thought to embody the values and concerns of metropolitan north London, where he has lived most of his adult life and where his constituency lies. Sunak is pro-private education; Starmer wishes to wage war on it. Sunak has several years' experience of high political office, yet Starmer, who is now in his sixties, has none. Who will prove preferable to the majority of the British electorate?

There is a moment in every parliamentary term, before a

general election, when the public pull down the shutters and stop paying attention to what politicians are saying because they have already decided what they think and which way they will vote. Nobody knows when this arbitrary point will be reached this time around, which is why Sunak and his party are already in election mode. One experienced politician who knows him well says that his path to the prize of winning his own mandate has three stages to it.

> The first stage was to stabilise everything post-Truss and show that a sensible government is back. I think he's done that. The second was to work through the problems resulting from Covid, inflation, industrial disputes and two changes of PM. He continues to do that pretty successfully. Having done those things, [the third stage will be that] he'll have earned the right to speak optimistically about the future and what the economic agenda is and the post-Brexit future of the country and he will have to paint an exciting picture of that. Labour's weakness is that they are not at all exciting. They've got rid of liabilities from Corbyn's era, but they haven't yet made themselves exciting in the way Blair was in '97 or Wilson was in '64 when Labour came in from opposition like a wave of the future. They are not yet that. The Tories must reinvent themselves and Rishi has to do that to be in with a chance.

Yet Sunak's political life was not made any easier thanks to a series of events that took place over an eight-day period in summer 2023. On 9 June, Boris Johnson announced he was resigning his Uxbridge and South Ruislip seat after receiving confirmation that he had been found guilty by the Commons

Select Committee of Privileges of deliberately misleading Parliament over his account of the Partygate scandal – an accusation he strenuously denied but which meant his parliamentary career up to that point ended in disgrace. Coincidentally, also on 9 June, Johnson's resignation honours list was published. Perhaps inevitably, it provoked debate. Seven allies received a peerage, including Charlotte Owen, Johnson's thirty-year-old former aide, and Ross Kempsell, aged thirty-one. Their youth and relative inexperience raised questions about their suitability for taking a seat in the House of Lords. Will Lewis, editor of the *Daily Telegraph* between 2006 and 2009 when Johnson wrote a weekly column for the newspaper, was given a knighthood for his 'political and public service' in Johnson's government. This was believed to amount to his membership of the shadowy Brains Trust group, a small unit set up in Downing Street in February 2022 with the aim of fortifying Johnson's shaky position. Lewis's role was to 'provide advice' to Johnson, but he never took a formal job in Number 10. His low profile in the Johnson operation meant that his receipt of such a high-ranking honour was greeted with some surprise. Several other supporters who received an honour were quickly identified as having been involved in Partygate events, triggering more complaints from Johnson's opponents. It was the fact that the House of Lords Appointments Commission (HOLAC) rejected eight of Johnson's nominations that prompted arguably the most damaging spat, however. For several days, claim and counter-claim from Johnson and Sunak appeared in newspapers, successfully turning the matter into a new episode of the soap opera in which they had played a starring role for the past three years. Sunak revealed that Johnson had asked him to 'overrule' the vetting advice on his

Lords nominations; Johnson accused Sunak of 'talking rubbish'. The row died down after several days, but, whatever the truth of why HOLAC blocked eight honours, those who cared about the reputation of the Conservative Party considered it an unedifying spectacle which served only to confirm that a significant amount of poison still existed within the ranks of its MPs.

On the same day Johnson bowed out, his colleague and friend Nadine Dorries announced her intention to quit as the MP for Mid Bedfordshire. She declared herself 'heartbroken' that the seat in the Lords which had been included in Johnson's resignation honours list had been denied her by HOLAC, and vowed to remain an MP while she investigated what lay behind this perceived snub. Within twenty-four hours, another Johnson loyalist, Nigel Adams, whose peerage was also thought to have been blocked by HOLAC, stated that he was standing down from his Selby and Ainsty seat with immediate effect. And, in an unconnected development, on 17 June, a fourth Conservative MP, David Warburton, who had been under investigation by the parliamentary authorities since April 2022 over allegations of sexual harassment and drug use, said he would resign as the member for Somerton and Frome. Suddenly four by-elections in what were usually considered to be solid Conservative-voting constituencies would have to be held – a number that potentially rose to five in early July after a withering parliamentary report into the conduct of another Tory MP, Chris Pincher. As detailed in Chapter 27, Pincher had been accused of inappropriate behaviour at the Carlton Club in June 2022. This story led ultimately to Boris Johnson's own defenestration. Pincher's eight-week suspension from Parliament meant that a by-election in his Tamworth seat could follow.

June 2023 also brought worrying news for the British economy, as sustained inflationary pressure caused the Bank of England to raise interest rates to 5 per cent (and then 5.25 per cent in August 2023). Inflicting bigger mortgage payments on millions of voters and fuelling forecasts of both a 'correction' in the property market and Britain entering a recession at a time when taxes were at a seventy-year high was politically toxic. As detailed in Chapter 23, however, Sunak had publicly voiced his fears of just such a rates rise back in December 2020, when most economists and politicians believed that the era of ultra-low borrowing would last far into the future. His allies argue that if the central conundrum facing British politics revolves around which politician is going to succeed in ridding the nation of the scourge of inflation, a fiscally conservative centre-right Prime Minister with a good understanding of economics such as Sunak is better placed to solve it than is the untested Keir Starmer. The electorate will have to make up its own mind.

The month ended with a double blow against Sunak's illegal immigration policy. On 28 June, peers did indeed defeat the government's plans via a series of amendments that watered down the legislation in key areas. And on 29 June, in a split decision, three Appeal Court judges blocked by two to one the much-vaunted Rwanda plan. They did so on the basis that there was a risk of asylum seekers who had been deported to Rwanda being sent back from there to their country of origin. As the deal with Rwanda was a key plank of Sunak's pledge to 'stop the boats', it left him with no option but to try to challenge the ruling in the Supreme Court. He issued a statement saying, 'It is this country – and your government – who should decide who comes here, not criminal gangs.' Many welcomed his fighting talk, but given how slowly the wheels of justice can turn, it appears that this row may drag on for months, potentially denying Sunak the opportunity to achieve his aim of stopping the boats in the calendar year 2023.

To cap it all, on 30 June, as the government launched its NHS long-term workforce plan, Lord Goldsmith – a long-term ally of Boris Johnson and his wife Carrie – stole the headlines by resigning as a Foreign Office minister. Goldsmith used a two-page letter to lambast Sunak's alleged 'apathy' towards climate change. Sunak responded immediately, pointing out in a public letter that Goldsmith had in fact refused to apologise for making critical comments about the Privileges Committee's investigation of Johnson, which were seen as incompatible with his position as a minister of the crown. In doing so, Sunak presumably wished to show voters that he would not be pushed around, but Goldsmith then retaliated in kind, and so yet another episode of the Conservative Party's soap opera was broadcast, almost certainly weakening still further its standing with the public. On 4 July, the ConservativeHome Cabinet League Table found that a record nine ministers had plunged into a negative approval rating. Among them was Sunak, whose standing had slipped to −2.7. It had been +49.9 in October 2022.

The by-elections in the former seats of Nigel Adams, David Warburton and Boris Johnson were contested on 20 July – the last day of the parliamentary session before the summer break. Adams's Yorkshire constituency, which had been held in 2019 with a majority of more than 20,000 votes, was overturned by Labour. This was not a surprise given the anger the abrupt resignation of this staunch Johnson loyalist had sparked there. Warburton's Somerset seat, where he had enjoyed a majority in excess of 19,000, was snatched by the Liberal Democrats. Again, this result was not entirely unexpected in light of the allegations that had prompted Warburton's departure.

The outcome in Johnson's former seat of Uxbridge and South Ruislip in west London, however, did come as something of a shock to most people. Ironically, given the amount of negative attention Johnson had forced on his party over such a long period of time, the constituency was retained by the Conservatives, albeit with a significantly reduced majority of just 495 votes. This result was attributed to local opposition to the mooted expansion by London Mayor Sadiq Khan of the controversial Ultra Low Emission Zone (ULEZ) scheme, by which motorists driving older polluting vehicles would be penalised financially. In what must count as a further irony, the Uxbridge result was also thought to provide a fillip to the Conservatives' flagging electoral fortunes more broadly. Many MPs and commentators agreed it demonstrated that pursuing expensive green measures would be unlikely to win votes, whereas reversing such policies might actively attract support and could even prove to be decisive at the polls. As noted in Chapter 24, since Sunak is not thought of by allies as being a 'hair-shirt green', modifying his party's environmental stance might not be as difficult for him as it would be for Sir Keir Starmer. Under the latter's leadership, the Labour Party has pledged to pursue a wide-ranging green programme, with some significant party donations seemingly being made on the assumption that Starmer will stick to this course.

More immediately for Sunak, though, by late July certain numbers reflected the reality of the situation. Two apparently safe seats had been lost; the parliamentary majority of eighty that had been secured by the Tories in December 2019 had been cut to sixty-two, taking into account Andrew Bridgen's defection to the Reclaim Party on 10 May; and more than forty Tory MPs had declared that they would not stand at the next general election. All this coming only nine months after Sunak's elevation to 10 Downing Street, it is hard to believe that even his natural drive and enthusiasm were not dented by the unstinting gloom and pessimism surrounding his party and government – despite the Illegal Migration Bill finally being ready to become law after the government eventually won a series of votes in the House of Lords. Sensing this perceived vulnerability, one intriguing possibility that has been floated by politicians on the right is that the Reform Party – a direct descendant of UKIP and the Brexit Party – might focus its general election campaign on twenty to thirty Red Wall seats. It would do so in the hope that, if it won them, it could form a coalition government with the Tories in the event of a hung parliament.

The key question, then, is: what is Sunak's vision for the future of Britain as we enter the second quarter of the twenty-first century? For while the differences between him and Starmer are clear on certain matters, Sunak's strategists will be aware that Labour does not scare large swathes of the electorate as it once did now that it has remodelled itself as a party of patriotism and equality. They will also know that many voters believe there is less and less to distinguish between the Tories and Labour. Both appear intent on a net zero future; both seem happy to hand ever greater amounts of taxpayers' money to the NHS without comprehensive reform; neither is prepared to expand the armed forces; both favour the extension of the 45p rate of income tax on higher earners; neither knows how to continue Thatcher's dream of creating a property-owning democracy; both are tolerant of net migration having passed 600,000 people annually; and neither has offered a realistic way of getting the quarter of the workforce that is inactive back into employment. If voters are willing to go along with all this, they may feel the time has come to give Labour another chance. After all, the last time the party won a general election was under Tony Blair in 2005.

Politics is, and always has been, an unforgiving business. You only have to remember that Winston Churchill won the Second World War in 1945 but lost the general election by a landslide two months later to know that. In this instance, Sunak may be more impressive than Sir Keir Starmer in certain respects. He may, therefore, deserve on paper to win his own mandate outright so that he can shrug off the problems of the past and refashion Britain as he sees fit. First, however, he needs to convince voters that the Conservative Party is worthy of the prize of a fifth successive term in office. This is an achievement that no leader has ever managed before. Despite Sunak's obvious personal qualities, he should not be surprised if the cards do not fall exactly as he hopes when the results of the next general election are declared.

INDEX